A GREAT LEAP FORWARD

———◦●●◦———

1930s Depression and U.S. Economic Growth

———◦●●◦———

Alexander J. Field

Yale

UNIVERSITY PRESS

New Haven & London

Published with assistance from the Louis Stern Memorial Fund.

Yale University Press books may be purchased in quantity for educational, business, or promotional use. For information, please e-mail sales.press@yale.edu (U.S. office) or sales@yaleup.co.uk (U.K. office).

Printed in the United States of America.

Library of Congress Cataloging-in-Publication Data
Field, Alexander J.
A great leap forward : 1930s Depression and U.S. economic growth / Alexander J. Field.
p. cm. — (Yale series in economic and financial history)
Includes bibliographical references and index.
ISBN 978-0-300-15109-1 (hardcover : alk. paper)   1. United States—Economic conditions—1918–1945.   2. Depressions—1929—United States.   3. United States—Economic conditions—20th century.   I. Title.
HC106.F46 2011
330.973'0917—dc22   2010038797

A catalogue record for this book is available from the British Library.

This paper meets the requirements of ANSI/NISO Z39.48-1992 (Permanence of Paper).

10 9 8 7 6 5 4 3 2 1

CONTENTS

v

PREFACE

I dedicate this book to Moses Abramovitz. Moe was chair of the economics department at Stanford when I was hired in 1974, just out of graduate school at the University of California at Berkeley, and I worked with him closely as associate editor of the *Journal of Economic Literature* between 1981 and 1987. In the first part of my academic career I did not entirely grasp the significance of his groundbreaking work. I was exploring other topics, and only in the 1980s and 1990s, as I developed greater interest in macroeconomic issues, did his research come into clearer focus for me. I made the first formal presentation of the material in chapter 1 on the last day of November 2000 at a seminar at Stanford. I remember it distinctly because I was bleary-eyed, having spent most of the previous night helping to upload my son's college application to the University of California's servers.

Moe had been sick and could not attend the seminar. He died the following day. I have always felt conflicted about this juxtaposition of events. Although we had had some preliminary discussions, I wish I could have engaged him more about this developing work. On the other hand, though there is some revisionism here with respect to the sources of growth in the nineteenth and twentieth centuries, I feel that in a way I contribute to his legacy by extending a style of research he pioneered. Moe was always a warm and gracious presence in the Stanford department, and I continue to run across his handwritten comments on various drafts of earlier work in my files. I miss him.

Many colleagues have given me valuable feedback as this research progressed. A special thanks to faculty at Santa Clara, in particular Kris Mitchener and Bill Sundstrom. It is not a stretch to say that Santa Clara has one of the finest economic history groups in the country. Most of the economics faculty is indeed research active, and the quality and impact of work it has produced rival that of many larger groups, including some with doctoral programs.

My friends at Stanford, including Ran Abramitzky, Paul David, Avner Greif, Petra Moser, Nate Rosenberg, and Gavin Wright, continue to provide a welcome sounding board for many of these ideas and are part of what makes the Bay Area and California such a great place to do economic history.

Thanks also to colleagues at other universities who have been especially helpful over the years. These include Greg Clark, Stan Engerman, Naomi Lamoreaux, Deirdre McCloskey, Tim Leunig, Peter Lindert, Joel Mokyr, Leandro Prados, Richard Sutch, Peter Temin, and Joachim Voth. Apologies to many others not explicitly mentioned.

Thanks to Michael O'Malley, who, by making me an offer I couldn't refuse, persuaded me to write this book and publish it with Yale.

And thanks to Ben Bernanke, who, as editor of the *American Economic Review*, had the good taste to accept my 2003 paper on the Depression.

Finally, thanks to my wife Valerie and our children, James and Emily, for tolerating the work habits of an academic and helping me make the work more accessible to a broader audience.

Early versions of material in this book benefited from presentations at numerous universities and conferences

These included seminars in the United States at Columbia, Dartmouth, Harvard, Indiana, Michigan, the New School, Ohio State, Rutgers, Stanford, UC Berkeley, UC Davis, UCLA, UC Riverside, Virginia, and Yale; in Canada at McGill, Queens, and Toronto; in Great Britain and Europe at the London School of Economics, All Souls College Oxford, Humboldt (Berlin), Sciences PO (Paris), Pompeu Fabreu/ CREI (Barcelona), and Carlos III (Madrid); and in Australia/New Zealand at Adelaide, Melbourne, and Canterbury.

Additional presentations were made at the Chicago Area Friends of Economic History seminar in 2004; the Economic History Association Meetings in 2004, 2006, and 2008; World Cliometrics meetings in Venice (2004) and Edinburgh (2008); BETA Workshops in Strasbourg in 2006 and 2008; and the ASSA meetings in 2008, 2009, and 2010.

Thanks to all who participated and gave me useful comments. This book is better for them.

Portions of this work are based on material appearing in previously published articles. I thank various publishers for permission to build on that work. Relevant book chapters are indicated at the end of each acknowledgement.

Field, Alexander J. 1992. "Uncontrolled Land Development and the Duration of the Depression in the United States." *Journal of Economic History* 52 (December): 785–805 (chapter 11).

Field, Alexander J. 2003. "The Most Technologically Progressive Decade of the Century." *American Economic Review* 93 (September): 1399–1413 (chapter 1).

Field, Alexander J. 2006. "Technological Change and U.S. Economic Growth in the Interwar Years." *Journal of Economic History* 66 (March): 203–236 (chapter 2).

Field, Alexander J. 2006. "Technical Change and U.S. Economic Growth: The Interwar Period and the 1990s." In *The Global Economy in the 1990s: A Long Run Perspective,* ed. Paul Rhode and Gianni Toniolo, 89–117. Cambridge: Cambridge University Press (chapter 5).

Field, Alexander J. 2007. "The Equipment Hypothesis and U.S. Economic Growth." *Explorations in Economic History* 43 (January): 43–58 (chapter 8).

Field, Alexander J. 2007. "The Origins of U.S. Total Factor Productivity Growth in the Golden Age." *Cliometrica* 1 (April): 63–90 (chapters 2 and 4).

Field, Alexander J. 2008. "The Impact of the Second World War on U.S. Productivity Growth." *Economic History Review* 61 (August): 672–694 (chapter 3).

Field, Alexander J. 2009. "U.S. Economic Growth in the Gilded Age." *Journal of Macroeconomics* 31 (March): 173–190 (chapter 6).

Field, Alexander J. 2010. "The Procyclical Behavior of Total Factor Productivity Growth in the United States, 1890–2004." *Journal of Economic History* 70 (June): 326–350 (chapter 7).

INTRODUCTION

This book is built around a novel claim: potential output grew dramatically across the Depression years (1929–1941), and this advance provided the foundation for the economic and military success of the United States during the Second World War, as well as for what Walt Rostow (1960) called the "age of high mass consumption" that followed. This view, if accepted, leads to important revisions in our understanding of the sources and trajectory of economic growth in the second quarter of the century and, more broadly, over the longer sweep of U.S. economic history since the Civil War.

The argument will strike some readers as implausible. Surely it was World War II that both brought us out of the Depression and laid the foundation for postwar prosperity. And if we insist on locating an era of strong growth in capacity in the interwar period, it must have been in the roaring twenties. If not then, what about the golden age, the quarter century from 1948 to 1973, the epoch of the strongest growth in the U.S. material standard of living? Finally (though this reaction would have been more common in March 2000 than in March 2011), what of the information technology boom of the late twentieth century? Surely all else pales before that.

To each of these questions this book responds with empirically supported answers. The 1920s did benefit from transformative organizational and technological progress involving both new products (especially the automobile and electrical appliances) and a revolution in factory organization and design in which traditional methods of distributing power internally via metal shafts and leather belts were replaced with electrical wires and small electric motors. But outside of manufacturing, there was little progress.

What made the 1930s (1929–1941) so unusual was the combination of still rapid advance in manufacturing with the effects of spillovers in transportation and distribution resulting from the buildout of the surface road network. Total factor productivity (TFP) growth within manufacturing slowed by almost half compared to its unparalleled record in the 1920s, though it remained world class by any standard of comparison other than the 1920s.[1] And the sector grew, so its weight was larger. Nevertheless, if the argument advanced here is correct, there had to have been significant progress elsewhere in the economy. And there was. The second pillar of the story involves the organizational and technological transformation of transportation and distribution (wholesale and retail trade) made possible by street, highway, bridge, and tunnel construction.

During the 1920s the expansion of car and truck production outpaced the modernization of the road network. Developing an infrastructure suitable for a transportation system rolling increasingly on rubber tires required overcoming political disputes about where the new U.S. route system would be located. These obstacles were largely resolved by November 1926, and if one looks at the data on street and highway improvements from then until the beginning of the Second World War, the effects of the Depression appear modest and short-lived, mostly affecting the years 1933, 1934, and 1935. In contrast, the building of private structures remained depressed throughout the decade.

The growth of public infrastructure resulted in large productivity gains in distribution and in transportation, where a striking complementarity developed between the rail system and the growing trucking industry. Together, the gains in manufacturing, transportation, distribution, and smaller sectors such as communication meant that the technological and organizational contribution to the growth of capacity across the Depression years was larger and more diversified in its sectoral origins than in other periods of U.S. history.

Although the Second World War provided a massive fiscal and monetary boost that eliminated the remnants of Depression-era unemployment, it was, on balance, disruptive of the forward pace of technological progress in the private sector. Military initiatives such as the Manhattan Project diverted scientific and engineering talent away from the private sector. And the economy was forced through wrenching changes as the military economy quickly expanded and then almost as rapidly shrank. The industrial buildup between mid-1942 and October 1943 was heavily unbalanced, focused on a small number of war-related sectors, such as iron and steel, chemicals, other transportation equipment, and electrical equipment. From 1944 onward, there was an almost equally rapid unwinding of the war economy. While the fiscal effect of war spending provided the final stimulus to bring the economy out of the Depression, the war experience, which involved in total perhaps forty months of serious war mobilization, with the peak effort lasting sixteen months, had a more muted and ultimately retardative effect on the growth of capacity. It was the expansion of potential output during the Depression, largely unappreciated because it took place against a backdrop of double-digit unemployment, that laid the foundation both for successful war mobilization and for the golden age that followed.

The golden age experienced the fastest sustained growth in the material standard of living in U.S. economic history. Much of this resulted from the revival of more "normal" patterns of physical capital accumulation (the acquisition of new structures and equipment), a process that had been disrupted by financial crisis during the Depression and distorted during the war. Organizational and technological progress per se proceeded at a respectable rate, but one that was more moderate than had been experienced during the Depression years. TFP growth in manufacturing continued to slow in comparison with the prewar period, but strong advance within such sectors as transportation and distribution persisted. Both the declining influence of progress within manufacturing (compared especially with the 1920s) and the significance of the continued transition within transportation and distribution reflected trends whose origins are to be found in the interwar years.

The causes of the slowdown in productivity growth during the "dark ages" (1973 through 1989 or 1995) remain an enigma. The retardation was broad-based; the continued slippage in the manufacturing TFP growth rate can account for only about a sixth of the TFP slowdown in the private nonfarm economy. The decrease in nondefense research and development spending probably played a role. Another influence was the conclusion of the buildout of the surface road infrastructure marked by the completion of the Interstate Highway System. Continued road construction would not necessarily have avoided retardation; by the early 1970s, the low-hanging fruit had largely been harvested. Nevertheless, exhaustion of potential gains from such infrastructural investments does help us understand why productivity growth slowed after 1973.

The economic and productivity history of the twentieth century up through 1995 can thus be thought of as a tale of two transitions. The first involved the electrification and reconfiguration of the American factory, a development that had its roots in the 1880s but blossomed only in the 1920s, producing enormously high rates of TFP growth in manufacturing during that decade. TFP growth rates in manufacturing then trended generally downward for the remainder of the century. The second transition, involving the movement of goods, peaked later. From the late 1920s through the early 1970s, trucking expanded its share of interstate ton mileage, while the rail sector shrank, specializing as it did so.

The information technology (IT) boom, which ran from 1995 to 2005, offered a respite from the doldrums into which productivity growth had fallen at the end of the golden age. The IT boom, and the technologies with which it was associated, have changed our lives. But from a historical perspective, advance was narrowly concentrated in the manufacturing sectors producing products such as computers, cell phones, and routers, as well as, at least initially, in a few sectors such as retailing and securities trading that used IT intensively. Compared to the Great Depression, the locus of revolutionary change was not as broad, and its overall impact on the growth of economic capacity has been more modest.

Many aspects of this narrative will challenge readers' preconceptions. A final part of the story, however, may be more easily accepted, particularly by non-specialists. It concerns the place of the post–Civil War period—roughly the last third of the nineteenth century—in U.S. economic and technological history. That epoch witnessed the expansion of railroad and telegraph networks, new steelmaking techniques, scientific progress across a broad frontier, and the birth of a genuinely new organizational form, the modern business enterprise, as chronicled by Alfred Chandler (1977). Yet pioneering growth economists such as Moses Abramovitz and Robert Solow downplayed the extent to which technological and organizational change during this period contributed to the growth of capacity beyond what resulted simply from the accumulation of new types of capital. They argued that most of the growth of output could be swept back to the growth of inputs conventionally measured—principally labor hours and the services of physical capital. And they contrasted this aspect of nineteenth-century growth with what they came to view as a defining feature of the twentieth century: increases in output far larger than what could be explained by the growth of inputs.

Their generalizations about twentieth-century growth were, however, made on the basis of only half a century of data (Solow, for example, based his conclusions on data from 1909 through 1949) and were heavily influenced by the extraordinary advance during the interwar period. With the twentieth century now complete, we can look back on almost a century and a half of U.S. economic growth and appreciate that the contribution of disembodied technological and organizational advance during the last third of the nineteenth century, though more modest than that experienced during the interwar years or the golden age, was nevertheless much higher than that enjoyed during the comparable portion of the twentieth century. In recognizing this, we can partially rehabilitate the idea that new blueprints such as the railroad and the modern business enterprise had a truly transformative impact on American economic history and growth.

The first half of the book (part I) makes the case for reorienting the history of U.S. growth around a very substantial increase in potential output between 1929 and 1941. The truly famous Great Leap Forward was, of course, a disastrous program of forced industrialization initiated by the Chinese leadership in the late 1950s. The expansion of capacity during the Depression years in the United States, in contrast, resulted largely from private initiative and creativity, augmented by what were historically modest government investments in infrastructure. This expansion nevertheless laid the foundation both for successful prosecution of the Second World War and for the quarter century of golden age growth that followed.

Part II of the book extends part I's analysis and reflects on some of its implications. Chapter 7 shows that the strong procyclicality of TFP during the Depression years was in fact a feature of the entire period 1890–2004. Chapter 8 revisits the equipment hypothesis, the view that producer durables, much more than structures, are carriers of technological change, that the social return to equipment investment exceeds the private return, and that such investment should be subsidized. Chapter 9 asks, in light of the narrative developed in part I, whether the practice of economic history could do as well without the now popular concept of a general purpose technology.

As work proceeded on this book in the fall of 2008, it was hard not to be transfixed by the astonishing chapter in economic history then unfolding. The last section of the book, part III, provides historical perspective on the almost catastrophic financial and economic meltdown experienced in the last part of the 2000s. Chapter 10 locates the origins of the crisis in the economy's growing financial fragility, a process with roots extending at least as far back as the administration of President Ronald Reagan. Chapter 11 considers in more detail what we can learn about real estate development and its consequences from the history of the interwar period. Finally, chapter 12 asks, in light of the experience of the 1930s, whether economic downturns may have a silver lining. An epilogue concludes.

Before proceeding, however, we must ask, in regard to the argument developed in part I, *how can we know these things?* How can we judge the comparative technological progressivity of different epochs? Qualitative accounts of invention and innovation are obviously important, and they play a role in the story that unfolds. But a substantial part of the argument relies on inferences from quantitative data. In order to appreciate the basis upon which they are drawn, an understanding of key concepts is essential. A number of the categories and methods used in this book are likely to be obscure, even for those who have some familiarity with economics. I review them now. Those with advanced training in economics can skip this material and go directly to the section discussing the history of growth accounting. Or they may wish to move straight to chapter 1.

CONCEPTS AND METHODS

There are two main productivity concepts used in this work. The first and more commonly encountered is labor productivity. Labor productivity is the ratio of output to labor input, measured as the number of employees or the number of labor hours (the latter measure is used in this book). Labor productivity means output per hour, and the growth rate of labor productivity is the difference between the growth rate of output and the growth rate of hours. The focus in the book is on aggregate and sectoral measures, but it can also be measured at the firm level. Labor productivity growth is critical in understanding improvement in the material standard of living, as measured by per capita output. Output per employee hour is not the same as output per capita—they have different denominators and may grow at different rates because of changes in labor force participation or the number of hours worked per person. But over the long run it is impossible to have a sustained increase in output per capita without a sustained increase in output per hour. That is one reason why we pay so much attention to labor productivity.

The second and less familiar concept, total factor productivity, lies at the core of the narrative. TFP is the ratio of output to a combined measure reflecting both capital and labor inputs. The growth of total factor productivity is the difference between the growth in output and a weighted average of the growth of capital services and labor hours, the weights corresponding to the shares of these factors in national income (typically about one-fourth to one-third for capital and the remainder for labor).[2] When, measuring between business cycle peaks, output grows more than a combined measure of the two key inputs, we can interpret the difference as a rough measure of the growth in capacity due to technological and organizational advance.

Since the end of the Civil War, the U.S. economy has grown at a long-term rate of a little more than 3 percent per year. Again, taking a very long view, we can decompose this into a long-term rate of population growth, and thus labor force, and thus hours, of roughly 1 percent per year, combined with a growth rate of output per hour (labor productivity) of about 2 percent per year.

The factors contributing to the growth of output and output per hour are related but not exactly the same. First consider output. The growth of output over a particular time period is decomposable into the contributions made by the growth of hours, the growth of the services of physical capital, and the growth in the power and efficacy of the recipes whereby these inputs are combined to generate output. The latter we call total factor productivity.

Here is an important illustration of the relevance of TFP. Between 1929 and 1941, labor hours in the U.S. private nonfarm economy were effectively unchanged. Because of population growth the labor force was larger in 1941, but the unemployment rate in 1941 was still several times what it had been in 1929, so total hours were about the same. Capital input by some measures had declined. For practical purposes, we can say that private sector inputs, conventionally measured, grew not at all between 1929 and 1941. No matter how we weight the growth rates of the two inputs, we will get combined private sector input growth close to zero. But real output was between 33 and 40 percent higher in 1941 as compared with 1929.[3] The difference between growth of inputs of zero and a growth of output of somewhere between 2.3 and 2.8 percent per year over the twelve-year period reflected improvement in total factor productivity. This empirical observation is one of the key findings of the book.

The growth of total factor productivity is one of two influences on the growth of labor productivity. The latter can be decomposed into a contribution from total factor productivity, representing in a very broad sense the benefits we get from technological and organizational progress, and a contribution attributable to saving and accumulation, or capital deepening, a process that results in members of the labor force cooperating with larger quantities of physical capital. Capital deepening (rises in the capital-labor ratio) by itself makes workers more productive. Ditch diggers using backhoes will move more cubic meters of earth per hour than those using shovels or hand tools. Moving from hand tools to backhoes (capital deepening) makes workers more productive, even if it is not reflective of any change in the available book of blueprints.

Separating the growth in output per hour into the respective and approximate contributions of innovation (the TFP portion) and thrift (the capital-deepening contribution) provides broad insights into the sources of labor productivity growth in different periods. Note an important implication about the Depression years: since the growth of both labor hours and physical capital in the private sector was close to nil between 1929 and 1941, there was no capital deepening (increase in the capital-labor ratio) over these years. Therefore, during this unusual period, virtually all of the increase in both output and output per hour is attributable to growth in total factor productivity.

A more formal treatment of these relationships, and discussion of some of the nuances of their interpretation, is included as an appendix. The key takeaway is that we aim to judge the comparative technological progressivity of different periods through comparisons of the annual average rate of total factor productivity growth in the private nonfarm economy, measuring, as best we can, between business cycle peaks.

OUTPUT MEASURES

Readers are likely acquainted with the concept of gross national or gross domestic product (GNP or GDP), consisting roughly of marketable goods and services produced during a given time period.[4] Most of the empirical work in this book involves a subset of GDP known as the *private nonfarm economy* (PNE). The main difference between GDP and the PNE is the exclusion from the latter of agricultural as well as federal, state, and local government production.[5] Although agriculture has shrunk during the periods with which this book is concerned, government has grown, so the share of the PNE in GDP has remained roughly constant at about three-fourths.

Much of this book's argument depends on using growth rates of productivity measures to make inferences about the relative technological progressivity of different periods. There are reasons for excluding agriculture and government from such calculations. Agricultural output is frequently influenced by shocks such as rainfall fluctuations, drought, flooding, and other natural events that are almost entirely unrelated to progress in technology or organization. The main exception to the book's exclusion of consideration of agriculture is chapter 6, which treats the late nineteenth century and concentrates on data for the *private domestic economy* (PDE), consisting of the private nonfarm economy plus agriculture.

Government output is not included in either the PNE or the PDE. Such output is not sold on the market and is typically valued at the cost of inputs. This accounting convention effectively precludes the sector's TFP from growing, which is why it makes sense to exclude it from productivity calculations.

Productivity tends to be easier to measure in manufacturing than elsewhere if for no other reason than that one can often benchmark by looking at physical output measures. But limiting oneself to manufacturing is problematic. How can we hope to construct a growth narrative for the economy as a whole by focusing on a small and declining sector? Value added in manufacturing peaked at about a third of the economy during the Second World War, averaging a little over 30 percent of GDP in the 1940s, 1950s, and 1960s. But its share declined thereafter, and today it generates a smaller fraction of national income, and employs a smaller fraction of the labor force, than it did in 1869.[6] Trends in manufacturing sometimes mirror what is happening in the rest of the economy, but not always. The study of manufacturing productivity forms part of the analysis that follows. But the focus is less on manufacturing productivity growth per se and more on the sector's contribution to productivity growth in the larger aggregates.

Note that the relevant output measure when one is considering an individual sector like manufacturing is not gross sales but value added. Value added is the difference between gross sales and purchased inputs, including energy, materials and subassemblies, and services other than those provided by employees. Value added represents a sector or firm's contribution to GDP. Purchased materials include the contributions of other sectors or firms. Safeway's contribution to GDP is not its gross sales, since that would inappropriately credit the supermarket chain with the value added by its suppliers. Since wage and salary payments as well as payments to owners of capital are made out of the flow of net revenue generated by value added, value added also represents a sector or firm's contribution to gross domestic income (GDI). It is because this equality must be true for every individual economic unit that in the aggregate, GDP must, subject to a statistical discrepancy, equal GDI.

Understanding what is included in the output measures is important. Equally important is understanding what is meant by *potential output* or *economic capacity*. Part I of the book is principally concerned with the growth of capacity. Potential output is not necessarily the same as GDP because actual output may fall below it. During a recession an *output gap* opens and, associated with it, increased involuntary unemployment. Capacity is sometimes called potential output, and sometimes, more technically, the non-accelerating inflation rate of output (or "natural" output), which has associated with it a non-accelerating inflation rate of unemployment (the NAIRU, or "natural" rate of unemployment). Because of the way capacity is defined, it is also possible, when the economy is experiencing sustained positive aggregate demand shocks, for output temporarily to exceed it.

Given an economy's labor force, capital stock, and technological and organizational blueprints and institutions, capacity or potential represents the highest level of output achievable without so stimulating the economy through expansionary fiscal or monetary measures that the inflation rate accelerates. Expansionary fiscal measures include tax cuts or increased spending; expansionary monetary policy results principally from open market operations during which the Federal Reserve System buys from the public previously issued Treasury debt in exchange for newly printed money or its equivalent. Either of these dynamics is considered a positive *aggregate demand shock*, or, for short, *demand shock*. If one is below potential output, positive demand shocks tend to increase output and employment; above potential their effect tends to shows up in inflation. In contrast, an *aggregate supply shock*, or *supply shock*, changes potential output. Demand shocks and supply shocks can be either positive or negative.

At a business cycle peak an economy is at or near capacity. In a downturn, output will fall below potential as an output gap widens and unemployment grows. Given the way the rate is calculated, some unemployment is socially beneficial. Individuals unemployed but actively seeking work are considered to be in the labor force. New entrants or reentrants, along with those who have quit or been fired from previous jobs, don't necessarily accept the first employment offer they encounter, and up to a point this search process is beneficial for both employees and employers. During recessions, however, unemployment and the unemployment rate rise to levels far above what can be rationalized on this basis.

In calculating long-run productivity growth rates, it is desirable, as much as is practically possible, to measure from business cycle peak to business cycle peak. The reason is that productivity measures tend to be *procyclical*: their levels or their rate of growth decline as one goes into a recession and rise as one comes out of it (see chapter 7). Measuring from a business cycle trough to a peak would likely give a misleadingly high estimate of the long-term or trend rate of growth. On the other hand, measuring from a peak to a trough will generally show that the actual levels of productivity are declining, even though one may be in a technologically progressive period. Measuring from peak to peak avoids these confounding influences on calculations of trend growth rates. These considerations are particularly relevant in thinking about the Depression years because of the steep drop in output between 1929 and 1933.

A NOTE ON MEASUREMENT

Sophisticated students of time series don't measure growth rates as simple percentage increases due to the asymmetry between decreases and increases. As those invested in the stock market ruefully appreciate, a drop in the Dow from ten thousand to eight thousand is a 20 percent decline. But a 20 percent increase from eight thousand won't return you to ten thousand. The solution is to calculate continuously compounded growth rates. Most of us recall problems in which we had to figure out whether 5.25 percent compounded monthly was better than 5 percent compounded daily. A continuously compounded growth rate is a rate of increase calculated such that the compounding interval has been reduced to an arbitrarily small period. Natural logarithms provide an easy means of calculating such rates. The rate of change over time of the natural logarithm of a magnitude is its continuously compounded growth rate. So the growth rate of a magnitude over five years, for example, can be calculated as the difference between the natural logarithm of the variable in the end period and the natural logarithm in the beginning period, divided by five. Mathematically equivalent is the natural logarithm of the ratio of end to beginning value, divided by five.

This is one reason why time series of economic magnitudes are typically plotted on what engineers called semi-log paper—with a logarithmic scale on the vertical axis and a linear scale for time on the horizontal. Then the continuously calculated growth rate is proportional to the slope of the line—rise over run. Thus a plot of U.S. real GDP since 1869 on semi-log paper will have a roughly constant slope, reflecting the long-term growth rate of the economy of a little over 3 percent. With a linear scale on the vertical axis we would see a curved line reflecting exponential growth, but we could not tell visually whether the increase reflected a true inflection point in the growth rate or simply the effects of compounding. Unless otherwise noted, reported growth rates in this book are continuously compounded, as described here.

ONLINE RESOURCES

The bibliography and source notes provide full documentation for all of the tables. Many of the more important statistical sources are now available online. For the pre-1948 period, the starting point for any serious study of productivity trends in the United States is Kendrick (1961).[7] Thanks to the National Bureau of Economic Research, the full text and all the tables from this book are available at http://www.nber.org/books/kend61–1. From 1948 onward I rely principally on data from two government statistical agencies: the Department of Labor's Bureau of Labor Statistics (BLS) (http://www.bls.gov) and the Department of Commerce's Bureau of Economic Analysis (BEA) (http://www.bea.gov). The BLS is the source for productivity and employment/unemployment data. The BEA provides information on output (click on the link for Gross Domestic Product; some tables extend back to 1929) and physical capital stock (click on the link for Fixed Assets; data extend back to 1925). Another very valuable set of online resources is the Bureau of the Census's annual *Statistical Abstract of the United States*, available at http://www.census.gov/compendia/statab/past_years .html. The bicentennial edition of *Historical Statistics of the United States* can also be accessed through this site.

A BRIEF NOTE ON THE HISTORY OF GROWTH ACCOUNTING

The discipline of growth accounting emerged as an effort to decompose increases in real output into the contribution of input growth (principally hours and physical capital) and a residual, and the statistical work in part I of this book adheres closely to the original implementation of this vision. Innovations in these chapters involve the choice of beginning- and end-period dates and what aggregates to use, not in basic methods. The aim is to produce a clearer picture of what actually happened across the course of American history.

As noted, in the 1950s Moses Abramovitz and Robert Solow both concluded, based in part on the yet unpublished work of John Kendrick, that economic growth in the twentieth century differed from the nineteenth in this sense. In the nineteenth century most of the growth of output could be swept back to the growth of inputs conventionally measured. With unrestricted immigration and physical capital accumulation fueled by domestic saving as well as capital account surpluses, both employee hours and physical capital, particularly in the form of railroads and housing, grew rapidly.[8] The increases in the two key inputs—labor and capital—weighted by their shares in national income, could account for most of the increase in output. In the twentieth century, in contrast, they argued, a large gap opened up between the growth of real output and the growth of inputs conventionally measured, and we shifted to what Abramovitz described as an era of "knowledge-based" growth. This gap became known as the residual.

Much of the subsequent work in growth accounting, such as that by Dale Jorgenson and Zvi Griliches (1967) or Edward Denison (1974), aimed to move beyond Abramovitz and Solow by allocating, explaining, decomposing, and, to the extent that this was possible, eliminating the gap between measured output and input growth. Part of the strategy was to augment or modify input series in ways that generally increased their growth rates—for example, by adjusting labor input to take account of increased schooling levels in the workforce or trying to quantify how much of the residual reflected unmeasured quality improvements in capital inputs. The remainder was attributed to such factors as shifts of resources from sectors with lower value added per worker to sectors with higher value added per worker or speculations about the contribution of investments in research and development.

In describing the way he measured inputs as conventional, Abramovitz alluded indirectly to these less conventional approaches, which often devolved into educated guesses about what underlay the twentieth-century gap between output and input growth he and Solow had identified. In characterizing the twentieth century as one of knowledge-based growth, Abramovitz associated the residual in general terms with improvement in technical and organizational competencies. But he also characterized it as a measure of our ignorance. Scholars such as Jorgenson and Griliches wished to eliminate these areas of ignorance, hoping as well that such retrospective research might provide insights that could inform policy. Their work nevertheless accepted—and indeed was premised upon—the view that there really had been a dramatic and irreversible change in the sources of growth in the twentieth century.

My argument in this book, in contrast, is that the twentieth century was not fundamentally different from the nineteenth in the ways suggested by Abramovitz and Solow. When inputs are measured conventionally, trend growth rates in total factor productivity varied substantially across different subperiods within both centuries, but the United States has not, at least since the end of the Civil War, moved systematically toward higher TFP growth rates. During the last third of the twentieth century, and in the absence of any of the multitudinous add-ons proffered by Denison or Jorgenson and Griliches, the residual, all by itself, almost completely vanished. Once again, and indeed to an even greater degree than at the end of the nineteenth century, the growth of output could be explained almost entirely as the consequence of the growth of inputs.

The Abramovitz-Solow characterization of twentieth-century growth, based as it was on data from only the first half of the century, turned out to have been premature. Their conclusions about the large role played by the residual were heavily influenced by its rapid growth across the Depression years and, to a lesser degree, during the 1920s (1919–1929). The claim of a fundamental difference between the character of nineteenth- and twentieth-century growth could be sustained through the golden age (1948–1973) but not as the residual melted away during the dark ages of slow productivity advance (1973–1995). As chapter 6 demonstrates, TFP growth in the last third of the twentieth century was slower than in the comparable period of the nineteenth. These statistics suggest that our challenge is less to explain why growth in the twentieth century was so different from what took place in the nineteenth and more to document and understand why, within both centuries, the trend rate of TFP growth has been so different in different subperiods.

Rather than starting from the presumption that twentieth-century economic growth was characterized by a comparatively larger residual and then devoting energy to explaining, decomposing, or eliminating it, this book begins with consideration of how trend growth rates of TFP varied over subperiods during the past century and a half. It assumes that differences in TFP growth rates can be used as very general indicators of the degree of technological and organizational progressiveness during different periods and finds, based on sectoral and industry-level data, much micro-level evidence consistent with the story told by the aggregate data.

Part I focuses almost exclusively on aggregate supply, and in particular on the trend growth rate of total factor productivity and potential output in different periods. The second half of the book extends the argument in new directions, explores more traditional questions associated with the Great Depression—questions of cyclicality—and places this work within the context of the near catastrophic meltdown of the U.S. and world economy in 2008–2009. Whereas part I aspires to set forth a robust narrative that will stand the test of time, parts II and III raise important questions that invite further inquiry.

Chapters 7, 10, 11, and 12 return to what are, from the standpoint of Depression scholars, more traditional concerns: the causes and consequences of cycles. The models and methods employed differ from those being developed at what John Cochrane (2009) and others would consider the frontiers of macroeconomic research. The framework utilized is what continues to be taught in intermediate macroeconomics courses: a blend of Keynesian aggregate demand analysis with an expectations-augmented Philips curve and explicit treatment of aggregate supply. This framework has the great merit of being useful for research in economic history, of helping us understand the current economic environment, and of offering assistance to policymakers when the economy is below potential.

The centrality of the Great Depression to this book is reflected in its organization. Part I begins with 1929–1941 and then moves roughly chronologically from the interwar period through the end of the twentieth and the beginning of the twenty-first century (chapters 1–5). Chapter 6 addresses the relationship of late-nineteenth-century development to what took place during the twentieth.

Part II develops extensions and implications of the narrative. Chapter 7 builds on the chapter 3 finding of strong Depression-era TFP procyclicality. It documents the pronounced procyclicality of TFP across more than a century (and the weaker procyclicality of output per hour) and explains it as resulting principally from aggregate demand shocks interacting with capital input that in the aggregate can't be decreased much during a recession. It rejects the view that procyclicality is a statistical artifact and contrasts the interpretation advanced with labor-hoarding stories as well as the approach associated with real business cycle models.

Chapter 8 considers implications for the equipment hypothesis—the view, popular in the 1990s, that investment in equipment, unlike that in structures, is a carrier of technological change and should be subsidized because its social rate exceeds its private rate of return. And yet, as the chapter shows, as the equipment share in gross investment and net capital stocks moved higher across the twentieth century, TFP growth moved generally lower, a reason for some skepticism.

Chapter 9 reflects, based on the argument of the first part of the book, on whether economic history could do as well without the concept of a general-purpose technology (GPT). Despite efforts to define the concept precisely, much ambiguity remains about what does and does not qualify and whether the criteria provide a good filter for identifying truly consequential innovations. As far as providing an organizing principle for writing economic history, the chapter notes that the most technologically progressive era of the twentieth century, the Depression years, cannot usefully be identified with any individual GPT, a particular breakthrough technology that gave its character to the age.

Part III considers ways in which Depression-era economic history can be relevant for understanding 2007–2010, and vice versa. Chapter 10 compares the Great Recession with the boom-and-bust economic history of the interwar period, focusing on an endogenously produced cycle of financial fragility and what might be done to control it. Chapter 11 looks at the real estate booms of the 1920s and their legacy in the 1930s. Uncontrolled land development in the 1920s was a response to new profit-making opportunities made possible by the automobile. The booms left physical and legal facts on the ground in the 1930s, including fractionated and uncertain ownership, premature subdivision, and poorly platted developments that hindered recovery in the Depression. The concluding chapter explores, looking particularly at railroads in the 1930s, whether depression can have a beneficial impact on long-run productivity growth. On balance, a boom/bust cycle is likely to impact long-run TFP growth negatively, but the dynamics engendered are mixed in their effects, and the answer to the question posed is nuanced: there can be positive influences. In particular, while much of the strong productivity performance of railroads during the Depression can be attributed to spillovers from street and highway construction, as described in chapters 1 and 2, some resulted directly from the sheer shock of adversity generated by the prolonged economic downturn.

A short epilogue considers the impact of the generally downward trend of TFP growth across the twentieth century on our cultural imagination.

With the exception of chapter 11, this book is based on research conducted over the past dozen years. But I have been working on topics related to the Great Depression for almost three decades. Its relevance for thinking about U.S. economic growth—and cycles—has, between 2007 and 2010, become even more apparent. The United States was fortunate at this juncture to have had a Federal Reserve chair (Ben Bernanke) and a chair of the President's Council of Economic Advisors (Christina Romer) who were both serious students of economic history and of this period.[9]

Part One

A New Growth Narrative

---●●●---

THE MOST TECHNOLOGICALLY PROGRESSIVE DECADE OF THE CENTURY

It was not principally the Second World War that laid the foundation for postwar prosperity. It was technological progress across a broad frontier of the American economy during the 1930s.

Because of the Depression's place in both the popular and academic imagination and the repeated and justifiable emphasis on output that wasn't produced, income that wasn't earned, and expenditure that didn't take place, it will seem startling to propose the view that the years 1929–1941 were, in the aggregate, the most technologically progressive of any comparable period in U.S. economic history.[1] The hypothesis entails two primary claims: first, during this period businesses and government contractors implemented or adopted on a more widespread basis a wide range of new technologies and practices, resulting in the highest rate of peacetime peak-to-peak TFP growth in the century, and second, the Depression years produced advances that replenished and expanded the stock of unexploited or only partially exploited techniques, thus providing the basis for much of the labor and total factor productivity improvement in the 1950s and 1960s.

The hypothesis does not imply that all of the effects of the advances registered in the decade were immediately felt in the productivity data, nor, on the other hand, does it dismiss the significance of larder-stocking during the 1920s and earlier, upon which measured advance built.[2] Rather, it draws our attention to the probability that progress in invention and innovation in the 1930s was significant, in ways not well appreciated, both in facilitating the remarkable U.S. economic performance before and during World War II and in establishing foundations for the prosperity of the 1950s and 1960s.

OUTPUT GROWTH, INPUT GROWTH, AND THE PRODUCTIVITY DATA

The starting point for this exploration is macroeconomic data on real output growth, labor force growth, and the growth of the real capital stock, series that underlie our conclusions about trends in labor productivity and total factor productivity growth. Major contributors to the construction, adjustment, and interpretation of these data have included Edward Denison, John Kendrick, Dale Jorgenson, Zvi Griliches, Robert Solow, Moses Abramovitz, Paul David, and Robert J. Gordon. Of these, only the last three have attempted systematic historically informed overviews of the twentieth century as a whole. There is agreement that, over the course of U.S. history, the period between roughly 1905 and 1966 experienced exceptionally high rates of total factor productivity growth, substantially higher than those evidenced in the decades preceding and following, when a much higher fraction of labor productivity growth is to be attributed simply to capital deepening (Abramovitz and David 1999, 2000; R. J. Gordon 1999, 2000a, 2000b, 2000c).

Within that plateau, the highest rates of TFP growth appear to have occurred in the second quarter of the century. Although the question of *when* within the 1905–1966 period peak TFP growth took place was not central to their research agenda, Abramovitz and David concluded that it happened in advance of mid-century.[3] Gordon zeroed in more intensively on the mid-century chronology, but his interpretations pose challenges because his narrative (and numbers) have changed somewhat in his publications. In Gordon (2000b), however, he continued to emphasize, consonant with the Abramovitz/David view, that "In the United States, in comparison to Japan and Europe, a substantial part of the great leap in the level of multifactor productivity had already occurred by the end of World War II" (Gordon 2000b, p. 22).[4]

Both the Abramovitz/David and Gordon analyses draw our attention to high and accelerating TFP growth in the second quarter of the century (see table 1.1). It was the data underlying what was then recent economic history that so surprised Robert Solow in his 1957 analysis, for which, in part, he received the Nobel Prize. Solow's work contributed to the development of the concept of the residual and its interpretation: since real output was growing much faster than could be explained by the growth of inputs conventionally measured, he (as did Abramovitz and others) suggested that the unexplained growth should be identified statistically with the contribution of a number of factors, the most important of which was technical change. Solow's seminal article was, however, published more than fifty years ago.

Table 1.1. Growth Rates of Private Nonfarm TFP,
United States, 1870–1996 (percent per year)

Abramovitz and David 1999		*Gordon 2000b*	
		1870–1891	.39
1890–1905	1.28	1891–1913	1.14
1905–1927	1.38	1913–1928	1.42
1929–1948	1.54	1928–1950	1.90
1948–1966	1.31	1950–1964	1.47
		1964–1972	.89
1966–1989	.04	1972–1979	.16
		1979–1988	.59
		1988–1996	.79

Sources: Abramovitz and David 1999, table 1: IV-A; Gordon 2000b, table 1, p. 28. The Abramovitz and David capital input estimates include an adjustment for vintage effects, based on the presumption that more recently installed capital embodies unmeasured quality improvements (see text). Their output series includes housing services, and their input series includes the housing capital stock, in contrast to Gordon, who excludes housing in both numerator and denominator. Gordon's data are before his adjustments for the composition of labor and quantity of capital; for discussion of these adjustments, see text.

Between 1973 and 1989 or 1995 Solow's residual—and indeed the total factor productivity growth to which it gives rise—all but vanished. It is true that labor productivity continued to grow, albeit at a markedly slower rate, but a very high percentage of this can be attributed to capital deepening (increases in the ratio of capital to labor), which continued at a slower rate than was true in the 1950s and 1960s in part because of an upward trend in hours per worker.[5] Still, to the degree that labor productivity has advanced in recent years, it has, with the exception of a ten-year period beginning in 1995, done so the old-fashioned way—through sacrifice of current consumption so that physical capital goods (mostly structures and equipment) could be piled up at a faster rate than the growth of labor hours.[6] Thus the economic history of the last three decades of the twentieth century recapitulated in the United States a pattern similar in some respects to that identified by Abramovitz and Solow for the late nineteenth century but quite markedly absent during the second quarter of the twentieth century and more generally over the five-to-six-decade period prior to the mid-1960s.[7]

The 1929–1948 period (I discuss the choice of beginning and end points below) is critical in understanding the long-term trajectory of technical change in the United States, both because of its direct effect on growth during the period and because of its lagged effect on TFP advance in the 1950s, which, when coupled with renewed capital deepening, produced what is often called the golden age of labor productivity growth and living standard improvement. If we are to put in perspective U.S. economic accomplishments over the past six decades, we need to understand what happened prior to mid-century to place the American economy in the position of world dominance it enjoyed after the war. Partly of course this involved wartime devastation in Europe and Japan. But partly it must have reflected the extraordinarily high rates of TFP growth over the second quarter of the century in the United States, and the question on this account comes down to how much of this was the direct result of wartime experience and how much is to be attributed to prior peacetime advances, particularly those achieved through 1941, both in measured productivity advance and in larder stocking.

TWO STORIES

This chapter is concerned specifically with what happened between 1929 and 1948 and when and, more particularly, with whether the bulk of total factor productivity advance over the period had already been achieved *before* full scale U.S. mobilization in 1942. Two competing hypotheses may be suggested with respect to this record. Either the growth in TFP is primarily attributable to an exceptional concatenation of technical and organizational advances across a broad frontier of the American economy during the 1930s, building on unexploited opportunities at the end of the 1920s, or it is principally the consequence of the production experience of World War II, a persisting benefit of the enormous cumulated output, as well perhaps of spinoffs from war-related research and development (R and D). For the latter hypothesis, the explanation of how we got to where we were by the end of the 1940s, to make reference to a classic article by Kenneth Arrow, is principally that the economy was one large C-47 factory, permanently reaping the gains from wartime learning by doing (Arrow 1962; Alchian 1963).[8]

Certainly the war experience left us with advances in such areas as radar, metalworking and materials science, microwave technology, aeronautics, and atomic energy, as well as additional experience in producing large quantities of aircraft, ships, aviation fuel, synthetic rubber, aluminum, and ordnance. Most of the growth accounting studies (this work is not an exception) focus on non-farm output, but we might add that the expansion of munitions plants led to a permanent decline in the real price of fertilizer in the postwar period, benefit-ing agriculture (Olmstead and Rhode 2000, p. 710).

Whether these advances were, in the aggregate, more significant in account-ing for the level of output and productivity achieved by 1948 than those already attained by 1941, or whose foundations were in place by that point, is a question that has not heretofore been asked. The alternative hypothesis is that the pre-ponderance of gains, both in the achievement of higher measured productivity levels and in the expansion of the larder, had already been attained by the out-break of war and indeed helped make possible its successful prosecution. This then implies that throughout the Depression, behind the dramatic backdrop of continued high unemployment, technological and organizational innovations were occurring across the American economy, especially but not exclusively in chemical engineering (including petrochemicals and synthetic rubber), aero-nautics, electrical machinery and equipment, electric power generation and distribution, transportation, and civil/structural engineering; that these trends have something to do with the rising real wages during this period of those who managed to stay employed, as well as rapidly increasing income to capital, especially after 1933; and that the sum total of these changes had, by the onset of World War II, increased the natural or potential output of the U.S. economy far beyond what contemporary observers and economists at the time believed possible. Some of these developments involved entirely new products, not just process improvements in the production of goods already in the market.

THE U.S. ACHIEVEMENT DURING THE SECOND WORLD WAR

There are several related reasons why economists have been inclined to attri-bute achieved productivity levels in 1948 to the experience of the war.[9] First, the sheer volume of military and total output produced between 1942 and 1945 was indeed remarkable. Second, there were extraordinary achievements in particu-lar sectors, most notably airframes and shipbuilding. Between the first quarter of 1942 and the last quarter of 1944, for example, airframe production increased by a factor of six, and labor productivity grew by 160 percent. Similarly in ship-building: in one ten-month period alone the number of hours required to build a Victory ship fell by half (U.S. Department of Labor 1946, pp. 897–898).

These successes, however, need to be kept in perspective. The War Pro-duction Board estimated that the overall increase in output per hour in the munitions industries was about 25 percent for the 1939–1944 period — certainly respectable but far below the increases registered in standout sectors. Look-ing back on the war from the perspective of 1949, Backman and Gainsbrugh concluded that the overall experience in the military sector "again reveals the extreme difficulties of securing 'miraculous' gains in productivity in any short term period" (1949, pp. 179–180).

And the period was relatively short. The United States declared war on Japan and Germany in December 1941, but it took time to formulate and agree on war production plans, pass budgets, and cut contracts. It was well into 1942 before the economy was on anything like a full-scale war footing (Edelstein 2000). So we are talking about a period of a little more than three years for the puta-tive effects of learning by doing to have established the foundations for postwar prosperity.

With respect to spillovers, there is at least as much evidence of transfer from civilian experience to military production during the war as there is for feed-back in the other direction afterward. The successes in planes and ships, for ex-ample, for the most part represented, in conjunction with massive government-funded infusions of plant and equipment, the application to the production of military hardware of organizational techniques that had been pioneered in the manufacture of radios, vacuum cleaners, and automobiles (Evans 1947, p. 217). Aside from advances in welding techniques, technologies for working with light metals such as aluminum, and radar (U.S. Department of Labor 1946), which benefited the commercial aircraft industry after the war, as well as the aforementioned drop in fertilizer prices, there is relatively limited evidence of beneficial feedback from wartime production to civilian activity in the postwar period.[10]

On balance, the war was detrimental to productivity growth in the civilian sector. It drained skilled workers, managers, and plant and equipment invest-ment from these industries, creating a productivity shortfall that had to be made up afterward. A 1946 Bureau of Labor Statistics study demonstrated that while output per hour in non-munitions industries continued to grow through 1939, 1940, and 1941, it declined in 1942 and 1943 before leveling off in 1944 and in-creasing in 1945 (U.S. Department of Labor 1946, p. 899). There was thus little net gain over the war years. This should be contrasted with a trajectory of rapid gains that might otherwise have persisted through the first half of the 1940s.

Finally, even if we set aside the difficulties in valuing wartime output (Higgs 1992), part of the apparent increase in output per hour was the consequence of the shift of output toward sectors that had traditionally experienced higher value added per worker. Labor productivity for the economy as a whole would have increased as a consequence of this reallocation alone even if there had been no improvement in productive efficiency in any individual sector (see Evans 1947). This effect, however, could not persist: it had to reverse itself with demobilization and the return to a less goods-intensive more consumer-oriented production set.

For all of these reasons there are grounds for doubting that the production experience of the Second World War was principally responsible for achieved productivity levels in 1948.

WHY 1941? WHY 1948? KENDRICK'S DATA AND THE IMPORTANCE OF PEAK-TO-PEAK COMPARISONS

Perhaps the most critical imperative in analyses of productivity trends is that comparisons be made between years in which the economy is at similar stages of the business cycle. As chapter 7 shows, total factor productivity tends to be strongly procyclical (and labor productivity weakly so). This means that productivity growth rates and often levels decline during recessions. Consequently, measurement from trough to peak, for example, may tell us little about long-term trends. The most straightforward way to avoid the contamination of cyclical effects is to choose business cycle peaks for both beginning and end points of a comparison.

Putting the rule into practice, however, is not always simple. The emphasis in this book on the technological progressivity of the Depression years would appear to conflict with Kendrick's conclusion that although private nonfarm economy TFP grew at a rate of 2 percent per year between 1919 and 1929, it did so at only 1.6 percent per year between 1929 and 1937 (Kendrick 1961, p. 72). Given the conventional emphasis on the boom of the 1920s and its contrast with the disastrous macroeconomic performance in the 1930s, we might be inclined to accept this differential and move on to more interesting matters.

The problem is that Kendrick compared a fully employed economy in 1929 (3.2 percent unemployment) with a 1937 economy in which 14.3 percent of the labor force was still out of work. Although large firms were doing well, thousands of medium and smaller ones were not. If we seek a peacetime peak-to-peak comparison, we are better served by choosing as an endpoint 1941, when unemployment, although still averaging 9.9 percent, was closer to what it was in 1929 but before war spending or production could seriously have influenced the economy.[11]

The choice of 1941 warrants further discussion given the two hypotheses developed above. It is true that a military buildup in anticipation of the Second World War had begun by 1941, a year in which federal military spending for rearmament, expansion of uniformed personnel, and Lend Lease and other programs totaled $6.3 billion. This represented about 5 percent of 1941 U.S. GNP, and both total military spending and active-duty military (1.8 million) were more than triple what they had been in 1940 (U.S. Bureau of the Census 1975; Lebergott 1964, table A-3, pp. 512–513).

This increased government spending undoubtedly contributed to higher employment and output levels before the war, through standard multiplier mechanisms (Vernon 1994). But cumulated military procurement was still minor compared to what would follow. Total federal military spending reached $22.9 billion in 1942, $63.4 billion in 1943, $76.0 billion in 1944, and $80.5 billion in 1945, when active-duty military peaked at 12.1 million (U.S. Bureau of the Census 1975; Lebergott 1964). By the end of 1941, only a small fraction (2.5 percent) of the $249.1 billion total military spending occurring between 1941 and 1945 inclusive had already been undertaken.

There would have had to have been extremely rapid spillovers from public to private production for the war buildup to have affected private sector productivity by this date through any mechanism other than bringing the economy closer to full employment. It seems difficult, therefore, to credit achieved productivity levels in 1941 to the effect of new management techniques learned or new technologies discovered as the result of cumulated war production (chapter 3 expands on this point). On the other hand, 1940 is a poor candidate for a peacetime peak, since unemployment (14.6 percent) was actually higher than it had been in 1937. Therefore 1941 is our best bet if we wish to differentiate between the two hypotheses set forth above.

Kendrick's 1961 book includes detailed appendices providing annual measures, in levels, of inputs, outputs, and productivity indexes.[12] It is thus particularly useful in addressing issues of timing. Using his data, I calculate a compound annual average growth rate of private domestic economy TFP of 2.27 percent per year between 1929 and 1941. In contrast, TFP grows at 1.51 percent per year between 1941 and 1948. The differential is larger for the private nonfarm economy: 2.31 percent per year across the Depression years versus 1.29 percent per year between 1941 and 1948 (see table 1.2) (Kendrick 1961, tables A-XXII, A-XXIII, pp. 334–335; 339–340).[13]

It is interesting in this light to reread Solow's 1957 article, which examined annual data for the years 1909 through 1949. The interpretation of his work has generally focused on the small fraction of improvements in output per hour that can be attributed to capital deepening over this period (in other words, the large fraction that is attributable to TFP growth). To my knowledge, his numbers have rarely been examined with an eye to comparative TFP growth

Table 1.2. Growth Rates of TFP, United States,
1919–1948 (percent per year)

Years	Solow (Private Nonfarm Economy)	Kendrick (Private Domestic Economy)	Kendrick (Private Nonfarm Economy)
1919–1929	.78	1.97	2.02
1929–1941	2.36	2.27	2.31
1941–1948	.89	1.51	1.29

Sources: Solow 1957, table 1, p. 315; Kendrick 1961, tables A-XXII, A-XXIII, pp. 334–335, 339–340.

rates within the four decades he looked at. It is striking, in this regard, and not entirely coincidental, to observe that the pattern evident in Kendrick's data for the entire private domestic economy was also apparent, in more extreme form, in Solow's original article. Solow intended his analysis (much of it based on Kendrick's preliminary data) as only a first cut. But he did note that with respect to total factor productivity, "there does seem to be a break at about 1930. There is some evidence that the average rate of progress in the years 1909–29 was smaller than that from 1930–49" (1957, p. 316). Although he did not use his data to examine growth within the latter period, they suggest (see table 1.2) that TFP growth was much higher between 1929 and 1941 as compared with 1941–1948.

ADJUSTMENTS TO THE CAPITAL INPUT SERIES

Although Gordon has repeatedly drawn attention to the extraordinary mid-century productivity record, his work poses special interpretive challenges because of the evolving character of his narrative. In his original emphasis on "one big wave," Gordon identified the 1928–1950 period as evidencing peak TFP growth, and it is this chronology that he featured in several editions of his macroeconomics textbook, beginning in 1993 and extending through the eighth edition published in 2000 (Gordon 2000a, table 10-1, p. 323). Subsequently he made adjustments to both capital and labor input that tipped the balance in favor of his 1950–1964 period (in Gordon 2000b, adjusted TFP growth is 1.13 percent per year for 1950–1964 and 1.05 for 1928–1950; see his table 7, p. 51).

It is important to understand what drives this switch in the top two TFP growth periods. Gordon's adjustments to labor input are straightforward and similar to those made by others; they create an "augmented" input series that takes into account the changing educational and demographic characteristics of the workforce. These changes have almost no impact on comparative TFP growth before and after the war, however, because they boost "effective" labor input by almost the same amount per year in the two periods (.5 vs. .4 percentage points per year).

Nor is the switch in peak TFP growth periods due to the adjustment to capital input for the increasing importance of equipment. Following Jorgenson, Gordon argues that the service flow from equipment tends to be higher because of its higher annual depreciation rates (this is different from the Abramovitz and David "vintage" adjustment, which involves the age of the equipment stock, not its share in total fixed assets). Thus using net capital stock data to proxy for service flow will understate capital input growth if the equipment share is rising. This adjustment, however, operates in favor of the 1928–1950 period since it increases capital input growth .85 percentage points per year between 1950 and 1964 but only .68 percentage points per year between 1928 and 1950.[14]

The toppling of 1928–1950 as the highest TFP growth period in Gordon's 2000 chronology is in fact driven entirely by the "Gordon quantity adjustment"— unique to the author—which boosts the annual average growth rate of capital input by .96 percentage points between 1928 and 1950 while *reducing* it .45 percentage points per year between 1950 and 1964.[15] It is scarcely surprising that such a large difference in the adjustment to input growth rates during the two periods reverses their relative dominance in terms of TFP growth.

The adjustment has three components. The first is the inclusion of street and highway capital. As argued below, there is good reason to believe that such capital was indeed complementary to private sector capital in industries such as trucking, railroads, housing, and wholesale and retail distribution. Including it works, however, in favor of 1928–1950 because street and highway capital grew faster between 1950–1964 than it did over the earlier period (4.62 percent vs. 2.89 percent; see U.S. Department of Commerce 2009, Fixed Asset Table 7.2a, line 10; accessed March 24, 2009).[16]

The second adjustment, which does favor 1950–1964, is for government-owned, privately operated (GOPO) capital, which grew rapidly between 1940 and 1945. During the war Washington funded the construction of large plants for the atomic bomb project (government-owned, government-operated). But it also used billions of dollars of taxpayer money to build structures and pay for equipment (especially machine tools) in a number of other industries critical to the war effort, including synthetic rubber, airframes and engines, aviation fuel refining, and aluminum production. These plants were owned by the government, operated by private firms during the war, and sold off to the private sector in its aftermath.

For decades Gordon has rightly insisted that we acknowledge the economic importance of these assets (Gordon 1969). The increase in GOPO capital between 1940 and 1948, however, is too small in relation to overall private sector capital stocks to account for the reversal in peak TFP periods. It is, moreover, counterbalanced almost exactly, in terms of its impact on comparative TFP growth in the two periods, by the effect of including street and highway capital (see Gordon 2000b, table 5).[17]

Finally, Gordon includes an adjustment for variable retirement rates. The conventional Kendrick/Bureau of Economic Analysis input series assume constant asset lives for each class. In making this adjustment, Gordon assumes instead that retirement rates varied directly with gross investment (Gordon 2000b, pp. 42–45), so that during the 1928–1950 period, when there was relatively little investment, structures and equipment were kept in service longer than would otherwise have been the case. As a consequence, Gordon suggests, the standard unadjusted series imply too small a rate of capital input increase.

There is little dispute that the capital stock aged over the 1928–1950 period and became younger between 1950 and 1964. The average age at year end of private fixed assets rose from 19.2 years in 1928 to 24.7 in 1950, then declined to 21.3 in 1964. Most of the increase in the second quarter of the century took place across the Depression years: average age in 1941 was 24.9 years. (see U.S. Department of Commerce 2010, Fixed Asset Table 1.9; accessed July 2, 2010). As a result, Gordon argues, capital input growth needs to be adjusted upward between 1928 and 1950.

Abramovitz and David, however, claim the reverse, arguing that newer assets are more likely to contain unmeasured or poorly measured quality improvements. Because the average age of assets increased over the second quarter of the century, the contribution to capital input growth of unmeasured quality improvements would have been smaller on this account than in the postwar period. This is the rationale for their vintage adjustment, which *reduces* capital input growth by .11 percentage points per year between 1929 and 1948 while increasing it by .16 percentage points per year between 1948 and 1966 (Abramovitz and David 1999, table 1: IV-A).

The argument they make is typically premised on the assumption that among the various components of the fixed asset stock, equipment is most likely to be characterized by unmeasured quality improvements. The big contributor to the rise in capital's average age, however, was not equipment, whose average age, according to BEA estimates, declined from 7.4 years in 1929 to

7.1 years in 1948 (it did rise over the Depression, standing at 9 years in 1941). The average age of residential structures, in contrast, rose from 23.8 to 29.9 years between 1929 and 1941 and to 31 years in 1948 (U.S. Department of Commerce, Fixed Asset Table 1.9; accessed July 2, 2010). Commercial structures increased from 18.4 years in 1929 to 23.9 years in 1941 to 25.3 years in 1948. The Abramovitz/David vintage adjustment therefore depends on substantial unmeasured quality improvement in newly built housing and commercial structures. That might have been the case, although it is not, I believe, what they had in mind in motivating the adjustment.

Whereas Gordon adjusts capital input growth rates *upwards* between 1928 and 1950 to account for assets being held in service longer because of the paucity of gross investment, Abramovitz and David adjust them *downward* between 1929 and 1948 because of the putative link between low gross investment and low unmeasured quality improvement due to the dominance of older vintages.[18] Gordon notes, but does not adjust for, the likelihood of unmeasured improvements in capital quality (Gordon 2000b, p. 42), which is somewhat ironic, given the emphasis he has given the issue elsewhere.

There is risk in simply assuming which category of fixed assets is most likely to carry unmeasured quality improvements or how much service lives may have changed as the capital stock became on average older. We may end up introducing noise into calculations already heavily contingent on assumptions, rather than improving our ability to draw inferences about the relative technological progressivity of different epochs.

To summarize, I believe that Gordon's original identification of the second quarter of the century as the period of highest TFP growth was correct. The switch to the postwar period in his work is entirely driven by his subsequent adjustment for the impact of an older capital stock on service flow, which has at least three components. In a relatively arbitrary fashion, Gordon made an imputation for one of them, without attempting to account for the counterbalancing effects of the other two. For this reason we should approach these adjusted estimates with caution. My expectation is that we will ultimately accept the broad ranking of peak TFP growth periods emerging from Abramovitz and David, as well as the earlier Gordon work, as the more appropriate one. The 1996 revisions of the BEA's National Income and Product Accounts (NIPA), which introduced the chained index method to measure economic magnitudes over time, result in an upward revision of the 1929–1948 output growth rates, reinforcing this conclusion, as will be discussed below (see chapter 3).

When all is said and done, however, the central issue in this book is not whether 1928–1950 or 1929–1948 had higher TFP growth rates relative to the postwar years. It is whether this was true of 1929–1941. And, particularly in comparison with 1948–1973, or for that matter 1919–1929 or 1995–2005, the case for this is very strong.

MICRO-LEVEL AND SECTORAL ANALYSIS

The macroeconomic evidence that the fastest rate of total factor productivity growth over the last century and a half took place in the 1929–1941 period is consistent with a variety of evidence at the micro level. Alfred Kleinknecht's study of product and process innovations from 1850 to 1969 provides a data set on fundamental innovations divided into product, process, instrumentation, and other. The peak for the total and two of the four components is in the 1930s and is particularly marked for product innovations (1987, p. 66). Jacob Schmookler's 1966 enumeration of basic and improvement innovations shows a similar peak in the 1930s, particularly the second half, as does the chronology provided by Gerhard Mensch (1979, p. 132). These studies have often been ignored in macroeconomic inquiry, in part because their results seem so at variance with our impressions of the economic "success" of the Depression years.[19]

These patterns, along with the aggregate data, are also consistent with David Mowery's study of R and D expenditures and employment in U.S. manufacturing (Mowery 1981). National Research Council data show that between 1919 and 1928 inclusive, companies founded an average of 66 R and D labs per year. Between 1929 and 1936 inclusive, a period that brackets the worst years of the Depression, such foundings rose to over 73 per year. During the 1930s, industry R and D expenditures more than doubled in real terms, with acceleration in the last years of the decade (Mowery and Rosenberg 1989, p. 69; see also Fano 1987, p. 262). Mowery and Rosenberg report that employment of research scientists and engineers grew 72.9 percent between 1929 and 1933 while employment totals in other occupational categories collapsed. Between 1933 and 1940, R and D employment in U.S. manufacturing almost *tripled*, from 10,918 to 27,777. In the Second World War, in contrast, R and D employment growth *slowed* as employment in other categories skyrocketed. Federal spending for nondefense R and D also fell substantially during the war (Mowery and Rosenberg 2000, pp. 814, 819).

Within manufacturing, advance took place across a variety of fronts (see chapter 2; also Bernstein 1987, esp. ch. 4). There were, to be sure, older industries such as textiles, leather goods, and apparel where productivity growth was slow or nonexistent. But there were also a remarkable number of dynamic sectors, generating new process and product innovations, with varying levels of

Table 1.3. TFP Growth in the Telephone, Electric Utilities,
and Railroad Industries (percent per year)

Years	Telephone	Electric Utilities	Railroads
1919–1929	1.60	2.51	1.63
1929–1941	2.01	5.55	2.91
1941–1948	0.53	5.87	2.56

Source: Kendrick 1961, tables G-III, H-IV, H-VI, pp. 544–545, 586–587, 590–591.

commercial exploitation before the war. Petrochemicals is an obvious example. At companies such as Dupont, advances in chemical engineering generated a host of new products, including Lucite (sold as Plexiglas by a rival manufacturer), Teflon, and nylon (Spitz 1988; Fenichel 1996). Even in an older industry such as automobiles, innovation and product quality improvement during the decade proceeded at a rapid rate. Indeed, Daniel Raff and Manuel Trajtenberg (1997) view the decade as the last one in which there were truly revolutionary improvements in vehicles powered by internal combustion engines.

But progress was not limited to manufacturing; communications services, electric utilities, and transportation were also standouts. TFP growth in the telephone industry accelerated significantly after 1929 before falling precipitously during the war years. In electric utilities, TFP growth more than doubled when we compare 1929–1941 with 1919–1929; in contrast to the telephone case, high rates persisted after 1941 (see table 1.3).

The railroad sector, which dominated the economy at the end of the nineteenth century in a way no single sector has before or since, continued to figure prominently in the second quarter of the twentieth. In 1941 railroad fixed capital still comprised almost one out of every four dollars (23.5 percent) of U.S. private fixed nonresidential assets (U.S. Department of Commerce 2010, Fixed Asset Table 2.1; accessed July 4, 2010). Labor productivity in railroads grew much more dramatically during the 1930s than it had in the 1920s, and as Spurgeon Bell wrote, "In the twenties, the increase was largely due to new capital investment, in the thirties to organizational economies" (1940, p. 64; see also chapter 12). Bell's analysis is consistent with Kendrick's data (see table 1.3). The strong TFP growth between 1929 and 1941 takes place in the context of a capital input series in railroads that declines after 1931. We see here at the sectoral level a major contributor to the unusual rise in the aggregate output–capital ratio during the

Depression years (Kendrick 1961, table G-III, pp. 544–545; on manufacturing, see Bernstein 1987, pp. 112–120).

The 1930s also witnessed important advances in structural engineering, particularly improved techniques for utilizing concrete in conjunction with steel in bridge, tunnel, dam, and highway design.[20] Perhaps of even greater importance, the decade saw the working out of a paradigm for building infrastructure suitable for an age of automobiles and trucks, with implications for the spatial configuration as well as design and construction of roads, highways, bridges, wholesale and retail distribution facilities, and residential subdivisions. Due to network effects, the design improvements in conjunction with infrastructural investment generated a boost in output in housing and wholesale and retail distribution beyond what can be swept back to the value of the physical capital formation itself. Much of the development work on these principles was done during the 1930s under the aegis of the newly formed Federal Housing Authority and diffused throughout the United States after the Second World War through the efforts of this agency in conjunction with local zoning authorities (see chapter 11).

A large portion of the infrastructure required for economically successful postwar housing construction was, moreover, put in place during the 1930s, as the consequence of the use of public funds to improve the road transport system. During the 1920s, infrastructure, particularly streets and highways, did not keep up with the burgeoning sales of private vehicles. Public expenditures during the 1930s substantially remedied this, in a manner that impacted the productivity of the housing sector as well as that of the economy as a whole. Denison's data show a surge in the real value of the service flow from the housing sector beginning in 1940 (1974, figure 3.1, p. 20). This may be partially attributable to a reduction in the vacancy rate, as Denison suggests, but it also coincides with the sharp increase in the streets and highways capital stock during the Depression (see below). After the war the increase in the real service flow from the housing stock continued apace, reflecting not only new investment, but also the full exploitation of new blueprints for organizing residential subdivisions and associated infrastructure tailored to the automobile (chapter 11).

The 1930s witnessed qualitative and quantitative changes in the nation's infrastructure, as well as its sources of funding. Ever since E. Cary Brown's 1956 article it has been commonplace to downplay the significance of public investment during the Depression as too small in relation to GDP to have "made much of a difference" in returning us to natural output.[21] What this point of view obscures is the likelihood that although insufficient in terms of its influence on aggregate demand to compensate for the drop in autonomous private spending, public investment nevertheless had significant impacts on the supply side, which is to say that it added to potential output even if its work-creating effects were far too small to bring us out of the Depression.

Reckoning the impact of public sector capital on productivity growth requires more than simply recalculating the residual after including in the overall capital input series a portion of public sector capital designated as complementary to private sector production. If we follow Gordon and adjust capital input to include both streets and highway and GOPO investment, this further widens the TFP gap between 1929–41 and 1941–48, because the increase in GOPO investment between 1941 and 1945 is significantly larger than the drop off in street and highway building over the same period (see U.S. Department of Commerce 2010, Fixed Asset Table 7.5A, lines 10, 28; accessed July 4, 2010). Although both types of government investment were complementary to private sector production, network effects and improved principles of street layout contributed to TFP growth in the 1929–41 period in a way GOPO investment between 1941 and 1948 did not.

The BEA fixed-asset stock data, which begin in 1925, show very rapid rates of public investment in automobile-related infrastructure in the second half of the 1920s that continued largely unabated through 1941 (see table 1.4). The real net stock of street and highway capital in the United States increased by more than two-thirds between 1929 and 1948, with virtually all of this increase occurring before U.S. entry into the war. Street and highway capital surged in value from 6.5 percent of the net private fixed capital stock in 1929 to 10.9 percent in 1941, a peak approached in 1973 (see table 1.5). Somewhat less dramatic patterns

Table 1.4. Growth Rates of Net Stock of Street and Highway, Sewer, and Water Supply Capital, 1928–2008 (percent per year)

Years	Street/Highway Capital	Sewer Capital	Water Supply Capital
1925–1929	6.00	6.88	4.91
1929–1941	4.32	3.69	2.66
1941–1948	0.08	0.43	0.66
1948–1973	4.15	3.85	3.29
1973–2008	1.63	2.76	2.36

Source: BEA, http://www.bea.gov, Fixed Asset Tables 7.2A, B; accessed July 5, 2010.

Table 1. 5. Street and Highway Capital as a Percent of the Net Fixed
Private Capital Stock, 1929–2008 (billions of dollars)

Year	Street/ Highway Capital	Private Fixed Capital Stock	Percent of Private Capital Stock
1929	$16.5	$253.9	6.50
1941	$30.9	$284.7	10.85
1948	$48.0	$567.8	8.45
1973	$290.5	$2,924.0	9.94
2000	$1,435.2	$21,240.5	6.76
2008	$2,465.2	$34,260.8	7.20

Source: BEA, http://www.bea.gov, Fixed Asset Tables 6.1, 7.1A, B; accessed July 5, 2010.

are seen for public investment in water and sewer systems. While spending on publicly owned capital has figured heavily in debates about the significance of declining infrastructure investment in the falloff in productivity growth in the last quarter of the century (Aschauer 1989; Gramlich 1994), little attention has been paid to its role on the supply side in the earlier period.

What is striking in retrospect about Depression-era technological progress is its broad base, both within and outside of manufacturing. In contrast, the 1995–2005 period of TFP acceleration in the United States saw advance initially rather narrowly concentrated within manufacturing; within manufacturing, within durables; and within durables, within computers, software, and telecommunication (Gordon 2000c; Oliner and Sichel 2000). TFP growth in IT-using sectors such as wholesale/retail distribution and securities trading contributed, but did so principally in the second half of this period, after the tech stock bubble peaked in 2000 and investment in information technology slowed. The estimates we have in the aggregate for TFP growth during what was optimistically called the "new economy" boom remain significantly below those evidenced during the Depression. These comparisons are discussed further in chapter 5.

ALTERNATE INTERPRETATIONS OF RISING LABOR PRODUCTIVITY IN THE 1930S

The disastrous record of capacity and labor force utilization in the Depression has overshadowed the comparatively high rate of TFP growth over the same period. Many authors, overlooking or unaware of the record of TFP advance, have nonetheless noted rapidly rising output per hour in the context of low rates of capital formation during the Depression. In developing idiosyncratic explanations for this, however, they have missed one that is more straightforward.

In a 1991 article, Ben Bernanke and Martin Parkinson described sharp procyclical movements in manufacturing labor productivity in ten industries over the 1929–1939 period. They rejected the possibility that supply side shocks might have played a role in producing this result: "We believe that it is quite unlikely that the preponderance of interwar cyclical variation (at least during the 1930s) was due to technological shocks to the production functions of individual manufacturing industries" (1991, p. 441). The authors were likely correct about the sources of cyclical variation in productivity—these weren't the result of technology shocks (see also chapter 7). But the contrary was true for the secular trend. What seems on its face implausible—technological and organizational improvement over the course of the Depression—was in fact the underlying cause of both higher output per hour and higher real wage rates comparing 1941 with 1929.

Harold Cole and Lee Ohanian (2004) noted rising real wages during the Depression but identified their causes as institutional. The National Industrial Recovery Act and, after it was declared unconstitutional, the effective continuation of its policies through the National Labor Relations Act (Wagner Act) and lax antitrust enforcement represented, in their view, significant governmentally induced negative supply shocks to the economy, which contributed to the severity of the downturn and the slow recovery.[22] Somewhat ironically, given that they work within the real business cycle tradition, with its strong emphasis on the importance of aggregate supply, Cole and Ohanian didn't explore the possibility that a considerable portion of the upward wage movement was in fact warranted by labor productivity improvement due to *positive* supply shocks.[23]

Claudia Goldin and Robert Margo also remarked on the high rate of labor productivity and real wage growth during the Depression years, asking how it was that high unemployment coincided with stable or increasing real wages.[24] Their explanation for why wages increased as employment fell has been selective retention. As demand declined, they argued, firms laid off their less skilled workers, and within occupational categories, they laid off their poorer performers, a selectivity that improvements in personnel and human resource management practices helped employers implement. Thus the high and rising wages that appear to have accompanied the downturn are largely a compositional effect (Margo 1991, p. 341).[25]

The type of effect Goldin and Margo describe, however, is a cyclical phenomenon, and whether or not it is important as the economy goes into recession, it should not be relevant peak to peak. As one comes out of a downturn, these effects would be unwound as labor markets tighten and the more marginal members of the labor force are rehired. Selective retention could have produced an upward movement in output per hour over time if the poorest workers were culled during recession *and never returned*. One might argue that 1941 output per hour was high because it had not yet been dragged down by the presumably still unemployed poorer quality marginal workers.

Employment began to rise again after 1933, and although private hours were about the same in 1941 as they had been in 1929, hours per worker were lower (part of a longer-term trend, as part of productivity increase was taken in shorter work weeks). The consequence was that there were actually more people employed. In spite of the 9.9 percent unemployment in 1941, 11.8 percent more people were employed in the private nonfarm economy in that year than in 1929 (Kendrick 1961, table A-XXIII).[26] It is true that some of those who lost their jobs in the 1929–1933 downturn may never have come back. And there could have been hysteresis due to loss of labor market attachment during the boom-bust cycle. But this would actually have slowed rather than increased the productivity growth rate.[27]

The last three years of the Depression provide an illustration at the aggregate level of why procyclical wage growth is inconsistent with the posited selective retention dynamic. TFP growth and labor productivity growth both accelerated as the unemployment rate fell after 1938. One did not see deceleration, as would have been the case if selective retention were the main force affecting productivity levels. As the unemployment rate dropped from 19.1 percent in 1938 to 14.6 percent in 1940, the increment to output per hour was less (4.18 percent) than that obtained (6.59 percent) in moving from 14.6 percent unemployment in 1940 to 9.9 percent in 1941 (Kendrick 1961, table A-XXIII). In each case we have a downward change in the unemployment rate of between 4.5 and 4.7 percentage points. If the selective retention mechanism were the main factor affecting labor productivity, with workers rehired in decreasing order of quality, the pattern of increments to output per hour should have been reversed.

A second factor that could have influenced labor productivity growth over the Depression years, not subject to this same critique, is secular improvement in the educational qualifications of the labor force. Goldin has called attention to the very rapid rise in high school graduation rates during the 1930s to levels not exceeded until the 1960s (1998, p. 359). As is suggested by the data on R and D employment, demand for scientific and technical personnel was very strong during the Depression, consistent with Margo's evidence (1993) that managerial, scientific, and professional-status or higher years of schooling provided substantial protection against unemployment during these years. The opportunity cost of high school attendance was also much lower during the 1930s since the likelihood of employment as a young worker without a high school degree was considerably lower than it had been in the previous decade. By the end of the 1930s, the United States was also benefiting from the influx of highly educated Europeans fleeing Hitler.

One way to estimate how much of the growth in output per hour might have been due to labor quality improvement between 1929 and 1941 is to look at the difference in that calculation when one substitutes in the denominator an index of "adjusted" labor hours. This index is constructed weighting different occupational or industrial categories by their respective wage rates. Kendrick's data show that although "raw" hours declined slightly between 1929 and 1941, augmented hours rose slightly, at about 0.12 percent per year. As a consequence, output per hour growth is about 6 percent lower over this period using adjusted as opposed to unadjusted hours (for data, see table 2.1 below, columns 2 and 3).

This calculation confirms my impression that the effect of labor quality improvement on growth in output per hour or TFP growth over the entire period 1929–1941 was dwarfed by other factors.[28] Margo accepted the conventional wisdom that technical change during the Depression was "concentrated in a few industries and modest overall" (1993, p. 49). The extent to which growth in output per hour, and perforce wages, is attributable to very rapid growth in TFP has not been fully appreciated, even by labor economists who have noted the trends in hourly wages and labor productivity.

If we seek to avoid cyclical confounds, 1941 (9.9 percent unemployed) is far better than 1937 (14.3 percent unemployed) or 1940 (14.6 percent unemployed). Still, for the purposes of my argument it would have been helpful had the Japanese delayed by eight to twelve months their attack on Pearl Harbor so that the U.S. economy could have returned to full employment, as it was in the process of doing, prior to full-scale war mobilization. Even in the absence of this more perfect historical experiment, there is enough evidence to suggest that whatever role selective retention may have played in measured productivity growth between 1929 and 1941, it was likely small in comparison with the influence of other factors.

The direction of and factors influencing the cyclicality of labor productivity have been debated extensively in the labor economics literature. Those arguing procyclicality have emphasized labor hoarding (the practice of retaining workers, even if they were underemployed, during recessions), whereas those arguing countercyclicality (the view that wage rates or their growth rates rise

Table 1.6. Output per Hour Growth, Private Domestic Economy (PDE) and Private Nonfarm Economy (PNE), 1919–1948 (percent per year)

Years	PDE	PNE
1919–1929	2.36	2.27
1929–1941	2.48	2.35
1941–1948	2.17	1.71

Source: Kendrick 1961, tables A-XXII, A-XXIII, pp. 334–335; 339–340.

during recessions) have emphasized selective retention. The aggregate evidence is solidly on the side of procylicality, particularly for the 1930s, although, as I will explain in chapter 7, I believe its main cause is neither labor hoarding nor the technology shocks emphasized in the real business cycle literature. Whatever the mechanism, the data for the private nonfarm economy show that when the unemployment rate rose, the level of TFP dropped, and when the unemployment rate declined, TFP rose. The cycle affected labor productivity in a similar although somewhat weaker fashion.

Superimposed on this cyclical pattern, however, was a sustained upward movement in output per hour. The average annual increase in labor productivity was almost as high over the Depression years as it was during the golden age (see tables 1.6, 2.1). Since neither capital deepening nor labor quality improvement can explain this, it must be attributed, at least in an accounting sense, to high TFP growth. Workers vary in their location, skills, training, and other attributes. It is quite possible for rising wage rates of those employed to have reflected a rise in output per hour from this cause, even though there were large pockets of labor—in construction, for example—suffering from prolonged unemployment. Even in the depths of the worst recession, one will still find numerous help wanted ads in the newspapers. As already noted, members of certain occupations—scientists, chemists, engineers, and managers, for example—remained in very strong demand throughout the 1930s.

If high TFP growth led to higher wages for those employed, it also made recovery from the recession more difficult because, given weakness in aggregate demand, it contributed to slower growth of employment in manufacturing, as well as continued declines in such sectors as railroads. The widespread concern during the Depression years with technological unemployment (see Bix 2000 for discussion)—a blessing in the long run but a serious problem for an economy operating below capacity—reflected dynamics similar to those experienced during both the early and late 2000s, when there was much discussion of jobless recovery.

Within manufacturing there is evidence that the downturn differentially affected high-and low-productivity firms, with a shakeout taking place as the least efficient establishments were culled out (Bresnahan and Raff 1991). This Darwinian mechanism—a version of selective retention applied to firms—may have reinforced the technological trends I identify in contributing to measured productivity growth between 1929 and 1941. But Bresnahan and Raff limit the source of productivity improvement to a between-firm (or plant) effect, much of which would have been reversed with the return to fuller employment before the war. I argue that the productivity outcome, measuring peak to peak, was due to more than temporarily losing the weakly performing tail of the firm or plant productivity distribution.[29]

In each of the instances discussed above, the authors' characterizations of the data (as opposed to their explanations) are consistent with a set of powerful positive supply shocks over the course of the Depression years that laid the groundwork not only for the remarkable Allied victory in the war, but also for postwar expansion. Profits and other income to capital, as well as wages, felt the beneficial impact of this advance (see chapter 10). Most of the corporations occupying the commanding heights of the economy, including RCA, AT&T, IBM, Dupont, Alcoa, GM, Kodak, and General Electric—companies that because of a strong commitment to organized privately funded R and D activity (Mowery and Rosenberg 1989, pp. 74–75) were contributing disproportionately to TFP advance—had returned to profitability well before the onset of World War II (Galambos 2000, p. 947). Overall, real proprietors' income surpassed its 1929 level in 1937; real corporate profits did so in 1940 (see chapter 10, table 10.9).

At the time of the Japanese attack on Pearl Harbor, a very substantial fraction of 1948 productivity levels had already been achieved. Moreover, almost all of the foundations for advance during the postwar period were already in place. These included a growing public infrastructure geared to automobiles and trucks, the technical foundations and physical capital investments necessary for producing and distributing cheap petrochemicals, gasoline, and electric power, and a range of new and improved materials and appliances that could take advantage of these inputs. The high rates of investment in street, highway, water, and sewer capital literally helped pave the way for the postwar suburbanization boom. In commercial aviation technical advance as well as government investment in municipal airports during the 1930s had fostered a nascent industry with much room for profitable expansion (the DC-3 was introduced in 1936). The defining new product of the third quarter of the century—television—was on the verge of explosive commercial exploitation. The Second World War had relatively little to do with any of this.

The Depression years experienced exceptionally high TFP growth rates partly as a result of serendipity. Technical advances do not necessarily arrive in a steady stream, and the 1930s were characterized by progressive programs in a remarkably large number of industries and sectors. The advances in chemicals, long-distance communication, electrical machinery, structural engineering, and aviation proceeded largely independently of the Depression. Many of these sectors relied upon and benefited from scientific advance in a way nineteenth-century industry leaders often did not. This type of economic progress was fostered by a system of largely privately funded R and D labs that reached maturity during this period and operated during the 1930s in a fashion relatively undistorted by the subsequent demands of the military. In other sectors—for example, railroads—the disruptions of financial intermediation and very low levels of capital formation associated with the downturn fostered a search for organizational innovations that enabled firms to get more out of what they had (chapter 12). Finally, government and university researchers played an important role in helping to work out and promulgate design principles for surface transport and residential subdivision in an automobile age.

The various studies discussed in the preceding section aim at reconciling otherwise anomalous labor productivity data with the apparently disastrous economic record of the Depression. But the performance of the economy between 1929 and 1941 was not disastrous from the standpoint of long-term growth. The reverse was true. In spite of his many contributions to our understanding of productivity trends, Kendrick led us astray by choosing 1937 as a reference peak in calculating productivity growth in the 1930s. If we use 1941 instead, it is clear that the bulk of the very rapid growth of TFP between 1929 and 1948 took place *before* U.S. entry into the war. Once this is recognized, labor productivity growth during the Depression in the absence of capital deepening ceases to be anomalous, and the conclusion drawn from the aggregate data finds strong support in microeconomic studies of the timing of key innovations, in sectoral studies of productivity change, and in data on private sector employment and expenditures on research and development. This finding requires rethinking our understanding of the broad contours and determinants of U. S. economic growth in the twentieth century.

2

———•●●—

THE INTERWAR YEARS

The acceleration of productivity growth during the Depression years and the expansion of potential output to which it gave rise are best appreciated when considered within the context of a broader overview of twentieth-century U.S. economic growth. This chapter brings together quantitative and qualitative material to tell the story of why TFP growth during the Depression years (1929–1941) was higher than it had been during the 1920s (1919–1929). It compares the sectoral sources of advance during the two periods and lays groundwork for chapters that follow. Chapters 3, 4, and 5 cover, respectively, the Second World War (chapter 3), the golden age and subsequent "dark ages" (chapter 4), and the information technology boom (chapter 5).

Table 2.1 provides a statistical summary of rates of increase of total factor, labor, and capital productivity between 1901 and 2008. Striking features of this table are that the fastest rates of peacetime peak-to-peak total factor productivity growth in the private nonfarm economy occurred during the interwar years and that there was, on balance, a downward trend in the second half of the twentieth century. While it is true that TFP growth between 1989 and 2000 was more than twice as fast as during the anemic years 1973–1989, it was less than a third the rate registered during the Depression years.

To give a more qualitative feel for what underlies the numbers, I begin by describing some of the key developments in manufacturing in the 1920s and 1930s and place them in historical perspective. I follow this with discussion of the changing share of manufacturing over the twentieth century, drilling down to identify which particular industries were expanding or contracting, which had

Table 2.1. Growth Rates of TFP, Labor, and Capital Productivity: Private Nonfarm Economy, United States, 1901–2008 (percent per year)

Years	TFP	Output/ Hour	Output/Adjusted Hours[a]	Output/Unit Capital Input
1901–1919	1.08	1.71	1.44	.01
1919–1929	2.02	2.27	2.33	1.09
1929–1941	2.31	2.35	2.21	2.47
1941–1948	1.29	1.71	1.42	1.32
1948–1973	1.88	2.75	2.64	.16
1973–1989	.36	1.28	1.06	−1.25
1989–2000	.79	2.07	1.57	−.91
2000–2007	1.38	2.59	2.25	−.43
1995–2005	1.46	2.89	2.38	−.93
2005–2008	.62	1.52	1.15	−.91

Sources: 1901–1948: Kendrick 1961, table A-XXIII. The unadjusted data for labor productivity are from the column headed "output per man-hour," the adjusted data from the column headed "output per unit of labor input."
1948–1989 (TFP and capital productivity): U.S. Department of Labor 2009.
1989–2008 (TFP and capital productivity): BLS, http://www.bls.gov. These data are from the productivity section of the website; accessed July 20, 2009.
1948–2008 (output per hour and output per adjusted hour): http://www/bls/gov; accessed January 7, 2010.
[a]Output per adjusted hour uses an hours index that has been augmented to reflect changes in labor quality or composition. In the creation of this index, different categories of labor are weighted by their respective wage rates. For the post-1948 data from the BLS Web site, the growth rate of adjusted hours is based on the product of the index for hours and the index for labor composition.

high TFP growth rates in different epochs, and which employed large numbers of scientists and engineers.

I then describe the changing contribution of the manufacturing sector to overall TFP growth in 1929–1941 and 1919–1929. The procedure for each interval is to multiply the estimated TFP growth rate for manufacturing by its share in the private nonfarm economy, thus generating an estimate of the percentage points contributed by the sector to the growth of private nonfarm economy TFP. Building on these calculations and using similar methods, we can then partition PNE TFP growth rates in the two periods (1929–1941 and 1919–1929) into the portions contributed by manufacturing, transport and public utilities, wholesale and retail distribution, and other.[1]

These exercises show that manufacturing was responsible for over four-fifths of PNE TFP growth in 1919–1929, as compared with only a little more than half during the Depression years. To understand TFP growth between 1929 and 1941, one must focus as well on the second pillar of the story: the high rates of advance in transportation and distribution. The final section of the chapter, returning to a more qualitative mode, describes the evolving relationship between roads and rails during the twentieth century, with an emphasis on the interwar period. Nonspecialist readers may wish to begin with the narrative material on manufacturing and then move to the last section, "Rails and Roads," before tackling the more quantitative sections.

THE MANUFACTURING REVOLUTION OF THE 1920S

The period 1929–1941 stands out in table 2.1 as having achieved the fastest rate of twentieth-century TFP growth. Advance during the 1920s was also impressive, but as I will show, it was more narrowly concentrated within manufacturing. Much attention has been focused on the extraordinary rise in manufacturing productivity during the 1920s, and rightly so. Between 1919 and 1929, TFP in the sector grew at 5.12 percent continuously compounded, accounting for 83 percent of the growth of the residual in the entire private nonfarm economy. If ever there were a period warranting the sometimes excessive attention devoted to this sector by economists, the 1920s qualifies.

The fundamental cause was a revolution in factory design and the distribution of power within it associated with a shift from steam (or in a few cases, still, water power) to electric power. Because of square-cube relationships involving cost savings associated with larger boilers and pistons, a single large steam engine as prime mover had, in prior years, almost always been the economically attractive option for a fixed installation. In a steam-powered factory motive force was generated centrally and distributed to workstations by means of a mechanical system of leather belts, pulleys, and rotating horizontal shafts. The economics of factory design required balancing the increased cost per square foot of multistory designs with the imperative to minimize the sum of runs from the prime mover to individual workstations so as to keep a lid on the substantial power losses attributable to friction when mechanical transmission was used.

The fact that power-driven factories in the nineteenth century were typically two, three, four, or five stories tall was not generally the result of high urban land values. This was obviously so in the case of water power, which dominated mechanized factories in the antebellum period. The early textile cities such as Lowell and Lawrence, Massachusetts, or Manchester, New Hampshire, were greenfield sites.[2] Water held on tenaciously in New England (in 1900 over 35 percent of the horsepower in the region was still generated by these means), but steam came to predominate elsewhere in the country, a change facilitated by advances in high-pressure engineering and the development of large, powerful, and energy-efficient engines such as the Corliss (Atack, Bateman, and Weiss 1980; Rosenberg and Trajtenberg 2001). The prime mover in a steam-powered factory was typically housed in its own room, with a leather belt (often several feet wide and several hundred feet long) connecting the flywheel to the main drive shaft. Although use of steam power allowed location of new factories closer to existing supplies of labor and transport facilities, the basic design of a plant remained fundamentally unchanged, and its height was driven by the same considerations involving the internal distribution of power as had dictated its profile in the age of water.

Thus for both water- and steam-powered plants, the multistory factory building of the nineteenth century was the result of a different economic imperative than that which pushed up the height of commercial office structures in central business districts. The most persuasive evidence for this is what happened in the twentieth century. With electrification and the eventual elimination of the old internal system for distributing power, factories went predominantly single-story, even though the population of the United States was larger and more concentrated so that in principle land was scarcer (more flexible surface transportation associated with the diffusion of the internal combustion engine and related infrastructure also played a role in this transition). To a very considerable degree, multistory factory construction in the nineteenth century reflected an engineering solution to the problem of distributing power mechanically from a central prime mover.

The first factory electrification (for power rather than illumination) involved simply replacing one large prime mover with another. The steam engine was removed and an electric engine substituted—but there were no changes in the mechanisms for distributing power mechanically within the factory. It took several decades for factory designers and electrical engineers fully to appreciate how, using a few large power-generating plants and a multitude of smaller electric motors, they could dispense with the onsite prime mover *and* the apparatus for mechanically distributing power, replacing the latter with a network of relatively cheap and flexible electric wires. An intermediate step (group drive) involved use of medium-sized motors to turn somewhat shorter drive shafts that in turn supplied power to groups of machines (Devine 1983).

The change in the way in which power was distributed removed a straight-jacket from factory design, allowing one-story layouts and a reconfiguration of internal work flow that went hand in hand with the diffusion of assembly-line techniques in such industries as transport equipment and electrical machinery. There are many features distinguishing twentieth-century factory buildings from those constructed in the nineteenth, but the most salient is that the twentieth-century structure, like Ford's River Rouge facility, is single-storied, whereas the nineteenth-century factory was not. Single-storied buildings had lower construction costs per square foot, but there were other advantages, particularly in industries based on mechanical or electrical engineering that required the assembly of many parts. The best way to engineer an assembly line, except in the few instances where gravity can be harnessed to particularly good effect, is to keep it on a single level. A bonus was a reduced risk of fire. Multistory factories with mechanical power distribution required openings between floors so that power could be transferred across drive shafts on different floors. These openings created natural avenues through which fire could spread, entailing higher fire insurance premiums and/or the costs of enclosures to mitigate the risk (Devine 1983, p. 361).

Electrical internal power distribution and the use of small electric motors made all floor areas of the factory—not just those close to an overhead shaft—of roughly equivalent economic value. In the steam-powered factory there was prime real estate near the overhead shafts and there were "dead" areas that could be used only for storage. Such areas could now also be used for stages of the manufacturing process. The dismantling or elimination of the mechanical system for distributing power internally, which had required brackets and rotating drive shafts hanging from the ceiling, made it much easier to install overhead cranes for moving subassemblies. The possibility of using portable tools powered by electricity was another contributor to productivity advance. Finally, new single-storied buildings could utilize skylights for illumination and ventilation—a rare feature in a nineteenth-century factory.

It was during the 1920s that much of this transition took place, and the decade is unique in the history of U.S. manufacturing. TFP growth rates in manufacturing were extremely high, and this was true across the board at the two-digit level.[3] The profits associated with this transition played a major role in fueling the stock market boom between 1925 and 1929.

As a result of this revolution in factory design, layout, and internal power distribution, the level of TFP in U.S. manufacturing was higher in all subsequent periods. But one of the lessons learned from analysis of the Solow growth model is that it is far easier to raise the trajectory of levels of productivity in a sector or economy than it is to permanently increase productivity growth rates. Of course, whenever levels increase, there will be a transition in which the rate of growth will accelerate. But the higher rates, whether due to a higher saving rate or the availability of new technologies, usually cannot be sustained.

And so it was in this case. U.S. manufacturing could not hope to sustain a rate of increase of TFP of over 5 percent per year in perpetuity from the electrification/assembly line/one-story transition. Eventually, as old factories were reconfigured and as new factories replaced old, there would be fewer and fewer opportunities to reap additional gains. As Devine shows, the transition from steam to electric power, which began around the turn of the century and accelerated after the First World War, was largely complete by the end of the 1920s. By 1929, electricity was responsible for driving about 79 percent of total capacity within U.S. manufacturing (Devine 1983, p. 349).

From this perspective, the puzzle is not so much why manufacturing TFP growth declined from 5.12 percent per year (1919–1929) to 2.76 percent per year between 1929 and 1941 as why it did not fall further. There are two effects that help account for this. The first reflects the residual influence—the tail end—of the electrification transition. In some cases, as Bresnahan and Raff (1991) have shown for the automobile industry, some older and less productive plants that had persisted in operation during the boom period of the 1920s simply shut down as the economy went into recession between 1929 and 1933, and it was the remaining (and higher-productivity) facilities that supplied output as the economy recovered. Some of the more marginally productive facilities were never brought back. The second and more important influence involved the maturing of a privately funded research and development system. Both R and D employment and spending soared during the Depression years, and as Margo (1991) has shown, scientists and engineers were largely protected from the risk of unemployment that fell so heavily on other job groups.

Thus one must use a light touch in contextualizing trends in manufacturing TFP during the interwar period. In the decades after 1929, TFP growth in manufacturing was substantially lower and less uniform across two-digit industries than it had been in the 1920s. Nevertheless, by any standard of comparison other than that of the 1920s, TFP growth in manufacturing during the Depression years was world class.

The 1941–1948 period saw manufacturing TFP growth become negative. Above and beyond war-related plants owned and operated by the government, the federal government paid for more than ten billion dollars of new capital, most of it in manufacturing and most of it equipment, located in Government Owned Privately Operated (GOPO) facilities (Reconstruction Finance Corporation 1946). Although labor productivity rose modestly (.20 percent per year) as a consequence of this rise in the capital-labor ratio, TFP in the sector fell at an annualized rate of −.35 percent per year, partly because of the very high growth rate of measured capital input.[4] In contrast with the 1920s, productivity advance during the Depression years and, to an even greater extent, the postwar period cannot be explained by focusing almost exclusively on manufacturing. That said, prior advances in manufacturing did help set the stage for the golden age of U.S. productivity growth following the war.

To recapitulate: the revolution in factory layout, design, and internal power distribution resulted in manufacturing TFP that was two-thirds higher in 1929 than it had been in 1919. The twelve Depression years saw almost a halving of the TFP growth rate in manufacturing, but this rate of advance was still far higher than rates obtained in any period of the twentieth century other than the 1920s. It was fueled in part by the final stages of the electrification transition and by the elimination, in some cases permanently, of low-productivity plants as output fell. That transition by itself, however, would have been insufficient to produce 2.76 percent per year over twelve years. An increasingly important ingredient was rising spending on R and D and rapid advances in science-based manufacturing, with which such spending was associated.

DISEMBODIED TECHNICAL CHANGE IN THE 1930S

What are some concrete examples of the largely disembodied technical change that raised both capital and labor productivity and was such a prominent feature of the Depression years? A canonical instance was perhaps the introduction of new chemical processes that increased the percentage of sugar extracted from beets during refining, raising output while requiring little increase in plant and equipment or labor input. Comparable innovations were common in the mining industry (Weintraub 1939, p. 23).

Another category of improvements involved the pursuit of thermal efficiency. A good example is from the electric-power-generating industry. In 1941 output of electricity was 86.5 percent above its 1929 level, an achievement associated with an increase in labor productivity of 126 percent and of capital productivity of 73 percent compared with 1929 (Kendrick 1961, table H-VI, p. 590). Partly this was made possible by the continuing trend toward larger-size boilers, for which kilowatt hour costs were lower. But partly it involved the diffusion of topping techniques, which used the exhaust steam from high-pressure boilers to heat lower-pressure boilers. Topping raised capacity on existing stations by 40–90 percent with essentially no increase in fuel costs or labor and only modest costs in upgrading parts of the plant (Weintraub 1939, p. 22). Other thermal-efficiency initiatives involved low-cost, high-payoff investments in insulation or captured exhaust gasses from stacks and used them to preheat air to improve combustion, preheat materials for subsequent fabrication, or generate steam. Innovative efforts pursued ways to make use of solid and liquid byproducts as well as gas. Finding commercial uses for waste was the equivalent of turning industrial excrement into gold and about as close to manna from heaven as one could get.

Advances in chemistry lengthened the life of equipment or structures. New treatments extended the life of wooden railroad ties from eight to twenty years (Temporary National Economic Committee 1941, p. 110). In the automobile industry, quick-drying lacquers reduced the time needed to paint a car from the more than three weeks it took in the early 1920s to a few hours, with big savings on inventory and storage costs. Stainless steel reduced oxidization on railway cars. Chrome plating lengthened the life of tools and moving parts (Weintraub 1939, p. 23).

Conveyer belts and other initiatives associated with the reconfiguration of factory layouts saved labor, but perhaps even more important, they saved capital, enabling economies "in floor space, inventories, in storage room, in machinery and auxiliary equipment and in cost of maintenance and repairs and through the elimination of waste, reduction of spoilage and shortening of the time in process" (Weintraub 1939, p. 26). Many such gains had been reaped in the 1920s, but there was still some juice in this fruit for the 1930s. In 1933 Cadillac consolidated its production of drive trains from four floors onto one, leaving the remaining three available for other uses. In 1934 Packard cut in half its floor space requirements per unit of output, freeing an entire building, and similar improvements were reported by Westinghouse and Western Electric (Weintraub 1939, p. 25). By rearranging machinery in a linear pattern and changing the way materials were handled, the textile industry garnered very high rates of TFP growth during a period in which the basic spinning and weaving technology remained largely unchanged.

The Depression years also experienced a continued trend toward larger units in the case of both equipment and fixed installations. Industrial locomotives sold between 1932 and 1936 averaged 11.4 tons, versus 7.4 tons for sales in the years 1924–1927. The average capacity of a power shovel rose from 1.73 cubic yards in 1920–1923 to 1.90 in 1924–1927 to 2.51 in 1928–1931 to 3.28 cubic yards in 1932–1936. Because of square-cube relationships, capital and operating costs per unit of output dropped when capacity increased, a phenomenon that could also be observed in electric-power-generating units, as well as in the spiral conveyer screws used to move materials in flour mills (Weintraub 1939, p. 17).

Finally, there were new or improved materials. The substitution of plastics for wood or metal parts involved savings in fuel, fabrication, and capital costs. Tungsten carbide blades wore out much less rapidly and reduced downtime.

In cutting phenol resins (plastics), carbon steel blades had to be removed and resharpened after sixty feet. A carbon alloy blade cut ten thousand feet without refitting, and what previously took a month to accomplish could now be done in a day.

The period was notable for an increasing emphasis on instrumentation. By facilitating automatic process control, instrumentation lengthened the life of equipment and reduced downtime and maintenance costs. The costs of the instruments were often trivial in comparison with the improvements in both capital and labor productivity they enabled. For example, in the 1920s cracking units in petroleum refining typically had to be cleaned every four to five days. Instrumentation lengthened the interval between cleanings to one or two months, with obvious savings in labor costs and capital costs reflected in higher utilization rates. Another example: Hand-controlled boilers required rebricking every three months; instrument controls eliminated the need to do so entirely (Weintraub 1939, p. 19).

MANUFACTURING'S CONTRIBUTIONS TO TFP GROWTH

To appreciate manufacturing's changing sectoral contributions to aggregate PNE TFP advance, it helps first to look back at how the share and composition of the sector evolved over the twentieth century. Data on the industrial or sectoral distribution of value added show that the shares of all goods-producing sectors of the economy, with the exception of construction, fell dramatically in the postwar period.[5] Between 1948 and 2000, agriculture dropped from 8.6 percent of GDP to under 1.0 percent, mining from 2.8 to 1.2 percent, and manufacturing from 26.0 percent to 14.5 percent. By 2008 industry's share was down to 11.5 percent. Most of the drop in manufacturing's share occurred after 1969.[6]

Within manufacturing, declining shares were evident at the two-digit level pretty much across the board and were especially notable in primary metals, textiles, apparel, and leather goods. At the two-digit level the only sectors to buck the trend were instruments and related products, electric and electronic equipment, chemicals and allied products, and rubber and miscellaneous plastic. All four had higher shares than in 1948, although all but the first declined in share after 1973. Three other sectors—non-electrical machinery, motor vehicles and equipment, and other transport equipment—increased in share between 1948 and 1973 but then declined rapidly so that their 2000 shares were significantly below those in 1948.

If one looks back at prewar numbers, it is clear that in 1941 manufacturing's share of national income—almost 32 percent—was close to its all-time peak (it would rise further, but only temporarily, during the war). Yet a great deal of economic analysis continues to be based on the history of manufacturing alone. Part of this is because the statistical data available for the sector are detailed. We need, however, to be careful searching for our keys under the lamppost simply because the light there is better. Even though manufacturing's share of national income was close to its peak during the Depression years, almost as much TFP growth originated in transportation, public utilities, and distribution as in manufacturing, as the next section will show.

The one period for which an almost singular focus on manufacturing is justi-fied is the 1920s. More than four-fifths of TFP growth was contributed by the sector. That proportion drops to 51 percent between 1929 and 1941. Between 1948 and 1973, only 27 percent of TFP growth in the private nonfarm economy can be attributed to manufacturing (see chapter 4).

Table 2.2 allows a disaggregated examination of TFP growth within man-ufacturing in different periods. It shows that whereas TFP growth rates were roughly comparable in durables and nondurables between 1949 and 1973 (1.48 vs. 1.32 percent continuously compounded), TFP advance virtually disappeared in nondurables between 1973 and 1995, aside from textiles.[7] There is a mod-est acceleration between 1995 and 2000, led by advance in leather goods and apparel, but these sectors were trivially small by the end of the century. The record in durables over the last quarter of the century is scarcely better, with the notable exceptions, as discussed, of SIC 35 and 36, where we see accelerating growth and the impact of revolutionary change in the IT-producing industries (see chapter 5).

This record can be compared with the manufacturing sector's performance during the 1930s. BLS data at the two-digit level for manufacturing extend back only to 1948, and Kendrick (1961) provides estimates at the two-digit level only for his benchmark years 1929, 1937, and 1948. In the absence of annual data we cannot calculate TFP growth at the two-digit level for 1929–1941 directly, although we can look at growth from 1929–1937, 1937–1948, or 1929–1948. If we compare the 1929–1948 numbers with the 1973–2000 data, they show first of all, for the latter period, a much slower advance of TFP across the board in nondurables: a very low .14 percent per year for 1973–2000 versus 2.22 percent per year between 1929 and 1948. In durables, the 1973–2000 period registers a slight advantage—1.57 versus 1.43 percent—but this is entirely accounted for by SIC 35 and 36. Aside from these two sectors and apparel (SIC 23), TFP advance in *every single* two-digit industry was higher over the years 1929–1948 than it was between 1973 and 2000, and often by a substantial amount.[8] Comparing 1929–1948 with 1948–1973, we find that the advantage again goes to the earlier

Table 2.2. TFP Growth within Manufacturing, 1919–2000 (percent per year)

SIC	1919–1929	1929–1937	1929–1948	1949–1973	1973–2000	1973–1995	1995–2000
Manufacturing	5.12	1.93	1.71	1.52	0.93	0.66	2.09
Durable goods	5.06	0.86	1.43	1.48	1.57	1.19	3.27
24 Lumber and wood products	2.49	0.41	1.42	1.67	0.65	0.98	−0.78
25 Furniture and fixtures	4.14	0.45	2.00	0.60	0.74	0.69	0.96
32 Stone, clay, and glass products	5.57	2.24	2.09	1.09	0.51	0.49	0.57
33 Primary metal industries	5.36	−1.26	1.30	0.39	−0.12	−0.36	0.95
34 Fabricated metal products	4.51	0.97	1.36	0.54	0.20	0.19	0.26
35 Industrial, commercial machinery, computer eq.	2.82	2.24	1.62	0.71	2.93	2.31	5.65
36 Electric and electronic equipment	3.45	3.14	2.55	2.07	3.85	3.09	7.18
37 Transport equipment	8.07	−0.37	0.39	1.47	0.18	0.05	0.72
38 Instruments and related products	4.47[a]	2.84	2.36*	1.75	0.97	1.07	0.54
39 Miscellaneous manufacturing industries				1.55	0.47	0.33	1.10

	Nondurable goods	4.89	3.34	2.22	1.32	0.06	0.47
20	Food and kindred products	5.18	1.47	1.47	0.67	0.39	−0.31
20	Beverages[b]	−0.23	14.14	6.94			
21	Tobacco products	4.28	6.15	4.19	−0.62	−2.92	−7.19
22	Textile mill products	2.90	4.45	3.28	2.29	2.32	1.87
23	Apparel and other textile products	3.90	2.47	0.63	0.72	0.91	1.41
26	Paper and allied products	4.54	4.22	2.33	1.58	−0.31	0.74
27	Printing and publishing	3.67	2.58	1.43	0.48	−0.94	0.22
28	Chemicals and allied products	7.15	3.00	3.36	2.51	−0.42	0.51
29	Petroleum and coal products	8.23	2.69	1.70	0.82	0.03	0.77
30	Rubber and miscellaneous plastics products	7.40	3.94	2.07	0.96	0.42	1.60
31	Leather and leather products	2.88	3.52	1.71	0.02	0.58	2.23

Sources: 1919–1948: Kendrick 1961, tables D-III, IV, pp. 466–475.

1949–2000: U.S. Department of Labor 2004.

Note: Definitions of SIC 35 and 36 change in the 1990s. The most important change is the inclusion of computer equipment in SIC 35: the old non-electrical machinery category.

[a]Includes miscellaneous manufacturing.

[b]For 1929–1948, data on beverages are reported separately from the remainder of food and kindred products.

period for every two-digit industry except lumber (SIC 24), transport equipment (SIC 37), and, again, apparel.

Table 2.2 shows that overall, manufacturing TFP grew faster between 1929 and 1937 than it did between 1929 and 1948, due to a slower growth rate within nondurables after 1937. Some of the slowness in durables between 1929 and 1937 is probably attributable to the poor showing in primary metals and transport equipment, which may reflect labor unrest and strike activity during 1937.

Kendrick's data do not allow one to calculate TFP growth rates within manufacturing for the 1929–1941 and 1941–1948 subperiods, but I have done so for the sector as a whole by combining his annual estimates for output and labor input with capital input data from the BEA's Fixed Asset Table 4.2.[9] This calculation shows TFP within manufacturing over the 1929–1941 period to have grown at the rate of 2.76 percent per year (table 2.3). This is higher than in any subsequent period of the twentieth century. It does, however, represent almost a halving of the 5.12 percent rate registered over the 1919–1929 period. This calculation also suggests, consistent with analysis developed in chapter 3, a negative rate of TFP advance in manufacturing over the 1941–1948 period. What this

Table 2.3. Growth of TFP, Labor, and Capital Productivity
in Manufacturing, 1889–2006 (percent per year)

Years	TFP	Output/Hour	Output/Unit Capital Input
1889–1919	.71	1.29	1.12
1919–1929	5.12	5.45	4.20
1929–1941	2.76	2.61	3.11
1941–1948	−.35	.20	−1.61
1949–1973	1.49	2.51	−.03
1973–1989	0.57	2.42	−1.22
1989–2000	1.58	3.56	.00
2000–2006	1.60	3.72	.00

Sources: 1889–1929: Kendrick 1961, table D-1, p. 464.
1929–1941 and 1941–1948: Output and labor input are from Kendrick 1961, tables D-1 and D-2. Capital input is based on the index for manufacturing fixed capital in BEA, http://www.bea.gov, Fixed Asset Table 4.2, line 19; accessed January 4, 2010. TFP growth is calculated based on an assumed share of .31 for capital.
1949–1989: U.S. Department of Labor 2004.
1989–2006: U.S. Department of Labor 2008.

implies, then, going back to table 2.2, is, on average, a pattern of sharp advance in TFP within the sector between 1937 and 1941, followed by retrogression to 1948.

Although it is difficult to make precise inferences about the loci of rapid advance between 1929 and 1941, the two-digit data through 1937 suggest that progress was particularly pronounced in beverages, tobacco manufacture, textiles, paper, rubber, leather, electric machinery, chemicals, instruments, and petroleum and coal products (Kendrick 1961, table D-IV, pp. 468–475). Chemicals was the only sector to attain TFP growth of 3 percent or more in both 1929–1937 and 1937–1948, although tobacco, textiles, and electric machinery came close. Textile mill products also turned in a surprisingly strong performance both pre- and postwar.[10] Notably absent from this group, however, is transport equipment, which had been the standout performer between 1919 and 1929, although, again, the 1937 numbers for this industry may be distorted by the effect of strikes.

The sources of TFP advance in manufacturing during the 1929–1941 period differed from those during the previous decade. In contrast to the 1920s, TFP growth took place in the absence of much net capital accumulation in manufacturing. According to the Bureau of Economic Analysis, the real net manufacturing capital stock was less than 10 percent higher in 1941 than it had been in 1929 while, according to Kendrick, hours had risen 15.5 percent over the same period.[11] Advance was also, in a number of subsectors, increasingly dependent on organized R and D. So at the same time that the aggregate capital-labor ratio in the sector was falling, the relative demand for scientists and engineers increased. It is quite astonishing, for those not inclined to think of the Depression as a technologically progressive era, to note the increase in R and D employment during the worst years of the downturn. Total R and D employment in U.S. manufacturing rose from 6,274 in 1927 to 10,918 in 1933 and then almost tripled in the following seven years of double-digit unemployment, reaching 27,777 in 1940 (table 2.4) (National Research Council; see Mowery 1981, 1983; Mowery and Rosenberg 2000, p. 814).

Margo (1991) has documented how much lower was the incidence of Depression unemployment among professional, technical, and managerial occupational classifications as compared, for example, with unskilled or blue-collar labor or workers with fewer years of schooling. This is indirect evidence that the sharp increase in R and D employment during the Depression was driven more by an outward shift in the demand for this type of labor than by a shift in its supply. The Depression years, unlike, for example, the more recent IT productivity boom, are not well characterized by what Goldin and Katz (1998) have

Table 2.4. Employment of Scientists and Engineers, United States, 1927–1940

Sector	Number Employed		
	1927	1933	1940
Chemicals	1,812	3,255	7,675
Electrical machinery	732	1,322	3,269
Petroleum	465	994	2,849
Nonelectrical machinery	421	629	2,122
Primary metals	538	850	2,113
Transport equipment	256	394	1,765
Food/beverages	354	651	1,712
Stone/clay/glass	410	569	1,334
Fabricated metal products	334	500	1,332
Instruments	234	581	1,318
Rubber products	361	564	1,000
TOTALS, 11 industries	5,917	10,309	26,489
TOTALS, manufacturing	6,274	10,918	27,777

Source: National Research Council, as cited in Mowery 1981, 1983, and Mowery and Rosenberg 2000, p. 814. For references to the original National Research Council reports, see Mowery 1983, fn. 12, p. 957.

described as capital-skill complementarity.[12] During the 1930s complementarity was between high-end labor and the disembodied technical change that was such an important feature of the period.

If one ranks two-digit manufacturing industries (see note 3) by the number of scientists and engineers employed in 1940 (table 2.4), chemicals tops the list by a wide margin, and, as noted, its TFP performance was stellar over the entire 1919–1948 period. Chemicals, electrical machinery, and petroleum account for almost half of R and D employment in 1940, and the eleven industries employing more than one thousand R and D workers in 1940 accounted for over 95 percent of the total in that year. Absent from this group were tobacco, textiles, apparel, lumber, furniture, paper, publishing, and leather—industries that, with the possible exception of tobacco manufacture, can be identified with the first, pre–Civil War industrial revolution. It should be noted, however, that a number of these latter industries, particularly tobacco and textiles, also turned in very respectable TFP performances over the entire 1919–1948 period, even though they were not R and D–intensive.

The overall trends revealed in these data are echoed in other R and D indicators. As noted in chapter 1, between 1929 and 1936 the annual rate of founding of new R and D labs (73) exceeded the comparable statistic between 1919 and 1928 inclusive (66), and real spending on R and D in manufacturing more than doubled during the 1930s, with an acceleration at the end of the decade (Mowery and Rosenberg 2000, pp. 814, 819).

DISAGGREGATION OF PRODUCTIVITY GROWTH, 1929–1941

Between 1929 and 1941, as noted, TFP growth in manufacturing fell by almost half (see table 2.4). There are really two questions to be addressed here, one focusing on the doughnut and the other on the hole. On the one hand, why did TFP growth fall from 5.12 percent per year to 2.76 percent per year when we compare the 1920s with the 1930s? The most likely explanation is that the extraordinary across-the-board gains from exploiting small electric motors and reconfiguring factories from the multistory pattern that mechanical distribution of steam power required to the one-story layout that was now possible were diminishing in aggregate magnitude by the end of the 1920s. They were not exhausted. It is simply that one could no longer hope to continue to generate 5 percent per year growth in the sector's residual from this source.[13]

The second question, then, is why didn't TFP growth in manufacturing fall even more? Here the answer has to do with the remaining mileage from reconfiguring factory floor layouts; a trend toward larger-capacity equipment and fixed installations; the use of new materials, particularly plastics and alloy steels; modest investments in instrumentation that saved both capital and labor; improved chemical processes for extracting minerals and processing agricultural materials; and a variety of advances that increased thermal efficiency. Many of these initiatives, and others, benefited from the contributions of a maturing and expanding privately funded R and D system that had begun with Thomas Edison at Menlo Park, New Jersey. The lion's share of private R and D spending was then and is now done in manufacturing, and a variety of new technological paradigms, most notably in chemical engineering, were ripe for exploitation.

Although the rate of TFP advance in manufacturing dropped by almost half if we compare 1929–1941 with 1919–1929, it remained at very high levels by the standards of the twentieth century. What is striking about the 1930s in comparison with the post-1973 period in the United States, including the recent IT productivity boom, is the broader base of productivity advance within the sector. Progress in individual industries was not, however, as uniformly distributed or as high as during the 1920s.

The growing importance of manufacturing—it generated about a quarter of national income in 1929, almost a third in 1941—helped counterbalance the within-sector decline in TFP growth in terms of the ability of the sector to contribute to high and indeed accelerating TFP growth in the aggregate economy during the 1930s. Still, this roughly 2.4 percentage point decline in the TFP growth rate in the sector worked in the opposite direction, reducing the overall importance of manufacturing in aggregate TFP growth. Clearly, one had to have substantial accelerations in TFP growth in other sectors in order to produce the 2.31 growth rate reported in table 2.1 for the private nonfarm economy.

That acceleration, as I will show below, came principally within transport and public utilities (about a tenth of the economy) and wholesale and retail distribution (about a sixth of national income). Transport and public utilities' TFP growth rate was higher—4.60 percent as compared with distribution's 2.39 percent per year—but because distribution was a larger share of the economy, it contributed about the same percentage of PNE TFP growth. Together, these two sectors were almost as important for TFP growth as was manufacturing, and along with manufacturing, they accounted for over 95 percent of advance in the private nonfarm economy during the Depression years.

These calculations are based on a division of the economy into four main subsectors: manufacturing, transport and public utilities, wholesale and retail distribution, and other. I begin by calculating each sector's share of national income and then calculate each sector's share of the private nonfarm economy. In 1941 agriculture, forestry, and fishing generated 8.06 percent of national income, and government 10.07 percent. Also excluded from the private nonfarm economy are the services of the owner-occupied portion of the housing stock and the nonprofit sector, defined as the sum of health, private education, and nonprofit membership organizations. Real estate's share of national income is partitioned into its owner-occupied portion and a remainder according to the ratios in the 1948 data. Taking into account these various exclusions, we find that the private nonfarm economy covers about three-fourths of the aggregate and approximates the BLS definition and that used by Kendrick. Thus, for example, whereas manufacturing contributed 31.9 percent of national income in 1941, it comprised 42.4 percent of the private nonfarm economy.

I begin with two critical numbers: the 2.31 percent per year growth of TFP for the private nonfarm economy reported by Kendrick and the estimate for manufacturing TFP growth from table 2.3 (2.76 percent per year).[14] I proceed by constructing an estimate for TFP advance in transport and public utilities (4.60 percent per year) and one for wholesale and retail trade (2.39 percent per year). I am then able to back out an implied net TFP advance in the remaining "other" sector of .22 percent per year. Table 2.5 summarizes these results.

Table 2.5. Sectoral Contributions to TFP Growth within the
Private Nonfarm Economy, United States, 1929–1941

Sector	1941 Share of National Income		1941 Share of PNE	Sectoral TFP Growth 1929–1941 (% per year)	Sector's Contribution to Aggregate PNE TFP Growth % Points	% of Total
Manufacturing	.319		.424	2.76	1.17	50.7
Transport and public utilities	.092		.123	4.50	0.55	23.8
Wholesale and retail trade	.167		.222	2.33	0.52	22.5
Other sectors (net)	.173		.231	.22	.07	3.0
Mining		.023				
Construction		.041				
Finance, insurance, real estate[a]		.051				
Other services[b]		.060				
TOTAL	.751		1.00		2.31	

Sources: Sectoral shares: U.S. Department of Commerce 1966, table 1.12.
Manufacturing TFP growth: See table 2.3.
Transport and public utilities TFP growth: See table 2.6.
Wholesale and retail trade TFP growth: See table 2.8.
Note: Subsector contribution to TFP growth lists the percentage point contribution of each subsector (share of covered subsector × subsector TFP growth rate). Subsector percent of TFP growth shows, for each subsector, the percent of the PNE's total TFP growth rate accounted for by that subsector.
[a]Excludes owner-occupied housing services, based on assumption that its share of real estate was the same as in 1948 (.619).
[b]Excludes health, private education, and nonprofit membership organizations. The private nonfarm economy also excludes the .35 percent of national income attributable to the rest of the world.

TRANSPORT AND PUBLIC UTILITIES

The calculations for transport and public utilities are the most complex. This sector constituted about 12 percent of the private nonfarm economy—a little more than half the share of wholesale and retail trade. But the estimated growth of TFP is approximately twice as high, and the rapid acceleration of TFP growth in this sector meant that it contributed slightly more to aggregate growth than did advance in distribution.

The 4.50 percent per year figure is based on estimates for eight subsectors: railroad transportation, local and interurban passenger transport, trucking and warehousing, water transport, air transport, pipelines, telephone and telegraph communication, and electric utilities. All told these eight sectors cover 92.5 percent of the entire transport and public utilities sector. Within the covered sectors, the largest weight is on railroads (.42), followed by electric utilities (.19), telephone and telegraph (.13), and trucking and warehousing (.12).

From Kendrick, we can obtain TFP estimates directly for railroads, local and interurban passenger transport, telephone and telegraph, and electric utilities. For the other subsectors, we can get output and persons employed from Kendrick on an annual basis. To obtain subsector capital input series, I go to the BEA's Fixed Asset Table 2.2. For trucking I use the real net capital stock data for trucks, buses, and truck trailers; for airline transport, aircraft; for water transport, ships and boats; and for pipelines, petroleum and natural gas pipelines. For trucking and water transport, my calculations are for 1942 and 1940 respectively because of the years for which Kendrick provides output and employment data.

These calculations (see table 2.6) reveal a stellar across-the-board productivity performance in transportation and public utilities between 1929 and 1941, with the exception of water transport. Of the 4.50 percent per year TFP growth in transport and public utilities, trucking and warehousing account for 32 percent of the total (1.46 percentage points), railroads an additional 27 percent (1.23 percentage points). Thus almost two-thirds of the advance in this sector took place in surface transportation. Electric utilities make the third largest contribution (24 percent) to sectoral growth.

In terms of subsector rates of productivity growth, airline transport and trucking top the list, with compound annual average growth rates of TFP over the period of 14.45 and 12.61 respectively. Both of these industries benefited from public spending, the airlines from subsidized airmail transport and the construction of airports during the 1930s, and trucking from the buildout of the surface road, bridge, and tunnel network during the Depression (see tables 1.4, 1.5, and 3.6). Since my analysis emphasizes the importance during the Depression of private sector spillovers consequent in part upon government infrastructural investment, one might ask by how much the PNE TFP growth rate for 1929–1941 would be reduced were one to add to private sector capital input a portion of government infrastructural investment complementary to private sector activity, and whether this would affect the rankings of time periods by TFP growth rates reflected in table 2.1, in particular the predominance of Depression-era growth rates. In other words, is the rate of TFP growth calculated for 1929–1941

Table 2.6. TFP Growth, Transport and Public Utilities, 1929–1941

Subsector	Share of NI 1941	Share of Covered Subsectors	Subsector TFP Growth	Subsector Contribution to Sector TFP Growth	Subsector Percent of Sector TFP Growth
Railroad transportation	.0361	0.424	2.91	1.23	27.3
Local and interurban passenger transit	.0056	0.065	3.02	0.20	4.4
Trucking and warehousing	.0099	0.116	12.61	1.46	32.4
Water transportation	.0041	0.049	1.69	0.08	1.8
Transportation by air	.0007	0.009	14.45	0.13	2.9
Pipelines	.0014	0.016	4.01	0.06	1.4
Telephone and telegraph	.0109	0.127	2.02	0.26	5.8
Electric utilities[a]	.0165	0.194	5.55	1.08	24.0
TOTAL	.0852	1.000		4.50	

Sources: Subsector shares of national income in 1941 are from U.S. Department of Commerce 1966, table 1.12. TFP growth for railroad, telephone and telegraph, local/interurban transportation, and electric utilities is from Kendrick 1961. For other subsectors, output and hours are from Kendrick 1961, and capital from BEA, http://www.bea.gov, Fixed Asset Table 2.2, lines 20, 24, 25, and 50; accessed August 1, 2010. See text for discussion. For trucking and water transport, my calculations are for 1942 and 1940 respectively because of the years for which Kendrick provides output and employment data.

Note: Subsector contribution to TFP growth lists the percentage point contribution of each subsector (share of covered subsector × subsector TFP growth rate). Subsector percent of TFP growth shows, for each subsector, the percent of the sector's total TFP growth rate accounted for by that subsector.

[a]TFP growth for electric, gas, and sanitary services is for electric utilities only; assumed .83 of the combined electric and gas utility national income share. This is the ratio of operating revenues of electric utilities to the sum of operating revenues of electric utilities and gas utilities in 1940. See U.S. Bureau of the Census 1951, tables 578 and 583, pp. 483, 485.

artificially inflated because of a changeover from privately owned infrastructural capital in railroads to publicly owned infrastructural investment in streets and highways?

Table 2.6 reports how much calculated TFP growth rates change if we augment the private sector capital input with government streets and highways capital plus "other" government structures (electric and gas facilities, transit facilities, and airfields),[15] likely, in contrast, for example, to military facilities, to be directly complementary to private sector production. Tables 2.1 and 7.1A of the BEA's Fixed Asset Tables provide annual estimates in current dollars of private and government capital stocks from 1925 onward.[16] The BEA's tables 2.2 and 7.2A provide chained index numbers for components of the real net stock starting in 1925.

The construction of a measure of private sector fixed capital augmented by these components of government infrastructure proceeds as follows. Start with the 1929 current values of the net stocks of private fixed assets, agricultural machinery, and farm structures from BEA Fixed Asset Table 2.1. Take the chained index numbers for the real net stock of each of these components for 1929 and 1941 from Fixed Asset Table 2.2. Using the ratio of 1941 to 1929 value, "grow" the 1929 current values to get 1941 real values (in 1929 dollars). Subtracting values of agricultural machinery and farm structures yields a fixed asset measure for 1929 ($244.8 billion) and 1941 ($251.1 billion in 1929 dollars) appropriate for calculations involving the private nonfarm economy. Then, using Fixed Asset Tables 7.1A and 7.2A, construct estimates for the real value of streets and highways plus other government structures. The sum, $18.6 billion in 1929 and $33.2 billion in 1941, is a measure of government infrastructure directly complementary to the private economy.

Using these data, one can calculate the growth rate of the real net stock of fixed private assets between 1929 and 1941 and the rate of growth of this stock augmented by government streets and highways capital and other structures, as described above.[17] Kendrick has the private nonfarm economy capital stock falling by –.14 percent per year between 1929 and 1941, but according to the calculations made with the more recent BEA data described above, it had a barely positive growth rate of .20 percent per year. The augmented stock, in contrast, grew by .63 percent per year, a difference of .43 percentage points. Man-hours in 1941 were basically unchanged from what they were in 1929 (Kendrick 1961, table A-XXIII). If we assume that it is reasonable to talk of private and government capital contributing additively to a combined capital measure, then

Table 2.7. Effect of Including Components of Public Infrastructure
on Calculations of TFP Growth, 1919–2000

Years	PNE TFP Growth	Change in Capital Contribution	Adjusted TFP Growth
1919–1929	2.02	.06	1.94
1929–1941	2.31	.13	2.18
1941–1948	1.29	−.05	1.34
1948–1973	1.88	.02	1.86
1973–1989	.36	−.04	.40
1989–2000	.79	−.02	.81

Sources: Table 2.1; BEA, http://www.bea.gov, Fixed Assets Tables 2.1, 2.2, 7.1, 7.2; accessed
January 4, 2010. See text.
Note: Public infrastructure includes streets and highways (federal, state, and local) and other public
structures, which include electric and gas facilities, transit systems, and airports. Capital share used
in calculating change in capital contribution = .3. For 1919–1929, I compare growth of fixed asset
stocks with and without public infrastructure between 1925 and 1929.

the augmented capital stock measure that includes this public infrastructure
does change the Depression years to a period of modest increase in the capital
stock and the capital-labor ratio. If we multiply the change in the rate of capital
growth (.43) by .3, an approximation of capital's share, we conclude that adding
in the services of this government infrastructural capital increases the contribution to growth attributable to capital by .13 percentage points per year.[18] Consequently, PNE TFP growth between 1929 and 1941 would be reduced from
2.31 to 2.18 percent per year on this account (see table 2.7).

Table 2.7 also reports how much difference this type of calculation would
make in other periods. For 1919–1929, I rely on capital data for the years 1925–
1929. Note that for 1941–1948, 1973–1989, and 1989–2000, the augmented capital stock grows more slowly than the private stock alone. In these instances
the effect of including government infrastructure is to raise estimates of TFP
growth. The largest adjustment to the capital contribution is for 1929–1941. For
the other periods, the growth of augmented and unaugmented capital stocks is
more similar, so the adjustments to the capital contribution are smaller.

The bottom line is that the main conclusion to be drawn from table 2.1
stands. Adding in these components of public infrastructure to private sector
capital input does not alter the preeminence of 1929–1941 in comparisons of
TFP growth across different periods in the twentieth century. It is not just the

physical capital deepening associated with government infrastructure spending in the 1930s that helps explain high labor productivity growth rates. It is also the positive production externalities such investment engendered in the private sector, especially in transport and public utilities and in distribution. In particular, public investment in the surface road network during the 1930s allowed very rapid TFP advance in trucking and warehousing and quite respectable productivity growth in railroads as the economy was reconfigured to take advantage of a transport system in which long-haul rail distribution could be more extensively integrated with local and regional use of trucks.[19] In turn, as is shown below, it was also associated with rising TFP growth in distribution, a trend that continued into the 1941–1948 period.

Even though some housing services—those of the owner-occupied portion of the housing stock—are excluded from the PNE statistical analysis, some discussion of the effects on this sector of the Depression-era surface road buildout is warranted.[20] With the exception of the years 1933, 1934, and 1935, street and highway construction proceeded at rapid rates during the Depression and then essentially ceased between 1941 and 1948. During the 1930s design principles for residential subdivision in an automobile age were worked out under the aegis of the Federal Housing Authority. A few demonstration projects were constructed, but the impact on housing sector productivity was small before the war because housing construction took so long to recover. Nevertheless, government- and university-financed research and development during the 1930s provided the foundation for the acceleration in both housing construction and housing productivity (flow of real rental services per unit of housing capital) that took place between 1948 and 1953 and continued at somewhat slower rates in the postwar period.

Denison's data show an index of housing sector real national income at constant (1958) occupancy rates growing from 40.7 to 70.8 over this five-year period (1974, table 3–6, p. 28; 1958 = 100). The BEA's Fixed Asset Table 5.2 shows an index of the net stock of private residential fixed assets growing from 17.8 in 1948 to 21.7 in 1953. In other words, the output of the housing sector between 1948 and 1953, adjusted for occupancy rates, grew at a compound annual growth rate of 11.1 percent a year while input grew at 3.99 percent per year, implying a sectoral productivity growth rate of over 7 percent per year.[21]

It is certainly true that some of the advance between 1929 and 1941 benefited from groundwork done in earlier decades. But if the Depression period drew from this larder, it also replenished it, establishing the basis for subsequent productivity advance. For example, almost all of the development work done by Phylo T. Farnsworth on the quintessential postwar consumer commodity—

television—was carried out during the Depression, supported by venture capital funding. The new product was introduced to a wide public in 1939 at the New York World's Fair, but the demands of war forestalled its full exploitation until after 1948. Thus while it is undoubtedly true that the technological achievements of the 1930s built on foundations put in place during the Depression years, as well as work done in the 1920s and earlier, it is also the case that the period laid the foundation for much of the productivity growth of the 1950s.

It is useful to contrast the effects of the boom in street, highway, and other infrastructure construction during the 1930s with those of the rather different government-financed capital formation boom that took place during the 1940s. The latter effort poured more than $10 billion of taxpayer money into GOPO plants. Almost all of this infusion was in manufacturing, and a large part of it went for equipment, particularly machine tools, in such strategic sectors as aluminum, synthetic rubber, aircraft engines, and aviation fuel refining (Gordon 1969). Most of this capital was then sold off to the private sector after the war.

The most spectacular expansion of equipment investment in U.S. economic history was associated with negative TFP growth in manufacturing between 1941 and 1948 and, partly as a result, a slowdown in PNE TFP growth overall (see tables 2.1 and 2.3). Outside of manufacturing, in sectors that were largely spared this infusion of equipment investment, productivity growth picked up speed somewhat during the 1941–1948 period.[22] Chapter 8 explores more comprehensively the implications of this experience for the equipment hypothesis—the view that equipment necessarily occupies a special place in capital formation as a carrier of technical change (DeLong and Summers 1991).

WHOLESALE AND RETAIL TRADE

Wholesale and retail trade comprised over a fifth of the private nonfarm economy during the Depression years, but Kendrick's data do not allow an estimate of TFP growth in the sector between 1929 and 1941. Key assumptions underlying my own estimate include the use of full-time equivalent (FTE) workers (rather than hours) to calculate input growth rates for labor and the use of the index of the net stock of commercial structures to calculate the growth of capital input. Table 2.8 shows a 2.39 percent growth rate in the sector, in the same range as in manufacturing but less than in transport and public utilities. Because of the sector's larger share, however, distribution contributed almost as much to the growth of PNE TFP as did transport and public utilities.

The Depression years present a complex picture in terms of advances in distribution. On the one hand, the sector experienced the high tide of such restrictive legislation as resale price maintenance (the Robinson-Patman Act),

Table 2.8. Compound Average Annual Growth Rates,
Wholesale and Retail Distribution, 1919–1948

Years	Output	Man-Hours	Output per Man-Hour	Capital	Output per Unit of Capital	TFP Growth
1919–1929	4.11	3.01	1.10	5.00	−.89	.50
1929–1941	3.37	1.45	1.92	.08	3.29	2.33
1941–1948	5.45	2.63	2.18	−.13	5.58	3.65

Sources: Kendrick 1961, table F-1, p. 506; U.S. Department of Commerce 1966, tables 1.12, 6.7A; BEA, http://www/bea.gov, Fixed Asset Table 2.2, line 41, accessed August 1, 2010; http://www.bea. doc.gov/bea/dn/FAweb/Index2002.htm; Bureau of Labor Statistics, Consumer Price Index (CPI) for urban workers, 1967=100; http://data.bls.gov.
1919–1929: Output and man-hours are from Kendrick 1961, table F-1, p. 506. Capital input growth rate is based on an adjustment to the growth rate of the net fixed stock of commercial structures from 1925 to 1929 (see text).
1929–1941, 1941–1948: Output growth is calculated from national income generated in the sector deflated by the CPI for urban workers, 1967=100. Man-hours input is based on the growth of FTE workers in the sector (U.S. Department of Commerce 1966, table 6.7A). The capital growth estimate is based on the growth in the chained index of commercial structures, from BEA Fixed Asset Table 2.2. *Note*: TFP calculations assume a labor share of .7, capital share of .3. Commercial structures include stores, restaurants, garages, service stations, warehouses, and other structures used for commercial purposes.

as well as various anti–chain store legislation at the state level (see Field 1996). At the same time, these legislative reactions are testimony to the inroads made by A & P supermarkets, Woolworth's, and other distributors who were taking advantage of the extension of the long-distance telephone network as well as a more flexible distribution system associated with the rapidly expanding surface road network.

Taking into account the contributions of manufacturing, transport and public utilities, and distribution, we conclude that the remaining (other) portion of the private nonfarm economy, which includes mining, construction, finance, insurance, and other services, experienced TFP growth of .22 percent a year and accounted for 2.2 percent of PNE TFP growth during the Depression. I do not attempt a detailed breakdown within this remainder category, some of whose components certainly experienced TFP advance higher than .22 percent per year and others lower and possibly negative rates.

Within the former category, mining is a promising candidate. If we follow procedures used within the transport and public utilities sectors, using Kendrick output and labor input data and a weighted average of mining equipment/oilfield machinery and mining structures and wells from BEA Fixed Asset Table 2.2, TFP growth within the sector comes in at 1.47 percent per year between 1929 and 1941.

My candidates for laggards would include construction, which took a very long time to recover from its collapse in the first part of the Depression.[23] Kendrick estimates that output per man-hour in the sector fell between 1929 and 1937, and in 1948 it was barely above its 1929 level (see Kendrick 1961, table E-1, p. 498). In a relatively non-capital-intensive sector this suggests low or perhaps even negative TFP growth over the period.

A second candidate would be the remainder of the finance, insurance, and real estate (FIRE) sector. Stock market trading volume plummeted, and there is no evidence of significant organizational or technological change during the 1930s. The basic system for ordering securities trades and receiving confirmation of execution, which developed after the Civil War, persisted for almost a century, breaking down only in 1968, the year in which peak 1929 daily trading volume was finally reattained and then repeatedly breached. Subsequent to the crisis, which forced Wednesday closings of the New York Stock Exchange for most of the second half of 1968 as brokerage houses struggled to deal with the backlog, technological and organizational changes in the sector have permitted average daily trading volume to increase by two orders of magnitude. But all this took place several decades after the end of the Depression (see Field 1998).

Banking, of course, was profoundly affected by the downturn, with failures of thousands of banks and persisting disruptions of the normal functioning of financial intermediation. The entire FIRE sector shrank in relative importance between 1929 and 1941, from 14.75 percent of national income in 1929 to 8.93 percent in 1941.

1919–1929 DISAGGREGATION OF TFP GROWTH

Using a similar approach, we can study how the drivers of TFP advance in the 1920s differed from those in the 1930s. We begin by using 1929 sectoral weights, making adjustments to real estate and other services similar to those made for 1929–1941.[24] From Kendrick, we have an estimate of annual TFP growth within manufacturing (5.12 percent per year). Based on the discussion above of wholesale and retail trade, I estimate TFP growth within the sector at .50 percent per year. What about transport and public utilities? How much had TFP growth in this sector accelerated during the 1929–1941 period in comparison with the 1919–1929 period?

Table 2.9. TFP Growth, Transportation and Public Utilities,
1919–1929 (percent per year)

Subsector	Subsector Weights	Subsector TFP Growth	Contribution to Sector TFP Growth
Railroad transportation	0.656	1.63	1.07
Telephone and telegraph	0.158	2.03	0.32
Electric, gas, and sanitary services	0.186	2.51	0.47
TOTAL			1.86

Sources: U.S. Department of Commerce 1966, table 1.12; Kendrick 1961.
Note: Subsector shares are based on 1929 data; electric utilities assumed to be .83 of combined electric and gas utilities. See text, table 2.6.

The absence of detailed subsector capital stock data for 1919 (the BEA fixed asset data begin in 1925) makes it difficult to estimate TFP growth in the sector in as comprehensive a fashion as is done for the 1930s. But from Kendrick we can calculate TFP growth rates for three of the subsectors: railroads, telephone and telegraph, and electric utilities. For the 1919–1929 period, these TFP growth rates clock in respectively at 1.63, 2.03, and 2.51 percent (see Kendrick 1961). Using 1929 subsector weights, we get an estimate of TFP growth in the sector of 1.86 percent per year between 1919 and 1929 (table 2.9).

Kendrick reports that output per hour in distribution between 1919 and 1929 rose at 1.1 percent per year, and the question is how much of this can be attributed to capital deepening. BEA Fixed Asset Table 2.2 shows that the net stock of non-office commercial structures grew at 5.87 percent per year between 1925 and 1929. How much can we assume it grew between 1919 and 1929? An acceleration of apartment and commercial office building construction followed culmination of the single-family residential housing boom in the mid-1920s (see chapter 11), so the end-of-decade rate was probably somewhat higher than that prevailing between 1919 and 1925. I have assumed an overall rate of increase of physical capital in distribution of 5 percent per year over the entire ten-year period 1919–1929. This implies 4.4 percent growth between 1919 and 1925, the first year for which the BEA data are available, with an acceleration to 5.87 percent per year between 1925 and 1929. If we assume a capital share of .3, we can then attribute .60 percentage points $[(5.00 - 3.01) \times .3]$ of the 1.1 percent per year labor productivity growth to capital deepening, leaving a residual of .50 percent per year in distribution for the 1919–1929 period.[25]

Combining this number with Kendrick's 5.12 percent figure for TFP growth within manufacturing between 1919 and 1929 and the estimate that TFP in transport and public utilities rose at about 1.86 percent, we can back out an implied net TFP growth for the remainder of the private nonfarm economy (33 percent of the total in 1929) of −.09 percent per year (see table 2.10).

We can now summarize the main distinctions between the 1919–1929 and the 1929–1941 periods with respect to aggregate TFP growth and its sources. First, TFP growth in the 1920s was almost entirely a story about manufacturing. There was a significant drop in the share of TFP growth in the private nonfarm economy accounted for by manufacturing, from 83 percent in the 1920s to

Table 2.10. Sectoral Contributions to TFP Growth within the Private Nonfarm Economy, United States, 1919–1929

Sector	1929 Share of National Income		1929 Share of PNE	Sectoral TFP Growth, 1919–1929 (% per year)	Sector's Contribution to Aggregate PNE TFP Growth % Points	% of Total
Manufacturing	.252		.329	5.12	1.69	83.5
Transport and public utilities	.108		.141	1.86	0.26	13.0
Wholesale and retail trade	.156		.203	0.50	0.10	5.0
Other sectors (net)	.250		.327	−0.09	−0.03	−1.5
Mining		.024				
Construction		.044				
Finance, insurance, real estate[a]		.110				
Other services[b]		.072				
TOTAL	.766		1.00		2.02	

Sources: Shares of national income: U.S. Department of Commerce 1966, table 1.12; sectoral TFP growth: see text, tables 2.3, 2.8, 2.9.

[a]Excludes owner-occupied housing services; assumes 1929 owner-occupied housing services were the same share of real estate as in 1948 (.619) (see text).

[b]Excludes health, private education, and membership organizations.

51 percent in the 1929–1941 period. This is due primarily to an almost halving of within-sector TFP growth, only partially compensated for by the expanding size of the manufacturing sector.

As noted, the extraordinary TFP growth in manufacturing in the 1920s was largely driven by floor space savings and improved materials flow associated with newly laid out factories, made possible by the removal of the straightjacket previously imposed by a mechanical distribution of internal power (Devine 1983; David and Wright 2003). Small electric motors were also important on the product side, driving such new consumer products as vacuum cleaners, refrigerators, and washing machines. Other new products associated with the consumer revolution of the 1920s exploited electricity to drive electronics, as in radios, or to provide heat, as in toasters or electric irons.

Aside from petroleum products, the standpoint performer at the two-digit level was transport equipment, with TFP growth of 8.07 percent annually over the 1919–1929 period (see table 2.2). This is hardly surprising, given what we know of the cost trajectory of a Model T Ford over these years—and what brought it about. What is striking about the first column of table 2.2 is how high TFP growth rates in manufacturing were *across the board* during the 1920s.

In order to generate a 2.31 PNE TFP growth in the 1930s, as compared with 2.02 percent during the 1919–1929 period, the economy had to experience accelerating TFP growth in sectors outside of manufacturing. Here the two major loci were wholesale and retail trade, which registered moderate acceleration (almost as fast as manufacturing) within a subsector with a relatively large weight, and transport and public utilities, which registered very rapid gains in a somewhat smaller sector. In both of these sectors public infrastructure investment generated positive externalities in private production that contributed to their high rates of productivity growth.

RAILS AND ROADS: HISTORICAL PERSPECTIVE

The growing complementarity between rails and roads is the second key pillar of the explanation of Depression-era TFP advance. An understanding of the evolution of this complementarity and its impact on transportation and distribution benefits from some historical background.

During the nineteenth century the construction and maintenance of roads had for the most part been a local responsibility. With the exception of expenditures for post roads and the construction of the National Road, which ran from Cumberland, Maryland, to Illinois and opened in 1818, the involvement of the federal government in the construction or improvement of highways was minimal prior to the passage of the Federal Aid Road Act (sometimes known as the Federal Highway Act) on July 11, 1916. It was also in that year that the first trackage of the rail system reached its all time peak. Although turnpikes had been built in the antebellum period (some private, some state supported), the extension of the railway network killed off most of this activity and resulted in an almost complete division of labor between the provision of local transport by horse-powered wagons traveling over mostly dirt roads and that of regional or interstate transport by steam-powered vehicles moving over rail and water. Aside from freight carried over water, longer-distance and in particular interstate transport of both goods and passengers was conducted overwhelmingly by rail.

The condition of American roads in the first decades of the twentieth century did not reflect the state of the technological art. Other countries at comparable stages of development had intercity road networks that were far superior. France, for example, had consistently devoted public resources to roads as well as rail and canals, and it had also invested in and benefited from the skills of a superb cadre of highway engineers, graduates of the Ecole des Ponts et Chaussées. In the early 1920s U.S. farmers paid twenty-one cents a ton-mile to haul crops over dirt roads, whereas French farmers paid ten cents a ton-mile to haul over paved roads. Proponents of highway spending in the United States referred to the poor state of U.S. roads as a "mud tax," arguing that it cost U.S. farmers over $500 million per year (Goddard 1994, p. 59).

The 1920s experienced a continuing and growing disjuncture between U.S. vehicle production and the country's surface infrastructure. Because of very rapid advance in manufacturing productivity, U.S. production and marketing of vehicles surged ahead of what was taking place in Europe, even though most of the underlying automotive technology had been perfected there. By 1919, U.S. automobile registrations had already risen to 6.6 million, and there were 898,000 trucks on the road. These vehicles were used, however, almost exclusively for local travel.

Trucks took advantage of the overburdened state of the railroads during the First World War to grab short-haul business. Urban firms welcomed trucks, which delivered door to door, obviating the necessity of running a horse and buggy down to the depot to pick up or drop off freight. To the degree one could arrange point-to-point truck shipment, thus bypassing the railroads entirely, businesses also found that breakage and wastage decreased because of the avoidance of intermodal transfer (Goddard 1994, p. 87).

But for interstate travel trucks still faced daunting challenges. The state of the U.S. road network at the end of the First World War was reflected in the experience of a fleet of army vehicles that attempted a cross-country transit in 1919.

It took them sixty-two days, averaging about fifty miles a day. If we assume they drove ten hours a day, this was an average speed of about five miles an hour—not that much faster than one can walk over level ground (three miles an hour). West of Kansas City, the roads were mostly dirt. Local roads outside of towns weren't much better (Paxson 1946, p. 244).[26]

During the 1920s the fleets of cars and trucks continued to expand as their costs of production declined. Between 1919 and 1929 automobile registrations more than tripled to 23.1 million, and truck registrations surged by a factor of four to 3.5 million. Although the states and counties labored mightily to respond to the growing political demand for taxpayer-financed road improvement and the federal government began some revenue sharing to this end, without an agreement on which state highways would be part of a national system, inter-state freight and passenger travel would be slow and uncertain at best, moving over roads of widely varying quality and capacity.

Agreement among the states about which routes would be stitched together into a national system was brokered by the federal government. The 1921 Highway Act pledged that paved roads should link every county seat (Goddard 1994, p. 91), but more important, it insisted that states identify which 7 percent of its roads should be linked together into a national system. The politics of doing so were contentious, however, and the list of U.S. routes was not finalized until November 11, 1926. Although the Great Depression began less than three years later, its impact on road construction figures was moderate and short-lived, having its most noticeable effects in 1933, 1934, and 1935 (see figure 3.6).

Because of the lag between the surge in vehicle production in the 1920s and the catch-up in infrastructure, it was primarily during the Depression years that the United States built its first national road network. The expenditures that made this possible, which included projects administered by the Public Works Administration (1933–1939) and the Works Progress Administration, have generally been interpreted as motivated by a Keynesian make-work rationale, and that is sometimes how they were justified politically after the fact. But these projects had very strong political support and a defensible economic rationale, and they probably would have been undertaken (with a supply-side[27] rather than a make-work justification) had the economy not headed south.

The tendency, under the pressure of new circumstances, to relabel the rationale of a program without changing its substance, is common and in this respect somewhat analogous to what happened with the Bush administration tax cuts of 2001. Those changes, which allowed disproportionate reductions in taxes to upper-income households, were justified initially as a saving-enhancing, growth-oriented program but were then repackaged in essentially unchanged form as a consumption-enhancing Keynesian stimulus package when the economy went into recession. The public road construction of the 1930s (an expenditure-increasing rather than a tax-reducing fiscal policy) had a less questionable supply-side rationale. Given the political agreement on the national road structure at the end of 1926 and the continued overhang of millions of new car and truck registrations, the United States probably would have gone forward with this construction whether or not the Great Depression had happened.

During the twelve Depression years, the stock of street and highway capital in the country almost doubled (see table 1.5), and the interstate (small "i") network whose outline had been agreed upon in 1926 was finished by the time the war began. As Frederic Paxson wrote, "When the attack at Pearl Harbor drew the United States again into war, the highways were a completed operating mechanism, needing at the last minute little more than a detail act for access and strategic roads" (1946, p. 238). The system of U.S. routes already enabled, prior to the Second World War, very substantial amounts of interstate ton mileage—almost 10 percent of the total—to be shipped by truck.

Road building then effectively ceased for six years, resuming again with a full head of steam in 1947. The Interstate Highway System, subsequently launched by President Dwight Eisenhower, significantly expanded the capacity of the system and changed some of its qualities, but its routes were built alongside of or literally on top of those of an already completed U.S. highway network. Interstate 95, for example, which runs from Maine to Florida, roughly parallels U.S. 1, which followed the same route; sections of several interstates have replaced U.S. 66, which, as the song says, ran from Chicago to Los Angeles. In 1956, the year in which ground was broken on the Interstate system, trucks already carried 18 percent of the ton mileage of interstate freight (up from 9.5 percent in 1940) (U.S. Bureau of the Census 1964, p. 561). In 1973, almost twenty years later, trucking's share had risen by only another five percentage points.

The outlines of the eventual truck/rail division of labor in carrying freight were not readily discernible in 1929, when trucks were responsible for less than 4 percent of interstate ton mileage (Stover 1997, p. 195). But they were by 1941. Postwar developments in surface transportation took place along lines that had been mapped out and essentially completed during the Depression.[28]

At the end of the First World War virtually all interstate freight not carried over water moved by rail, and the rail/water division of labor that this reflected had been in place at least since the 1850s. Just as the reconfiguration of American manufacturing in the 1920s represented a major departure from patterns that had prevailed for decades, so too did the transition in interstate shipments from a rail/water system to one that involved rail, road, water, and pipelines. That shift took off during the Depression and continued during the golden age.[29]

This transition is part of the explanation for the high economy-wide TFP growth rates that prevailed in the United States during the Depression years and the golden age. The growth of trucking's share of interstate shipments from under 4 percent as late as the end of the 1920s to 18 percent in 1956 was predicated both on infrastructural capital accumulation and on a number of important technical advances, which included the pneumatic tire and (more arguably) the internal combustion engine. This complex of innovation and accumulation facilitated the development of a complementary and symbiotic relationship between a growing trucking industry and a pared-down rail sector.

A very substantial portion of this transition had already occurred by the time the first concrete for the Interstate highway system was poured. That massive public works project helped extend the good times, at least for another decade. But the mechanisms and magnitude of productivity advance in the transport/distribution sector in the postwar period represented a continuation of trends and processes begun during the Depression.

Road improvements contributed to productivity growth in the trucking industry in a number of easily understood ways. With paved roads stopping at a city's edge, as they generally had in 1919, trucks faced a tough go of it if they ventured beyond, particularly in the winter and during the spring thaw. Improved roads meant trucks could travel at higher average speeds and cover longer distances in a day. As routes got longer and trucking traffic grew, network externalities resulted in greater likelihoods that truckers could snag a backhaul, which increased capacity utilization and raised the productivity of both capital and labor.

Quality improvements in the reliability and durability of trucks complemented improvements in the roads. Perhaps the most important of these was the borrowing of the pneumatic tire from the bicycle industry. Indeed, one can make a case that the tire was a more important technological precondition for a successful truck industry than were advances in the internal combustion engine—since alternate power sources, such as steam, might have achieved comparable range and reliability had they received similar levels of R and D attention (Arthur 1989).[30] In the absence of the pneumatic tire, however, vibration and shocks made any but short distances and low speeds unbearable for the driver. Wear and tear on the vehicle as well as the driver was far greater, and there were higher costs in damaged freight and broken containers. The problem of absorbing shocks transmitted from the road surface was more serious for trucks than cars because of the greater weights involved. After more than a century, no serious alternative to the use of inflatable rubber tires for cushioning surface road transport has emerged.

The pneumatic tire was first used on bicycles in 1889. Just as many automobile manufacturers benefited from their experience building bicycles, so too did political pressure from bicyclists for better paved roads lay the foundation for subsequent lobbying by automobile and truck interests toward the same end (Finch 1992, pp. 24–25.). The emerging political coalition for "good roads" brought together automobile and bicycle enthusiasts and a growing trucking industry with automobile, truck, and tire manufacturers, road contractors, asphalt and cement producers, the petroleum industry, insurance companies, and the motor lodging industry (Goddard 1994, p. ix).

There is now an extensive literature on the impact of general-purpose technologies (GPT) on economic growth. Despite the efforts of Bresnahan and Trajtenberg (1995) and Lipsey, Bekar, and Carlaw (1998) to be more precise about its characteristics, there are good reasons to be skeptical that the concept has added much to our toolkit (see chapter 9). Nevertheless, there are clearly some innovations and innovation complexes that are more important than others. A number of writers (Gordon 2000b; David and Wright 2003) have speculated about the "internal combustion engine" as a potential GPT. Careful consideration suggests that this new engine design was only part of a consequential innovation complex and not necessarily its most important part. It is true that in the event the vast majority of vehicles on America's highways were powered by gasoline or diesel engines, in which combustion took place within rather than outside of cylinders. But the particular design of the engine is not what was critical. It was the use of self-propelled vehicles on rubber tires running over a paved and improved infrastructure that was the key contributor to the second wave of TFP advance identified here. Whether these vehicles were powered by external combustion (steam) or gasoline-fueled internal combustion engines was a matter of secondary importance.

While it is clear that better roads benefited trucking, it is not so obvious that they promised and in fact yielded significant benefits to the rail industry. How did improving the surface road network lead to complementary improvements in productivity in the railroad sector? One important mechanism was the smoothing out of seasonal fluctuations in the demand for freight cars. Rural free delivery had brought mail and mail order goods to millions of farm households, and the insistence by the post office that roads be minimally passable in order to institute the service had resulted in some improvements in local roads and bridges. But, as noted, as late as the mid-1920s paved roads tended to end at the edges of towns and cities with the exception of major metropolitan centers on the two coasts and a few interior cities such as Chicago. Consequently shipments to and from rural households dropped precipitously when the roads were bad. Prior to the railroad, freezing temperatures shut down interior commerce in much of the Northeast and Midwest for as much as five months during which canals and rivers were impassable. Railroads were largely unaffected by changing weather conditions, but they still relied on trucks or horses and buggies for the trip from depots to farm households. These miles, dependent on a dirt roadbed, remained more vulnerable to the weather than had interregional canal and river traffic prior to the railroad.

The flip side of the collapse of shipments during winter and spring months was that shippers deluged the railroads with business during the dry season. Carriers had to balance the benefits of being able to meet this surge in demand with the costs of holding excess capacity the rest of the year. As one might expect, their solution represented a compromise, with the result that prior to road improvements and the growth of the trucking industry, railroad shipments were backlogged during four or five months while many freight cars ran close to empty during the remainder of the year (Goddard 1994, p. 52).

In the 1920s railroads could not imagine trucks making runs of more than twenty miles a day, and they anticipated that better roads would smooth their shipment flow and they would enjoy a symbiotic relationship with the trucking industry in which they (the railroads) would enjoy the role of senior partner. That was one reason for their support of the "good roads" movement for the better part of several decades. Another was their expectation that they could earn money by shipping construction materials—asphalt and concrete—for new roads. They cheerfully hauled the materials that would improve the highways; they hauled the steel, glass, tires, and subassemblies to Detroit, where the trucks and cars were built; and they hauled the completed trucks and cars from Midwest factories to retail markets around the country. Slowly, shipment by shipment, they contributed to the building of a competitive transport mode that eventually took away most of their passenger business and much of their freight traffic.

The railroad industry simply did not fully appreciate the extent to which the burgeoning trucking industry would eventually eat much of its (the railroad industry's) lunch. Conventional wisdom for several decades was that trucks helped railroads; they were the servants of railroads because they either delivered from the depot to the final destination (where railroads could not) or, in cases where roads might parallel rails, trucks were suitable only for short hauls on which railroads couldn't make money anyway. But entrepreneurial truckers had other ideas, pushing the edge of the envelope to fifty miles, then one hundred, then even longer runs. Low barriers to entry and the lack of regulation prior to 1935 created an environment in which the industry could grow rapidly in response to burgeoning profit opportunities made possible by improvements to the roadbed and to the durability, reliability, and size of trucks.

The economics of trucking were fundamentally different from those of railroads. Because railroad companies enjoyed decreasing average costs over much of their output range, the industry tended toward monopoly. Pricing at marginal cost might be allocatively efficient but could not hope to cover fixed costs. The consequence was a byzantine system of freight classes through which rail companies tried to apply price discrimination based on the value of the product being shipped rather than what it cost to move it. Charging what the market would bear was a practical necessity if bankruptcy was to be avoided, but it was arbitrary and inherently discriminatory. Complaints about discrimination and political agitation against railroads led to the creation of the Interstate Commerce Commission and a system of regulated prices.

Truckers, who did not own their roadbed or have to pay for it directly, had low fixed costs and faced cost structures more closely approximating the canonical competitive firm. They did not have to segregate their freight into categories. They charged by weight and could respond to changing market conditions by quickly adjusting rates, whereas railroads had to go through a complicated and time-consuming administrative process to do so.[31] That was one reason why truckers were running circles around railroads, literally and figuratively. Another was that trucking had much greater flexibility in terms of changing routes and batching jobs to deal with geographically dispersed pickup and delivery, so that while railroads struggled with increasing numbers of less-than-carload shipments, network externalities allowed truckers to increase their load factors.

Nevertheless, there remained much that was defensible in the railroad's justification for supporting the construction of better roads. Both labor productivity and TFP went up in the railroad sector faster during the 1929–1941 period than they had between 1919 and 1929, even though there was much more capital deepening in the 1920s (see chapter 12). The total mileage of the railroads reached its high-water mark in 1916, the year of the first federal highway bill, but the shrinkage of trackage was slow in the 1920s and began to accelerate only during the 1930s. Spurs to inactive mines were abandoned, and lightly used freight and passenger routes were increasingly abandoned as well. To the degree that the rail system shut down its least productive activities, productivity went up.

Total mileage for single or first main track for all reporting railways peaked at 266,381 miles at the end of 1916. By 1929 first track mileage had dropped only marginally to 262,546. By 1941, however, it had fallen to 245,240, about a 9 percent decline from the peak (U.S. Bureau of the Census 1942, p. 477.) In 1973 it had fallen to 216,000 miles (U.S. Bureau of the Census 1978, p. 660), as the industry continued to seek and receive permission to abandon unused or lightly used lines.

Between 1929 and 1941 TFP advance in trucking and warehousing was nothing short of phenomenal, growing at a compound annual rate of 12.6 percent. The sector was responsible for almost 8 percent of the entire PNE TFP growth during this period ($(1.46/4.50) \times 23.8$). TFP in railroads rose at 2.91 percent per year between 1929 and 1941. Even though this was only a fourth of the blistering pace in trucking and warehousing, the substantially larger weight of rails in the economy meant that railroads accounted for about 6.5 percent of the 2.31 percent per year TFP growth in the private nonfarm economy (again, this is in comparison with the 51 percent contributed by manufacturing; see tables 2.5 and 2.6).

By 1941, then, a significant reconfiguration of the U.S. surface transportation system had already taken place. The network of national routes that remains with us to this day, although subsequently expanded and paralleled by the Interstate system, was essentially complete. The key infrastructural components (bridges and tunnels) for the major East and West Coast port complexes had been built. Trucking was already responsible for close to 10 percent of interstate ton mileage, and the railroads had abandoned more than twenty thousand miles of first track. And relative to 1929, they had cut employees by almost a third and locomotives, freight cars, and passenger cars by 27, 24, and 29 percent respectively. Yet in 1941 the rail system generated 6 percent more revenue ton-miles and produced almost as many passenger miles as it had in 1929 (see chapter 12, table 12.1). The intertwined history of the iron rail and the pneumatic tire, of railroads and trucking, puts flesh on the skeletal story told in tables 2.5 and 2.6 and provides a foundation for exploring sources of growth in the postwar period (chapter 4).

3

THE SECOND WORLD WAR

The historiography of the Great Depression in the United States has been overwhelmingly concerned with the sources of the deficiencies in aggregate demand responsible for more than a decade of double-digit unemployment over the twelve-year period 1929–1941. The narrative has been infused with leitmotifs of failure and loss: of output, of employment, and of expenditure. In contrast, the macroeconomic history of the golden age, the quarter century following the end of demobilization, has, on balance, radiated the bright glow of success. The emphasis has been on an American economic colossus standing astride the world in a position of dominance not realized before or, in quite the same way, since (Ferguson 2004, p. 18).

Awkwardly situated between Depression-era "failure" and postwar "success" has been the Second World War, a disruption to the "normal" path of economic development every bit as significant, although in different ways, as was the Depression. As a consequence of its temporal location, the conflict has acquired almost mythological significance in bridging these two story lines, although it has in fact received relatively little detailed examination from macroeconomists and economic historians. Conventional wisdom credits the war both with "bringing us out of the Depression" and with "laying the foundations for postwar prosperity."[1]

There can be little doubt that the war administered a huge demand shock to the economy, especially from 1942 onward, the result of a massive increase in deficit spending and an expansionary monetary policy committed to pegging both short- and long-term rates at low levels.[2] The standard interpretation, how-

ever, couples the demand story, at least implicitly, with emphasis on a powerful supply shock, one resulting from learning by doing in military production
(Searle 1945; Alchian 1963; Gemery and Hogendorn 1993) and spinoffs from
military research and development (Ruttan 2006). That posited supply shock
has to be a main underpinning of the claim that the war "laid the foundations
for postwar prosperity."

My concern in this chapter is principally with delving more deeply into
the second part of the conventional wisdom, that which credits much of the
achieved level of potential output in 1948 to war-induced positive supply shocks.
To what degree was the war responsible for establishing the technological, organizational, and infrastructural preconditions for the golden age? Chapters 1 and
2 have laid out the argument that productivity advance between 1929 and 1941
was far stronger than has been traditionally appreciated. A corollary is a greater
skepticism about the rosy supply-side picture typically painted of the impact of
the war years.

The conventional (Kendrick 1961) productivity data for the private nonfarm
economy show that TFP, which had been growing very rapidly between 1929
and 1941, continued to increase from 1941 to 1948 but at a markedly slower rate
(see table 2.1). The data do show TFP higher in 1948 than it had been in 1941,
although as I show at the end of this chapter, much of the gap is eliminated if
one makes a cyclical adjustment to take account of the fact that the economy in
1941 had not yet fully reattained potential output. The question I wish to pose is
whether 1948 levels were higher than they would have been in the absence of
the war. Stated alternately, one can ask whether these productivity levels might
have been reached earlier in the absence of the conflict.

There is a strong case to be made—and this chapter will attempt to make
it—that whatever positive shocks may have been associated with progress in
the mass production of airframes, ships, penicillin, or munitions/fertilizer were
largely counterbalanced by the negative shocks associated with the disruptions
to the economy resulting from rapid mobilization and demobilization. Chapters 1 and 2 have established that the years 1929 through 1941 were marked by an
exceptionally high rate of TFP growth, with the consequence that a significant
fraction of the productivity foundations of the postwar epoch were already in
place by 1941, before full-scale war mobilization. Thus the rate of increase of
TFP between 1941 and 1948, even without a cyclical adjustment, is lower than
is commonly realized.

Why? Mobilization/demobilization delivered a one-two punch, whipsawing
the economy, as it first force-fed very rapid expansion in a limited number of war-
related sectors, such as other transport equipment, and then imposed equally

rapid contraction. The conflict diverted the cream of American scientific and engineering talent, who had *not* been experiencing high unemployment rates during the Depression (see Margo 1991), into military work such as the Manhattan Project. Mobilization required that managers and workers pay attention not only to the wrenching tasks of reorienting production within and between sectors, but also to a panoply of regulations associated with government contracting and resource allocation in what, within the military and much of the civilian sector, approached a command economy (Civilian Production Administration 1947).[3] There was certainly some learning by doing in high-profile sectors, such as airframes and shipbuilding, and some war-related R and D spinoffs, such as microwaves and advances in electronics that benefited the nascent computer industry. But there were opportunity costs, and the overall effect of the Second World War was probably to slow the growth of TFP and potential output. The best way to describe the supply-side effects of the war is that they represented, in the aggregate, a retardative supply shock, slowing down the breakneck pace of advance of potential output that had been achieved during the Depression years, largely fueled by advance of TFP.[4]

THE TIMING OF ECONOMIC MOBILIZATION

The supply shocks associated with mobilization and demobilization were short; they were sharp; and whether they were positive or negative, they were experienced almost entirely after the United States entered the war.[5] The military buildup, which was only beginning when Pearl Harbor was attacked in December 1941, led to a massive ramp-up in military and naval construction in 1942, a surge in equipment and ordnance production that peaked in 1943, and an expansion of employment in the federal government, both civilian and military, that peaked in 1944. By 1948, with demobilization largely complete, nonmilitary production revived, and unemployment at 3.8 percent, these changes had been almost entirely unwound.

Either of these shocks alone would have imposed substantial transition costs on the economy. Together they represented something of a double whammy. The war put the economy through a wringer, not once, but twice. From this perspective, it is hardly surprising that total factor productivity grew much more slowly between 1941 and 1948 than it had between 1929 and 1941.

Although it was commonly believed during the conflict and immediately thereafter that the war was associated with large positive productivity effects, a more nuanced and pessimistic evaluation was shared by economists familiar with the effects of mobilization and demobilization. Solomon Fabricant was an exemplar of this group; his general pessimism is echoed by Jules Backman and Martin Gainsbrugh (1949). Here's what Fabricant wrote in 1952:

> Despite beliefs frequently held to the contrary, little contribution to the defense effort may be expected from productivity. . . . The composition and even the volume of output undergo radical transformation. Speed rather than cost is the criterion. And fundamental changes occur in the organization of the economy. In a word, attention is diverted from the mainsprings of progress.
>
> In such a situation, the energy of businessmen is devoted not to new improvements and additions to knowledge, but to adapting standard mass production methods to the munitions industries. And they are under the necessity of learning new rules. Price, production, and other controls have to be studied and the very rapid and radical changes in them require attention. Little time or energy is left for improving efficiency. . . .
>
> The new workers are inexperienced; and some are handicapped. Some of the new equipment brought into production is standby equipment, not worth operating in normal times, and the flow of new and up to date equipment is slowed to a trickle. The mines reopened are low grade or high cost mines. . . . Inventories are inadequate, and delays in receiving materials hold up production lines. Ersatz materials frequently require more labor for processing. Long hours cut the strength of labor and management.
>
> As a result, national output per man hour fails to rise at the peacetime rate. (1952, p. 30)

Fabricant went on to note that railroads were an exception to this rule because of their unusual cost structure (but see also chapter 12) and that productivity declines in trade and services were sometimes disguised because they took the form of deterioration in quality. But "in most peacetime and manufacturing industries . . . , actual and palpable declines occur. For skilled labor is pulled away, transport is choked, and materials come hesitatingly and in meager quantity" (1952, p. 30).

Fabricant concluded his analysis by acknowledging that some munitions manufacturing did experience rapid productivity gains. He referred to the famous case of shipbuilding, noting a doubling of output per hour in the three years following Pearl Harbor. But he also observed that these increases were from very low levels immediately following conversion so that "even the wartime peak in productivity may be below the level of the industry's peacetime productivity" (1952, p. 31).

Some of Fabricant's arguments address why one cannot expect, overall, a big contribution to wartime output growth from productivity advance. Many of the retardative forces, such as disruptions to production from erratic inventory control, would in principle disappear with the cessation of hostilities, with no permanent ill effects. But other factors identified help explain why war imposed a persisting cost in terms of the trajectory of long-term productivity advance. Technical, scientific, and managerial energies were diverted from commercial pursuits toward the war effort. There was invention and learning by doing as a result, but not all of it was relevant when peace returned. And there was an opportunity cost. When scientists and engineers devoted their time to building atomic bombs, when businessmen were preoccupied with learning new administrative rules, and when success was measured by one's ability to produce large quantities of ordnance quickly in an environment of cost-plus contracts, it is scarcely surprising that the overall rate of commercially relevant innovative activity slowed down.

Table 2.1 reports the rates of total factor and labor productivity growth before, during, and after the period of war mobilization and demobilization, calculated from the conventional data. The choice of 1941 as a breakpoint is critical, and chapter 1 discussed why using this more fully employed year is preferable to the local peak of 1937 privileged by Kendrick. Because productivity is strongly procyclical (see chapter 7), measuring from 1929–1937, with its 14.3 percent unemployment, gives too low an estimate of the trend growth rate of TFP. The year 1941, with 9.9 percent unemployment, is better, though not ideal. The penultimate section of this chapter discusses an adjustment for the remaining cyclical effect and how much it would increase our estimates of trend TFP growth.

For the moment, the contrast between 2.31 percent per year (1929–1941) and 1.29 percent per year (1941–1948) is quite enough to motivate discussion. We begin with the striking observation that high TFP growth during the Depression years meant, according to these numbers, that achieved productivity levels in 1941 were much higher than they had been in 1929. Because of the absence of capital deepening over this period, this was true for both labor productivity and TFP. Readers may have the impression that with Lend-Lease and other expenditures in anticipation of war the United States was already on something like a full-scale war footing by the time of Pearl Harbor. If this were true and if one were an "optimist" about the effects of war on productivity growth, one might argue that some of the productivity levels in 1941 were attributable to the defense buildup that had already been under way for two years.

It is important to appreciate how small a share of total war spending had actually taken place at the time Pearl Harbor was attacked. The U.S. Departments of the Army and the Navy spent $1.8 billion on military manpower, structures, equipment, and other ordnance in 1940 and $6.3 billion in 1941 (table 3.1, column 2; these figures exclude veterans' benefits). If one wanted to emphasize the extent of the buildup in 1941, one could say that spending had more than tripled compared to the previous year. But the 1941 figure is clearly dwarfed by what followed. Combined army and navy spending in 1940 and 1941 represented just 3.2 percent of the 1940–1946 cumulative total.[6] Adjusting for price changes makes virtually no difference in these calculations. Column 1 of table 3.2 reports the price index for national defense expenditures, rescaled so that 1940 = 100. This index rises 6.7 percent in 1941 but then trends slightly downward, presumably reflecting some learning by doing and productivity improvement in the production of ordnance. The combined share of 1940 and 1941 spending in real terms (column 3) is still just 3.2 percent of the cumulative 1940–1946 total.[7]

The picture is slightly modified if one considers a broader measure of spending on national defense, including Lend-Lease and spending by the Defense Plant Corporation, a subsidiary of the Depression-era Reconstruction Finance Corporation. By this measure, a total of about 5 percent of cumulative 1940–1945 military spending had taken place prior to Pearl Harbor (table 3.1, columns 4 and 5).

Like total military spending, and not coincidentally, the average number of U.S. military personnel also more than tripled, comparing the calendar year 1941 with 1940. But one needs to appreciate both that the U.S. economy had been almost completely demilitarized during the Depression and that much mobilization was still to come. Figure 3.1, drawn from the 1951 *Statistical Abstract of the United States* (U.S. Bureau of the Census), make this point vividly. The uptick in military personnel in 1941 looks large in comparison with 1940 but is dwarfed by what followed. And the 1.8 million average military personnel in 1941 seems trivially small in comparison with the armed forces of Germany, Japan, and Italy, each of which already had more than 7 million men in uniform, including reserves, at the beginning of 1940 (Nelson 1946, p. 30).

The pattern observed in military manpower is also evident in the time series for U.S. military aircraft production (figure 3.2). Output of 19,455 planes in 1941 was more than three times the 6,028 produced in 1940 but barely a fifth of peak production of 95,272 in 1944.

This pattern is even more pronounced for ship production (table 3.2), in part because of the country's urgent need after 1941 to make good on the losses suffered at Pearl Harbor. Starting from low levels, production of combatant ships peaked in 1943, at more than seventeen times 1941 levels. The surge in production of landing craft in 1944, however, pushes the peak in total ships produced to that year.

Finally, let's consider the division of industrial production between war and non-war activity. Figure 3.3, which is based on indexes compiled by the Federal

Table 3.1. U.S. Military Spending, Nominal and Real,
1940–1945 (billions of dollars)

Year	1 Price Index National Defense, 1940 = 100	2 Army and Navy Nominal	3 Real	4 All National Defense Nominal	5 Real
1940	100.0	$1.8	$1.8	$2.5	$2.5
1941	106.8	6.3	5.9	14.3	13.4
1942	104.5	22.9	21.9	51.1	48.9
1943	105.5	63.4	60.1	84.2	79.8
1944	103.8	76.0	73.2	94.5	91.0
1945	104.5	80.5	77.0	81.9	78.4
TOTAL		250.9	239.9	328.6	314.0

Sources: Column 1: BEA, http://www.bea.gov, National Income and Product Accounts, table 1.5.4; accessed July 15, 2010. Price index has been rescaled so that 1940=100.
Column 2, sum of outlays by the Departments of the Army and the Navy: U.S. Bureau of the Census 1975, series Y-458, 459, p. 1114.
Column 3: Column 2/Column 1.
Column 4, total national defense spending: http://www.bea.gov, National Income and Product Accounts, table 3.9.5; accessed July 13, 2006.
Column 5: Column 4/Column 1.

Reserve Board, shows that in 1941 military production accounted for less than a fifth of the total, and civilian industrial production was still increasing. In 1942, 1943, and 1944, on the other hand, civilian production declined, and military production accounted for more than half of the total.

Federal Reserve Board data also show that the wartime expansion of industrial production was almost exclusively a durable goods phenomenon (see citations in U.S. Bureau of the Budget 1946, p. 104). These data show industrial production, both total and war-related, peaking in 1943. Total industrial production peaked in October, when manufacturing accounted for a larger share of U.S. value added than it ever had before or ever would again, and it fell precipitously after February 1945.[8]

Individually and in the aggregate, these data show that although the United States may have been gearing up for war prior to 1942, it was doing so from a very low base, and what had been accomplished through the end of 1941 was

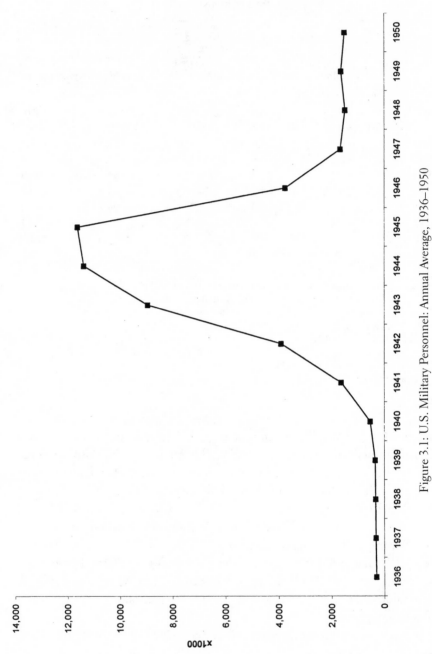

Figure 3.1: U.S. Military Personnel: Annual Average, 1936–1950
Source: U.S. Bureau of the Census 1951, p. 210.

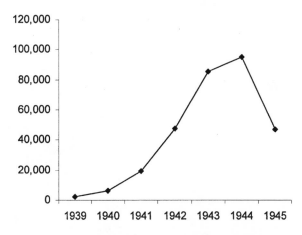

Figure 3.2: U.S. Military Aircraft Production, 1939–1945
Source: U.S. Bureau of the Census 1975, series Q-566, p. 768.

Table 3.2. U.S. Military Ship Production, 1941–1946

Category	Number of Ships					
	1941	*1942*	*1943*	*1944*	*1945*	*1946*
Combatants (total)	33	141	568	420	152	73
Battleships	2	4	2	2		
Aircraft carriers	1	1	15	8	5	7
Aircraft carriers (large)					2	
Aircraft carriers (escort)	2	13	50	37	13	4
Battle cruisers				2		
Heavy cruisers			4	2	8	4
Light cruisers	1	8	7	11	7	6
Destroyers	16	81	128	84	74	38
Destroyer escorts			306	197	6	
Submarines	11	34	56	77	37	14
Patrol and mine craft	167	743	1,106	640	238	6
Auxiliaries	83	184	303	630	402	43
Landing craft	1,035	9,488	21,525	37,724	17,958	21
District craft	261	786	677	577	661	48
TOTAL	1,579	11,342	24,179	39,991	19,411	191

Source: U.S. Bureau of the Census 1947, p. 222.
Note: Data for 1945 include a total of 457 converted ships: 5 patrol and mine craft, 240 auxiliaries, 127 landing craft, and 85 district craft.

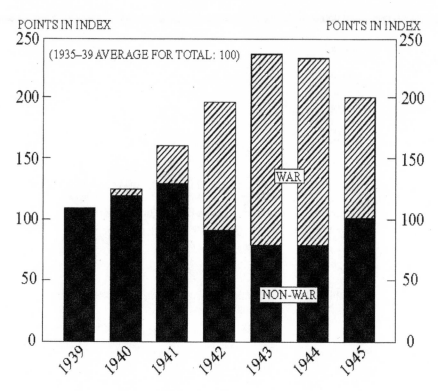

Figure 3.3: War and Non-War Industrial Production, United States, 1939–1945
Source: U.S. Bureau of the Budget 1946, p. 104.

small compared to what would come subsequently. Achieved levels of production, total factor productivity, and output per hour in 1941 cannot have had much to do with learning by doing from military production or spillovers from military R and D.

SECTORAL REDISTRIBUTIONS OF LABOR

This section takes a broader look at the effects of mobilization and demobilization on the economy, in particular on its manpower requirements.[9] Tables 3.3 and 3.4 are based on data on FTE workers from the *National Income and Product Accounts* (U.S. Department of Commerce 1986). I have divided the major sectors of the economy into those acquiring and those releasing workers between 1941 and 1943 (table 3.3) and between 1943 and 1948 (table 3.4). Although total military spending and military manpower continued to rise in 1944, 1943 represented the peak of industrial production and economic mobilization per

Table 3.3. Labor Releasers and Labor Acquirers, United States, 1941–1943

	FTEs (thousands)	
Nongovernment:		
Labor releasers	*FTEs Released*	*1941 FTEs*
Motor vehicles and equipment	(330)[a]	655
Contract construction	(208)	1,774
Wholesale trade	(200)	1,952
Farms	(179)	2,201
Retail trade	(109)	5,075
Sum, above 5 sectors	(1,026)	
Total labor releasers	(1,580)	
Labor acquirers	*FTEs Acquired*	
Other transportation equipment	2,596	675
Iron and steel and their products, incl. ordnance	819	1,641
Machinery, except electrical	370	1,087
Electric and electronic equipment	353	607
Chemicals and allied products	269	580
Railroad transportation	249	1,285
Sum, above 6 sectors	4,656	
Total labor acquirers	5,302	
Government:		
Labor releasers	*FTEs Released*	
Work relief	(1,317)	1,364
State and local	(132)	2,922
Labor acquirers	*FTEs Acquired*	
Military	7,349	1,680
Federal civilian, except work relief	1,553	944
Government enterprises	74	431
Net inflows from unemployed, NILF[b]		
Nongovernment sector	3,722	
Government sector	7,527	
TOTAL NET INFLOWS	11,249	

Source: U.S. Department of Commerce 1986, table 6.7a, p. 275.
[a]Parentheses indicate negative numbers (outflows from the sector).
[b]NILF: Not in labor force.

Table 3.4. Labor Acquirers and Labor Releasers, United States, 1943–1948

	FTEs (thousands)	
Nongovernment:		
Labor acquirers	FTEs Acquired	1943 FTEs
Retail trade	1,511	4,966
Services.	756	5,226
Contract Construction	712	1,566
Wholesale trade	676	1,752
Motor vehicles and equipment	441	325
Finance, insurance, and real estate	281	1,389
Telephone and telegraph	202	490
Total labor acquirers	6,099	
Labor releasers	FTEs Released	
Other transportation equipment	(2,800)	3,271
Iron and steel and their products, incl. ordnance	(588)	2,460
Chemicals and allied products.	(126)	849
Electric and electronic equipment	(73)	960
Agriculture, forestry, fisheries	(56)	2,121
Nonferrous metals and their products	(32)	508
Railroad transportation	(31)	1,534
Total labor releasers	(3,709)	
Government:		
Labor acquirers	FTEs Acquired	
State and local	1,062	2,790
Labor releasers	FTEs Released	
Federal civilian, except work relief	(1,119)	2,497
Government enterprises	(294)	505
Work relief	(47)	47
Military	(7,485)	9,029
TOTALS		
Government net releases	(7,883)	
Nongovernment net acquires	2,390	
Total outflows to unemployed, NILF	5,493	

Source: See table 3.3.

se (see figure 3.3). For the sake of consistency I have used it as the breakpoint for the analysis of both government and nongovernment employment.

For the nongovernment sector we find the following major sectors releasing workers between 1941 and 1943: the motor vehicle industry, construction, wholesale and retail trade, and agriculture. Together, these five sectors accounted for 1.026 million of the total 1.580 million FTEs contributed by releasing sectors over this two-year period.

We then identify six major sectors acquiring workers. The largest by far was other transportation equipment (not motor vehicles). This sector, which was producing the ships and planes already discussed, as well as a variety of other vehicles, acquired over a two-year period a mind-boggling 2.6 million FTEs, a 384 percent increase over its 1941 employment of 675,000 FTEs. The second-biggest acquirer of labor was iron and steel and their products, including ordnance, followed by nonelectric machinery, electrical machinery, chemicals, and railroad transportation. Together these six sectors accounted for 88 percent of the total increase of 5.302 million FTEs in the acquiring sectors.

It is striking how narrowly concentrated were the sectors acquiring labor. Other transportation equipment accounted for 49 percent of the increase in FTEs in the acquiring sectors. Adding in iron and steel products, including ordnance, one gets to 64 percent. In contrast, the two largest releasing sectors (motor vehicles and construction) accounted for barely 34 percent of the total FTEs contributed by releasing sectors. FTE acquisitions were therefore much more highly concentrated than FTE releases. Economic mobilization for war was very far from a balanced, across-the-board expansion of the economy.

This methodology does not capture flows within sectors. For example, automobile production effectively ceased in February 1942, and workers remaining in the motor vehicles industry were producing military vehicles such as jeeps and trucks.

We now turn to the government sector, where between 1941 and 1943 we find 1.317 million released from work relief and 132,000 released from state and local government employment. Between 1941 and 1943 the U.S. military acquired 7.349 million FTEs and federal civilian employment another 1.553 million. Finally, government enterprises acquired 74,000.

Overall, summing the nongovernment sector consolidated acquisition of 3.722 million and the government sector consolidated acquisition of 7.527 million, we have a net inflow from the ranks of the unemployed or not in the labor force of 11.249 million.

Taken together, mobilization led to a rapid expansion of the economy, but one that represented a very sharp distortion of the "normal" channels of such an expansion.

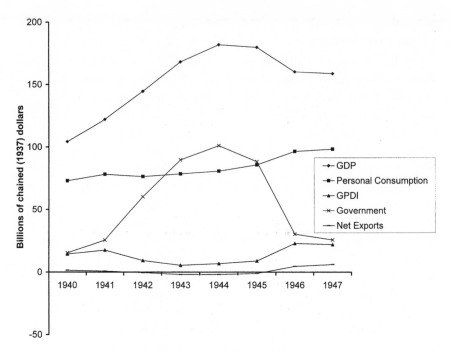

Figure 3.4: Components of GDP, United States, 1940–1947
Source: BEA, NIPA Table 1.1.5, http://www.bea.gov.

Although nongovernment FTEs peaked in 1943, total FTEs peaked in 1944 at 54.982 million (1.3 million above the 1943 total), largely because of an additional increment of 2.3 million military FTEs, which counterbalanced the declines beginning elsewhere. Military equipment had to be produced before it could be used. By the time of D-Day, the military goods production machine had already begun to wind down.

In the short span of two years, between 1941 and 1943, the U.S. automobile industry shut down and reconverted to defense production. Nondefense construction largely ground to a halt, as military and naval construction soared. People streamed out of farms and wholesale and retail trade into defense factories and the military, and they were joined by hundreds of thousands, indeed millions, from the ranks of the unemployed and not in the labor force. Billions of dollars were spent by the Defense Plant Corporation to build GOPO plants and equip them with machine tools to jump-start the airframe and shipbuilding industries and produce aviation fuel, synthetic rubber, and aluminum (Reconstruction Finance Corporation 1946). Then, before the economy could catch its breath, most of the ordnance was expended, the war was won, and full-scale demobilization was underway.

Table 3.4 uses the same methodology to study demobilization from 1943 to 1948. What we see here is a rough reversal of the trends associated with mobilization. The two biggest acquirers of labor during mobilization—other transportation equipment and iron and steel and their products, including ordnance—were the two biggest releasers during demobilization, and the FTEs released by these two sectors (3.388 million) were almost exactly equivalent to those acquired during mobilization (3.415 million). Symmetrically, the biggest acquirers of labor during demobilization were largely the sectors that had released the most during mobilization, in particular motor vehicles, retail and wholesale trade, and construction. Another big acquirer was finance, insurance, and real estate. Home building and nonresidential private construction, as well as other forms of physical capital accumulation, revived in the postwar period, finally surpassing 1929 rates after two decades in which investment had been depressed (the Depression years) or largely government-controlled (the war years). Employment in intermediation and brokering correspondingly increased. Agriculture, on the other hand, continued to lose FTEs, reflecting a long-term trend.

The analysis understates the impact of demobilization in the government sector since government FTEs peaked in 1944. The military added an additional 2.336 million FTEs between 1943 and 1944, although other components of government FTEs were largely unchanged. Federal civilian FTEs went up 23,000, government enterprises went down 26,000, state and local governments lost another 79,000, and the remaining 47,000 on work relief left this category. The huge increase in the military would make the outflows from government larger for an analysis based on a 1944–1948 transition.

Expenditure data (figure 3.4) show that during the war rising government spending crowded out domestic private investment and, to a lesser degree, consumption and net exports (the current account went into deficit largely because of unilateral transfers, including Lend-Lease).[10] These numbers do show the absolute value of consumption rising in real terms throughout the war, except in 1942, although Higgs (1992, 1997, 1999) has argued that this is misleading because the price deflators used do not correctly measure the increasing real costs of goods in the context of rationing or simple unavailability. In other words, Higgs would have the series for real personal consumption spending dip substantially during the war years before reviving.

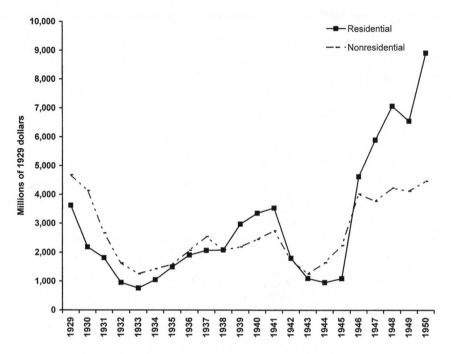

Figure 3.5: Real Private Construction Spending, 1929–1950
Sources: See text. Nominal values for 1929 from U.S. Council of Economic Advisors
1951, table A-18, p. 188 (nonresidential includes "other private," mostly spending
on gas and electric facilities). Real values calculated by linking 1929 nominal
values to data from BEA Fixed Asset Table 2.8, "Chain Type Quantity Index
for Investment in Private Fixed Assets."

Although the question of how much real consumption rose or dropped during the war remains at issue (see Rockoff 1998; Edelstein 2000, p. 400), there is
little dispute that government spending increased and that private investment
in the country declined, not just as shares of GDP, but in absolute terms. There
were also significant changes in the composition of public investment. Figures 3.5 and 3.6 show trends in public and private construction expenditures.
The nominal data for 1929 are taken from U.S. Council of Economic Advisors
(1951, table A-18, p. 188). Real values are calculated by linking 1929 nominal
values to data from the Bureau of Economic Analysis (Fixed Asset Tables 2.8
[for private construction] and 7.6A [for public construction], at http://www.bea
.gov; accessed July 7, 2009).

Several conclusions are apparent from these figures. First, residential construction—the sick child of the U.S. economy throughout much of the Depres-

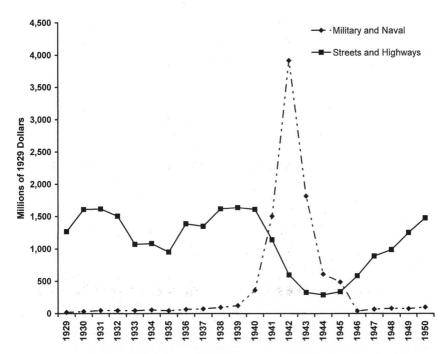

Figure 3.6: Real Public Construction Spending, 1929–1950
Sources: See text. Nominal values for 1929 from U.S. Council of Economic Advisors
1951, table A-18, p. 188. Real values calculated by linking 1929 nominal values
to data from BEA Fixed Asset Table 7.6A, "Chain Type Quantity Index
for Investment in Government Fixed Assets."

sion (see chapter 11)—had by 1941 laboriously climbed back to within striking
distance of its 1929 level. The war took the steam out of this forward movement,
and by 1944 private housing construction was at an even lower level than it had
been at the depths of the Depression in 1933. It was not until 1946 that residential construction surpassed its 1929 rate, soaring past the previous 1926 peak in
1947. Nonresidential private construction was also depressed during the war,
driven almost to the vanishing point in 1943. Other private construction, largely
public utilities, was less dramatically affected by the war, principally because
energy, especially electric power, was critical to the war effort.

If we look at public construction, we are first struck by the big peak for 1942
in military and naval construction and other public nonresidential building.
Mobilization for war can be thought of as consisting of three waves, each crest-
ing respectively in 1942, 1943, and 1944. The year 1942 saw massive military construction; 1943, the peak in military industrial production, and, finally, 1944, the

peak in military FTEs. Build the production facilities, produce the ordnance, and then let the military use it.

A second point to note, already emphasized in chapter 1, is the high rate of street and highway construction during the Depression years. Spending increased sharply from 1929 levels in the years 1930, 1931, and 1932. Although outlays then declined in the years 1933, 1934, and 1935, when they bottomed out, they had, by 1938, 1939, and 1940, reattained the levels of the early 1930s. The cumulative effect of this spending was the building of a modern surface road infrastructure that was, as noted, essentially complete by the outbreak of the war. Military spending crowded out highway construction during the war: street and highway construction outlays fell to extremely low levels in 1943, 1944, and 1945, and this spending came back more slowly than housing production immediately after the war. Also reflected in figure 3.6 are outlays on bridges, dams, tunnels, and other non-highway public infrastructure spending during the Depression. This too was crowded out during the war years, although the magnitude of the drop was lower, partly because recovery had been less dramatic

Public infrastructure spending in the 1930s had already begun to generate spillovers in transportation, distribution, and housing before the war.[11] It continued to do so afterward. Thus the case that it was a combination of product and process innovation during the Depression and Depression-era infrastructure building, far more than the war, that was responsible for 1948 productivity levels.

SENSITIVITY ANALYSIS: ADJUSTMENTS TO 1941 AND 1948 PRODUCTIVITY LEVELS

The purpose of this penultimate section is to consider a cyclical adjustment for 1941 productivity, an adjustment to 1948 productivity based on inadequate accounting for GOPO capital sold to the private sector after the war, and how such adjustments might affect the relative magnitude of productivity growth during the period of mobilization and demobilization. The section also considers how the use of output and capital input data based on chained indexed methods would affect estimates of TFP growth across the Depression and war years.

The standard of the business in measuring productivity change over time is, if possible, to calculate from peak to peak so as to control for cyclical confounds. With its 9.9 percent unemployment, 1941 is not ideal in this respect. The question is whether productivity levels in 1941 would have been higher or lower had

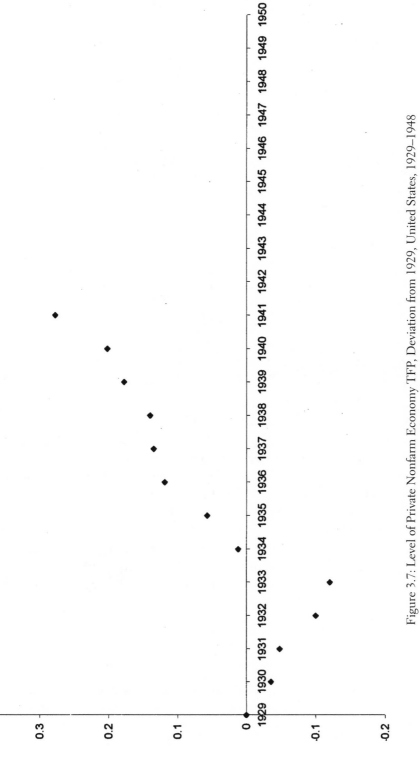

Figure 3.7: Level of Private Nonfarm Economy TFP, Deviation from 1929, United States, 1929–1948
Source: See table 2.6. Data points plotted are ln (t) – ln (1929).

Table 3.5. Cyclical Effects on Total Factor Productivity, 1929–1941, 1948

Year	PNE TFP (Kendrick)	Change from Prior Year (ln(t)–ln(t–1))	Unemployment Rate (%) (Lebergott)	Change (percentage points)
1929	100.0		3.2	
1930	96.5	−0.0356	8.7	5.5
1931	95.3	−0.0125	15.9	7.2
1932	90.5	−0.0517	23.6	7.7
1933	88.7	−0.0201	24.9	1.3
1934	101.2	0.1318	21.7	−3.2
1935	105.9	0.0454	20.1	−1.6
1936	112.6	0.0613	16.9	−3.2
1937	114.4	0.0159	14.3	−2.6
1938	115.0	0.0052	19.1	4.8
1939	119.4	0.0375	17.2	−1.9
1940	122.4	0.0248	14.6	−2.6
1941	132.0	0.0755	9.9	−4.7
1948	144.5	0.0905	3.8	−6.1

Sources: Kendrick 1961; Lebergott 1964.

the economy been at full employment, and if so, by how much. The Depression years experienced strongly procyclical productivity, as figure 3.7 shows. Table 3.5 provides the underlying data. The first column shows Kendrick's index of total factor productivity for the private nonfarm economy. Column 2 shows the continuously compounded rate of change in that index from one year to the next. Column 3 is the national civilian unemployment rate from Lebergott (1964), and column 4 the change in percentage points in that rate.

If we regress the change in the natural log of TFP ($\Delta\ln$ TFP) on the change in the unemployment rate in percentage points (ΔUR), we get the following results:

$$\Delta\ln\text{TFP} = .0283 - .0092*\Delta\text{UR}$$
$$R^2 = .647 \quad (3.02) \quad (-4.28)$$

(t statistics in parentheses; data are for 1929–1941; n = 12)

The intercept term can be interpreted as showing that TFP had a trend growth rate of approximately 2.83 percent per year over this twelve-year period.

The coefficient on ΔUR suggests that every percentage point decrease in the unemployment rate raised TFP growth by about .92 percent, or close to a percentage point, with every percentage point increase in the unemployment rate doing the reverse. We can use this equation for two closely related exercises, first to make a cyclical adjustment to the 1941 productivity level and second to imagine what one more year of peacetime growth and declining unemployment would have meant for productivity in the United States.[12]

If one is a war-productivity optimist, one thinks of 1948 as the first year in which a demobilized peacetime economy benefited from all the new production knowledge generated during the war, and this influences one's interpretation of its achieved productivity level. A better way to think of 1948, in my view, is that it is 1941 with full employment. As noted in chapter 2, the major new consumer product, television, had had all of its development work done before the war but had had its commercial exploitation delayed until after the war. One can tell a similar story about nylon, over which women went wild when it was first introduced in 1939 before the war; diverting its use from stockings to parachute and tent production made it a scarce civilian commodity. The 1948 surface transport infrastructure, which underlay productivity levels in distribution, transportation, and housing, had been almost entirely completed before 1942.

All of this suggests that if we imagine a world without the disruptions of the war, with the economy continuing a rapid progression toward full employment in 1942, productivity levels in 1942 could well have approached those achieved in 1948. In a closely related exercise, we can ask what productivity levels would have been in 1941 had unemployment been at 1948 levels (3.8 percent).

Unemployment in 1948 was 6.1 percentage points lower than it had been in 1941. Using the estimated coefficient from the above regression, we can predict that had unemployment in 1941 been as low as it was in 1948, TFP would have been 5.61 percent higher than it was ($-.0092 \times -6.1 = .0561$). TFP in 1948, measuring by using natural logs, was 9 percent higher than in 1941. So close to two-thirds of the productivity gap between 1941 and 1948 would be eliminated if we were to make a cyclical adjustment to the 1941 data (table 3.6).

Any positive cyclical adjustment to measured 1941 productivity to account for the fact that the economy had not yet reached capacity would raise the estimated TFP growth rate between 1929 and 1941 and lower it between 1941 and 1948. Kendrick's TFP index for the private nonfarm economy stands at 132.0 for 1941. If we make the 5.61 percent adjustment implied by the above analysis, we are at a cyclically adjusted 1941 level of 139.6. The level for 1948 is

Table 3.6. TFP Growth, 1929–2000, with Cyclical Adjustment
for 1941 and Chained Index Output Estimates for 1929–1948

Years	TFP with 1941 Cyclical Adjustment	TFP Using Chained Index Output with 1941 Cyclical Adjustment
1929–1941	2.78	3.29
1941–1948	.49	2.59
1948–1973	1.90	1.90
1973–1989	.34	.34
1989–2000	.78	.78

Sources: See table 2.1 and text.
Note: Data are for the private nonfarm economy and are annual growth rates.

144.5, implying less than half a percent growth (.49 percent) per year between 1941 and 1948, as compared with 2.78 percent per year between 1929 and 1941.[13] Table 3.6 revises the numbers reported in table 2.1 to include rates of growth based on a cyclically adjusted productivity level for 1941. It is notable, and quite remarkable, that if we go back to table 2.1 and calculate output per hour growth between 1929 and 1941, taking into account the higher 1941 TFP that would have prevailed with a lower unemployment rate, cyclically adjusted labor productivity growth would exceed that achieved during the golden age.

The 1941–1948 TFP growth rate would be further reduced were one to make an adjustment to 1948 TFP for the value of formerly GOPO capital, much of which was already in the hands of the private sector by 1948 (the major exception was synthetic rubber, which was not completely privatized until 1955). Gordon has argued that this capital was often sold off in sweetheart deals and that its value has not been adequately included in the standard capital stock measures (see Gordon 1969; Rockoff 1998, p. 106). If the capital stock input should be higher for 1948, the level of TFP in that year would have to be lower, and so, consequently, would its rate of growth between 1941 and 1948. A nod in Gordon's direction on this account would further reduce the cyclically adjusted rate of growth of TFP for the private nonfarm economy between 1941 and 1948.[14]

We can also ask, counterfactually, what might have happened had the Japanese attack been delayed twelve months. Due to the disruptions associated with conversion and war mobilization, TFP in actuality grew hardly at all between 1941 and 1942 (132.5 vs. 132). But suppose the economy had experienced one more year of peacetime growth in which it benefited from the 1929–1941 trend growth rate in TFP and the unemployment rate fell to 1948 levels. The regression results suggest that in this case, 1948 productivity levels would have been approached in 1942. This conjecture is based on adding the 2.83 intercept term from the equation, for one year of additional growth based on the peacetime trend growth rate, to the 5.61 percent cyclical adjustment, the predicted increase in TFP from a drop in the unemployment rate of 6.1 percentage points. Summing these two terms leads to a predicted level of TFP in 1942 that is 8.4 percent higher than 1941, just shy of the measured 1948 level.[15]

On average, there were 5.560 million unemployed in 1941. Had the unemployment rate been at its 1948 level of 3.8 percent, with higher employment in construction, motor vehicles, other manufacturing sectors, wholesale and retail trade, and finance, insurance, and real estate, 3.547 million of them would have been at work. Unemployment was falling rapidly during 1941. In the fourth quarter it was down to an average of 3.4 million, with a civilian labor force of 53.9 million, yielding an unemployment rate of 6.3 percent (U.S. Bureau of the Census 1946, p. 173).

Had trends persisted in the absence of war, employment, TFP, and labor productivity would all likely have been higher in 1942. As figure 3.6 shows, housing construction was robust and growing in 1939, 1940, and 1941, and when the postwar housing boom emerged with full force in 1946, it took off from where it had been arrested in 1941. Since the failure of residential construction to revive fully was one of the major contributors to the persistence of low private investment spending during the Depression, its signs of revival in the years immediately preceding the war suggest that had peace continued, investment, output, and employment growth would have continued as the economy reapproached capacity.

One concludes from this analysis that the 1.29 percent per year cumulative growth in TFP per year between 1941 and 1948 calculated from Kendrick, a rate of growth already lower than that recorded between 1929 and 1941, substantially overstates productivity advance across the period of mobilization and demobilization. Both of the adjustments discussed strengthen the relative importance of productivity advance between 1929 and 1941 and weaken its likely magnitude between 1941 and 1948.

There is an additional reason to believe that strict reliance on Kendrick's numbers understates the extent of TFP (and capacity growth) across the Depression years. In 1996 the Bureau of Economic Analysis began providing real output estimates based on chained indexed methods. When calculating real growth between two years, it can make a big difference whether we use initial-year or end-year prices. One of the problems with the old procedures was that changes in the base year for real output series required periodic rewriting of economic history. The chained index method "solves" the index number problem by calculating real growth first using initial-year and then using end-year prices and then taking a geometric average of the two growth rates (multiplying them together and taking the square root). These year-over-year growth rates are then linked to create a real output series. The Bureau of Economic Analysis now provides estimates of real GDP based on these methods going back to 1929.

These revisions substantially increase the growth of output between 1929 and 1941 and between 1941 and 1948. The chained index series shows output in the private nonfarm economy rising 40 percent over the twelve-year period between 1929 through 1941 and an additional 42.5 percent between 1941 and 1948 (some of this represents the completion of cyclical recovery).[16] Converting to a continuously compounded annual rate, we have PNE output growing at 2.80 percent per year between 1929 and 1941.

The Bureau of Economic Analysis also provides updated Fixed Asset Tables, which report index numbers for the real value of various components of the physical capital stock, along with current price values, going back to 1925. These offer the basis for a modest upward revision in Kendrick's capital input numbers (as discussed in chapter 2; see table 2.7). The BEA numbers suggest a small positive (.2 percent per year) rate of growth of the private nonfarm economy capital stock over the twelve-year period, as compared with Kendrick's small negative rate (−.1 percent per year).

Taking zero percent as the growth rate of hours (from Kendrick; the hours series has not been updated by the BLS) and +.2 percent as the growth of capital and using an estimate of .3 as capital's share, we get a weighted average of combined input growth rates of +.06 percent annually. Subtracting .06 percent per year from the 2.80 percent per year chained index estimate of output growth yields 2.74 percent per year as a revised estimate of TFP growth for the private nonfarm economy between 1929 and 1941, before a cyclical adjustment.

The previous calculations in this section suggest that a cyclical adjustment for 1941 raises the TFP growth rate between 1929 and 1941 by about 20 percent (2.78/2.31 = 1.20). Combining a cyclical adjustment with the TFP estimate based on the revised BEA numbers for capital and output, we can make a plausible case for a "true" growth rate of PNE TFP between 1929 and 1941 exceeding 3 percent per year (1.20 × 2.74 = 3.29).

For 1941–1948, PNE output based on chained index methods grew at 5.06 percent annually. Hours grow at 1.80 percent per year and capital at 1.45 percent, yielding a TFP estimate without a cyclical adjustment of 3.37 percent per year. With a cyclical adjustment for 1941, this falls to 2.59 percent; an adjustment for the undervaluation of GOPO capital in 1948 would reduce this further.

These results, summarized in table 3.6, reinforce the conclusion that PNE TFP growth was more rapid across the Depression years than during the 1941–1948 period and that estimates of TFP growth for the Depression years from Kendrick represent a lower bound.[17]

By 1948 the U.S. economy had demobilized, the civilian economy was booming, and unemployment stood at the low peacetime rate of 3.8 percent. Housing and private nonresidential building had finally risen above their 1929 levels, as had automobile production. Between 1941 and 1948, TFP in the private nonfarm economy grew at a respectable rate in comparison with 1973–1989, but one that was below the rapid advance before (1929–1941) or after (1948–1973).

We come back to the question posed at the start of this chapter. How much of the achieved productivity level of the 1948 civilian economy should reasonably be attributed to the war? The two main components of the "war stimulates productivity growth" thesis involve learning by doing in military production and spinoffs from military research and development.

Much attention has been paid to the success stories in producing ships and airframes. There are several reasons, however, why one should be skeptical that this success had much to do with how the economy performed in 1948. First, as Fabricant (1952) noted, the initial productivity levels immediately following conversion to military production were often low (see also U.S. Bureau of the Budget 1946, p. 433). Some of what one is seeing is improvement from this base. Second, much of the success here involved the application to these military goods of mass production methods that had been pioneered in the 1920s and 1930s in the civilian economy. In other words, organizational and technical advances prior to 1942 probably made a greater contribution to the success of economic mobilization than the latter did to postwar productivity levels. Even on the technical (as opposed to production) side, it is notable that there was not a single combat aircraft produced during the Second World War and seeing major service that was not already on the drawing boards before the war began.[18]

Finally and most important, whatever commodity-specific learning by doing took place between 1942 and V-J (Victory over Japan) Day in 1945 was largely irrelevant by 1948 because most of it applied to the other transport equipment sector, and that sector, having practically quadrupled in size between 1941 and 1943 (based on FTEs), was smaller in 1948 than it had been in 1941. Few of the ships and aircraft about which so much has been written (Liberty Ships or B-29s, for example) were produced after the war.[19] Even those for which the production of civilian counterparts continued, such as the C-47/DC-3, had much smaller postwar production runs. Other dual-use vehicles, such as trucks, had fewer units produced annually between 1942 and 1945 than had been the case in 1941 or even 1937 (U.S. Bureau of the Census 1975, series Q-150, p. 716). Here again, it is much more likely that success in producing these vehicles in volume derived from prewar experience in civilian manufacturing, as opposed to the war contributing dramatically to postwar capabilities.

To the degree learning by doing took place in war industries, it involved innovations in workplace organization, materials flow, sequencing of tasks, and the acquisition of job- and product-specific human capital. Because of the shrinkage of the other transport goods sector and the disappearance of many of the wartime products from the postwar output mix, little of this learning would have had much influence on 1948 productivity levels.[20]

The second component of the thesis emphasizes spillovers from military research and development. Items often referenced include microwaves, advances in electronics benefiting the computing industry, atomic power, and techniques for mass-producing penicillin. Unlike learning by doing producing Sherman tanks, the penicillin experience clearly had more peacetime applicability, as did improved techniques learned on the battlefield for treating trauma. But with computers, microwaves and atomic power, and many of the other putative spillover candidates, one has to ask how much the war accelerated a scientific and technological trajectory that was proceeding very well prior to it.

The scientific and engineering community, in cooperation with government officials, managers, and workers had, by all accounts, and based on the U.S. experience with war mobilization, done a superb job in helping to expand the potential output of the economy between 1929 and 1941. This community was then asked to drop much of what it was doing and focus on challenges central to the war effort. In the process, some discoveries and learning useful for civilian production took place. But these were incidental to the war effort and entailed opportunity costs in the forms of disruptions of the trajectory of technical advance in the civilian economy. It is unlikely on balance that the stock of economically relevant knowledge (both technical and production knowledge) was on balance higher compared to what it would have been in the absence of war.

There continues to be a popular perception that war is beneficial to an economy, particularly if it does not lead to much physical damage to the country prosecuting it. The U.S. experience during the Second World War is the typical poster child for this point of view. Detailed research into the effects of armed conflict, however, has usually produced more nuanced interpretations. For example, an earlier tradition (Hacker 1947) saw the Civil War as a tremendous stimulus to the Northern economy, whereas more systematic quantitative inquiry has led to an emphasis on its retardative effects on growth (Goldin and Lewis 1975). In that spirit, the research reported in this chapter represents a revisionist approach to the analysis of the Second World War, although one that is not entirely unanticipated.[21]

The Golden Age and Beyond

The quarter century running from 1948 through 1973 has come to be known as the golden age of U.S. productivity growth. Over these years output per hour in the private nonfarm economy grew at a compound annual average rate of 2.75 percent per year. The distinctiveness of this achievement, as well as its implications for the U.S. material standard of living, is reflected in the fact that the long-run growth rate of U.S. *output* for over a century has been a little over 3 percent per year.

Of this 2.75 percent, approximately .9 percentage point per year can be attributed to the effects of capital deepening associated with the revival of private sector physical capital accumulation following its sharp decline after 1929. Although accumulation revived after 1941, it was only following the war that it could do so in a fashion less distorted by the demands of war. The remainder of growth in output per hour between 1948 and 1973, 1.88 percent per year, reflects increase in total factor productivity.

The purpose of this chapter is to examine the sources of this advance in light of a narrative of twentieth-century U.S. economic growth that places the Depression years in a more prominent position than they have heretofore occupied. The new emphasis on the Depression's contribution to growth of potential output is a prism through which the experiences of the rest of the century are refracted in new ways. It places the achievements of the 1920s and the 1995–2005 period in a different light (chapters 2 and 5). It overturns the conventional wisdom attributing achieved 1948 productivity levels principally to the war (chapter 3). And—the thesis of this chapter—the golden age (1948–1973) no longer has to be understood sui generis but can be seen as a period reflecting the extension and persistence of trends and technological foundations established during the interwar period.

What were these trends? The first was a continuing decline in the rate of advance of TFP within the manufacturing sector. The second was the persistence of high rates of TFP growth in transportation, communication, public utilities, and trade. In both the 1930s and the golden age, these sectors benefited from complementary investments in government infrastructure. The 1930s saw a high rate of street and highway expenditure, in which the paved highway network of the United States caught up with the rapid expansion of automobile and truck production and registrations that had taken place during the 1920s. This allowed the emergence of a transformed system of moving goods that involved an integration of rails for long-haul and trucks for local and regional distribution. These changes underlay extremely high rates of TFP advance in trucking and warehousing and to a lesser degree railroads during the Depression years (see chapter 2) and the persistence of advance in these sectors during the postwar period. TFP growth was much lower during the dark ages (1973–1989 or 1995).

MANUFACTURING

The golden age decline in TFP growth, relative to what took place during the Depression years, is almost entirely accounted for by manufacturing. The sector had enjoyed unprecedented gains in the 1920s based on electrification and new products and somewhat weaker although still strong R and D–based advance during the 1930s (chapter 2). During the Second World War manufacturing benefited from, but was also bloated and distorted by, the increase in military procurement and the injection of GOPO capital. American industry nevertheless emerged from the conflict in a position of world dominance. Technical frontiers had been expanded by a host of new product and process innovations during the 1930s, and some of this potential had begun to be realized prior to the war. In other cases, such as television (as noted), all of the development work had been done before the war, and the new products were poised for rapid exploitation with the ending of controls after V-J Day.

With European and Japanese manufacturing hobbled by war damage, U.S. manufacturing faced extraordinary global opportunities and challenges in helping to rebuild foreign industries and in satisfying their domestic markets while this took place. Continued high levels of military spending during the Korean and Cold Wars meant a stream of direct orders for defense contractors and a stimulus to and stabilization of aggregate demand for the rest of the economy.

Such was the environment in which the manufacturing corporations described in John Kenneth Galbraith's *New Industrial State* (1971) consolidated
their distinguishing characteristics. Galbraith described them as islands of
planned economy within an ostensibly market-based system. Many corporations offered something equivalent to lifetime employment security. Through
marketing and planned obsolescence, the disruptive force of technological
change—what Joseph Schumpeter called creative destruction—had largely
been domesticated, at least for a time. Whereas large corporations had funded
research leading to a number of important innovations during the 1930s, many
critics now argued that these behemoths had become obstacles to transformative innovation, too concerned about the prospect of devaluing rent-yielding
income streams from existing technologies. Disruptions to the rank order of the
largest U.S. industrial corporations during this quarter century were remarkably
few. And the overall rate of TFP growth within manufacturing fell by more
than a percentage point compared with the 1930s and more than 3.5 percentage
points compared with the 1920s.

The view of the quarter century following 1948 as one of more moderate
innovative advance within manufacturing is consistent with the enumerations
of basic innovations by Kleinknecht (1987), Schmookler (1966), and Mensch
(1979). All of their series show peaks in the 1930s, particularly in the second
half. Kleinknecht's analysis, which runs through 1969, shows a big peak in total
and product innovations in the 1930s, although process innovations peak in
the 1950s. Schmookler's data, which run through 1959, show a peak of forty-
eight basic innovations in the 1935–1939 period, dwindling to zero in 1955–1959.
Mensch's series on basic innovations also peaks in 1935–1939 (at 13) before declining to zero in 1955–1959.

Bureau of Labor Statistics (2004) data show that the rate of increase of TFP in
manufacturing fell (in comparison with the Depression years) to 1.49 percent per
year between 1949 and 1973. Kendrick and Grossman (1980) report that the total
(not annual average) TFP increment in manufacturing when measured from
1948 to 1973 was 1 percent less than when measured from 1949 to 1973. Making
a small allowance for this difference, I have used 1.48 percent per year as an estimate of TFP growth in the sector between 1948 and 1973. This is 1.28 percentage
points lower than the rate experienced in the Depression years and 3.64 percentage points lower than the blistering pace realized in the 1920s (see table 2.3). An
important conclusion follows: the golden age of American labor productivity
growth was associated with a deceleration of TFP advance within manufacturing.

Here are some ways to consider manufacturing's diminishing contribution to
TFP growth. On average manufacturing constituted about a third (.334) of the

private nonfarm economy over this period (see table 4.2). Suppose TFP growth in manufacturing had continued at the same rates it had evidenced during the Depression. With an imagined golden age growth rate of 2.76 percent per year and the actual share of output, manufacturing would have contributed .922 percentage points to PNE TFP growth (.334 × 2.76). In actuality, with TFP rising at 1.48 percent per year, it contributed .494 percentage points (.334 × 1.48), a difference of .43 percentage points. The hypothetically higher manufacturing TFP growth would have boosted golden age PNE TFP growth to 2.31 percent per year (1.88 + .43), equal to the record (unadjusted) rate calculated from Kendrick's data for the Depression years. Most of the slowdown in PNE TFP growth, in a comparison of the postwar period with the Depression years can therefore be attributed to the reduction in the growth rate in manufacturing.

We can also consider the effect of declining TFP advance in manufacturing by looking at the proportion of PNE TFP growth it contributed. Manufacturing accounted for 26.3 percent of TFP advance in the PNE during the golden age (.494/1.88), as compared with 50.7 percent during the 1929–1941 period. This decline was the result of a reduction in the sector's share of output and its TFP growth rate. Had the share but not the sector growth rate decreased, manufacturing's contribution would have fallen only from 50.7 percent to 39.9 percent of PNE TFP growth (.922/2.31).

However we parse manufacturing's contribution, we are impelled to look elsewhere in the economy for a full understanding of productivity advance within the United States during the golden age. An obvious strategy is to examine sectoral TFP growth rates across the economy. Begin with the rate of growth of TFP in manufacturing (1.48 percent per year) and for the PNE as a whole (1.88 percent per year). The latter number is higher, which means that within the private nonfarm economy TFP advance outside of manufacturing had to have been, on average, higher than it was within it. The large bureaucratic corporations that dominated manufacturing (and were described in Galbraith's *The New Industrial State*) generated rates of TFP advance that were historically modest by the standards of the 1920s or 1930s.

The rate of overall TFP growth in the PNE will be approximated by a weighted average of sectoral TFP growth rates, the weights corresponding to the shares of the sectors in PNE value added. A good rule of thumb for the twentieth century is that the PNE constituted three-fourths of GDP. For TFP calculations applicable to the PNE, the BLS excludes from GDP the value added of agriculture, general government, government enterprises, nonprofit institutions, paid employees of private households, and the rental value of owner-occupied

Table 4.1. GDP Excluded from the Private Nonfarm Economy (percent shares)

	1948	1973
Agriculture	8.89	3.97
Government (incl. government enterprises)	11.17	14.77
Educational services	0.34	0.72
Social services	0.05	0.27
2/3 of nonfarm housing services	3.03	4.67
Private households	0.88	0.35
TOTAL	24.36	24.75

Source: U.S. Department of Commerce 2004.

dwellings (U.S. Bureau of Labor Statistics 1997, ch. 10). In table 4.1 I sum the value added of agriculture, government (including government enterprises), educational institutions (almost all of which are private and nonprofit; government-funded schools and universities would already be excluded because they are part of general government), social services, and two-thirds of nonfarm housing services. These exclusions approximate a quarter of GDP in both 1948 and 1973, and in the calculations that follow, as in previous chapters, I use 4/3, or 1.333, as the markup factor to convert a GDP share into a share of the PNE.

Manufacturing's share of value added was .276 in 1948 and .231 in 1973.[1] Averaging beginning- and end-year shares, we conclude that manufacturing constituted about a quarter of GDP (25.4 percent) in the golden age and about a third of the private nonfarm economy (25.4 × 1.33 = 33.8 percent). Multiplying manufacturing's weight by the sectoral TFP growth rate (.338 × 1.48) yields the sectoral percentage point contribution of .494 to the total PNE TFP growth of 1.88 percent. Thus, as noted, manufacturing was responsible for 26.3 percent of PNE TFP growth (.494/1.88) during the golden age, compared with the 83 percent contributed between 1919 and 1929 and the 51 percent contributed between 1929 and 1941.

So where is the remainder of TFP advance coming from during the golden age? Neither the BLS nor the BEA, unfortunately, provides detailed sectoral calculations outside of manufacturing. There are two sources that do, although they are not based on the most recent revisions to the national accounts. The first is Kendrick and Grossman (1980). The second is a study by the American Productivity Institute (API) cited by William Nordhaus (1982). We will use these data (see table 4.2) to examine relative productivity advance in the following subsectors of the PNE: manufacturing, trade, public utilities, communication, transportation, construction, services, and FIRE (finance, insurance, and real estate), keeping in mind that the absolute rates of growth are somewhat higher than a complete reworking of the numbers based on more recent revisions to the national accounts would likely suggest. Both of these sets of estimates imply TFP growth in the PNE of about 2.2 percent per year, whereas the current (2010) BLS estimate has it at 1.88 percent.

If we sum the shares of the six subsectors with higher TFP growth rates than manufacturing, they account for 43.9 percent of the PNE, in comparison with the 33.6 percent share attributable to manufacturing. Using the Kendrick/ Grossman data, a weighted average of the TFP growth rates of these six subsectors is 2.66, in comparison with 2.30 for manufacturing. With the API data cited by Nordhaus, the weighted average is 2.75, in comparison with 2.2 percent for manufacturing. A more definitive analysis awaits a full reworking of the sectoral estimates to bring them in line with the BLS's more recent estimates for manufacturing and the PNE as a whole. Such a reworking would likely strengthen the emphasis on progress in sectors outside of manufacturing emphasized here. That is because the current BLS numbers show an even larger differential than do these two accountings between TFP growth in the PNE as a whole and manufacturing alone.

Most of the remainder of this chapter focuses on transportation and distribution and the implications of a several decades–long transition from a surface system dominated by a rail/water division of labor to one in which roads, and to a lesser degree pipelines, also played important roles. According to table 4.2, transport accounted for an average of 6.4 percent of the PNE during the golden age. But the significance of technological and structural change in the sector is broader because changes within it contributed to the ability of distribution (trade) and real estate to enjoy TFP growth rates above those experienced within manufacturing. I have less to say here about the sectors generating the very highest rates of TFP growth—communication and public utilities—except that what was going on in these sectors also represented a continuation of trends already evident during the Depression years. Their direct contribution to TFP advance was smaller than that of transport or trade because even though their rates of advance were higher, their shares in the economy were smaller.

As we seek to understand what forces outside of manufacturing were responsible for achieved productivity gains during the golden age, it is helpful to go back to the Depression years and consider them in relation to what transpired during the 1920s. As previously noted, the TFP growth rate in manufacturing dropped by almost half when we compare 1919–1929 with 1929–1941. The

Table 4.2. Sectoral TFP Growth Rates, United States,
1948–1973 (percent per year)

Sector	Share PNE	TFP Growth (Kendrick/Grossman)	TFP Growth (API/Nordhaus)
Communication	.025	4.13	4.6
Public utilities	.026	3.79	4.1
Transportation	.064	2.87	2.8
Real estate	.063	2.74	2.8
Mining	.034	2.39	2.5
Trade	.227	2.33	2.4
Manufacturing	.334	2.30	2.2
Services	.122	1.70	1.8
Construction	.061	.91	1.2
Finance, insurance	.042	.00	.2

Sources: Kendrick and Grossman 1980; Nordhaus 1982, p. 134, citing American Productivity
Institute (API).
Note: Share of PNE is based on average of share of value added in 1948 and 1973, divided by .7593,
the share of PNE in total value added. The shares are calculated from a 2004 spreadsheet from the
Bureau of Economic Analysis entitled "GDP by Ind_VA_SIC.xls." See note 1 for this chapter.

Depression years enjoyed a TFP growth rate higher than was registered in
1919–1929 because of advance in transportation, communication, and public
utilities, and to a lesser degree in wholesale and retail distribution (chapter 2).
Within this general area of nonmanufacturing TFP advance, transportation was
a standout. The very rapid buildout of government-funded highways during the
Depression years facilitated high TFP growth rates in such sectors as trucking
and railroads.

Both road and rail transport continued to experience healthy productivity advance after the war. Remarkably, between 1948 and 1966, rail productivity rose
even faster than it had during the Depression and faster than productivity in
the rest of the transportation sector. The shrinkage of the railway sector and the
corresponding expansion of trucking in the golden age are vividly illustrated
in the BEA's "persons employed" series. Railway employment dropped from
1.503 million to 565,000 between 1948 and 1973, while employment in trucking
expanded from 655,000 to 1.303 million over the same period.[2] Between 1973
and 1989, while persons employed in railways dropped further to 262,000, trucking expanded to 1.546 million. By 1989 there were as many people employed in

trucking as there had been in railroads in 1948 but less than half as many people employed in railroads as there had been in trucking at the earlier date.

The relationship between highway construction and productivity in the U.S. rail industry is complex. There is no question that (along with air transport) improved surface roads ultimately killed most of the rail passenger business and that roads (along with pipelines) did the same for much of the railways' freight business. But it is also true that rail productivity increased sharply during the Depression years (chapter 12). It did so even more rapidly after the war in the context of capital deepening caused in part by a very rapid decline in labor input (see Kendrick and Grossman 1980, p. 133). And for several decades railroads remained part of a political coalition demanding federal support for the expansion of roads. The buildout of the surface road network led to spillovers—network externalities and innovations in running rail systems and trucking operations—that boosted Depression-era TFP growth and continued to do so in the postwar period.

The historical trends that emerged during the Depression were temporarily interrupted by the Second World War, as the trucking sector shrank and railroads expanded in the face of wartime exigencies. It was a triumphant period for the U.S. rail system, which performed far better than it had during the First World War, when, jammed with shipments from the industrial Midwest to East Coast ports, a railroad sector beaten down by a hostile public and tough Interstate Commerce Commission rate regulation had been ignominiously taken over by the government. Trucking, on the other hand, had received something of a boost during the First World War. Even though the roads were terrible, the United States was still the world's largest petroleum producer and fuel availability was not a problem, so trucks were able, heroically in some instances, to come through where the bottlenecked rail system could not.

The situation was quite different during the Second World War. Petroleum was scarcer. Fuel was now needed for thousands of aircraft, tanks, jeeps, and other military vehicles since the scale of mechanized warfare far exceeded what had been true in the earlier war. Truck tonnage shrank, while rail tonnage expanded. Because the war was fought on both a Pacific and a European front, freight (and passengers) moved both east and west, a situation that benefited rail performance by attenuating the backhaul problem that had plagued the system in 1917–1918. Both passenger and freight traffic hit record levels and the railroads made substantial profits, emerging from the war in better financial shape than they had enjoyed in more than two decades.

After the war trends from the 1930s reasserted themselves. Public infrastructural expenditure resumed and, in conjunction with innovations such as piggybacking and containerization, continued to throw off spillovers in the transport and distribution sector. But it was now rail rather than trucking that experienced the highest rate of productivity growth. TFP in the shrinking rail sector more than doubled between 1948 and 1966, growing at a compound annual rate of over 4 percent per year (Kendrick and Grossman 1980, p. 133).

A growing contributor to productivity advance in the transport sector in the postwar period was innovation in intermodal transfer, particularly piggybacking and containerization. Piggybacking involved placing the trailer part of a tractor-trailer on a flatbed railcar, shipping it over long distances, and then re-connecting the trailer to a truck to be taken to its final destination. In 1958 about 1 percent of railway car loadings (278,081) were piggybacked trailers. By 1986 that share had risen to 15 percent (Duke et al. 1992, pp. 52–53). Containerization, launched in 1956 in the ocean-borne freight industry, expanded rapidly during the 1960s and even more rapidly thereafter. The development of a standard-sized container, carriers built to accommodate them, and transshipment facilities that could quickly handle them meant dramatically reduced labor and capital costs associated with transfers between water, road, and rail.

For the railroads and trucking industries, containerization represented a more flexible generalization of the principle of piggybacking. Some commodities, such as coal, oil, grain, or iron ore, remain best suited, whether shipped over water or rails, to specialized bulk carriers. And some other types of packaged but non-containerized cargo continue to be shipped in the breakbulk portion of the industry. But for a wide range of general freight, the innovation of a standard-sized container (originally 20 feet × 8.5 feet × 8.5 feet; now usually 40 feet long) that could be stacked on a ship, a railcar, or the back of a tractor-trailer dramatically cut the costs and time required to effectuate transfers.

Containerization began in 1956, when the Sealand Corporation ran a modified tanker stuffed with containers from New York to Houston. The innovation took off in the 1960s, as new port facilities were built in places such as Port Elizabeth, New Jersey; Oakland, California; and, in Europe, Rotterdam. Although originally developed to reduce turnaround time and labor costs in loading and unloading ships, containerization rapidly evolved to the point where it could equally well facilitate road-to-rail transfers (or vice versa). Containerization and its predecessor, piggybacking, represented an important part of the continuing and evolving symbiosis between railways and the trucking industry.

As Wilfred Owen observed, the innovation saved both labor and capital (1962, p. 410). The labor saving was obvious: fewer hours required to break or transship cargo. And although containerization required investments in both structures and equipment, capital saving resulted from increases in the rate of throughput, meaning faster rates of inventory turn and higher utilization rates on fixed capital (see Field 1987 for historical analogies). In terms of its contribution to PNE TFP growth during the golden age, containerization was probably more important than any single innovation coming out of the manufacturing sector during the period.

THE END OF THE GOLDEN AGE

A full understanding of the post-1973 productivity slowdown—a global phenomenon—has eluded the best efforts of many economists. But the study of retardation after 1973 benefits from a search for the sources of advance in the golden age, just as our understanding of economic growth in the golden age benefits from a study of its roots in the Depression years. Growth in TFP began to slow in many sectors after 1966 and dropped precipitously after 1973. The slowing in TFP growth, the major cause of the retardation in growth in output per hour, coincides with a tapering off of gains from a one-time reconfiguration of the surface freight system in the United States. After declining sharply for decades, the share of rails in intercity ton mileage stabilized after 1973 in the 37 percent range, actually rising slightly in the 1990s (the 2000 figure was 41 percent). This stabilization, in turn, coincided roughly with the completion of the Interstate Highway System.

Productivity advance in transportation did not cease after 1973. Although progress was weak in all modes in the 1970s, it came back strongly in rail and air transport in the 1980s and 1990s. Rail productivity benefited from changes in work rules that eliminated cabooses and reduced manpower requirements. Crews on intercity trains dropped from four or five to two people. Electronic sensors rather than humans now warned of avalanche slides or high-water flows over bridges. Computer-assisted dispatching, combined with track sensors and other electronic devices, reduced labor requirements in marshalling yards. The 1980 Staggers Rail Act made it easier for lines to abandon lightly used track and to merge. Mergers, in turn, allowed more intensive utilization of consolidated and shared facilities (Duke et al. 1992, pp. 52–53).

Railroads became highly specialized and highly productive "pipelines" for coal, grain, chemicals, and even the movement of new vehicles, a business they now recaptured to a significant degree from trucks. They rounded out their portfolio with containerized shipments, which grew dramatically in the last third of the century. Railroads initially opposed containerization, but they ultimately appear to have benefited from it more than did trucking. One of trucking's big early advantages over rails had been that it could offer point-to-point transit without the need for breaks in cargo. Because the use of standard-ized containers reduced the cost and time required for transfers, rails could now recapture some of this business. Rails also benefited from periods of high energy costs, in a manner somewhat analogous to what had happened during the Second World War. Railroads are more energy efficient in carrying freight long distances; higher energy costs also increased the demand for coal ship-ments, rarely carried by truck.

Although productivity growth in trucking eventually revived after the dol-drums of the 1970s, the glory days were behind it. The sector could no lon-ger anticipate spillovers from infrastructure enhancement, as it had to such an extraordinary degree in the 1930s. Just as the unprecedented TFP gains in manufacturing slowed as the share of electrified manufacturing approached 80 percent at the end of the 1920s, so too did the surface road spillovers within transportation slow as the capacity enhancements of the road net were com-pleted in the early 1970s. After 1973, productivity growth in trucking slumped. Productivity growth in airlines and railways, on the other hand, revived at a strong pace during the 1980s (Baily and Gordon 1988, p. 419).

At least through the 1960s, highway construction was, on balance, benefi-cial to the U.S. standard of living. For several decades spillovers and network externalities outweighed any tendency toward diminishing returns. This does not mean, however, that such a result could necessarily have continued indefi-nitely. There are grounds for questioning both the social and economic benefits of the final stages of the building of the interstate system, which rammed free-ways into the hearts of central business districts, reducing the urban tax base as they destroyed often viable neighborhoods, and contributing to the decay of in-ner cities. These projects were extraordinarily expensive on a per-mile basis and improved road access to a core whose economic viability was simultaneously being eroded by the construction projects themselves. It took several decades to reconfigure urban areas to adjust to these shocks (in some cases more success-fully than others), with renewed investments in mass transit and reintroduction of light-rail technologies abandoned several decades earlier.

With the exception of services, there was an across-the-board decline in TFP growth rates, if we compare 1966–1973 with 1948–1966 (see table 4.3), presaging deceleration over the 1973–1989 period, which experienced the worst (peak-to-peak) productivity growth in the twentieth century. Most students of the slowdown (Abramovitz was an exception) dated it from 1973, but as the above data show, the deceleration did begin earlier. The emphasis on 1973 led to a lot of early work on the role of the oil shocks of 1973–1974 and 1979, and oil retains appeal as the one obvious explanation for the global character of the

Table 4.3. Sectoral TFP Growth Rates, United States, 1948–1966 and 1966–1973
(percent per year)

Sector	Share PNE, 1948–1973	TFP Growth, 1948–1966 (Kendrick/Grossman)	TFP Growth, 1966–1973 (Kendrick/Grossman)
Communication	.025	4.62	2.84
Public utilities	.026	4.79	1.24
Transportation	.064	2.99	2.08
Real estate	.063	3.32	1.26
Mining	.034	3.20	.32
Trade	.227	2.44	2.04
Manufacturing	.334	2.46	1.89
Services	.122	1.50	2.20
Construction	.061	2.46	−3.10
Finance, insurance	.042	.40	−.88

Sources: Kendrick and Grossman 1980. Share of PNE: see note to table 4.2.

slowdown (see also chapter 7). But real oil prices collapsed in the 1980s, and productivity growth remained slow through the remainder of that decade.

Within the United States, Vietnam and the malaise and discontent—as well as dislocations of the economy with which it was associated—may have played a role. But a more concrete influence was the end of the era of large private sector spillovers from government-funded highway programs. Whether higher levels of infrastructural spending following the completion of the Interstate Highway System could have forestalled lower productivity growth rates on this account, and if so, by how much, is an open and much debated question. There is no inconsistency in pointing out that the productivity slowdown coincided with the completion of the Interstate Highway System and remaining agnostic or even skeptical about whether continued high levels of infrastructural spending could have forestalled the deceleration.

In accounting for the decline in PNE TFP growth following 1973, we should also pay some attention to the continued decline in TFP growth within manufacturing compared with the golden age. TFP growth in manufacturing dropped from 1.48 percent per year (1948–1973) to .57 percent per year between 1973 and 1989.[3] Over the same period TFP in the private nonfarm economy declined from 1.88 percent per year to .36 percent a year, a stunning drop of

1.52 percentage points. How much of this can be attributed to the slowed rate of growth of TFP in manufacturing? Manufacturing's share of value added declined after the Second World War, dramatically so after 1973.

Averaging beginning (.2324) and end-point (.1843) share, we have a manufacturing share of .2084 of value added over the 1973–1989 period, thus a manufacturing share of about .277 of the PNE. Had TFP growth within manufacturing persisted at the 1948–1973 rate of 1.48 percent per year, we would have had a contribution from manufacturing to PNE TFP growth in 1973–1989 of .41 percentage points a year (.277 × 1.48), instead of the .16 percentage points (.277 × .57) actually contributed. The difference represents manufacturing's contribution to the collapse of PNE TFP growth: .25 percentage points per year.

But since PNE TFP growth declined, between the two periods, by 1.52 percentage points, manufacturing can account for at best a sixth of the slowdown. As has been noted, there is a general and persistent downward trend in TFP growth within manufacturing from its peak during the 1920s. Some of the retardation, which is already evident in the last years of the golden age and continued during the 1973–1989 period, may be associated with the slowdown in non-defense R and D spending that is apparent starting in the 1960s and continuing in the 1970s (see Mowery and Rosenberg 2000). But whatever its causes, only a small fraction of the slowdown in the economy as a whole after 1973 can be attributed directly to productivity slowdown within manufacturing.

The remainder has to have originated elsewhere, and a prime candidate is the retardation in productivity advance in transport/distribution coincident upon the exhaustion of the extraordinary productivity advances made possible by the shift from rail to truck that had begun in the late 1920s. The rough post-1973 stability of road/rail shares in intercity ton mileage, after four decades in which trucking had risen at the expense of rails, testifies powerfully to the coming to the end of a transition comparable in significance to the electrification of U.S. manufacturing.

John Fernald's analysis supports this interpretation. He finds a close correlation between road construction and changes in productivity in vehicle-intensive sectors, such as transportation and trade. Prior to 1973, productivity growth in those sectors was higher than the economy-wide average. Subsequent to 1973, when the U.S. street and highway capital stock essentially stopped growing, the reverse was true. Fernald also finds that at the margin, highway construction does not appear to be unusually productive. Thus he concludes that "Road building . . . explains much of the productivity slowdown through a one time, unrepeatable productivity boost in the 1950s and 1960s" (1999, p. 619). Fernald's argument is consistent with mine, although because his statistical work is limited to the second half of the century, he is not able fully to highlight the extent to which advances in the golden age represented a continuation of trends first manifested in the 1930s.

Jovanovic and Rousseau (2005) attribute the end of the golden age to the first stages of the IT revolution, arguing that when one has a transformative technology, productivity growth must first deteriorate before it can improve. The logic involves transition and the reality that users often don't initially know how best to take advantage of a new technology.

While their argument is theoretically coherent, it is empirically implausible. In the late 1960s, when the slowdown began in the United States, the use of mainframe computers for accounting and billing and time-shared systems for airline reservations were already well established, whereas the disruptive effects of personal computers and the Internet were still decades away. In 1966 the current cost value of IT equipment and software was just 2.5 percent of private fixed assets and 3.1 percent of the total in 1973. Another perspective: the real stock of IT capital in 1966 stood at just 3.25 percent of its value in 2000 (the latter calculation is based on chain type quantity indexes of the net stock; see Bureau of Economic Analysis, Fixed Asset Tables 2.1 and 2.2).

At the time the productivity slowdown began, the uses of IT capital were limited, relatively well established, and concentrated in a few sectors. The slowdown in productivity advance was significantly broader. Without a more detailed explication of exactly how and where IT investments were responsible for the slowdown, it is difficult to give the Jovanovic-Rousseau hypothesis credence. The exhaustion of the gains from the second transition emphasized in this chapter—from a rail/water duopoly in surface transport to the new modality of road/rail/water/pipelines is a more promising candidate in helping us understand the decline in growth in both TFP and output per hour after 1973.

Again, it is quite possible that the slowdown in infrastructural spending was a justifiable response to the reduced potential for incremental gains from additional investment. The logic here is similar to the argument made with respect to factory electrification/redesign: a paradigmatic transition will raise growth rates while it is in process and propel the economy to a higher level of productivity, but it cannot be expected permanently to sustain the high growth rates. Thus it may be misleading to suggest that the slowdown after 1973 is directly attributable to the demonstrable decrease in such spending (Aschauer 1989), with its suggestion that had the slowdown not occurred, the deceleration in economy-wide TFP growth would have been prevented.

Here is an illustration of the relevance of diminishing returns. The 1930s were a great age of bridge, hydroelectric, and tunnel construction. The last major suspension bridge built in the United States crossed the Verrazano Narrows and was completed in 1964. That does not mean that U.S. productivity growth would necessarily have been higher had bridge construction continued at the same pace into the 1970s and 1980s.

A TALE OF TWO TRANSITIONS

A consideration of TFP growth in the United States during the golden age raises related questions: on the one hand, why was it so strong, and on the other hand, why were TFP growth rates lower than they were during the Depression years? A continuing downward trend in TFP growth within manufacturing and its declining share after World War II help provide answers to the latter question. A persisting productivity windfall associated with the buildout of the surface road infrastructure helps answer the former question. We can also understand the retardation of productivity growth after 1973 as in part associated with, if not necessarily caused by, the decline in infrastructure spending following the completion of the Interstate Highway System.

As noted in the introduction, the economic and productivity history of the twentieth century can be seen, broadly, as a tale of two transitions. The first involved the electrification and reconfiguration of the American factory, a development that had its roots in the 1880s but blossomed only in the 1920s, producing enormously high rates of TFP growth in manufacturing during that decade. Rates in that sector trended generally downward for the remainder of the century. The second transition, involving the movement of goods, peaked later. From the late 1920s to the early 1970s, trucking expanded its share of interstate ton mileage, while the rail sector shrunk, specializing as it did so. Within the four decade period identified above, the strongest TFP growth occurs across the Depression years, with performance in the quarter century after 1948 a runner-up.

As we step back from the subperiods and consider the 1929–1973 years as a long swing characterized by exceptionally high TFP growth, we should appreciate the extent to which developments in the postwar period—both the declining influence of advance within manufacturing (compared especially with the 1920s) and the significance of the continued transition within transport and distribution—reflect the extension of trends already evident during the interwar years. In doing so, we can move beyond the inclination to treat the golden age sui generis and see within it the unfolding of developments that, although temporarily disrupted by the war, had their origins in the interwar years.

5

THE INFORMATION
TECHNOLOGY BOOM

Between 1989 and 2000, TFP in the U.S. private nonfarm economy grew more than twice as rapidly as it had during the years 1973–1989. Between 2000 and 2007 TFP growth inched higher still—driven by strong gains in the years 2002–2004. Much of this revival, both before and after the tech stock market crash, can be credited to information technology. But the close identification of the boom with IT is reflective of why economy-wide TFP growth was so much lower than during the Depression years: the locus of advance was much narrower than it had been between 1929 and 1941.

This book's thesis that the Depression years experienced the highest TFP growth of the twentieth century was developed in the heart of Silicon Valley during the height of the tech stock market enthusiasm. No one who did not live through this period in this place can fully understand the true meaning of mania. Imbued once again with the belief that this time it was in fact different, many asked, sometimes skeptically, whether the claim about TFP growth included consideration of the "New Economy" boom. Obviously, given the data in table 2.1, it does. The upwardly spiraling equity valuations of the tech bubble were propelled by human enthusiasms and one of the most formidable marketing machines ever constructed. With assists from research departments of brokerage firms; IT companies celebrating their own prospects; independent public relations firms; radio, television, and print media; and (at times) government officials and academic economists, warm air fanned speculative fires fueled by dreams of Dow 36,000.[1] For better or worse, the drumbeat led to a reorganization of the federal government's statistical apparatus in an effort to make it more sensitive to the possible contributions of IT to growth.

The NASDAQ stock index topped out in March 2000 and more than a decade later had recovered to barely 40 percent of its peak level, absent any adjustment for inflation.[2] Following the crash, the number of tech IPOs (initial public offerings) shriveled compared with the heady days of the late 1990s, and the venture capital industry in 2010 remained a shadow of its former self. The hoopla, and the revulsion against it that followed collapse, seem at the time of this writing both familiar yet at the same time distant in light of what turned out to be the much more serious financial/real economy crisis of 2007–2009.

The tech boom is part of a long history of asset price bubbles, and as much as the real estate and stock booms of the 1920s or the real estate mania of 2001–2006, it benefited and suffered from the cheerleading and excessive optimism characteristic of such enthusiasms. The all-too-common will to believe, which insists against evidence on the uncommon uniqueness of each historical episode, is well chronicled in Carmen Reinhart and Kenneth Rogoff's book, *This Time Is Different* (2009).

The reality is that during the last decade of the twentieth century, revolutionary technological or organizational change — the sort that shows up in TFP growth — was concentrated within distribution, securities trading, and a narrow range of industries within a shrinking manufacturing sector. TFP advance in industry was largely localized within the old SIC 35 and 36, sectors that included the production of semiconductors, computers, networking, and telecommunications equipment.[3] This technical advance, though evident in the many ways it altered our lives, was more localized and smaller in its aggregate impact than what took place during the 1930s. Following the deflation of the stock bubble, productivity growth, particularly in IT-using industries, remained strong through 2005, providing support for those who had maintained that, as had been the case with electricity, the benefits of these new technologies might take some time fully to realize (David 1990). But even putting the IT boom in its most favorable light, by measuring from 1995 to 2005, TFP growth was substantially slower than during the Depression years.

THE NARROW BASE OF TFP ADVANCE DURING THE IT BOOM

After years in the doldrums, manufacturing productivity growth moved sharply upward starting in 1993 and, with the exception of a cyclical downturn in 2001, remained on this trajectory through 2004. Prior to 2000, however, TFP advance within industry took place almost entirely within NAICS 334 (the old SIC 35 and 36). Strong advance in IT-intensive distribution and securities trading complemented this. The .79 percent per year PNE TFP growth over the eleven years between 1989 and 2000 was, however, less than a third that registered across the Depression years.

After 2000, the story needs to be modified, though the basic conclusion about the breadth and magnitude of the tech boom relative to Depression-era productivity growth remains. Between 2000 and 2007, TFP in the private nonfarm economy grew at 1.38 percent per year, almost double that experienced between 1989 and 2000, though still less than half the cyclically adjusted rate for the Depression years (see table 3.6). The pace of gains in IT manufacturing—NAICS 334—decelerated, as it did in securities trading and in wholesale and retail distribution. This was counterbalanced by accelerating advance in the manufacture of machinery, electrical equipment, and transportation equipment, as well as in nonmanufacturing sectors such as mining, broadcasting and telecommunications, health care, credit intermediation, and real estate.

Table 5.1 reports TFP growth within manufacturing for durables and nondurables and for various three-digit NAICS manufacturing industries for the periods 1989–2000 and 2000–2006. As can be seen, between 1989 and 2000, all of the advance in manufacturing came from durables, and within durables, virtually all of it from within computers and electronic products.

After 2000, TFP growth within IT manufacturing remained strong (6.4 percent per year between 2000 and 2006) but declined by almost half as compared with the 11.5 percent per year between 1989 and 2000. TFP growth within durable manufacturing was, however, slightly higher in 2000–2006 than in 1989–2000 because of a move from negative to positive advance in machinery, electrical equipment, and transportation equipment (NAICS 333, 335, and 336). Particularly important, because of the size of the sector, was the turnaround in transportation equipment.[4] Much of this can plausibly be attributed to spillovers from the diffusion of IT hardware into IT-using manufacturing sectors (Basu, Fernald, Oulton, and Srinivasan 2003).[5]

Following procedures used in chapters 2 and 4, we can estimate the contribution of different subsectors to PNE TFP growth by combining data on sectoral growth rates with estimates of the share of each sector's value added in GDP. To calculate percentage point contributions between two dates, such as 1989 and 2000, we average sectoral shares for the beginning and end years. Since the share of the PNE in GDP has remained stable at about three-fourths, I continue the practice of multiplying GDP shares by 1.333 to get an approximate share of each sector in the PNE.[6] The contribution of a sector's TFP growth rate to the overall PNE TFP growth rates can then be estimated by multiplying the sector's growth rate by its sectoral share, and we can explore how sectoral contributions changed by comparing 1989–2000 with 2000–2006, as well as earlier periods.

Table 5.1. Manufacturing Subsector Contributions to PNE TFP Growth Rate, 1989–2000 and 2000–2006

NAICS Code		TFP Growth Rate (percent per year)		Share of GDP		Percentage Points Contributed to PNE TFP	
		1989–2000	2000–2006	1989–2000	2000–2006	1989–2000	2000–2006
	Nondurables	0.0	0.6	6.36	5.37	0.00	0.04
311, 312	Food and beverage and tobacco	−0.6	0.3	1.68	1.42	−0.01	0.01
313, 314	Textile mill and textile mill products	0.9	0.8	0.33	0.21	0.00	0.00
315, 316	Apparel and leather and applied products	1.7	2.0	0.37	0.19	0.01	0.01
322	Paper products	0.0	1.1	0.67	0.47	0.00	0.01
323	Printing and related support activities	0.0	1.1	0.57	0.42	0.00	0.01
324	Petroleum and coal products	0.4	−0.6	0.36	0.39	0.00	0.00
325	Chemical products	−0.5	1.0	1.68	1.70	−0.01	0.02
326	Rubber products	0.8	0.4	0.69	0.58	0.01	0.00
						0.00	0.00
	Durables	2.3	2.4	9.36	7.75	0.29	0.25
321	Wood products	−0.5	1.2	0.35	0.27	0.00	0.00
327	Nonmetallic minerals products	0.8	−0.1	0.46	0.43	0.01	0.00

331	Primary metals	0.5	1.1	0.62	0.47	0.00	0.01
332	Fabricated metal products	0.5	0.7	1.30	1.13	0.01	0.01
333	Machinery	−1.3	1.7	1.28	1.01	−0.02	0.02
334	**Computer and electronic products**	**11.5**	**6.4**	**1.81**	**1.48**	**0.28**	**0.13**
335	Electrical equipment, appliances, components	−1.7	0.7	0.61	0.47	−0.01	0.00
336	Transportation equipment	−0.3	2.0	2.02	1.63	−0.01	0.04
337	Furniture and related products	0.4	0.3	0.34	0.29	0.00	0.00
339	Misc. manufacturing	1.0	1.6	0.56	0.56	0.01	0.01
311–339	*Manufacturing*	1.4	1.6	15.72	13.12	0.29	0.28

Sources: TFP growth rates: U.S. Department of Labor 2008.
Sectoral shares: U.S. Department of Commerce 2009.

Notes: Sectoral shares for each of the two time periods are an average of the share for the beginning and end years. Private nonfarm economy is assumed equal to three-fourths of GDP. Thus percentage point contribution for each of the two time intervals is equal to the sectoral TFP growth rate × the sectoral share × (1.33/100), and is a contribution to TFP growth.

Overall PNE TFP advance was .79 percent per year between 1989 and 2000. Nondurable manufacturing contributed almost nothing to this, but durables contributed .29 percentage points, of which .28 is attributable to NAICS 334. So IT manufacturing alone contributed slightly more than a third of overall PNE TFP growth. Wholesale trade, retail trade, and securities trading made up most of the rest, contributing .15, .24, and .14 percentage points respectively (a total of .53 percentage points). Along with manufacturing, this sums to more than .79 percent per year. The explanation for the surfeit is that some sectors saw negative productivity growth. Construction, for example, contributed −.04 percentage points, and ambulatory health care and hospitals each contributed −.04 percentage points.

Analysis of 2000–2006 is more tentative. Ideally, we would measure through 2007, to match the peak-to-peak estimate for the private nonfarm economy. At the time of this writing, disaggregated data were available only through 2006. The Bureau of Labor Statistics, moreover, treats almost all its disaggregated estimates outside of manufacturing as unpublished, signaling reservations about their quality.

That said, we can discern some characteristics of supply-side advance across the initial business cycle of the twenty-first century. First, manufacturing made almost the same percentage point contribution to TFP growth as it had in 1989–2000 and thus played no role in acceleration between the two periods. Nondurables experienced modest TFP growth, rising from 0 percent per year to .6 percent per year; their percentage point contribution rose from 0 to .04.

Within durables, whereas NAICS 334 was responsible for almost all of manufacturing's contribution between 1989 and 2000, between 2000 and 2006 it was responsible for only .13 percentage points, about half the overall contribution made by durables. This was counterbalanced by faster TFP growth in other durable manufacturing sectors, in particular machinery, electrical equipment, and transport equipment. Because of a decline in their share of value added, the overall percentage point contribution of durables was .25 percentage points, .04 percentage points less than in 1989–2000. Their contribution declined by roughly the amount that of nondurables increased, so there was no change in manufacturing's contribution to PNE TFP growth. Overall, manufacturing-sector TFP grew at 1.37 percent per year between 1989 and 2000 and at 1.60 percent per year between 2000 and 2006, its percentage point contribution remaining unchanged because its share fell.[7]

Acceleration, in a comparison of 2000–2007 with 1989–2000, had to have come largely from outside of manufacturing, suggesting some broadening in the areas of forward movement. Where were these gains? They did not come from the nonmanufacturing standouts in the 1989–2000 period. TFP growth in wholesale and retail trade and securities trading decelerated—in wholesale trade from 1.7 to 1.2 percent per year, in retail from 2.6 to 1.8 percent per year, and in securities trading from 8.4 to 6.1 percent per year (see table 5.2). This meant that the percentage point contributions dropped in wholesale trade from .15 to .09 and in retail trade from .24 to .16. In securities trading the percentage point contribution remained steady, due to an increase in the size of the sector. Still, there was a net percentage point loss in these three sectors of .14. Sectors with accelerating TFP growth had to have compensated for this as well as contributed to the net increase in PNE TFP growth rate.

Some of the biggest contributors on the plus side appear to have been sectors related to the real estate boom. NAICS 521, Federal Reserve Banks, and 522, credit intermediation and related activities, swung from negative TFP growth of −2.3 percent per year between 1989 and 2000 to positive growth of 3.6 percent per year between 2000 and 2006. Given the large and growing size of this sector, this meant a move from contributing −.09 percentage points to PNE TFP growth between 1989 and 2000 to .17 percentage points, a net swing of .26 percentage points. The next biggest contributor was real estate, which swung from .2 to 1.1 percent per year growth and a percentage point contribution of .03 to .17. Together these gave us .40 percentage points. Information and data-processing services swung from −1.7 percent per year to 5.0 percent per year, which engendered a net percentage point contribution of .104.

Other sectors improved as well. Mining moved from TFP growth of −.99 to 4.09 percent per year, thus contributing .105 percentage points to the acceleration of TFP. The health sector also generated gains. Ambulatory health care (NAICS 621) swung from −.09 to .06 percent TFP growth, which meant a net swing in terms of percentage point contribution of .064. Hospitals and nursing homes (NAICS 622 and 623) didn't improve, but they stopped deteriorating, moving from −1.2 to −.01 percent per year; this accounts for a net percentage point improvement of .032. Still, other sectors, such as construction and utilities, experienced decelerating (and negative) TFP growth.

Table 5.2 is constructed by taking every non-industrial subsector for which the BLS provides KLEMS estimates and calculating the percentage point contribution of the sector to PNE TFP growth between 1989 and 2000 and then between 2000 and 2006, using the methods described for table 5.1.[8] Summing the percentage points contributed, both positive and negative, we account for .70 of the .79 annual increase in PNE TFP between 1989 and 2000 and 1.17 of the 1.38 percent PNE TFP growth between 2000 and 2007, and thus .47 of the .59 percentage point acceleration between the two periods. The remainders are partly attributable to the fact that the BLS does not provide disaggregated analyses for all portions of the non-industrial economy.

Table 5.2. Contributions to PNE TFP Growth Rates, 1989–2000 and 2000–2006

NAICS Code	TFP Growth Rate (percent per year)		Share of GDP		Percentage Points Contrib. to PNE TFP		2000–2006 vs 1989–2000
	1989–2000	2000–2006	1989–2000	2000–2006	1989–2000	2000–2006	
Durable manufacturing	2.33	2.41	9.36	7.75	0.291	0.249	−0.043
Nondurable manufacturing	0.03	0.59	6.36	5.37	0.002	0.042	0.040
21 Mining	−0.99	4.09	1.31	1.61	−0.017	0.088	0.105
22 Utilities	1.26	−0.24	2.20	1.98	0.037	−0.006	−0.044
23 Construction	−0.72	−1.68	4.45	4.43	−0.043	−0.099	−0.057
42 Wholesale trade	1.89	1.17	6.09	5.93	0.154	0.092	−0.062
44, 45 Retail trade	2.61	1.82	6.92	6.61	0.241	0.160	−0.081
48, 49 Transportation and warehousing	1.08	1.67	3.03	3.01	0.044	0.067	0.023
511 Publishing industries (includes software)	2.18	1.60	1.04	1.10	0.030	0.023	−0.007
512 Motion picture and sound recording industriesc	−1.99	2.42	0.32	0.32	−0.008	0.010	0.019
513 Broadcasting and telecommunications	0.76	3.73	2.57	2.62	0.026	0.130	0.104
514 Information and data processing services	−1.69	5.00	0.32	0.42	−0.007	0.028	0.035
521, 522 Fed. Res. Banks, credit intermediation	−2.32	3.60	3.06	3.45	−0.095	0.166	0.260
523 Securities, commodity contracts, invest.	8.40	6.10	1.26	1.71	0.141	0.139	−0.002
524 Insurance	−.10	−2.7	2.30	2.42	−0.003	−0.087	−0.084
531 Real estate	0.20	1.11	11.01	11.26	0.030	0.166	0.136

Code	Industry							
532, 533	Rental and leasing services	-2.05	-4.15	1.06	1.03	-0.029	-0.057	-0.028
55	Management of companies, enterprises	-0.32	-0.64	1.78	1.92	-0.008	-0.016	-0.009
561	Administrative and support services	-0.87	1.38	2.27	2.69	-0.026	0.050	0.076
5411	Legal services	-1.98	-2.76	1.42	1.41	-0.037	-0.052	-0.015
5415	Computer systems design, related services	4.09	0.73	0.90	1.25	0.049	0.012	-0.037
5412–19	Misc. scientific, prof., and technical services	0.10	0.59	3.90	4.42	0.005	0.035	0.030
621	Ambulatory health care services	-0.95	0.56	3.06	3.37	-0.039	0.025	0.064
622, 623	Hospitals, nursing, residential care	-1.18	-0.15	2.36	2.57	-0.037	-0.005	0.032
624	Social assistance	1.24	1.89	0.45	0.58	0.007	0.015	0.007
711, 712	Performing arts, spectator sports, museums	1.36	0.40	0.36	0.43	0.006	0.002	-0.004
713	Amusements, gambling, recreation	-0.47	0.22	0.45	0.51	-0.003	0.001	0.004
721	Accommodation	1.80	-1.32	0.85	0.90	0.020	-0.016	-0.036
722	Food services and drinking places	-0.36	0.29	1.77	1.81	-0.008	0.007	0.016
81	Other services except government	-0.84	0.00	2.39	2.31	-0.027	0.000	0.027
	TOTALS					0.698	1.169	0.47

Sources: TFP growth rate: For manufacturing, see table 5.1; for nonmanufacturing, U.S. Department of Labor 2008.
Sectoral value added shares of GDP: U.S. Department of Commerce 2009.

Notes: Sectoral shares for each of the two time periods are an average of the share for the beginning and the end years. Private nonfarm economy is assumed equal to three-fourths of GDP. Thus percentage point contribution for each of the two time intervals is equal to the sectoral TFP growth rate × the sectoral share × (1.33/100).

Table 5.2 provides insights into the likely sources of acceleration in productivity growth, both when we compare 1989–2000 with the "dark ages" and when we compare advance during this period with that which took place following the end of the tech boom (2000–2007). Given that much recent progress was due to gains in credit intermediation and real estate, sectors that imploded during the 2007–2009 recession, there are some grounds for forecasting slower progress over the second decade of the 2000s. As the process of deleveraging continues and debt to income levels (in the household and business, not government, sectors) decline to more sustainable levels, credit intermediation activity will likely persist at lower levels. If we interpret the post-2000 TFP acceleration as principally due to spillovers in IT-using sectors, a broader question is whether this dynamic still has legs. It is one achievement to propel the economy to higher levels of TFP. It is another to sustain a higher level of growth in those levels.

MANUFACTURING'S CONTRIBUTION: HISTORICAL PERSPECTIVE

Manufacturing's TFP growth was faster than the PNE average in both 1989–2000 and 2000–2007. This pattern has been evident for most of the twentieth century, with the important exceptions of the Second World War (when it was negative) and the golden age. Table 5.3 consolidates the story line introduced in

Table 5.3. Manufacturing's Contribution to PNE TFP Growth Rate, 1919–2007

Years	PNE TFP Growth	Manu. TFP Growth	Manu. Share of PNE	Percentage Points Contrib. to PNE TFP Growth	Manu. Share of PNE TFP Growth
1919–1929	2.02	5.12	0.33	1.68	0.83
1929–1941	2.31	2.76	0.43	1.19	0.51
1941–1948	1.29	−0.35	0.39	−0.11	−0.08
1948–1973	1.88	1.49	0.33	0.49	0.26
1973–1989	0.36	0.57	0.26	0.15	0.42
1989–2000	0.79	1.37	0.21	0.29	0.37
2000–2007	1.38	1.60	0.17	0.28	0.20

Sources: See tables 2.1, 2.3, and text.
Note: 1929–1941 and 1941–1948 calculations are based on unadjusted Kendrick 1961 data (see chapter 1). For 2000–2007 calculated TFP growth and sectoral share for manufacturing are based on data for 2000–2006.

chapter 2. TFP growth in manufacturing was broadest and most uniformly high during the 1920s. Advance across the Depression years was at a sharply reduced pace but was still higher than during any subsequent period and was taking place across a broader frontier than was true in the two cycles stretching from 1989 through 2007. For 1989–2000, manufacturing's contribution was about 37 percent of total PNE TFP growth (.29/.79); for 2000–2007 it looks to have been about 20 percent (.27/1.38).

What made the interwar period unique was a combination of strong forward movement in both labor and capital productivity. Although labor productivity growth in manufacturing since 1989 was stronger than during any period save the 1920s, there was no improvement at all in capital productivity, which explains, in an arithmetical sense, why TFP growth in the sector was lower than it was during the Depression years or the 1920s (see table 2.3).

ATTEMPTS TO RESOLVE THE SOLOW PARADOX

The mania surrounding the run-up in stock prices in the 1990s created unusual pressures favoring arguments or statistical practices that could resolve, or appear to resolve, the Solow Paradox. The Solow Paradox was that for the better part of two decades computers seemed to be showing up everywhere except in the productivity data. Success in resolving the puzzle promised stronger analytical underpinnings for soaring equity valuations, particularly in companies that had yet to show much (or in some cases anything) in the way of profits.

As noted in chapter 1, cyclical influences on productivity levels mean that it is desirable in historical research to restrict calculations of productivity growth rates to those made from the peak of one business cycle to the peak of another. For the most recent episodes, this requires, taking our lead from the National Bureau of Economic Research, that we measure from 1989 to 2000 and from 2000 to 2007. Why 1989 rather than 1990? And why 2000? TFP data are available only on an annual basis. According to the NBER business cycle chronology, the peak of activity in July 1990 was followed by a recession that bottomed out in March 1991, followed by the long expansion of the 1990s, culminating in the peak 120 months later in March 2001. But 2001 was also a year of economic downturn, with the trough reached only 8 months later in November 2001. Similarly, 1990 included 5 post-peak months. Since we are using annual data, I prefer to measure from the last full year of expansion before a downturn (1989) to the subsequent final full year of expansion before a downturn (2000).[9] According to the NBER, the first cycle of the twenty-first century peaked in December 2007.

For the private nonfarm economy as a whole, TFP growth rates remained sluggish through 1995, increased moderately between 1995 and 2000, hesitated during the recession year 2001, and then moved strongly upward in 2002, 2003, and 2004 before returning to a slower pace after 2005. PNE TFP growth between 1989 and 1995 was .51 percent per year; between 1995 and 2000 it was 1.14 percent per year; and between 2000 and 2005, it rose at 1.78 percent per year. Between 2005 and 2007 growth was anemic: .36 percent per year. Measuring between 1989 and 2000, we have, as noted, an annual rate of increase of .79 percent per year and between 2000 and 2007, 1.37 percent per year.

During the boom period of the 1990s, many scholars and cheerleaders for information technology advocated measuring from 1995. Although 1995 is not a business cycle peak, the acceleration in output growth that started in that year makes the IT-based productivity revival look more impressive, yielding 1.46 percent per year if we measure through 2005, thus including the advances among IT users that continued even after the end of the boom in networking, fiber optic cables, computers, and software investment.[10]

Whether it is desirable or appropriate to choose one's start and end dates with the objective of showing IT in its best light is an open question.[11] It was a big issue during the second half of the 1990s because of political and economic pressures to rationalize rising stock market valuations. The argument against using 1995 is that it is not a business cycle peak, a point related to Gordon's initial claim that much of the end-of-century improvement reflected cyclical acceleration in both labor and total factor productivity common in later stages of a business expansion (Gordon 2003). The basic story of productivity acceleration can be told well while still adhering to the convention of measuring from business cycle peak to peak, a procedure that protects against the charge that what we are picking up are cyclical effects.

Nevertheless, in deference to this tradition, because the cyclical behavior of productivity has been unusual in the most recent cycle and because the strong productivity performance over these years is plausibly linked to advances in information technology, table 2.1 also includes calculations of growth rates of various productivity measures between 1995 and 2005. When all is said and done, they still show that although TFP growth in the private nonfarm economy was almost four times higher than it had been between 1973 and 1995, it was substantially less than what was registered between 1929 and 1941 or even between 1919 and 1929.[12]

A second consequence of the attempt to resolve the Solow Paradox was pressure on government statistical agencies to make the influence of IT in the data more apparent by rearranging presentation and making greater use of hedonic prices (see below) to capture unmeasured quality improvements in computers and other IT goods. One result was a change in the way data on fixed assets are collected, classified, and presented. In the BEA's Fixed Asset Tables, the assets produced by IT industries are now listed first. One might ask why, on a dollar-for-dollar value, saving flows congealed in IT goods and software are more or less important than those congealed in structures, machine tools, vehicles, nuclear fuel rods, or any of the other fixed asset categories, and thus why they deserve pride of place. A likely reply is that IT is a special type of capital good, one with a greater propensity to carry or embody or stimulate technical innovation within using sectors. Perhaps so, although, as chapter 8 suggests, the evidence on this is mixed.[13]

Another illustration is to be found in the "Gross Domestic Product by Industry Accounts" (http://www.bea.gov/industry/index.htm), where the publishing sector has been removed from manufacturing and combined with motion picture and sound recording, broadcasting and telecommunications, and information and data processing services to form a new category simply called "information." Changes such as these can be interpreted as responses by government statisticians to advocacy from new economy proponents, long after the cheerleaders moved on to other things and long after most recognized some of the exaggerated claims reflected in the "New Economy" ideology. The utility of these particular changes may be validated in the future; their consequence in the present is to complicate historical comparisons.

Hedonic pricing, which uses regression analysis to estimate the separate values of product attributes, is an attempt to account for otherwise unmeasured quality improvements. Its use addresses a real concern, but it has a potential to overshoot and can be particularly problematic for TFP calculations when the products are capital goods. The methods can result in an overestimate of real product growth and, where the products are producer goods, the growth of the real capital stock as well. The difficulty is that in products whose quality has improved, users are typically forced to purchase bundles of attributes, not all of which they may actually desire or value. Unmeasured quality improvement and the introduction of new products present challenges in constructing estimates of real product growth. But some of the resulting estimates push the boundaries of what is reasonable or plausible.

For example, hedonic methods yielded end-of-century estimates in the range of –27 percent per year for the rate of decrease of quality-adjusted computer prices (Berndt, Dulberger, and Rappaport 2000). This rate of price decrease would reduce a 1999 computer priced at $2000 to $500 over five years. Thus, if I used a laptop in 1999 and another in 2004 selling at the same nominal price (say $2,000), the BEA would have concluded, based on the price data received from the BLS, that there had been a fourfold increase in the ratio of capital services to hours in my intellectual work, even though, aside from the increased storage and slightly faster speed, there were many bundled hardware and software improvements I left untouched.

To the extent these methods credited computers and IT devices for features and performance gains that few end-users actually used or valued, overestimation of the *decline* in the IT deflator would have led to an overestimate of the *increase* in the real value of the output of NAICS 334, thus increasing the apparent TFP growth rates in this subsector of manufacturing. Those hungry for evidence of the impact of computers in the productivity statistics might have applauded this result.

But any boost in measured TFP growth in the IT-producing sector had the effect, at least initially, of lowering TFP growth in IT-using industries since the huge increases in their adjusted real capital inputs meant it was much harder in those sectors to show any positive TFP growth. For the broader economy, what the overadjustment gave in boosting TFP in the IT-producing sector, it took away by reducing measured TFP growth in the using sector. If one of the appeals of the introduction of hedonic methods (it also had the effect of reducing measured inflation) was the promise of resolving the Solow Paradox, it ran the risk in the aggregate of being partly self-defeating.[14]

HOW MUCH LABOR PRODUCTIVITY GROWTH SHOULD BE ATTRIBUTED TO IT?

A third consequence of the quest to resolve the Solow Paradox was, among researchers, a willingness to attribute to IT, in terms of its influence on labor productivity growth, not only its contribution to the acceleration in economy-wide TFP growth, but also that portion of capital deepening associated with investments in IT goods themselves.[15] The standard of the business as it developed in the late 1990s and early 2000s was to estimate a tripartite contribution of IT to labor productivity growth: sum the contribution of TFP growth in the IT-producing industries, TFP growth attributable to IT diffusion in the IT-using industries, and labor productivity growth due to the capital deepening in IT-using industries associated with information capital itself (Oliner and Sichel 2000, or Jorgenson, Ho, and Stiroh 2003). There are few objections to the first two of these contributions. It is the third leg of the stool that I wish to question, even though it has been endorsed by many—for example, Barro and Sala-i-Martin (1995, p. 352) or Klenow and Rodriguez-Clare (1997, p. 608).

If one wants to take the measure of IT innovation, one needs to try and imagine a world in all respects similar save for the availability of these enabling technologies. In their absence and assuming that the forces affecting aggregate saving were largely independent of those determining investment, saving flows would have been congealed in other *not quite as good* capital goods. Output and productivity growth rates would have been somewhat lower, and we would like to know by how much.

We would, in effect, be trying to estimate the social saving of the IT revolution. In its absence, saving flows would have been congealed in a slightly less beneficial array of physical capital goods. Breakthroughs such as the integrated circuit and continuing advances in the manufacture of semiconductors, display screens, and mass storage devices saved us real resources in generating quality-adjusted IT services. That saving shows up in TFP growth in the IT-producing sectors (NAICS 334; see table 5.1). The very rapid TFP growth here, particularly between 1989 and 2000, is one of the reasons why the relative prices of semiconductors and goods embodying them plummeted.[16]

We would also need to ask whether the fact that saving flows were congealed in this slightly superior range of physical capital goods, as opposed to others, enabled a set of resource savings in other parts of the economy. This we would pick up in TFP growth in the IT-using sectors (often referred to as spillovers or productive externalities), which, as noted, played a growing role after 2000.

But unless we make the argument that the enabling technologies of IT raised the rate of return to new investment projects at the margin *and* that there was a response of aggregate saving rates to this rise, the capital-deepening effect should ultimately be credited to saving behavior and not to the enabling technologies.[17] It is of course conceivable that the enabling technologies, by raising the incremental return to investment and perforce saving, or by redistributing income to households with higher saving propensities, increased the total flow of accumulation as a percent of GDP at either the U.S. or the world level, in which case it becomes conceptually difficult cleanly to distinguish between the roles of saving and technical change in fostering labor productivity growth (see appendix). Versions of these arguments, for example, have been made for the post–Civil War period in the United States, where, it has been suggested, such innovations as the railroad and Bessemer/Siemens-Martin steel elicited an upward surge in aggregate saving behavior that propelled the economy on a "grand traverse" to higher labor productivity levels as predicted by the Solow model (David 1977; Williamson 1973, p. 591).[18]

The evidence is, however, that investments in IT goods did not crowd out consumption goods by causing U.S. households to save more. Rather, they crowded out other not quite as good capital goods within the United States and outside of it. Although we can posit some upward influence of IT innovations on marginal returns to investment and thus saving (this was after all the rationalization for rising stock market values during the 1990s), we would also need to argue, in order to justify the inclusion of the third component, that saving responded. And we would be hard pressed to do so.

There is a large literature on the responsiveness of saving to after-tax interest rates. Theoretically, as in the case of the response of labor supply to increases in after-tax wages, we face the possibilities of both income and substitution effects. Empirically, the evidence is inconclusive, although consistent with a conclusion of little net effect (see Elmendorf 1996). As far as the income distribution mechanism is concerned, there is no question that there was a trend toward greater inequality in the last quarter of the century, particularly in the United States, and that it was marked by a widening gap in the wages of highly and less highly educated workers. But there is little evidence that this redistribution resulted in any increase in private sector saving.

Some have argued, particularly in the late 1990s, that saving rates were improperly measured because they did not include unrealized capital gains. But the conventionally measured saving rate was largely invariant to both the expansion of stock market valuations in the 1990s and their collapse in the early twenty-first century. U.S. household saving rates, after declining below zero, began to increase only following the financial sector/real economy crisis that unfolded in 2008.

Figure 5.1 is designed to show the changing sources and uses of saving in the United States between 1989 and 2008. All nominal values have been deflated by the implicit GDP deflator from the BEA's NIPA Table 1.1.9. In order to limit the amount of information presented to what can easily be comprehended, only four series appear here. We look first (starting at the top of the left-hand side of the figure) at domestic investment net of depreciation. This includes government investment, which grows relatively steadily. Thus most of the variation here is due to variation in private net investment. The series bottoms out in 1991 and then rises sharply and steadily through the year 2000. Broadly speaking, this is the tech boom as manifested in its impact on capital formation. The series then declines through the year 2002 before rising again, at a very sharp rate, through the year 2006. This, broadly speaking, is the real estate boom.

How were these booms financed, and in particular, is there any evidence that for the United States the tech boom was associated with a rise in saving rates? As we move downward from the top of the left-hand side of figure 5.1, the second series shows personal saving. As can be seen, there was more than

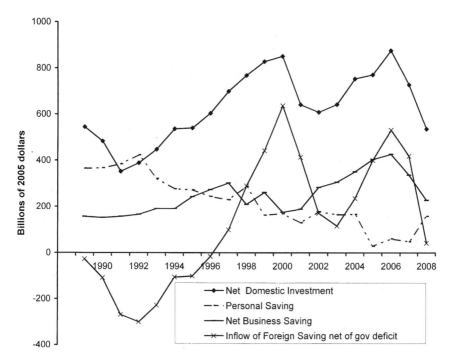

Figure 5.1: Investment and Saving Flows, United States, 1989–2008
Source: Nominal magnitudes are from BEA, NIPA Table 5.1, http://www.bea.gov;
accessed July 25, 2009. All nominal magnitudes have been deflated by the
implicit GDP deflator, 2005 = 100, from http://www.bea.gov, NIPA
Table 1.1.9; accessed July 25, 2009.

enough of such saving to finance all net domestic investment in 1991 and 1992,
but household saving then declined steadily before reaching a trough in 2005.
Net business saving (third series down from the left) does pick up in the middle
of the tech boom, but by the year 2000 it was back below where it had been
in 1993. There is no indication here that domestic private saving (the sum of
household and business saving) increased in the United States in response to a
posited IT-produced increase in the rate of return.

As the tech boom proceeded, domestic private saving fell, and consumption
rose not just absolutely, but also as a share of a rising GDP. Consumption spending was 65.6 percent of GDP in 1989, 68.7 percent in 2000, and 70.3 percent
in 2007 (http://www.bea.gov, NIPA Table 1.1.5). The boom in tech investment
did not crowd out consumption. What it did do was crowd out other types of
investment goods, both in the United States and outside of it, that might have

been accumulated in an alternate world without the enabling technologies of the IT revolution.

Since the tech boom was not paid for, in the aggregate, by an increase in U.S. private or business saving, how was it financed? To a large degree, by inflows of foreign saving. The final series in figure 5.1, fourth down on the left, represents foreign saving inflow (capital account surplus) net of government saving. In years when consolidated federal, state, and local governments ran a deficit, the series shows how much foreign saving inflow was left over to pay for U.S. domestic private sector capital accumulation after the government deficit had been covered. When government ran a surplus, as was the case in 1998, 1999, 2000, and 2001, government saving added to the inflow of foreign saving to produce the very large peak in the series during those years.[19] The end-of-century tech boom was thus enabled, on the one hand, by the willingness of foreign wealth holders to divert their saving flows from investment in their own countries or elsewhere and make it available to the United States, and, on the other hand, by the tax policies of the Clinton and George H. W. Bush administrations. Their fiscal policies—in particular modest tax increases in conjunction with an economy operating at close to capacity—provided the foundation for the increase in government saving that augmented the inflow of foreign saving as a source of funding.

It is conceivable that although the IT accumulation spurt was not associated with a rise in the private saving rate within the United States, it was associated with a rise in the *world* saving rate. Any such upward pressure in this regard, both in the late 1990s and the early 2000s, however, appears to have had more to do with the legacy of the 1998 Asian financial crisis as well as the run-up in commodity prices, particularly oil prices, and the need of oil exporters to recycle their current account surpluses. We are left with the conclusion that by and large, the IT capital accumulation spurt in the United States represented a substitution not away from consumption but away from other not quite as good capital goods, both within the United States and abroad.

Whether the flows necessary to finance capital accumulation came from national saving or from outside the country is irrelevant from the standpoint of productivity trends within the United States. But it does have welfare implications for U.S. residents. Reliance on foreign borrowing meant that the United States was able to forego the sacrifice of current consumption that otherwise would have been, assuming one was close to potential output, the price of capital deepening. The borrowing was a good deal for the country if the increases in output per hour associated with the additional capital deepening exceeded the increases in debt service per hour of labor input. As in any investment boom, there were excesses leading to wasted capital (the billion dollars spent by Webvan come to mind), and some of the real investment was built ahead of demand (fiber optic capacity in the early 2000s comes to mind). However we ultimately reckon it, the gains in output per hour obtained through foreign borrowing will not be manna from heaven, given the obligation of debt repayment.

Within the United States, there was a modest end-of-century acceleration in the rate of capital deepening. Thus the slowdown in non-IT capital accumulation was more than compensated for by the rising rate of IT capital accumulation. One might argue that the drop in U.S. private saving simply compensated collectively for the rise in government saving (Ricardian equivalence in reverse). But this seems doubtful since the saving rate trended downward for decades through periods of government deficit and surplus, particularly after 1980, when the household debt-to-income ratio began its sharp rise. More likely, had the tax increases of the early 1990s not been enacted, the deterioration of the current account would have been even worse.

If the enabling technologies of the IT revolution diverted toward the United States some portion of world saving flows that would not otherwise have come this way *even though U. S. and world saving rates remained largely unaffected,* it would technically be correct to say that we should grant to the IT revolution that part of the growth in labor productivity associated with IT's share of capital deepening. But if we care about labor productivity because we care ultimately about consumption per person in the United States, this misleads. Much of the capital deepening has associated with it a liability tied to increased foreign indebtedness. This is in sharp contrast with the contributions to labor productivity growth of the first two components of the traditional triad used to measure IT "contributions." It is for this reason that the insistence on attributing a substantial portion of the capital deepening effect on labor productivity to IT is problematic. In calculating the impact on labor productivity, it is reasonable to credit IT with the spillovers in the using sectors that may have resulted from such capital deepening, but not the direct effects of the capital accumulation itself.

THE IT CONTRIBUTION AND SOCIAL SAVING CONTROVERSIES

The suggested framework for reckoning the impact of IT on labor productivity emphasizes TFP advance in the IT-producing and IT-using sectors but not the portion of the increase in labor productivity attributable to IT's share of capital deepening. Its merits can be better appreciated by comparing the challenge of coming to terms with IT in the 1990s with one of the critical disputes that gave rise to the new economic history. That dispute involved an attempt to estimate the social saving of the U.S. railroads. Rostow (1960) had argued that railroads were "indispensable" to American economic growth. Both Robert Fogel (1964) and Albert Fishlow (1965) wanted more precision. They tried to imagine worlds otherwise similar save for access to the blueprints needed to build railroads. They calculated alternate channels for saving flows (into canal building and river dredging, for example) and ultimately how much lower U.S. GDP would have been in this alternate world.

The social savings calculations that came out of those debates four decades ago were designed to impress upon us first of all the fact that because saving flows were congealed in railroad permanent way and rolling stock (as opposed to other forms of physical capital such as canals), GDP was indeed higher than it otherwise would have been. *But not by a whole lot.* Fogel argued, for example, that 1890 U.S. GDP was about 4 percent higher than it would have been in the absence of the availability of the railroad. What kind of an increment to TFP over a quarter of a century would one have needed to produce a GDP (or output per hour) in 1890 4 percent higher than it otherwise would have been? About .15 percent per year, continuously compounded.

The key message of the work by Fogel and Fishlow was that in the absence of the railroad, saving flows would have been congealed elsewhere, with results for the economy that would have been almost, but not quite, as good. It would make little sense to suggest that economic historians underestimated the contribution of the availability of railroad blueprints to growth in living standards in the nineteenth century because they did not account for the share of the increment to output per hour attributable to that portion of capital deepening associated with investments in locomotives, rolling stock, and permanent way.[20] We should take the same approach to reckoning the contribution of information technology.

Some labor productivity growth in the 1990s was certainly, in an accounting sense, attributable to capital deepening. And a large fraction of capital deepening, particularly at the end of the 1990s, was indeed associated with the accumulation of physical IT goods: computers, servers, fiber optic cable, routers, etc.[21] But since the counterfactual I have in mind imagines saving behavior largely unaffected by the presence or absence of the IT blueprints, our estimate of the portion of labor productivity growth we attribute to saving (as opposed to technical innovation) should be largely independent of the particular forms in which saving flows were congealed.

It should, to be fair, also be independent of the sources of that saving. With respect to the labor productivity growth caused by capital deepening, it is irrelevant whether the saving came from outside of the country. But from the standpoint of their contribution to U.S. standards of living, labor productivity gains from capital deepening financed by foreign borrowing, as noted, came encumbered in a way that similar gains financed by domestic saving did not.

It is true that if we are operating below capacity and a new attractive invention offers profitable opportunities for new investment, it is reasonable to talk about the extent to which the innovation increases real output through its effect on the amount of real capital formation. From an aggregate perspective, such investment will be largely self-financing (just as, in the presence of accommodative monetary policy, will be government deficits). Under these circumstances, we can argue that it is investment that drives saving, a point of view that has been a staple of traditional Keynesian analysis.

But this has not been the argument of advocates of the tripartite framework. Once we reach potential output—and the economy was close to it throughout most of the tech boom—the old rules of microeconomics apply. Choices have opportunity costs, and saving constrains investment rather than the other way around. This has always been the rationale for policy changes designed to increase the after-tax return to saving, and, if the elasticities are right, saving flows—policies that make sense from a long-range growth perspective but are contraindicated if one is below capacity. By and large, in growth accounting, we are trying to abstract from cyclical effects and study the effect of saving and innovation on the increase of potential output. We want to know, in the long run, what was the effect of the IT-enabling technologies on the growth of potential output. If we are concerned with contributions to long-run growth, an appeal to the role of IT capital formation in "contributing" to increases in real output based on these shorter-run Keynesian arguments, which involve moves from within the production possibility frontier toward it, would not be appropriate.

It would be analogous to emphasizing, as did Rostow (1960), the stimulus to the iron and steel and lumber industries from late nineteenth-century railroad construction. That emphasis obscured the fact that once we were at potential output, these resources had alternate uses, and the enormous costs of constructing the railroads raised the hurdle they had to overcome to make a positive contribution to GDP. They managed to do so, as Fogel and Fishlow demonstrated, by speeding up the turnover of inventories in the economy and by enabling a superior exploitation of regional comparative advantage. But it was close.

TFP GROWTH VS. THE CAPITAL-DEEPENING EFFECT

How much of a difference could this alternate framework for reckoning the impact of IT make? We can examine this by considering how important, in terms of their impact on labor productivity, were the respective roles of TFP and capital deepening over the 1989–2000 period, comparing this to 1973–1989 as well as 2000–2007. There are a couple of ways of approaching the data. The first is to ask how much of the *acceleration* in labor productivity growth between the different periods can be attributed to each factor (see table 2.1 and the bottom three panels of table 5.4). For the private nonfarm economy, labor productivity growth accelerated from 1.28 percent per year between 1973 and 1989 to 2.07 percent per year between 1989 and 2000, an acceleration of .79 percentage points. About 54 percent of this (.43 percentage points) was attributable to TFP acceleration. Some of the remainder (.28 percentage points) was due to faster growth in labor quality (labor composition), which rose at .50 percent per year between 1989 and 2000, versus .22 percent per year between 1973 and 1989. The balance (.08 percentage points) resulted from a somewhat faster rate of capital deepening.

TFP is the entire story in explaining the acceleration in labor productivity growth when we compare 2000–2007 with 1989–2000. Output per hour grew at 2.59 percent per year in the latter period versus 2.07 percent during 1989–2000. The acceleration of TFP growth was responsible for virtually all of this since, along with a slight acceleration in the rate of capital deepening, it had to cover both the net acceleration and the negative contributions associated with deceleration in the growth of labor quality.

Looking back over the performance of the economy since 1973, one notes the relatively modest differences in rates of capital deepening in the three periods examined. This reinforces the point that the accumulation of IT capital was largely not on top of but in lieu of other nor quite as good producer durables that would probably have been accumulated in the absence of IT's enabling technologies.

We can also slice the data differently, looking at the role of TFP and capital deepening in explaining rates of labor productivity growth (as opposed to acceleration). The top three panels in table 5.4 take this perspective. As can be seen, capital deepening contributes about the same percent per year to labor productivity growth in each of these three periods. TFP is responsible for most of the change when we compare 1989–2000 with 1973–1989 and all of it when we compare 2000–2007 with 1989–2000. As we have shown, the data are consistent with a major role for IT, both in sectors producing it (NAICS 334) and in sectors

Table 5.4. Sources of Growth and Acceleration in Growth
of Labor Productivity, United States, 1973–2007

Labor productivity growth, 2000–2007	2.59
TFP[a]	1.38
Capital deepening[a]	0.87
Labor composition[a]	0.34
Labor productivity growth, 1989–2000[a]	2.07
TFP[a]	0.79
Capital deepening[a]	0.78
Labor composition[a]	0.50
Labor productivity growth, 1973–1989	1.28
TFP[a]	0.36
Capital deepening[a]	0.70
Labor composition[a]	0.22
Labor productivity growth acceleration, 2000–2007 vs. 1989–2000[b]	0.52
TFP[b]	0.59
Capital deepening[b]	−0.09
Labor composition[b]	−0.16
Labor productivity growth acceleration, 1989–2000 vs. 1973–1989[b]	0.79
TFP[b]	0.43
Capital deepening[b]	0.08
Labor composition[b]	0.28

Sources: 1973–1989: U.S. Department of Labor 2009.
1989–2007: BLS, http://www.bls.gov, multifactor productivity section of the site; accessed January 7, 2010. Data apply to the PNE.
Note: Contribution of capital deepening is calculated as a residual after the effects of TFP and labor composition are subtracted from the rate of growth of output per hour.
[a]Percent per year.
[b]Percentage points.

using it. We don't need to try and put our hand on the scales by attributing to IT that portion of the growth in labor productivity due to the capital deepening associated with the accumulation of particular IT goods.

TAKING THE MEASURE OF THE IT REVOLUTION

I came of age in the 1960s. Advances in IT have, over the past decades, changed how I work and how I spend my leisure time. These changes are probably more salient than any others wrought by technological progress during my lifetime.[22] I am not quite with my daughter, who, with some hyperbole, says she cannot imagine how people lived before smart phones, computers, global positioning satellites, and the Internet, but I can understand why she feels this way. And yet the degree to which the rapidity of advance in these areas stands out so strongly testifies itself to the relative narrowness of the frontier of advance. The cars I drive, the planes in which I fly, the clothes I wear, the appliances I use, the house I live in: all of these may have experienced quality improvements and may be produced somewhat more cheaply than was true four or five decades ago, but in most respects the experience of using them has not changed greatly over these years.

What was incontrovertibly revolutionary about the IT revolution was the operation of Moore's Law: the ability to manufacture computers, peripherals, and telecommunications equipment in such a fashion that output rose much faster than inputs conventionally measured. The plummeting costs of producing quality-adjusted CPUs, memory, mass storage, and display devices have been for the late twentieth and early twenty-first centuries what spinning jennies and water frames were for the late eighteenth century in Britain, although the rates of productivity advance have been far more dramatic and the spillovers from IT have been greater.

The revolutionary character of what happened in the IT industries shows up as higher and accelerating TFP and, perforce, labor productivity growth in NAICS 334. Even allowing for the possibility of overshooting in the estimate of output growth resulting from the use of hedonic techniques, we can happily and uncontroversially credit the revolution with most of these gains, which flow directly through to improvements in the material standard of living.

It is also likely that some—although by no means all—of the TFP advance in securities trading and wholesale and retail distribution in the 1990s, as well as acceleration in sectors such as transportation equipment, mining, health care, and credit intermediation in the 2000s, is attributable to spillovers from IT investments, and we should credit the enabling technologies of the IT revolution with some fraction of these gains as well. But I cannot see a compelling reason also to attribute a portion of the effect of capital deepening on labor productivity to IT innovation.

An intellectual legacy of the IT boom has been the popularity of the concept of a general-purpose technology. IT or computers have been the inspiration because of their use in multiple applications and potential to generate spillovers in using industries (Bresnahan and Trajtenberg 1995). But multiapplication innovations can sometimes have a superficial economic impact, while single-purpose devices, such as the cotton gin, can be consequential. It is undoubtedly true that some advances are more important than others, but to call something a GPT has in many instances been to suggest about a class of innovations or industries that there was more to them than apparently met the eye or showed up in aggregate statistics. The enthusiasm for the concept runs the danger of placing too much emphasis on specific innovations awarded this designation, and it is not clear that the attempt to generalize from the IT experience has produced a good filter for separating consequential innovations from those that are less so (see chapter 9).

It is important to distinguish between the proposition that it sometimes takes a long time for the productivity benefits of new technological complexes to be reaped and the concept of a GPT. One can accept the former without necessarily embracing the usefulness of the latter. The full benefits of IT may indeed have involved delay before they were realized. My intent, however, has been to focus not on hope and promise (the ultimate drivers of the tech stock boom) but on what the statistical record shows was actually achieved, in both the 1990s and the early 2000s. The end-of-century productivity revival needs to be understood in these terms, not as the reflection of the arrival of some quasi-magical force unlike anything the world had seen before.

There is quite enough to be impressed about with IT without trying to make it more than it is or was by jiggering the benchmark dates, rearranging the presentation of the data, or crediting it with the effects of capital deepening, most of which would have taken place, albeit in different forms, in an imagined world lacking the IT innovations.

———————————●●●———————————

FIN DE SIÈCLE: THE LATE NINETEENTH CENTURY IN THE MIRROR OF THE TWENTIETH

In this chapter, we return to an issue first addressed in the introduction: how the character and drivers of late nineteenth-century growth may have differed in relationship to what took place in the twentieth. In the immediate postwar period, Moses Abramovitz and Robert Solow both examined data on output and input growth for the United States and reached similar conclusions. The pattern of disembodied technical change appeared to be markedly different in the twentieth century as compared with the nineteenth. In the twentieth century, a much smaller fraction of real output growth could be swept back to the growth of inputs conventionally measured; the residual, correspondingly, was much larger. Abramovitz published his findings in 1956, Solow in 1957, and their generalization rapidly became accepted as identifying a permanent change in the sources of economic advance. At the end of his career, Abramovitz continued to characterize the twentieth century as experiencing "Growth in the Era of Knowledge-Based Progress," distinguishing it from the nineteenth (Abramovitz and David 2000).

Solow's 1957 study examined data covering the four decades between 1909 and 1949; Abramovitz's 1956 study examined growth up through an end period that averaged data between 1944 and 1953. The big acceleration in TFP growth during the interwar years surely colored their conclusions. Yet as chapters 4 and 5 make clear, their generalization about the nature of twentieth-century growth was premature. After a lag during the war period (1941–1948), TFP growth persisted at high, although somewhat more moderate, rates during the golden age. But it then ground to an almost complete halt between 1973 and 1989 or 1995. Output per hour continued to rise, albeit much more slowly, but this was almost entirely attributable to physical capital deepening. Data are now available for the entire century, and it is no longer possible to interpret the high rate of TFP advance during the interwar years that prompted the Abramovitz/Solow generalization as a defining characteristic of the century as a whole.

The collapse of TFP growth after 1973 is, however, only one aspect of the difficulty with the Abramovitz/Solow claim. Another is that TFP was in fact quite robust between the end of the Civil War and 1906, as was in fact acknowledged by Abramovitz (1993). It looks modest only in comparison with the exceptional performance in the second and third quarters of the twentieth century, but that would be true of almost any other period held up for comparison. The available data simply do not support the suggestion that almost all growth in the last third of the nineteenth century can be swept back to inputs conventionally measured.

As noted in chapter 1, Kendrick's (1961) work has been the starting point for almost all research on U.S. productivity growth prior to 1948. In the 1950s both Abramovitz and Solow worked with his then unpublished data. Abramovitz and David (1973) used Kendrick for their post-1909 analysis, and Gordon (2000b) also began with Kendrick, as do I. In contrast with chapters 2–5, I focus here on data for the private domestic economy as well as the private nonfarm economy because of the important contribution of agriculture in the late nineteenth and early twentieth centuries.

What does it mean empirically to say that "almost all" growth can be swept back to inputs conventionally measured? Abramovitz and David wrote that "over the course of the nineteenth century the pace of increase of the real gross domestic product was accounted for largely by that of the traditional, conventionally defined factors of production. . . . The long term growth rate of total factor productivity lay in a low range from .4 to .6 percent per annum" (1973, p. 429).

Abramovitz and David did not argue that technological change was unimportant in raising output per hour. Rather, they maintained that its effects weren't necessarily apparent in TFP growth. Instead, they saw technical change as inducing a rise in the post–Civil War saving rate by increasing the return to investment and thus influencing the growth in output per hour by affecting the rate of capital deepening. Whatever the merits of this position and whether or not a rise in the saving rate was a response to higher returns, an aim of this chapter is to show that TFP growth was in fact robust from the 1870s through the first decade of the twentieth century.[1]

Abramovitz and David reported TFP growth of .5 percent per year between 1855 and 1905, with approximately .3 percent per year up through 1890, accelerating to .8 percent between 1890 and 1905 (1973, p. 430). The authors presented their results in growth rates rather than levels, making it difficult to ask of the data questions others than those they posed.[2] They promised that "the full body of data [would] be presented for examination in a later publication" (1973, p. 431), but the data in levels remain unavailable. Some modifications in reported growth rates were made in subsequent publications. The main change was recalculation for the private domestic economy, as opposed to a somewhat larger aggregate in the earlier work. They reported TFP growth rates for the private domestic economy between 1855 and 1890 as .36 percent per year (Abramovitz 1993, p. 223) or .37 percent per year (Abramovitz and David 2000, p. 20).

A rate of TFP increase of .37 percent per year for thirty-five years is low and implies a total rise in the level of TFP over the period of less than 14 percent. Can this rate of growth be made consistent with the estimate of 1.22 percent per year between 1873/1874 and 1892 derived from the Kendrick data (see table 6.1)? (Since Kendrick's initial observation is for 1869/1878, I've described it as centered on the midyears of that interval.) That rate running from 1873/1874 to 1890 would have raised the level of TFP by a total of more than 22 percent. So for the Abramovitz and David numbers to be consistent with those reflected in table 6.1, derived from Kendrick, TFP would have had to have fallen between 1855 and 1873/1874 at a rate approaching −.4 percent per year.

Precisely that possibility is acknowledged in Abramovitz (1993, p. 228), where he breaks down the 1855–1890 epoch into two subperiods, reporting TFP growth for the private domestic economy (PDE) of − .4 percent per year between 1855 and 1871 and 1.00 percent per year between 1871 and 1890 (with .91 percent per year between 1890 and 1905). Abramovitz acknowledged that these subperiod calculations presented potential problems for his interpretation: "Those who prefer to form their view from the shorter long swings would look instead to the figures in Table 2. One might then tell a somewhat different tale. One might then say that the years when the growth of capital intensity was the dominant contribution to labor productivity growth were the mid century years, from 1835 to 1871. One might argue that a transition toward a development pattern resembling that of the present century began during the last quarter of the last century. And one would be supported in this view by the facts that in those years TFP became much larger" (Abramovitz 1993, pp. 227–228).

Reference to a possible alternative to what had become the standard narrative was, however, absent in Abramovitz and David (2000), which again gave us data only for the very long periods 1855–1890 and 1890–1927.[3] The low reported TFP growth between 1855 and 1890 obscures robust gilded-age TFP advance because it combined the influence of the years 1855–1871, in which TFP fell, with a post-1871 period in which it rose.

Table 6.1. TFP Growth Estimates, Private Domestic Economy,
1869/78–2007 (percent per year)

1869/78–1892[a]	1.23
1892–1906	1.24
1906–1919	.85
1919–1929	1.97
1929–1941[b]	2.66
1941–1948[b]	.84
1948–1973	2.20
1973–1989	.56
1989–2000	.87
2000–2007	1.45

Sources: 1869/78–1948: Kendrick 1961, table A-XXII; 1948–2007: U.S. Department of Labor 2009.
[a]The estimate for these years is based on a regression of logged values of TFP from 1869–1878
through 1907 that yields a trend growth rate of 1.23 percent per year. The first two observations are
averages for ten-year periods. Since some procyclicality of TFP over these decades is likely, this is
probably a slight overestimate of TFP growth since the initial period included almost two complete
peak-to-trough cycles (see text). A direct growth calculation for this period from the Kendrick data,
centering 1869–1878 on 1873/1874 as the starting point, yields 1.59 percent per year, which may
partly reflect some procyclicality in TFP or remaining recovery from the Civil War. The 1892–1906
calculation is defensible as peak to peak since both years represented troughs in the annual unemployment series. The main conclusion is that TFP advance in the post–Civil War decades prior to
1892 was not dissimilar to that experienced between 1892 and 1906.
[b]Growth rates for these years are based on a cyclically adjusted TFP level for 1941. Unemployment
in 1941 was still 9.9 percent, and TFP was strongly procyclical over the years 1929–1941 (as it has
been for more than a century; see chapter 7), suggesting that its level would have been higher had
the economy been closer to full employment in the last year before full-scale war mobilization. The
adjustment is made, using data from 1929 to 1941, by regressing the TFP growth rate from the previous year (difference in natural logs) on the change in the unemployment rate (percentage points)
and then using the coefficient on the change in unemployment to calculate what 1941 PDE TFP
would have been had the economy been at potential output, defined as the 3.8 percent unemployment experienced in 1948. The regression results are as follows:

$$\Delta\text{TFP} = \quad .0270 \quad - .0077 * \Delta\text{UR}$$
$$R^2 = .660 \quad (3.53) \quad (-4.41)$$
(t statistics in parentheses; data are for 1929–1941; n = 12)

There is a 6.1 percentage point difference between actual 1941 unemployment (9.9 percent) and
unemployment at potential output (the 3.8 percent of 1948), implying that 1941 TFP would have
been 4.7 percent higher than in fact it was had the economy been fully employed. The unadjusted
growth rates, calculated directly from table A-XXII of Kendrick, are 2.27 percent per year for
1929–1941 and 1.51 percent per year for 1941–1948. For application of this methodology to data on
the private nonfarm economy, see chapter 3.

As noted, the first part of this period, 1855–1871, is one in which, according to Abramovitz (1993), TFP fell at −.4 percent per year, which means that the level of TFP was about 6 percent *lower* in 1871 than it had been in 1855. Why might this have been? The impact of the Civil War is a plausible explanation. War can push technological frontiers forward in certain areas, but its overall impact is likely to be retardative. With over six hundred thousand fatalities in a population of roughly 31 million, with widespread physical destruction in the South, and with the wrenching changes associated with the demise of the peculiar institution (slavery), it is hardly surprising that the progress of innovation was set back. War requires sharp but transient dislocations of an economy, and while it is true that challenge or adversity can sometimes stimulate invention, war, on balance, does not generally provide a fertile environment for scientific, technical, and organizational progress.[4]

Understanding Abramovitz's estimate of .37 for TFP growth in the PDE between 1855 and 1890 as resulting from the combination of −.4 percent per year TFP growth from 1855 through 1871 followed by 1.00 percent per year from 1871 through 1890—numbers that are similar to those in table 6.1 below—we have the foundation, as Abramovitz recognized, for a rather different narrative. As Kendrick's data show and as Abramovitz acknowledged in 1993, TFP growth following the Civil War was robust by absolute standards. And as I will show, it was substantially higher than that experienced in a comparable period of the twentieth century.

Before moving to that task, let's take a quick look backward, prior to the Civil War. It's clear from the analysis of the subperiod data that the post-1871 TFP growth rates pose difficulties for the Abramovitz-Solow narrative. This is less true for the 1835–1871 data, as presented by Abramovitz. The growth rate over that thirty-six year period also reflects the combined influence of two subperiods, the first between 1835 and 1855, in which growth of output per hour was largely attributable to capital deepening, and the second, as noted, in which TFP fell. Abramovitz reported TFP essentially unchanged between 1835 and 1855, dropping at −.01 percent per year over the period (1993, p. 228). Perhaps this was due to the relatively modest rate of advance (compared to the postbellum period) in scientific, technical, and organizational knowledge and practice.

Prior to the bombardment of Fort Sumter, the fundamentals of telegraphic and railroad technology were well established, and the country had begun to build nationwide networks for both. But only thirty thousand miles of rail had been put in place on the eve of the Civil War (as opposed to a quarter million miles of main track on the eve of the First World War), and the first transcontinental telegraph line was completed only in 1861. The influence of modern business enterprise was still modest. Railroads, the most important sector in which that organizational innovation would be applied, still generated a relatively small portion of overall output. And until nationwide networks of railroad and telegraphic communication were filled in, the technical preconditions for the spread of modern business enterprise to distribution and some sectors of manufacturing were incomplete. The Abramovitz/David calculations, relatively more conjectural for the earlier part of the nineteenth century, show TFP roughly unchanged between 1835 and 1855 before declining across the Civil War period.

But the concern of this chapter is with the postwar years—the period imprecisely known as the gilded age—extending from the mid-1870s through the business cycle peak in 1906. The basic data in Kendrick—and Abramovitz and David's analysis of subperiod data—support a conclusion of robust TFP growth over these years. Kendrick provided us with annual data starting in 1889 and prior to that, with estimates for 1869–1878 and 1879–1888. Figure 6.1 displays the logged values of Kendrick's TFP estimates for the first two decadal averages and then annually through 1907, along with the logged values of PDE TFP for 1973–2007 from the Bureau of Labor Statistics. The relative position of these two groups of data is not of interest here because the index numbers in the two clusters of data use different base years. What is relevant are the relative slopes evident in the two groups. Visual inspection suggests a steeper slope, and thus a faster rate of growth, in the earlier period, an impression confirmed by running a time trend through each cluster.

Ideally in comparing growth rates in different periods, we would like to measure peak to peak, with each peak at or close to potential output, so as to control for the procyclicality of TFP (see chapter 7). The NBER dates a strong business cycle peak in May 1907; Lebergott's (1964) annual unemployment series, as well as Christina Romer's (1986) filtered series for unemployment, bottom out in 1906. This is clearly the end of an important expansion. Because the 1869–1878 observation includes roughly two complete peak-to-trough cycles according to the NBER chronology (June 1869–December 1870 and October 1873–March 1879), an estimate for the average over that period cannot be interpreted as corresponding to a business cycle peak. A calculation from the initial observation (treating it as corresponding to 1873/1874) to 1906 shows compound annual growth of TFP of 1.44 percent per year. If TFP was procyclical, however, this growth rate estimate will be biased upward because the initial data point cannot be treated as corresponding to a peak, and thus the initial observation would likely be cyclically depressed.

A better estimate is obtained by regressing the log of TFP from 1873/1874 through 1907 on a time trend, which yields an estimate of annual TFP growth

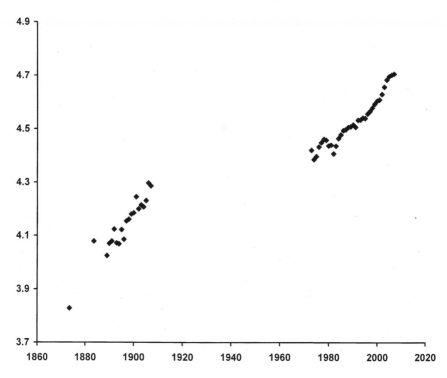

Figure 6.1: Natural Log of Private Domestic Economy
TFP, 1873/1874–1907 and 1973–2007
Source: Kendrick 1961, table A-XXII; U.S. Department of Labor 2009.

of 1.23. A relatively straightforward peak-to-peak estimate runs from 1892 to 1906 (both troughs in the annual unemployment estimates). This yields a rate of 1.24 percent per year for that subperiod, at least 50 percent higher than the .8 percent suggested by Abramovitz and David (1973) for 1890–1905 and substantially higher than rates registered over a comparable period at the end of the twentieth century (.84 percent per year from 1973 through 2007).[5] Abramovitz and David used five-year averages centered on years they considered peaks. The choice of beginning and endpoints matters in avoiding cyclical confounds, and on this score 1892 and 1906—both troughs in annual unemployment series— are on this score more defensible than 1890 and 1905.[6]

The rate of TFP growth implied for the period from after the Civil War to 1892 is more than three times higher than what Abramovitz and David (1973) report for the entire period 1855–1890, although it is much closer to the 1 percent per year Abramovitz (1993) reported for 1871–1890. These data also suggest the absence of a major discontinuity in TFP growth rates from the end of the Civil

War to the 1906 business cycle peak.[7] In contrast with the rapid growth prior to 1906, there follows afterward a substantial slowdown in TFP growth through 1919, prior to the TFP experience of the 1920s, which (see chapter 2) is almost entirely due to advance in manufacturing.

TFP for the private domestic economy displays its fastest growth between 1929 and 1941. The calculated growth rates over the periods 1929–1941 and 1941–1948 are based on a cyclically adjusted level for 1941, but this characterization holds even without the adjustment (see chapters 1–2 and footnote a to table 6.1). From 1948 onward, data are from the Bureau of Labor Statistics. The logged values of TFP levels from the BLS Web site from 1973 through 2007 are also plotted on figure 6.1. Peak-to-peak calculations for 1973–1989 yield .56 percent per year, increasing to .87 percent per year from 1989 to 2000 and to 1.45 percent per year between 2000 and 2007. For the entire 1973–2007 period, the compound annual growth rate is .84 percent per year.

These data show that TFP growth rates in the last part of the nineteenth century were far stronger than the narrative we have come to accept suggests and substantially higher than they were during corresponding years in the twentieth century. This comparison and reframing is important because it offers the possibility of reconciling what has become a troubling disconnect in the teaching of U.S. economic history. How could it be that the buildout of the transcontinental railway and telegraph networks and the development of modern business enterprise (Chandler 1977; Field 1987), which both enabled and were in turn enabled by the new technologies, had so little imprint on the TFP data? How could it have been that the new technologies of the second industrial revolution—such as Bessemer and Siemens-Martin open-hearth steel, the Bonsack cigarette-making machine, or the disassembly line pioneered by Swift in meatpacking—left so little trace on the data? Add to this David and Wright's (1997) argument that advance in mineral extraction was heavily dependent on a knowledge base developed and transmitted in universities, schools of mines, and professional associations, as well as the dependence of the growth of American agricultural output on biological innovation resulting from government-sponsored R and D (Olmstead and Rhode 2002), and there is a real puzzle.

How can we reconcile the influence of all these factors with the suggestion that TFP growth averaged just .5 percent a year from the end of the Civil War into the first decade of the twentieth century? This number obscures the relatively high post-1871 TFP growth rates by combining them with the period of falling TFP between 1855 and 1871. The commonly quoted generalization that TFP grew at about half a percent a year in the post–Civil War nineteenth century is inconsistent with the post-1871 data and with what we know qualitatively and at the sectoral level about the evolution of the economy after the war.

Consider again the railroads and Fogel's 1964 study of their social saving. Fogel concluded that had saving flows been congealed in somewhat inferior capital investments (canals, river dredging), U.S. GDP would have been about 4 percent lower in 1890 than it was. Now, 4 percent is not a large number, but neither is it zero, and, as noted, it can be translated into an increment to TFP growth. Over a twenty-five-year period (1865–1890), a .15 percent per year increment to TFP growth, continuously compounded, yields a 4 percent boost to GNP in 1890. Suggesting that total TFP growth up through 1890 was in the range of .37 percent per year, as did Abramovitz and David, leaves only .22 percent per year for everything else. We should not, however, feel obliged to construct our narrative within such a tight TFP budget.

Consider next that the buildout of the railway network, combined with the construction of a transcontinental telegraph network, gave rise to perhaps the greatest organizational innovation of the last two centuries—what Chandler (1977) called modern business enterprise (MBE). Is there any type of innovation that would be more likely to show up in the residual, a measure of disembodied change, than this? The new organizational form was critical for the operation of large railway and telegraph corporations. These technologies were also what allowed MBE to be extended from transport and communications to distribution and ultimately manufacturing (Field 1987). The .15 percent per year does not account for the spillover effects of the railroad in using sectors, most particularly its enabling of MBE. It will therefore underestimate the railroad's overall contribution to TFP.

If we accept the traditional narrative, MBE had apparently little measurable impact on TFP growth prior to the First World War. When is it supposed to have had an impact? Data from table 6.1 for the PDE show TFP growth falling off after 1906. Data from table 6.2 for the private nonfarm economy show some deceleration in TFP in a comparison of 1892–1906 with 1869–1892, and Kendrick's incomplete data for manufacturing (see table 6.3) show some retardation in that sector as one goes into the first years of the twentieth century. By the time we get to the extraordinary TFP growth in manufacturing of the 1920s (1919–1929), MBE is already well established, and the explanatory focus is less on organizational innovation. Rather it is on the delayed effects of electrification, particularly the use of wires as a substitute for mechanical gears and shafts in distributing power internally within the factory (Devine 1983; David and Wright 2003). The 1920s manufacturing revolution, moreover, was an across-the-board phenomenon–evidenced in the uniformly high rates of TFP advance

Table 6.2. TFP Growth Estimates, Private Nonfarm Economy, 1869/78–2007

1869/78–1892[a]	1.95
1892–1906	1.11
1906–1919	1.12
1919–1929	2.02
1929–1941[b]	2.78
1941–1948[b]	.49
1948–1973	1.88
1973–1989	.36
1989–2000	.79
2000–2007	1.38

Sources: 1869/78–1948: Kendrick 1961, table A-XXIII; 1948–2007: U.S. Department of Labor 2009.
[a]The estimate for these years is based on a regression of logged values of PNE TFP from 1869–1878 through 1907 that yields a trend growth rate of 1.59 percent per year. One needs 1.95 percent per year TFP growth from 1873/1874 to 1892 to make the trend growth rate through 1907 consistent with the peak-to-peak calculation for 1892–1906.
[b]Growth rates for these years are based on a cyclically adjusted TFP level for 1941 (see chapter 3; table 3.6).

at the two-digit level (chapter 2). The impact of MBE in manufacturing prior to the First World War was far less uniform — quite important in a few key sectors, not so important elsewhere. The same was true for distribution — but not for rail transportation, where one had to have it. The data show higher TFP growth in the private nonfarm economy in the period from the end of the Civil War through 1892. This is the more relevant aggregate if one is interested in the likely effects of MBE, and the data are consistent with its having played a contributing role in robust TFP growth then. Again, this is where Abramovitz's 1993 pre–World War I subperiod data show the fastest TFP growth.

To what degree could the discrepancy between the low TFP rates associated with the conventional narrative and those in table 6.1 have to do with differential accounting for the growth of land input? Kendrick does include land in his estimates of farm capital, which are derived from Tostlebe (1957). If Kendrick's numbers do not adequately account for the growth of land input in agriculture, then TFP growth estimates for the private domestic economy for the end of the nineteenth century might be too high. One way to explore this possibility is to examine trends in TFP growth rates for the private nonfarm economy, for which the growth of land inputs is presumably less directly relevant.

To estimate TFP growth rates for the private nonfarm economy from the end of the Civil War up to 1892 I employ a methodology similar to that used for the private domestic economy. First, run a time trend through the logged values of Kendrick's PNE data, centering 1869–1878 on 1873/1874 and 1879–1888 on 1883.5. This yields 1.59 percent per year, continuously compounded, from 1873/1874 through 1907. Second, do a relatively clean peak-to-peak measure between 1892 and 1906, which yields 1.11 percent per year. Third, ask what growth rate one would have needed between 1873/1874 and 1892 to be consistent with the results of the first calculation. The answer is 1.95 percent per year. This suggests strong TFP growth in the private nonfarm economy before 1892, moderating thereafter. Keep in mind that 1.11 percent per year between 1892 and 1906 is still substantially higher than what was registered in the U.S. twentieth-century economy from 1973 onward. Whereas the Abramovitz and David narrative proposes accelerating TFP growth after 1890 (.8 percent per year rather than .3 percent earlier), table 6.2 suggests some deceleration for the private nonfarm economy in a comparison of the years before and after 1892. Table 6.1 shows rough constancy for the private domestic economy; the differences have to do with some acceleration in TFP growth in agriculture comparing 1892–1906 with the earlier period.[8] Neither table 6.1 nor table 6.2 is consistent, however, with notable acceleration after 1890. The Abramovitz and David suggestion of .3 percent up through 1890 and .8 percent from 1890 through 1905 is, again, potentially misleading because the .3 (or .37) percent from 1855 through 1890 is a productivity growth estimate dragged down by declining productivity across the Civil War period.

The data on sectoral productivity trends are less complete than those for the aggregate measures, but what are available help us flesh out the underpinnings of what we are picking up in tables 6.1 and 6.2.

Table 6.3 shows rates of TFP growth in mining, manufacturing, and telephone and telegraph. These data suggest that the biggest gains in manufacturing came in the 1880s, after which growth slowed before the huge acceleration after 1919. In mining, the 1890s appear to have been a particularly fertile period (see David and Wright 1997), and we also see an acceleration for agriculture. Progress in communication remains relatively strong throughout.

The relatively strong gains in manufacturing during the 1880s likely reflect the contribution of modern business enterprise. As noted above, the 1880s were a big decade for the expansion of such MBE-intensive subsectors as steel, cigarettes, meatpacking, and petroleum refining. Use of this organizational form required the availability of reliable railroad and telegraph service and was necessary in manufacturing to exploit economies dependent not just upon scale per se but also on high levels of capacity utilization and rates of inventory turnover.

Table 6.3. TFP Growth in Mining, Manufacturing, and Telephone and
Telegraph, 1869–1919 (percent per year)

Years	Mining	Manufacturing	Telephone and Telegraph
1869–1879	n.a.	.86	n.a.
1879–1889	1.24	1.94	2.30
1889–1899	2.49	1.12	1.27
1899–1909	.77	.72	3.98
1909–1919	1.39	.28	1.35

Source: Kendrick 1961, tables C-III, D-I, H-III.

Finally, the growth of TFP in railroads was very strong throughout the post–Civil War period—higher than the rate of growth in the economy-wide aggregates and thus a significant contributor to them. Much of this represented the consequence of a continuing process of technical change resulting in larger locomotives and rolling stock, air brakes, and automatic couplers (Fishlow 1966). But much, including the economically successful exploitation of such improvements, reflected and depended upon the contribution of modern business enterprise—the organizational form that allowed the operation of private enterprises whose size and dominance in the economy had never been witnessed before and has never been seen since. MBE was an absolute requirement in the business of railroad transportation, especially on a largely single-tracked system, whereas MBE was adopted only in portions of the distribution and manufacturing sectors (Field 1992a). The high penetration within the railroad sector was unmatched elsewhere, with the possible exception of the telephone and telegraph sector, which also exhibited TFP growth above that registered in the economy-wide aggregates (see table 6.3).

Table 6.4 also includes data for the railroad sector on the growth rates of labor and capital productivity (TFP growth rates are a weighted average of the two). Readers may be surprised by the relative rates of increase of labor and capital productivity, as well as the respective sectoral increases in capital and man-hours associated with them. Although the capital-output ratio for the economy rose (in other words, capital productivity went down), in part as the consequence of the enormous accumulation in railroads, the situation within the sector itself was quite different. The sector of the economy most thoroughly

Table 6.4. Productivity Growth in Railroads, 1873.5–1919 (percent per year)

Years	TFP	Output/Hour	Output/Unit of Capital
1873.5–1883.5	4.25	3.58	5.75
1883.5–1892	2.33	1.86	4.98
1892–1906	2.56	1.82	5.31
1906–1919	3.02	3.33	1.70

Source: Kendrick 1961, table G-III.

penetrated by MBE generated rates of increase of capital productivity averaging over 5 percent per year from 1873/1874 through 1906. Aside from assuring that trains didn't collide—an event that is, one might say, capital-using—advanced logistical control contributed to rises in capital productivity by enabling higher utilization rates on fixed capital and rolling stock. One can interpret this simply as a scale economy, but the ability of a system to generate low costs at high volume is beside the point if volume cannot be managed and sustained at those levels. This required increases in labor input even more rapid than those of capital.

Whereas capital in railroads grew at 1.96 percent per year between 1873/1874 and 1906, man-hours rose at 4.92 percent per year (Kendrick 1961, table G-III, p. 543).[9] In other words, in railroad enterprises, the capital-labor ratio declined at a rate of about 3 percent a year, one of the reasons capital productivity went up so much. In contrast, for the private domestic economy as a whole, capital grew at 3.76 percent per year and man-hours at 2.75 percent per year between 1873/1874 and 1906, so capital was deepening at a rate of about 1 percent per year (Kendrick 1961, table A-XXII).[10] The trends within the railroad sector are testimony to the degree to which modern business enterprise is a capital-saving innovation. MBE uses labor and saves capital (Field 1987), and this characteristic is especially evident in sectors where the organizational form had its deepest penetration.

The need to ensure high volume flows is central to Chandler's emphasis on the importance of throughput, whether he is discussing transportation, communication, distribution, or manufacturing. Modern business enterprise, in the context of the new railroad and telegraph technologies, represented a decisive break with prior modes of business practice. There were no modern business enterprises in 1840. In The Visible Hand (1977) Chandler suggested that if a contemporary business manager were transported back to 1910, he would be more or less at home in the organizational and management environment, but if he were transported back to 1840, he would be in a different world and might as well go back to the fifteenth century.

Modern business enterprises employ a multidivisional structure, depend on management information systems, and are run by a cadre of professional managers. Nineteenth-century MBEs used the telegraph to move information quickly, the typewriter to create and maintain administrative office records, and the vertical file to store them. The linotype machine and innovations in making cheap paper from wood pulp spelled dramatic reductions in the cost of mass media, which were in turn increasingly utilized by department stores, mail order houses, and manufacturers to stimulate demand for their products or services through advertising.

MBE developed first in the railroads. The telegraph industry also faced an imperative to manage high-speed traffic and employed MBE as well. The organizational form then spread to wholesale and retail distribution, giving rise to such new institutions as the department store and the mail order house. Finally, it was adopted in a limited number of subsectors of the industrial sector—in such businesses as steel, cigarette manufacturing, petroleum refining, meatpacking, and sewing machines/typewriters. MBE made possible, and in turn was technologically dependent on, nationwide systems of telegraph communication and railroad transportation. You could not have MBE without the telegraph, and there was no rationale for it without the railroad (Chandler 1977; Field 1987).

The hypothesis that the diffusion of MBE is implicated in TFP increases leads to testable predictions. The historical narrative is reasonably clear with respect to where the organizational form did and did not take root prior to World War I. The hypothesis predicts that in sectors wholly or partially penetrated by MBE, one should see TFP growth stronger than in the economy as a whole. The data in tables 6.3 and 6.4 are largely consistent with this hypothesis. TFP growth in railroads and telegraphs was above the economy-wide average throughout the period in question. In manufacturing this was so in the 1880s and especially the 1890s. Data for the distribution sector are also consistent with this view (see Field 1996).

Chandler's principal focus was on organizational innovation. In a somewhat similar vein, Vaclav Smil (2005) explored the contributions of late-nineteenth-century scientific and technical advance to twentieth-century growth. His main thesis, which bears similarities with Chandler's, is that the four decades prior to the First World War contributed to a decisive break with the past: "The fundamental means to realize nearly all of the 20th century accomplishments were put in place before the century began, mostly during the three closing decades of the 19th century and in the years preceding WW1. That period ranks as history's most remarkable discontinuity not only because of the extensive sweep of its innovations but also because of the rapidity of fundamental advances that were achieved during that time" (2005, pp. 5–6).

A good deal of what Smil went on to describe represented larder stocking: the establishment of foundations upon which was predicated future progress. But much of the advance had an immediate impact: "Many pre WW1 innovations were patented, commercialized and ready to be diffused in a matter of months (telephone, lightbulbs) or a few years (gasoline powered cars, synthesis of ammonia) after their conceptualization or experimental demonstration" (2005, p. 9). Thus TFP growth between the Civil War and First World War can be interpreted as reflecting the influence of contemporaneous scientific and technical progress combined and sometimes interacting with the effect of evolutionary improvement of systems such as the railroad and the telegraph, whose foundations had been established prior to the Civil War. Rapidly commercialized breakthroughs and progress building upon earlier foundations meant that scientific, technical, and organization advance during this period had an impact on the way people lived then, as well as on how they would live after the First World War.

In language similar to Chandler's, Smil wrote that "The enormity of the post 1860 saltation was such that people alive in 1913 were further away from the world of their great-grandparents who lived in 1813 than those were from their ancestors in 1513." He made a similar point about scientific progress, arguing that if one transported the distinguished French chemist Lavoisier forward to the early twentieth century, much of what he would have seen would have been incomprehensible to him. In contrast, he suggested, transport Edison, Fessenden, Haber, or Parsons (developer of the turbogenerator) to the early twenty-first century and they'd be on top of what they were seeing—indeed, they would have provided the scientific and technical foundations for much of it (2005, pp. 28, 296).

TFP advance in any given period results from the exploitation of technical systems whose foundations have been laid earlier and from the rapid commercialization of new products and processes resulting from contemporaneous scientific and technical progress. Some of that progress will, however, not be immediately exploited, thus replenishing the cupboard for subsequent periods. One can acknowledge the importance of larder stocking and also recognize that gilded-age scientific and technical progress influenced living standards or productivity growth rates prior to the First World War and that this is reflected in the growth of TFP.

Clearly, the mix of larder stocking and immediate impact varied across the different areas of advancement examined by Smil. For example, his exposition gave pride of place to electricity, and we can consider its impact in providing motive power in manufacturing. A small steam engine, he argued, could convert only about 4 percent of coal's energy into power, of which 60 percent was lost in the process of mechanical transmission to the workstation via overhead shafts and belts. The transmission system, moreover, had to be shut down typically for about 10 percent of the time for maintenance. So steam-generated power distributed mechanically within a factory implied an energy efficiency of about 1.4 percent ($.04 \times .4 \times .9$).

In contrast, by the time of the First World War, electricity produced with a turbogenerator had an energy conversion efficiency of about 10 percent. If we assume 10 percent of this was lost in transmission and if we also assume the use of a direct-drive electric motor with 85 percent efficiency, we have overall energy efficiency of almost 8 percent ($.1 \times 9 \times .85$)—a fivefold improvement. Removing the straightjacket of mechanical distribution of power also allowed substantial savings on floor space and the possibility of moving to single-story rather than multiple-story installations.

The conventional narrative argues persuasively, however, that most of the gains from this source were not realized until the 1920s and indeed underlay the fabulous—more than 5 percent per year—growth of TFP in the manufacturing sector between 1919 and 1929 (Kendrick 1961; Devine 1983; David and Wright 2003). So whereas it would be fair to say that prewar advances in systems of power generation laid the foundation for post–World War I advance in manufacturing TFP, it is unlikely that a great deal of the prewar TFP growth can be attributed to the electrification of industry, at least with respect to motive power. Note that within manufacturing, the Kendrick data suggest the fastest gains in the 1880s, certainly well before any of this could have had much effect.

The situation is quite different, however, with respect to space lighting and traction. By 1900 there were over one thousand central power stations in the United States. Much of the demand these stations satisfied was residential, but some was also in commerce and manufacturing, particularly in industries such as textiles, where electric lighting offered much lower probabilities of inducing explosions than did gas lighting and facilitated expanded shift work. By absolute standards incandescent bulbs were and still are quite inefficient in turning energy into light, but in comparison to candles or gas, they represented a big improvement. Smil estimated that candles converted .01 percent of paraffin's chemical energy into light and coal gas no more than .05 percent. By 1913 tungsten filaments converted 2 percent of electric energy into light. With 10 percent generation efficiency and 10 percent transmission losses, energy efficiency had risen to .18 percent (.1 × .9 × .02), still very low but more than three times that of coal gas. The efficiency of converting coal into electric power benefited from very rapid gains in the electricity-generating sector, involving the switch from the use of steam engines to drive dynamos to the use of steam turbines linked inline with a generator or alternator. As the result of improvements in bulbs and power generation, as well as reductions in loss due to transmission, the cost of household lighting fell 90 percent in just two decades between 1892 and 1912. Steam engines themselves underwent substantial improvements, with energy efficiency for new, large, stationary installations rising from 6–10 percent in the 1860s to 12–15 percent after 1900 (Smil 2005, pp. 289–290).

If direct-drive motors were slow to find their way into manufacturing, that was not true in traction. Edison's Pearl Street Station opened in 1882. By 1893 fourteen out of sixteen cities with a population greater than two hundred thousand had electric-traction streetcars, as did forty-one out of forty-two cities with a population between fifty thousand and two hundred thousand (Dyer and Martin 1929; cited in Smil 2005, p. 94).

A second area upon which Smil focused is materials. David Landes (1969, p. 259) noted that the real cost of steel fell 80–90 percent between the early 1860s and the mid-1890s. Crude oil in the United States in 1910 cost 10 percent of what it had in real terms in the 1860s. With the invention of the Hall-Herout reduction process, the real cost of aluminum fell 90 percent between 1890 and 1913, although the use of this advanced material in the economy was still very small (Smil 2005, pp. 155, 292). These cost reductions are the duals of productivity advance in the respective sectors, and they are the consequence of more simply than the effects of capital deepening.

All of the foundational work on the gasoline-powered internal combustion engine was done prior to the First World War. Although this was largely larder stocking, with most of the big productivity gains in the use of self-propelled vehicles yet to come, some gains were already beginning to be reaped prior to the war. In 1913 the operating cost of a truck was 40 percent that of a horse-drawn vehicle; garaging costs alone were barely 15 percent of the analogous space requirements for a horse (Perry 1913; cited in Smil 2005, p. 288). The same economics can be applied to the use of electric power for purposes of traction. Ultimately, the replacement of horsepower with the gasoline engine would free a substantial portion of American crop acreage for purposes other than producing feed for animals.

Similarly, although the scientific and technical foundations for radio and moving pictures were established prior to the war, much of the realization of gains associated with them took place subsequently.

Smil argued that most of the important scientific and technical foundations for twentieth-century economic growth had been established in the two generations prior to World War I. We can acknowledge that much of the impact on aggregate productivity of nineteenth-century technical advance was not felt until later in the twentieth century, particularly the interwar years, and also recognize that much, such as Bessemer and Siemens-Martin steel, did have an immediate impact. We can also acknowledge that much productivity growth and living standard improvement in the years from 1871 through 1906 was influenced by spillovers from the buildout of the railroad and telegraph networks, technologies whose foundations were laid pre–Civil War, as well as rapid productivity growth within those sectors themselves.

Spillovers took the form of innovations in business organization that allowed new ways of doing business in using sectors. Some examples: the telegraph enabled the development of a system of stock trading after the Civil War that persisted in essentially unaltered form for almost a century—breaking down only in 1968 (Field 1998). The telegraph and the railroad were essential technical preconditions for the revolution in meatpacking and distribution engineered by Swift and its competitors. Carnegie's steelmaking revolution depended on the railroad and telegraph for its logistical operation (and railroads played an important role in stimulating the demand for his product). The development of the American Tobacco Company and exploitation of the Bonsack cigarette-making machine are inconceivable without the railroad and the telegraph, as is Rockefeller's success with Standard Oil. In all these cases, we see very substantial declines in real prices.

In the two generations prior to the First World War scientific advance became increasingly important as an underpinning of economic growth. For the first time in history technological progress depended substantially on an understanding of scientific principles, including modern chemistry, which underlay the Haber-Bosch process for synthesizing ammonia; the laws of thermodynamics, which were critical in improvements in the efficiency of steam engines, as well as the development of steam turbines; and advances in understanding electromagnetism, which underlay breakthroughs in wireless communication, as well as the development of improved electric motors. If modern business enterprise was the most important institutional innovation in this period, a good candidate for the second would be the industrial research laboratory, which played a role in all of the above developments. As Abramovitz (1993) acknowledged, once one looks at the subperiod calculations, there is no longer a disconnect between narratives such as Smil's and the aggregate data. Strong TFP advance after 1871 is consistent with the importance of "knowledge-based progress" in the last part of the nineteenth century, as it is with the major acceleration in per capita patenting rates in the United States after the Civil War (Khan and Sokoloff 2001, p. 239).

Together, this qualitative and quantitative evidence makes implausible the suggestion that economic growth in the gilded age can almost entirely be explained as the consequence of the growth of inputs conventionally measured or that labor productivity and living standard advance is virtually entirely to be attributed to capital deepening. The aggregate numbers don't show this, and such a conclusion is contrary to the impression of contemporary observers such as Edward Byrn (1900) that they were living and had lived through a historically unique transition, a conclusion affirmed in the judgments of writers such as Chandler and Smil.

Productivity advance in any period is the consequence of the exploitation of technical foundations that have been established earlier and breakthroughs that are rapidly commercialized and have their impact within the same epoch. The period 1871–1913 is no different in this regard. The technical foundations for the railroad and the telegraph were pre–Civil War, although the proximately significant advances that allowed for the plummeting prices of steel and aluminum took place after the war. The rapid progress in scientific, technical, and organizational knowledge during the two generations prior to the First World War laid the foundations for twentieth-century advance, particularly that remarkable period between the two world wars. But it also underlay the qualitative and quantitative changes that characterized the epoch—the multifaceted improvements that in the minds of so many observers irrevocably separated the world of 1910 from that a half century earlier.

Perhaps Byrn can be forgiven some millennial enthusiasm when he wrote the following in 1900 about the century just ending:

> The Philosophical mind is ever accustomed to regard all stages of growth as proceeding by slow and uniform processes of evolution, but in the field of invention the nineteenth century has been unique. It has been something more than a merely normal growth or natural development. It has been a gigantic tidal wave of human ingenuity and resource, so stupendous in its magnitude, so complex in its diversity, so profound in its thought, so fruitful in its wealth, so beneficent in its results, that the mind is strained and embarrassed in its effort to expand to a full appreciation of it. Indeed the period seems a grand climax of discovery, rather than an increment of growth (1900, p. 3).

Edward Bellamy, H. G. Wells, and Jules Verne would have agreed. Macroeconomic data are consistent with this interpretation. They do not support the view that the last part of the nineteenth century exhibited exceptionally low rates of increase in total factor productivity. TFP growth averaged, for the private domestic economy, above 1.2 percent per year from the early 1870s through 1906. Such growth was substantially more robust than that experienced in the last part of the twentieth century, although still well below the record pace during the interwar period. Revision in our growth narrative for the years between the Civil War and First World War is necessary to reconcile it with these numbers and with what we know about organizational, scientific, and technological progress at the sectoral level during the same period. And it is needed to complete the process of placing twentieth-century success and failure within a longer-run historical perspective.

Part Two

EXTENSIONS AND REFLECTIONS

7

—●●—

PROCYCLICAL TFP

This is the first of three chapters extending or reflecting upon the narrative developed in chapters 1–6 as a way of shedding light on issues of broader macroeconomic or historical significance. This chapter asks how generalizable is the phenomenon of Depression-era TFP procyclicality. Chapter 3 showed that total factor productivity growth was strongly procyclical across the Depression years. When the unemployment rate went up, the level or rate of growth of TFP went down, and vice versa, with this cyclical dynamic overlaid upon a very strong trend growth rate. That relationship was used to make a cyclical (and upward) adjustment to the 1941 level of TFP based on the less than full employment during that year.

The Depression years were an unusual economic period in many ways, and it is natural to ask whether this was one of them. The answer turns out to be quite striking. Between 1890 and 2004, TFP growth in the United States was strongly procyclical (and labor productivity growth mildly so). For over a century TFP growth varied systematically with the business cycle, and the elasticity of TFP growth with respect to a change in the unemployment rate was remarkably stable in the years both before and after the Second World War and in a variety of subperiods during which trend growth rates of TFP were quite different.[1]

I argue that these results are not simply a statistical artifact, as Matthew Shapiro (1987, 1993) and others have suggested. Procyclicality resulted during the Depression and in most other periods principally from demand shocks interacting with relatively invariant capital services, thus generating short-run economies of scale. This account contrasts with explanations emphasizing labor hoarding, as well as those offered by the real business cycle (RBC) program, which attributes economic cycles to technology shocks as measured by deviations in TFP from trend.

THE EVIDENCE FOR PROCYCLICAL TFP

The evidence for the persistence of procyclical TFP and the stability of the cyclicality coefficient comes from a series of regressions of the change in the natural log of TFP ($\Delta\ln\text{TFP}$) on the change in the unemployment rate in percentage points (ΔUR):

$$\Delta\ln\text{TFP} = \alpha + \beta\,\Delta\text{UR} + \mu$$

The estimated constant term in the equation (α) can be interpreted as an estimate of the trend growth rate of TFP over the period studied. The coefficient (β) describes the relationship between the TFP growth rate and the change in the unemployment rate and is thus a measure of cyclicality. This is the specification used in the initial investigation in chapter 3.

Prior empirical work on productivity has tended to involve shorter data runs or focus on the manufacturing sector alone. The statistical analysis here covers more than a century of data for the U.S. private nonfarm economy. Although data for manufacturing are more detailed than those available for the rest of the economy, trends within the sector do not necessarily offer an accurate guide to what is happening in the economy as a whole. Manufacturing has contributed a declining share of U.S. GDP, particularly since the 1970s. Even at its high point in the mid-century decades, that share barely exceeded one-third, and in the first decade of the twenty-first century it contributed less than one-sixth.[2]

Over more than a century TFP was procyclical and in a remarkably consistent fashion: a fall in the unemployment rate by one percentage point led to an increase in the growth rate of TFP of about 0.9 percent per year.[3] The procyclical relationship held across all time periods, even the World War II years, despite the fact that nearly half of all production went to the military and there were shortages and rationing in the civilian sector (Higgs 1992). Nor did the size of the procyclicality coefficient depend on whether one was close to potential output or substantially below it. A comparison of regressions 1.10 and 1.11 shows that inclusion of the level of unemployment (UR) along with its change (ΔUR) has little effect on the originally estimated coefficient.

It is striking that the estimates before and after World War II are so similar. Although Kendrick felt comfortable publishing annual TFP estimates, Simon Kuznets worried about the use of his early national income estimates for cyclical analysis, primarily because of unease about the inventory investment series he had constructed.[4] There are many ways in which inaccurate data might lead to spurious conclusions. But if the process producing short-run procyclicality was similar pre- and postwar and if there was simply more noise in the prewar data, we might have expected the estimated prewar relationship to be weaker. It is not.

Table 7.1. Growth Rates for Subperiods, 1890–2004: Regression Analysis

			Dependent Variable: ΔlnTFP[a]			
Regression	Years	N	Constant	ΔUR[b]	UR[c]	R^2
(1.1)	1929–1941	12	.0283	−.0092		.647
			(3.02)	(−4.28)		
(1.2)	1900–1941	41	.0197	−.0091		.337
			(2.83)	(−4.45)		
(1.3)	1900–1948	48	.0175	−.0091		.307
			(2.65)	(−4.52)		
(1.4)	1890–1948	58	.0166	−.0084		.289
			(2.75)	(−4.77)		
(1.5)	1890–1948[d]	58	.0165	−.0103		.255
			(2.68)	(−4.38)		
(1.6)	1948–1973	26	.0195	−.0082		.294
			(6.51)	(−3.16)		
(1.7)	1973–1995	23	.0053	−.0098		.319
			(1.57)	(−3.14)		
(1.8)	1948–2004	56	.0129	−.0083		.235
			(6.08)	(−4.11)		
(1.9)	1890–2004	114	.0148	−.0084		.283
			(4.59)	(−6.65)		
(1.10)	1890–2004[e]	114	.0148	−.0100		.252
			(4.50)	(−6.14)		
(1.11)	1890–2004	114	.0105	−.0087	.0006	.288
			(1.79)	(−6.64)	(.889)	

Sources: TFP data for 1890–1948 are from Kendrick 1961, table A-XXIII; data for 1948–2004 are from U.S. Department of Labor 2009. Variant 1 of the unemployment rate for 1890–1948 is from Lebergott 1964, and variant 2 for 1890–1948 is from Weir 1992. See also Weir 1986. The unemployment rates for 1948–2004 come from the Bureau of Labor Statistics, "Employment Status of the Civilian Noninstitutional Population, 1940 to Date," at http://www.bls.gov/cps/cpsaat1.pdf; accessed August 14, 2009.

Notes: The figures in parentheses are *t* statistics. All data are for the private nonfarm economy. The convention followed is to calculate the 1947–1948 growth rate from historical data (Kendrick, Lebergott, or Weir) and to calculate the 1948–1949 growth rate from Bureau of Labor Statistics data.
[a]$\Delta lnTFP$ is the difference in the natural log of TFP between year t and year t–1. It is thus a measure of the continuously compounded annual rate of increase of TFP. The dependent variable is therefore logged and differenced, mitigating autocorrelation problems. Durbin-Watson statistics are within acceptable ranges.
[b]ΔUR is the change in the unemployment rate in percentage points between year t and year t–1.
[c]UR is the level of the unemployment rate in year t.
[d]Uses Weir rather than Lebergott unemployment data.
[e]Uses Weir unemployment data through 1948, BLS thereafter.

Table 7.1 also illustrates how much TFP growth rates varied in different historical epochs, a finding emphasized in the work of Abramovitz (1956) and other pioneers in the study of TFP growth rates and consistent with the peak-to-peak calculations reported in chapters 1–6. This variation in trend growth rates measured between business cycle peaks is consistent with a view that the arrival of economically important innovations may be quite discontinuous and may cluster in particular epochs, rendering some periods more technologically progressive than others. A contrasting perspective underlies the use of the Hodrick-Prescott filter to separate trend from cycle in real business cycle studies. These studies are not concerned with identifying business cycle peaks, nor do they use such identifications to calculate varying trend growth rates. They envision a relatively smooth long-run process of technological change, perturbed by deviations upward and downward from trend in the growth rate of TFP. These deviations are considered to be exogenous, rather than the consequence of demand shocks that might widen or shrink an output gap, and are assumed to be the impulses generating cyclical movements in GDP.[5] I explore below more fully the challenges faced by the RBC approach in interpreting short-run movements in TFP.

PROCYCLICALITY IN TFP AND OUTPUT PER HOUR

Interest in the procyclicality of TFP, as opposed to output per hour, is relatively recent.[6] Since the 1960s and the work of Hultgren (1960), Eckstein and Wilson (1964), and Kuh (1965), empirical macroeconomists have taken it as a stylized fact that the growth of labor productivity is procyclical: the growth rate of output per hour (like TFP) is negatively related to changes in the unemployment rate.[7] The majority of these studies have dealt with data from manufacturing, but Gordon (1979; 1993, p. 275) makes the claim more generally for the private nonfarm economy.

Table 7.2 explores the cyclicality of output per hour and related measures, as well as their long-run growth paths. Its regressions replace the TFP growth rate in table 7.1 with several other dependent variables, including the growth rates of output per hour, the capital-labor ratio, hours, capital, output per unit of capital, and total output. The results show first (regressions 2.1–2.4) that although output per hour, like TFP, is procyclical, the relationship between its growth rate and the change in the unemployment rate is weaker, and for the period after 1973 (regression 2.3), one cannot reject the hypothesis of acyclicality. In an arithmetical sense, the procyclicality of labor productivity is due to the fact that the response of output to a change in the unemployment rate (regressions 2.18–2.20) is stronger than the response of hours (regressions 2.9–2.11).

Table 7.2. Labor and Capital Productivity and Their Components: Growth Rates for Subperiods, 1890–2004, Regression Analysis

			Dependent Variable: $\Delta\ln(Y/N)$		
Regression	Years	N	Constant	ΔUR	R^2
(2.1)	1890–1948	58	.0210 (3.58)	−.0052 (−3.01)	.139
(2.2)	1948–1973	26	.0253 (8.68)	−.0060 (−2.37)	.189
(2.3)	1973–2004	32	.0154 (5.69)	−.0028 (−1.12)	.009
(2.4)	1890–2004	114	.0203 (6.48)	−.0051 (−4.15)	.133
			Dependent Variable: $\Delta\ln(K/N)$		
(2.5)	1948–2004	56	.0275 (16.65)	.0190 (12.10)	.727
(2.6)	1890–1948	58	.0121 (3.02)	.0147 (12.57)	.738
(2.7)	1900–1941	41	.0073 (1.67)	.0162 (12.68)	.805
(2.8)	1890–2004	114	.0195 (8.49)	.0151 (16.70)	.713
			Dependent Variable: $\Delta\ln N$		
(2.9)	1890–1948	58	.0163 (7.53)	−.0152 (−17.88)	.741
(2.10)	1948–2004	56	.0164 (14.18)	−.0213 (−19.36)	.872
(2.11)	1890–2004	114	.0163 (7.53)	−.0152 (−17.88)	.741
			Dependent Variable: $\Delta\ln K$		
(2.12)	1890–2004	114	.0346 (18.08)	−.0001 (−.167)	.000
(2.13)	1948–2004	56	.0416 (27.93)	−.0029 (−2.04)	.071
(2.14)	1890–1948	58	.0283 (8.62)	−.0001 (−.115)	.000

(continued)

Table 7.2. *(continued)*

Regression	Years	N	Constant	ΔUR	R^2
			Dependent Variable: Δln(Y/K)		
(2.15)	1890–2004	114	.0020	−.0200	.654
			(0.61)	(−14.52)	
(2.16)	1948–2004	56	−.0052	−.0212	.579
			(−.2.00)	(−8.70)	
(2.17)	1890–1948	58	.0090	−.0199	.671
			(1.41)	(−10.68)	
			Dependent Variable: ΔlnY		
(2.18)	1890–2004	114	.0366	−.0203	.690
			(11.20)	(−15.81)	
(2.19)	1948–2004	56	.0361	−.02458	.777
			(18.38)	(−13.84)	
(2.20)	1890–1948	58	.0373	−.0198	.684
			(6.09)	(−11.01)	

Sources: Data for real output, capital services, and labor hours for the private nonfarm economy for 1890–1948 are from Kendrick 1961, table A-XXIII; for 1948–2004, they are from U.S. Department of Labor 2009.

Notes: The figures in parentheses are *t* statistics. *ΔlnY, ΔlnN, and ΔlnK* are defined as the change in the natural log of output, hours, and capital input respectively between year t and year t–1. They are thus a measure of the continuously compounded growth rate of these variables from one year to the next. *Δln(Y/N)* is the difference between the growth rate of output and the growth rate of hours; it is thus a measure of the growth rate of labor productivity. *Δln(K/N)* is the difference between the growth rate of capital and the growth rate of hours; it measures the growth of the capital-labor ratio. *Δln(Y/K)* is the difference between the growth rate of output and the growth rate of capital. It measures the growth rate of capital productivity (the inverse of the capital-output ratio). *ΔUR* is the change in the unemployment rate in percentage points.

Whereas both output and hours change systematically with a change in the unemployment rate, the coefficient in the capital growth rate equation is so small that the growth rate in capital appears to be essentially acyclical (regressions 2.12.–2.14). Why? There are substantial lead times in acquiring some types of producer durables (aircraft, for example), as well as virtually all categories of structures (factories, warehouses, houses, and any type of infrastructure). These long gestation periods, in which projects are completed in an uncertain future and where the strength of aggregate demand down the road can only be guessed at the time the projects are begun, is part of the explanation. It is true that optimism in expansions tends to boost planned investment, but central banks often attempt to lean against the wind by raising interest rates and dampening enthusiasm. Cyclical fluctuations in the cost of materials and availability of construction labor can also make recessions attractive times in which to initiate expensive projects. That said, there is a slight negative correlation between the unemployment rate and an index of gross private investment spending, but it is too weak to influence the overall acyclicality of the capital stock numbers, from which our estimates of service flow are drawn.[8]

Because capital is acyclical and hours are procyclical, labor hours grow more than capital input in expansions, so that the capital-labor ratio is countercyclical (regressions 2.5–2.8). That means that the capital-labor ratio tends to decline as one comes out of a recession. If changes in the capital-labor ratio were the only operative factor in an expansion, its decline would cause the marginal product of labor to fall as an output gap closed.[9] Operating by itself, this effect would mean that output per hour should fall as the unemployment rate falls. Since the results in regressions 2.1 through 2.4 in table 7.2 show the contrary, some other factor must provide a counterweight.

Labor hoarding is the most common explanation for why labor productivity rises with declines in unemployment (see, for example, Hall 1988, p. 929). As Christina Romer put it, "Firms tend to be slow to fire workers in bad years and slow to hire workers in good years" (1986, p. 6). Because of fixed costs associated with turnover and hiring, it is argued, firms retain labor during downturns and seek increased work intensity per man-hour during upturns. The rise in intensity of work is not initially reflected by increases in employment or hours, and the consequence is that output rises more rapidly than hours as unemployment declines.

The dynamics of employment, hours, and output are, however, more complex than the labor-hoarding story suggests. First, while firms may sometimes retain underemployed workers in bad times, they are ultimately not averse to putting them on temporary layoff or firing them. Second, during the postwar period the evidence is that firms typically completed the more intensive exploitation of already hired labor well before the end of an expansion. In the last one or two years before a peak, they tended to hire additional workers at a rapid rate. Robert J. Gordon (1979, 1993) suggested that this "end-of-expansion" effect slows growth in output per hour and attenuates the overall procyclicality of labor productivity. Since the growth of capital is acyclical, the end-of-expansion effect causes the capital-labor ratio to decline as one completes recovery from recession. The resulting downward pressure on the marginal product of labor helps explain why the procyclicality of output per hour is weaker than that of TFP. But we need to understand why it is procyclical at all.

The Solow growth-accounting framework (see the appendix) is often used to decompose the growth rate in output per hour $(y - n)$ into the sum of the TFP growth rate (α) plus capital's share (β) times the growth rate in the capital-labor ratio $(k - n)$:

$$y - n = \alpha + \beta (k - n)$$

The equation can also be used to explore the influences on the cyclicality of growth in output per hour by differentiating with respect to a change in the unemployment rate. Tables 7.1 and 7.2 establish empirically the signs of the relevant relationships. First, $d(y - n)/d(UR)$ is negative: when the unemployment rate declines, the rate of growth of output per hour rises. Second, $d\alpha/d(UR)$ is negative: when the unemployment rate declines, the TFP growth rate rises (table 7.1). Finally, $d(\beta (k - n))/ d(UR)$ is positive: when the unemployment rate declines, the growth rate of the capital-labor ratio declines.[10]

When the unemployment rate falls as the economy comes out of recession, the fall in the capital-labor ratio tends to reduce growth in output per hour while procyclical TFP advance increases it. During the period 1890–2004, for example, reductions in the unemployment rate by 1 percent were associated with increases of 0.5 percent in the growth rate of output per man-hour (regression 2.4). This is a smaller effect than the average TFP rise of 0.84 percent associated with a one percentage point decline in the unemployment rate in regression 1.9. Assuming a capital share (β) of roughly one-fourth, the decomposition suggests that this difference can largely be explained by a fall in the growth rate of the capital-labor ratio of 1.5 percent per year (regression 2.8) associated with a one percentage point decline in the unemployment rate. Thus for each percentage point decline in the unemployment rate the TFP growth rate rises by .84 percentage points per year, but the growth rate of output per hour increases by this amount less an offset of .33 (.25*1.5) due to declines in the growth of the capital-labor ratio. The strong procyclicality of TFP—and capital productivity, which in an arithmetical sense is driving this—keeps labor productivity growth mildly procyclical.

The argument advanced here is that labor productivity and TFP are both procyclical because of the inability of the private business sector to get rid of capital in a downturn. Unlike labor, capital cannot be fired. It must be held by someone who incurs real holding costs and real depreciation costs largely unaffected by utilization. This involuntary "hoarding" of capital is thus more important in my view than the voluntary hoarding of labor in explaining procyclicality in TFP and any tendency in that direction for labor productivity.

Not only are the costs of holding existing capital unavoidable, but for most asset categories, total user cost is largely independent of how intensively the stock is used. The capital costs of a warehouse, hotel, or airplane, for example, do not depend much on how full each is.[11] As a result, as unemployment declines, the average cost of capital declines because utilization-invariant depreciation charges and the largely fixed costs of holding capital are spread over a larger flow volume of output. The productivity dual of these cost reductions is that TFP increases. Meanwhile, the effect on output per hour in the aggregate is closer to a wash because the rise in TFP is partially offset by the effect on output per hour of the reduction in the capital-labor ratio as one approaches potential output from below.

A STATISTICAL ARTIFACT?

Is TFP procyclicality a statistical artifact due to the failure to make a cyclical adjustment to capital input? In all of these calculations capital services are proxied by estimates of its stock. Beginning with Solow (1957), a number of economists have attempted to make a utilization adjustment for capital when calculating TFP. Solow used the unemployment rate for labor as a proxy. The magnitude of such an adjustment may not make much difference if one is interested in long-term growth, but it can make a big difference if one is concerned with the cyclicality of productivity. In particular, if the cyclical adjustment to capital input is large enough, it will reduce or even eliminate the finding of procyclicality.

Matthew Shapiro (1993), for example, used unpublished data on hours per day and days per week of plant operation to adjust capital input in manufacturing. After the adjustment, the procyclicality of measured manufacturing TFP over the period 1978–1988 disappears. The result is not surprising since reducing capital input in recessions, when facilities are operated less intensively, will raise calculated TFP levels in troughs.[12] But such adjustments are too large. If any adjustment is warranted, it is in the aggregate small, and treating the service flow as proportional to capital stock will probably give a better first approximation of economically meaningful capital input than the adjusted series suggested by Solow or Shapiro.

It is important to understand why cyclical adjustments such as those made by Solow or Shapiro are too large. In a non-slave economy capital and labor are not on an equal footing in terms of the options available to business owners in the event of a downturn. Firms may choose, but are not required, to hoard labor. Insofar as capital is concerned, the private business sector is in the same position as were antebellum southern plantation owners with respect to their field hands. The private business sector must hold existing capital irrespective of the stage of the business cycle. It can, in principle, adjust the rate of accessioning, but for a variety of reasons, including lead times, the estimates in table 7.2 show that the growth rate of the capital stock is basically acyclical.

This acyclicality would be less relevant here if the aggregate cost of capital fluctuated proportionately with utilization. But it does not because the preponderance of the user cost of capital is unaffected by utilization. That proportion varies by asset category but is particularly high for structures, such as warehouses, factory buildings, commercial and retail office structures, hotels and apartment buildings, railway permanent way, pipelines, telephone landlines and microwave installations, and fiber optic cable.[13] It should be noted that structures account for a large majority of capital assets in the economy. Since 1925, the first year for which the BEA provides fixed-asset data, the value of structures has never fallen below 80 percent of the value of fixed assets (see Field 2010b).

The majority of the user cost of capital is unaffected by utilization for other asset classes as well, including producer durables in the transportation sector such as aircraft, railroad rolling stock, busses, and barges. Even for producer durables for which depreciation is a larger portion of the user cost, decisions about when the asset has been fully depreciated are largely unrelated to utilization for many assets. This is particularly true for items like computers, cellular telephones, and software, where technological obsolescence is far more important than how many hours of operation the equipment has experienced.

In the case of durables such as aircraft or vehicles, it is true that depreciation will rise with operating hours or miles. But the relevant output or scale variable is passenger or ton-miles, not simply miles. In an airline system, for example, much of the increase in passenger miles as one comes out of recession is accommodated by a rise in load factors, not necessarily an increase in aircraft operating hours. Consequently, the rise in output as one approaches potential can have little effect on aggregate capital costs. The situation is even more dramatic for structures such as hotels, apartments, warehouses, or retail and commercial office buildings. The user cost of a warehouse or hotel is largely the same whether it is full or half empty. We can attribute the reductions in unit costs as the output gap closes to short-run economies of scale, provided we recognize that we are indexing scale to output (cubic meters of goods stored or moved per year), not to a combined input measure.

Ignoring the possible effect of capital gains and losses, we can, following Jorgenson and Griliches (1967, p. 256), characterize the annual user cost of capital C as the capital stock K times the sum of the interest rate r and the rate of depreciation δ.

$$C = (r + δ)K$$

User costs are therefore the sum of rK, the pure cost of holding physical capital, and δK, depreciation costs. The first term is entirely unaffected by utilization. Much depreciation is also unrelated to utilization because it reflects technological obsolescence or exposure to the elements, rather than the direct effects of wear and tear related to utilization.[14]

Since the aggregate annual user cost of holding the existing stock of capital is largely unrelated to utilization and since the growth rates of capital inputs are basically acyclical in table 7.2, the economy experiences rising output per unit of capital and rising TFP as it comes out of a recession. As aggregate output goes up, unit costs go down, principally because the largely fixed costs of holding capital are spread over a larger flow volume of output. Procyclical TFP is not simply a statistical artifact produced by failure to make an adequate utilization adjustment to capital input. It is real and economically meaningful.

AGGREGATE SUPPLY AND THE CYCLICAL BEHAVIOR OF TFP

If in fact the growth rate of TFP has behaved procyclically in the United States, there are differences over how this is to be interpreted. Real business cycle theory provides an alternative account. RBC theorists view business cycles as "small deviations in trend" of real output (Kehoe and Prescott 2008, p. 11), and they view productivity shocks, defined as deviations from a detrended TFP series, as the impulses causing the cycles (Prescott 1986). Rather than demand shocks causing short-run TFP movements and procyclicality being something one could test empirically, TFP is by definition procyclical.

A unifying precept in RBC modeling is that sources of measured productivity change, in both the short and long run, lie outside of economics–in the realm of politics or in an independent dynamic of technological advance. The large drops in TFP associated with depressions must, therefore, according to this way of thinking, be the result of technological regress or, in the absence of plausible candidates, bad government supply-side policies.[15]

RBC research has merged into a broader umbrella known as dynamic stochastic general equilibrium (DSGE) analysis, which includes neo-Keynesian variants. Many DSGE models escape from the narrow strictures of the original RBC initiative. Some adopt features of macroeconomic research from over half a century ago, exploring the influence of monetary or fiscal policy shocks within the context of nonmarket clearing imperfections and returning to an empirical strategy relying on the estimation of structural equations rather than calibration (Woodford 2009).[16]

The main issues in macroeconomics, however, particularly after the almost catastrophic meltdown of the U.S. and world economy in 2007–2009, don't revolve around the respective merits of calibration as opposed to statistical estimation as a means of determining model parameters. They involve the degree to which one approaches the study of short-term fluctuations with a prior belief that they are almost entirely caused by technological progress or regress or, absent that, changes in government supply-side policies. This, along with a novel methodology, defined the original RBC tradition, one within which writers such as Harold Cole and Lee Ohanian, for example, continue to operate. This is true as well for the broader Great Depressions project run by Timothy Kehoe and Edward Prescott at the Federal Reserve Bank of Minneapolis.[17] For these writers, the assumption that short-run TFP fluctuations are exogenous is part of the maintained hypothesis.

In contrast, the view maintained here is that cycles are caused principally by aggregate demand fluctuations, with the output gap as proxied by the unemployment rate reflecting the strength of negative demand shocks.[18] TFP declined with recession and depression because as the output gap widened, output fell, but capital inputs and costs generally didn't.

These approaches involve different understandings of the primary causes of business cycles, differences reflected in the competing principles used by the NBER's Business Cycle Committee in its ex post dating of cycles. The committee places "substantial weight" on movements in real GDP but acknowledges that one can also look at the output gap in which case the unemployment rate would be a "critical guide."[19] An RBC perspective leads one to put most weight on the former criterion, and indeed some have suggested that cycles can be dated mechanically and a committee is not needed.

The various approaches pursued within the DSGE umbrella have had mixed success in dislodging prior beliefs. The fact that one's model can track the actual data reasonably well doesn't preclude the likelihood that other parameterizations will as well. As a consequence, historical narrative has taken on an important role in attempts to persuade those not already committed. A challenge for the RBC approach has been to provide plausible stories consistent with the periodic and often substantial declines in TFP associated with recessions. Variations in the arrival rate of innovations might account for alterations in a

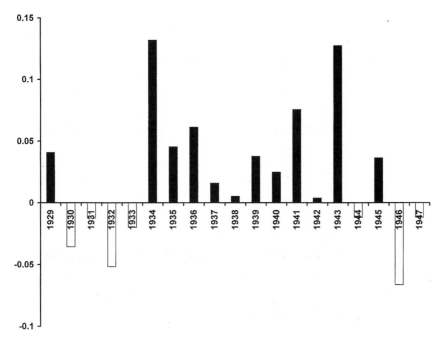

Figure 7.1: TFP Growth Rates, 1929–1947
Source: See source note for table 7.1.

positive rate of growth of TFP, but it is more difficult to see how such variations would periodically cause it to go negative.[20] Data for the years 1890 through 2004 indicate an average annual rate of PNE TFP growth of 1.46 percent with a standard deviation of over four percentage points. There are many years in which TFP didn't just grow more slowly but actually declined, often sharply (see figure 7.1).

For 1948 and earlier, average annual TFP growth was 1.7 percent per year, and the standard deviation was 5.4 percent. TFP declined in twenty-three of the fifty-eight years: 1893, 1894, 1896, 1898, 1902, 1904, 1907, 1908, 1910, 1912, 1914, 1917, 1920, 1922, 1925, 1927, 1930, 1931, 1932, 1933, 1944, 1946, and 1947. On the face of it, it seems unlikely that all of these declines can be attributed to negative technological shocks or, absent those, innovations in bad government supply-side policy, with the implied counterfactual that within a less interventionist state these declines would not have occurred.

The three most serious twentieth-century output gaps developed in 1929–1933, 1974–1975, and 1979–1982. In each of these episodes, TFP declined sharply. The most striking and problematic declines prior to the Second World

War took place in 1930, 1931, 1932, and 1933 in the context of the worst output shortfall in U.S. economic history. Twelve percentage points of the more than 30 percent drop in real output between 1929 and 1933 is attributable to downward movement in TFP.

Although there is much we do not understand about what happened between 1929 and 1933, we do have well-established narratives detailing the effects of collapsing banks, a shrinking money supply, the interactions of debt and deflation, and plummeting velocity due to declines in spending on consumer durables and investment goods (Friedman and Schwartz 1963; Temin 1976; Bernanke 1983; Field 1984; C. Romer 1990; Eichengreen 1992).[21] These accounts differ in terms of their relative emphasis on national and international factors or on monetary versus velocity shocks, but they reflect a shared view that the Great Depression was principally the consequence of aggregate demand shocks.

Lee Ohanian (2009) has suggested that a meeting with President Herbert Hoover in November 1929 persuaded industrialists to maintain high nominal (and thus in the context of deflation real) wages in manufacturing, and that this explains part of the shrinkage in that sector through 1931. Much of the decline in manufacturing took place in durables. There is considerable evidence that overextended, overindebted, and uncertain consumers cut back sharply on this category of their spending (Mishkin 1978; C. Romer 1990; Olney 1999). To this can be added the decline in orders attributable to the drop in the producer durables portion of investment expenditure.[22] These demand-side shocks were the primary cause of the drop in manufacturing up through the banking crisis of October 1931. At issue here are not increases in nominal wages from prior levels but rather their persistence; the actions or inactions of manufacturing wage setters should not therefore be considered an affirmative shock to the system. At best, a failure of nominal wages to decline faster can be seen as an institutional factor contributing to the non-neutrality of a negative aggregate demand shock.

Moreover, a more rapid decline in nominal wages in manufacturing—Ohanian's posited counterfactual—would have worsened the debt deflation problem. There is nothing in the modeling to capture the threat posed to output and employment by deflation in a world in which most borrowing and lending involved instruments with fixed nominal repayment obligations. There are many institutional features of an economy that can contribute to non-neutrality, and, as historical and contemporary experience indicates, the most significant of these may lie in financial as opposed to labor markets (see chapter 10).

The other shocks emphasized by Cole and Ohanian, such as the National Industrial Recovery Act or the National Labor Relations Act, all took place after

1933, during a period of very rapid TFP growth (see figure 7.1). They might possibly account for why TFP growth wasn't even faster after 1933, but they could not have played a role in the cumulative 12 percent decline in TFP under President Hoover.

There are well-known historical instances in which large declines in output can plausibly be linked to negative supply shocks. Russian/Soviet GDP, and presumably TFP, declined sharply after 1913 and did not reattain its prewar level until 1926. But a historical narrative can point to large negative shocks, including the disastrous participation of the Russians in the First World War, the Treaty of Brest-Litovsk (which reduced Russian territory), the March 1917 revolution, the October 1917 Bolshevik Revolution, the civil war between the Reds and the Whites, foreign intervention, and the political turmoil associated with the death of Lenin and the rise of Stalin.[23] We lack any comparable supply-side narrative for the productivity declines during the worst years of the Great Depression in the United States.

For the 1948–2004 period, average TFP growth was lower and less variable (figure 7.2). The mean growth rate was 1.4 percent with a standard deviation of

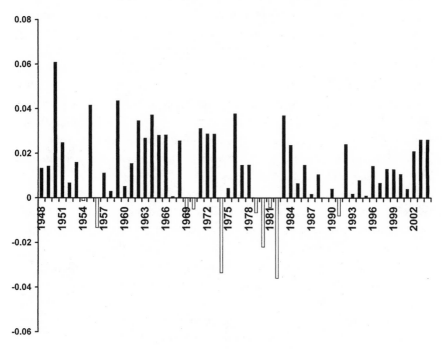

Figure 7.2: TFP Growth Rates, 1948–2004
Source: See source note for table 7.1.

1.8 percent. The reduced cyclical volatility of TFP during this period was arguably because cycles were weaker, at least between the 1982 recession and the 2007–2009 downturn. In the quarter century prior to 2008, the U.S. economy experienced only two relatively minor recessions. Even with a lower ratio of standard deviation to mean, however, the level of TFP, not just its rate of growth, declined in 1954, 1956, 1969, 1970, 1974, 1979, 1980, 1981, 1982, and 1991. All but one of these declines correspond to at least part of an NBER business cycle downturn.

For the second half of the twentieth century, the largest output gaps developed in 1974–1975 and 1979–1982. TFP declined in 1974 by 3.3 percent and by .7 percent in 1979, 2.2 percent in 1980, .4 percent in 1981, and 3.6 percent in 1982.[24] In contrast to the Depression years, we can identify a source of negative supply shocks, particularly between 1972 and 1985, that might have contributed to output retardation or decline during these episodes. Sharp increases in the price of oil resulting from decisions made by the Organization of Petroleum Exporting Countries (OPEC) produced deteriorations in the efficiency of the machine (foreign trade) whereby the United States transformed wheat, soybeans, plywood, and aircraft into oil. Prior to mid-century, when the United States was still the world's largest oil producer, oil shocks were of little relevance in understanding the aggregate economy. And, in part because of controls, there was relatively little change in the real price of a barrel of crude oil from the end of the Second World War through 1970. Between December 1973 and January 1974, however, that price more than doubled as a direct consequence of OPEC actions. And in April 1979, the price again began rising rapidly. Following a peak in April 1980, at which point the price had more than doubled from a year earlier, it then began a steady decline before bottoming out in 1985. Aside from a brief spike during the first Gulf War, the real price of oil then remained relatively steady until after 2005.

It is commonly argued that in contrast with 1980 or 1981–1982, the 1974–1975 recession was made in Vienna and Riyadh, not Washington. Still, the Federal Reserve, which had kept the federal funds rate under 5 percent as late as September 1972, allowed the rate to more than double over the next ten months. It remained above 10 percent between July 1973 and November 1973 and then again between April and October 1974. The discount rate, a less accurate measure of monetary tightness but a signal of Federal Reserve intentions, was raised in a series of steps from 4.75 percent in February 1971 to 7.5 percent in August 1973 to a peak of 8 percent in April 1974. The role that monetary stringency played in inducing this recession has been perhaps underplayed. It was clearly implicated in the decline in investment spending that marked this downturn as well as so many others.

The NBER identifies the six months between January and July 1980 and the sixteen months between July 1981 and November 1982 as recessions. The proportional increase in the real price of oil was actually larger in 1979–1980 than between December 1973 and January 1974. But its disruptive impact was less because, as a consequence of the first oil shock, the U.S. economy had begun moving toward a more energy-efficient capital stock. A review of the sequence of oil price, interest rate, and unemployment rate movements between 1979 and 1982 helps explain why, in spite of the coincidence of the second oil shock, the recessions of 1980 and 1981–1982 are almost universally attributed to changes in aggregate demand conditions resulting from the tightening of monetary policy to fight inflation (figure 7.3).

Even before the real price of oil began its year-long upward movement in April 1979, the federal funds rate began a climb into historically unprecedented territory. Following the seven-month period in 1974 when it had exceeded 10 percent, the rate declined to a trough in January 1977 at 4.71 percent, then began a gradual upward movement. In December 1978 it broke 10 percent again, hit 11.4 percent in September 1979, and then 13.8 percent in October, when Federal Reserve chairman Paul Volcker announced a new monetary regime in which the Fed would target monetary aggregates and allow the funds rate to seek its own level. By April 1980 the rate had increased to an eye-popping 17.6 percent.

Unemployment began to rise sharply, from 6.3 percent in March 1980 to a peak of 7.8 percent in July. Concerned that the unprecedented monetary stringency would take the real economy into a major recession, the Fed relented, slashing the funds rate by almost half to a low of 9 percent in July 1980. In reaction to monetary easing, the unemployment rate stopped rising and remained in a range of 7.2–7.6 percent through September 1981.

In the meantime, however, reconsidering the impact of its easing on inflationary expectations in both the bond and labor markets, the Fed again allowed the funds rate to move upward. It reached a new and unprecedented peak of 19.1 percent in January 1981. The rate dropped to 14 percent in April but then rose again to 19.1 percent in June.[25] In July 1981 the unemployment rate began a relentless year and a half rise to a peak of 10.8 percent in November and December 1982—as of this writing still the highest unemployment rate experienced since the Great Depression.

Economists such as Robert Lucas, a pioneer of rational expectations theory, predicted that we could have costless disinflation, forecasts that proved to be far

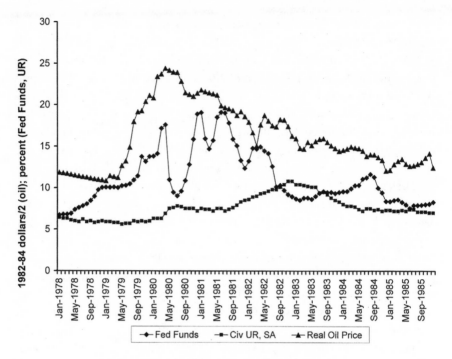

Figure 7.3: Real Oil Price, Federal Funds Rate, and
Civilian Unemployment Rate, 1978–1985

Sources: Nominal spot oil price for West Texas Intermediate: http://research
.stlouisfed.org/fred2/series/OILPRICE; accessed October 24, 2009. Seasonally adjusted consumer
price index for urban areas (CPI-U, SA), 1982–1984 = 100: http://www.bea.gov, accessed October
24, 2009. Federal funds rate: http://research.stlouisfed
.org/fred2/data/FEDFUNDS.txt; accessed October 24, 2009. Civilian unemployment rate,
seasonally adjusted: http://www.bls.gov; accessed October 24, 2009.
Notes: The monthly real oil price is calculated by deflating the nominal spot oil
price for West Texas Intermediate by the seasonally adjusted consumer price index for urban
areas, 1982–1984 = 100. To improve the readability of the table, the plotted data are one-half the
calculated values in 1982–1984 dollars. For the federal funds
rate and the unemployment rate, the vertical scale is percent. Unemployment
values refer to the seasonally adjusted civilian unemployment rate.

off the mark. The rise in the unemployment rate from 7.2 percent in July 1981
to its peak of 10.8 percent a year and a half later can't be attributed to negative
supply shocks because the real price of oil had been declining steadily since
April 1980. Yet we continue to observe declines in the level of TFP (not just its
rate of growth) characteristic of recession.

With the possible exception of 1974–1975, the most serious economic down-turns of the twentieth century, including and especially the 1929–1933 and 1979–1982 episodes, were precipitated by aggregate demand shocks and marked by negative TFP growth. The most plausible explanation for TFP declines during these periods is that demand shocks widened the output gap, and as the output gap widened, output fell, while capital input and costs largely didn't.

SHORT-RUN ECONOMIES OF SCALE
AND INCREASING RETURNS

This section extends discussion of the microeconomics underlying procyclicality and argues against interpreting the empirical results as reflecting a more general phenomenon of increasing returns to scale. If we assume that the capital stock is optimized for production levels at or close to potential output, unit costs will fall (productivity will rise) as the output gap closes. Falling unit costs are driven by reduced unit costs within firms, by production synergies or externalities at the industry level, and by externalities that may be reaped between sectors and thus at the level of the aggregate economy. These declines in costs should be understood as short-run economies of scale, not necessarily the same as increasing returns.

The costs faced by firms in the short run may not solely be a function of their own decisions about output; costs but can also be influenced by levels of output in other firms (Caballero and Lyons 1990). The findings of Ciccone and Hall (1996) on the impact of increasing density on output per hour are consistent with the importance of such external effects.[26] An additional consideration that may bias or push minimum short-run average cost (SRAC) toward or even above natural output is a tendency in industries that are potentially oligopolistic or monopolistic for firms to invest in or to retain excess productive capacity as a deterrent to entry.

These effects mean that the economy benefits from short-term economies of scale, where the index of scale is understood to be output.[27] The economies are short term because they are based on an installed capital base optimized for output close to the economy's current potential, and the economies will, in the aggregate, diminish in importance as the economy approaches potential.[28]

Learning by doing as a result of cumulated output could, over time and in a world in which some capital installations are very long-lived, have the effect not only of shifting average costs curves down but also of moving their minimum points to the right. To the degree that we interpret such learning as positive supply shocks, we can acknowledge that they play a role in conditioning the firm demography that results in short-run economies of scale in response to aggregate demand fluctuations. Thus while supply shocks play little direct or immediate role in determining the ups and downs of TFP in the short run, they do play a role in creating the environment of firm cost structures in which fluctuations in aggregate demand generate procyclicality.

Of course, a dynamic economy, even one with a steady rate of growth of aggregate demand, would be subject to relative demand shifts (often unanticipated at the time facilities were constructed) that would push some firms on to the upward sloping portions of their cost curves even when the economy was close to potential. What we would expect to find, then, at any moment of time, is a preponderance of individual firms experiencing short-run economies of scale in a range of output below potential. But this would not be true for all firms or sectors. This is the pattern found by Hart and Malley (1999) in their study of U.S. manufacturing.

When an economy drops below potential output, the fraction of firms pushed to the left of their minimum average cost point increases, which means costs rise and productivity falls. The corollary is that unit costs decline as output increases within a range of output below natural output. Some of the productivity gains/cost reductions are not necessarily experienced at the firm level but represent spillovers—externalities—at higher levels of aggregation, not just at the sectoral level—for example, within manufacturing—but between sectors, particularly manufacturing, on the one hand, and transportation/distribution on the other. These show up as procyclical TFP growth at the level of aggregates such as the private nonfarm economy.

When hours continue to rise above levels associated with natural output, the sources of these TFP gains dissipate, as the fraction of firms operating to the left of their minimum SRAC point declines. The inflationary acceleration that is by definition experienced above natural output is due to a combination of upward pressure on input prices, particularly labor, as the result of scarcity, and a short-run deterioration in productivity growth.

Natural output can thus be interpreted as representing a sweet spot in the struggle to achieve maximum levels of output and employment while controlling inflation, with increased cost pressures due to deterioration of productivity growth likely to be experienced above and also possibly below it. If there is some downward nominal wage rigidity, there will be an asymmetry in the sources and inflation correlates of these deteriorations because above natural output the productivity deterioration will be augmented by the upward pressure on wage and materials prices resulting from scarcities and tightness of markets in other inputs.

Potential or natural output is a barrier beyond which the main contributors to procyclical TFP have greatly diminished empirical importance. Factories, warehouses, hotels, and airplanes are close to full, and pools of available labor have been exhausted. Output can be sustained above this level in the short run only by tolerating continued accelerations in the inflation rate. That barrier is relaxed over the longer run by positive supply shocks, including growth in the size and quality of the labor force, growth in the capital stock through accumulation, and advance of knowledge.

Endogenous growth theorists, like RBC proponents, attribute both cyclical and secular changes in TFP to the same causes. But these causes differ for the two groups: for RBC theorists it is technology shocks; for endogenous growth theorists, economies of scale or increasing returns (P. Romer 1986). Short-run economies of scale are not, however, necessarily the same thing as increasing returns. And there is reason to question how much long-term trend growth rates are due to increasing returns. The historical (time series) evidence, particularly from the Depression years, suggests that that they are not, in the sense that if, starting from potential output, we were suddenly provided with an increase of x percent of all inputs, we would be able, using today's technological and organizational knowledge, to increase output by more than x percent (see, for example, Jones 1995, p. 702).[29]

Although the distinction between the effects of advance of knowledge and increasing returns is not sharp, the implication of this view is that if the economy had been larger at an earlier date, we could have enjoyed current productivity levels earlier. Proponents of the (exogenous) advance of knowledge view would dispute this: the recipes we have available today simply weren't known earlier. Discriminating econometrically between advance of knowledge and long-run increasing returns to scale is often difficult because inputs grow historically alongside of technical and organizational advance.

The Depression experience provides an unusual historical experiment whose outcome is consistent with the view that secular TFP growth, as opposed to its cyclical component, is mostly driven by technological and organizational innovations. Note that there are two subtly different definitions of increasing returns. The most general indexes scale to output and identifies increasing returns with a reduction in unit costs associated with higher output. A more frequently encountered definition, however, indexes scale to inputs and refers to a situation where all inputs increase by x percent but output goes up by more than x percent.

Consider the second definition. Should it make a difference if the growth rate of inputs is zero rather than some positive number? Formally, it should not. But in practice, it can matter in terms of our ability to isolate the effects of advance of knowledge. If combined inputs rose 5 percent over a decade and output rose 10 percent, it is hard to tell whether this was due to true advance of knowledge or to increasing returns to scale. If one attributes this entirely to scale, one is implicitly saying that if, ten years ago, given then existing knowledge levels, we had increased inputs by 5 percent, we could have had 10 percent more output. Without being able to run the experiment, however, we can't tell whether or not this would have been true.

If we index scale to inputs, a situation in which all inputs increased by zero percent (in other words, did not change) would not represent an increase in scale. Therefore, any output increase associated with a zero percent increase in combined inputs would have to reflect the advance of knowledge. The Depression experience coupled a very high rate of TFP advance with virtually no growth in private sector inputs (see chapter 2). Because the growth of inputs was so small, true increasing returns cannot be said to have had much to do with this.

Extending the findings of strong TFP proyclicality during the Depression years, this chapter identifies a striking empirical regularity in U.S. economic history, advances an original explanation for it, and contrasts this with other possible accounts. A stable and systematic relationship between the business cycle as manifested in the unemployment rate and total factor productivity endured in the United States for over a century. The gains in total factor productivity as the economy came out of recessions were real. They represented short-run economies of scale as hotels, warehouses, transportation systems, and other capital assets experienced higher load factors.

RBC models provide an alternate interpretation in which deviations in TFP from trend are cause, not consequence, of business cycles. The difficulty with this approach is that TFP did not just experience retardation in its growth rate during recessions. It declined. TFP declined between 1929 and 1933 and has declined during almost every economic downturn since 1890. Narrative history, at its best integrating the analysis of qualitative and quantitative data, plays an important role in efforts to persuade that a particular explanatory framework is preferable. RBC proponents have difficulty providing compelling narratives consistent with the observation that TFP often declines during recessions, rather than simply experiencing growth retardation.

An unresolved question at the time of this writing is whether the empirical regularities discussed in this chapter ceased to be relevant at about the time they were first identified. Gordon (2010) has suggested that the historically inverse relationship between the output gap and productivity may recently have disappeared. There is increasing evidence, however, that economic downturn in the first decade of the twenty-first century will in fact be associated with weak or negative TFP growth as was the case between 1929 and 1933, and more generally throughout the entire period from 1890 to 2004. Advance between 2007 and 2008 — the worst year of the Great Recession — was very slow: .1 percent per year. And although there appeared to be some recovery in 2009, TFP growth throughout the period 2005 through 2009 was just .42 percent per year, barely above rates during the dark ages (http://www.bls.gov, accessed October 29, 2010).

THE EQUIPMENT HYPOTHESIS

In several articles published in the 1990s, Brad DeLong and Larry Summers argued that investment in producer durables had a high propensity to generate externalities in using industries, resulting in a systematic and substantial divergence between its social and private return. They maintained, moreover, that this was not the case for structures investment. Together, these claims constitute the equipment hypothesis. This chapter explores the degree to which the growth narrative for the United States in the twentieth century developed in chapters 1–5 actually supports it.

Equipment—producer durables—has long enjoyed a privileged position in thinking about economic growth, in spite of the fact that throughout most of recorded economic history its importance has been dwarfed by structures both in flows of net investment and in shares of the capital stock (Field 1985). Machinery—with its roots in mechanical and electrical engineering, its intricacies, and its interplay of finely wrought moving or changing parts—may simply be more interesting than structures to the typical economist.

But there is a serious economic argument as to why we should pay special attention to machinery. Many scholars believe that machinery, unlike structures, is an important carrier of or stimulus for the type of technological change that shows up in measures of TFP growth. This means that machinery is particularly likely to generate uncompensated spillover effects in using sectors — uncompensated in the sense that the producers of the machinery do not reap the full benefit of the incremental contribution to value added for which their product is responsible.

Another way of stating this is that there is a divergence between the private and social return to investment in machinery, which in turn leads to the conclusion that tax policies favoring equipment (investment credits, accelerated depreciation schedules) are desirable. If growth is the objective, it follows that equipment investment should be subsidized, either directly or through tax policy, and organizations contributing to the formation of different types of capital should not face a level playing field. In particular, those producing equipment, and their customers, should be favored.

The equipment hypothesis has deep roots in classic works in economic history and theory that placed great emphasis on the productivity implications of mechanical innovations. It received renewed attention with the papers by DeLong and Summers (DeLong and Summers 1991, 1992; DeLong 1992). Although these papers are often understood to be concerned primarily with developing economies, the authors viewed their conclusions as applicable to developed countries as well as those aspiring to become so. It is appropriate, therefore, to reexamine what the economic history of the world's largest developed economy tells us about the hypothesis.

THE MODERN STATEMENT OF THE EQUIPMENT HYPOTHESIS

In 1991 DeLong and Summers reported the results of cross-country regressions on data from sixty-one countries over the years 1960–1985. These regressions showed a statistical relationship between the share of equipment investment in GDP and the rate of growth of output per hour. Based on these data, they maintained that "the social rate of return on equipment investment is 30 percent per year, or higher. Much of this return is not captured by private investors. . . . The gains from raising equipment investment through tax or other incentives dwarf losses from any nonneutralities that would result. A 20 percent wedge between the social return to equipment and other investments has implications for all policies affecting saving and capital allocations" (p. 485).

This passage contains two empirical claims and a policy implication: the social return to equipment investment is high, it is largely uncompensated, and it warrants subsidization. Elsewhere in the paper DeLong and Summers make clear both their view that this 30 percent social return applies to advanced as well as developing economies[1] and their belief in an asymmetry between the effects on growth of equipment investment as opposed to investment in structures.[2]

The DeLong and Summer analysis, as well as that of this chapter, is developed within the context of a version of the Solow growth model and the growth-accounting tradition with which it is associated (Abramovitz 1956; Solow 1957; see appendix). DeLong and Summers maintained that some types of investment—equipment investment—contributed to the growth of the residual in a way that investment in structures did not. They intended their work as a counter to the "investment pessimism" implied by the original Abramovitz and Solow analyses, which attributed a substantial portion of growth to factors other than inputs conventionally measured. If Abramovitz and Solow were right, then one couldn't necessarily expect much boost to economic growth from boosting saving rates and physical capital accumulation.

The DeLong and Summers analysis implied that while this pessimism might be warranted for the accumulation of structures, it was not so for equipment. Within the standard growth-accounting framework, focusing only on the rate of equipment accumulation (weighted by its share in national income) would understate the contribution to growth of such investment because it would not take into account the role of new producer durables in generating positive production externalities, which would also be responsible for part of the increase of the residual. This double-barreled impact on growth was not applicable, in contrast, to that portion of capital accumulation associated with investment in structures.

In 1992, following additional empirical work, DeLong and Summers reduced their estimate of the social rate of return to equipment investment from 30 to 20 percent but reaffirmed the earlier conclusions, in particular the applicability of these conclusions to advanced countries such as the United States.[3] Even if the estimated wedge between the total return to equipment investment and that of other investments had been 10 rather than 20 percentage points, this would still have been a very large wedge.[4] If the spillover effects were as large as DeLong and Summers suggested, they would have justified far more than a "modest" bias toward equipment investment. If we truly believed these numbers, the government should have been sending out checks—and they should have been large—to firms and perhaps even households installing more equipment. Obviously, there were companies, including many in Silicon Valley, who would have found this a very congenial policy.

DeLong and Summers wrote at the start of the 1990s, at the beginning of the longest economic expansion in U.S. economic history. During this boom, the United States experienced a continued decline in the relative price of equipment, led by the operation of Moore's Law in computers and semiconductors, and a surge in physical capital formation coinciding with a rising share of equipment in gross and net capital formation and in the capital stock. Finally, after 1995, this was matched by an acceleration in both labor and total factor productivity growth (see chapter 5). From the vantage point of 2000, with the NASDAQ approaching its all-time high, the coincidence of rising equipment investment and an increase in the growth rate of the residual appeared to confirm the validity of the equipment hypothesis, as well perhaps as justify stratospheric stock valuations. But the NASDAQ remained only briefly at its March 2000 peak of 5,048. Subsequently there was greater receptivity to a more nuanced view of the impact of IT investment.

WHAT CAN WE LEARN FROM THE ECONOMIC HISTORY OF THE UNITED STATES?

Many analyses of recent productivity advance, if they look back in history at all, do so no further than 1948, the start date for the productivity series maintained by the Bureau of Labor Statistics. This chapter, as do DeLong and Summers (1992) and DeLong (1992), takes a longer view, with particular focus in my case on the interwar period. It argues, based on a reconsideration of the patterns of economic growth, investment, and technical change in the United States between 1919 and 2007, that the social returns to equipment investment claimed as a general principle by DeLong and Summers are too high. And it argues that the claimed asymmetry between the ability of equipment as opposed to structures investment to generate TFP growth is not clearly established. The rise in equipment investment and its share of total investment in the United States represents a trend that began after the end of the Second World War. It coincided with a long-term downward trend in TFP growth, as the economy moved away from the very rapid advances registered for the private nonfarm economy during the interwar period.

Empirical analysis buttressed the DeLong and Summers argument. DeLong and Summers (1991) examined data for sixty-one countries over the period 1960–1985. DeLong and Summers (1992) extended the cross-country investigation backward to 1950 and forward to 1990. DeLong (1992) analyzed a pooled cross-section time series analysis of six advanced countries extending back to 1870.[5]

My purpose here is not to offer a comprehensive critical analysis of the post-1950 econometric work and its interpretation, which has already been provided by others. Auerbach et al. (1994) argued that the 1991 DeLong and Summers results were statistical artifacts resulting from the inclusion of outliers (particularly the diamond mining country of Botswana, which had the highest equipment to GDP ratio). More generally, the critics argued, it was inappropriate to include high-income, low-income, and newly industrializing economies in the same regression since not all of these countries had access to the same production possibilities as advanced nations; many indeed were in the process of moving toward that access. Most important, Auerbach et al. questioned the relevance of the conclusions for the United States—in particular that equipment warranted special tax treatment because the spillovers meant that it had a higher social than private return. DeLong (1992) can be seen in part as an anticipatory response to the type of objections raised by Auerbach et. al.

My interest is in what countries aspiring to be developed can learn from the economic history of the world's largest and most important economy and in how our history should inform tax policies in advanced countries. In 1992, De-Long and Summers wrote that "in assessing the determinants of growth, there is little alternative to examining natural experiments provided by the different policies, investment outcomes, and growth rates found in various different nations" (p. 158). This chapter explores the lessons to be learned from the natural experiments provided by the last century of U.S. economic history.

DeLong also undertook a longitudinal analysis. He examined advanced performance in six countries over eight time intervals: 1870–1885, 1885–1900, 1900–1913, 1913–1929, 1929–1938, 1938–1950, 1950–1965, and 1965–1980. He acknowledged a goal of examining growth rather than cyclical phenomena, remarking that "the 15 year frequency of observation, with some dates offset to better match the cycle and the eras of war and peace, was chosen to reveal long run shifts in growth rates instead of short run cyclical fluctuations" (1992, p. 309).

The standard in growth accounting is to restrict growth rate calculations as closely as possible to peak-to-peak measures. The choice of start and stop dates for the calculations is quite important because of the powerful cyclical influences on productivity advance (see chapter 7). At least with respect to the United States, and probably for other countries, DeLong's intervals deviate substantially from this standard. It is largely by accident that many of his beginning and end points are business cycle peaks.

The choice of 1938 as a benchmark date is particularly problematic. Unemployment in the United States in 1938 was 19.1 percent, the worst performance in the entire twentieth century save 1932–1935. Therefore 1929–1938 is a peak-to-trough calculation, and 1938–1950 is approximately a trough-to-peak calculation.[6] TFP growth in the private nonfarm economy between 1929 and 1938 was 1.55 percent per year, as compared with an unadjusted rate of 2.31 percent per year between 1929 and 1941 and a cyclically adjusted rate of 2.78 percent per year (see chapter 3). In 1938–1948 growth was 2.28 percent per year (even higher to 1950, the end year used by DeLong), as opposed to the 1.29 percent per year one gets when measuring from 1941 to 1948 (see Kendrick 1961, table A-XXIII; the cyclically adjusted estimate in table 3.6 is only .49 percent per year). The fact that Angus Maddison chose 1938 as a breakpoint in many of his calculations (see, for example, Maddison 1982), perhaps because of availability of data in a variety of countries, and the fact that it was the last year before war in Europe, cannot be grounds for ignoring these cyclical influences, particularly in analyses of the economic history of the United States.

SEVEN PEAK-TO-PEAK EPISODES, 1919–2007

I analyze seven peak-to-peacetime-peak periods in U.S. economic history for which relatively complete data can be obtained: 1919–1929, 1929–1941, 1941–1948, 1948–1973, 1973–1989, 1989–2000, and 2000–2007. Most of the beginning and end dates will be familiar to students of U.S. economic history, and the rationales for the others are discussed in preceding chapters.

For the purposes of this analysis, we can focus on the numbers themselves rather than the nuances in their interpretation since the equipment hypothesis claims, without a great deal of nuance, that high rates of equipment investment will be associated with high rates of TFP growth. While, for given rates of capital deepening, higher TFP growth rates will mean higher growth in output per hour, it makes more sense in evaluating the hypothesis to focus on TFP directly, rather than on the output per hour or output per capita measures that are the dependent variable in the DeLong and Summers studies. As figure 8.1 (based on data in the first column of table 8.1) makes visually apparent, for the last eighty years of the twentieth century, TFP growth rates in the United States trended generally downward.

To consider the applicability of the equipment hypothesis to U.S. economic experience, we now need to examine relative and absolute trends in equipment capital formation. For these purposes, I have constructed series for the real net stock of both equipment and structures from data in the BEA's Fixed Asset Tables. As noted, the BEA provides estimates in current dollars of components of private and government capital stocks from 1925 onward. It also provides chained index numbers for the components of the real net stock starting in 1925. From these index numbers, growth rates of the individual components can be calculated. And from the current dollar estimates of the net stocks, ratios of components can be constructed for any particular year. But since these ratios are based on current year prices, their use presents problems if comparisons are made over time. For example, if the real net stock of structures is growing

Table 8.1. TFP Growth (percent per year) and Investment in Equipment,
1919–2007

	1	2	3	4	5
Years	TFP Growth, PNE	Growth of Real Net Equipment Stock	Growth of Real Output (PNE)	Growth of Equipment/ Output Ratio	Average Ratio, Equipment/ Nonresidential Structures
1919–1929	2.02	2.72	3.97	−1.25	0.336
1929–1941	2.78	−0.27	2.80	−3.07	0.300
1941–1948	0.49	4.80	5.44	−0.64	0.354
1948–1873	1.88	4.79	4.11	0.68	0.554
1973–1989	0.36	3.95	3.16	0.79	0.804
1989–2000	0.79	4.57	3.56	1.01	0.952
2000–2007	1.38	3.40	2.53	0.87	1.241

Sources: Column 1: See tables 2.1, 3.6.
Column 2: BEA, http://www.bea.gov, Fixed Asset Table 2.2, line 3, accessed October 16, 2009.
Column 3: PNE, 1919–1929—Kendrick 1961, table A-XXIII; 1929–1948—Bureau of Economic Analysis, NIPA table 1.3.6, line 3; accessed August 22, 2009; 1948–2007—U.S. Department of Labor 2009.
Column 4: See sources for columns 2 and 3.
Column 5: Bureau of Economic Analysis, Fixed Asset Tables 2.1 and 2.2, lines 3 and 37; accessed October 16, 2009.

at a steady rate but real equipment investment (and the net stock) is growing more rapidly during a period in which the relative price of equipment is falling, one could in principle register no change in the current dollar ratio of the net stocks of the two components. To address this problem, I start with chained indexes and then obtain series for the real net equipment and structures stock as the product of this transformed index number and the 1925 current dollar start value.

Figure 8.2 plots the logged value of the real net stocks of the main components of private nonresidential fixed assets. A first conclusion is that there is no clear trend in the equipment stock between 1925 and 1944. The real net stock of equipment rose moderately between 1925 and 1929, declined sharply through 1935, and then rose moderately through 1944. The net equipment stock was lower in 1941 than it was in 1929.

Starting in 1945 and continuing through the end of the century, the equipment stock grew, sharply between 1945 and 1948 as GOPO equipment capi-

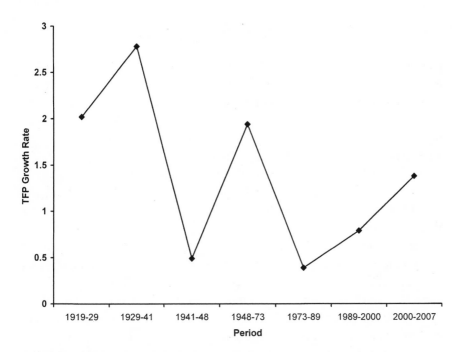

Figure 8.1: TFP Growth Rate, Private Nonfarm Economy, United States, 1919–2007
Source: Table 8.1, column 1.

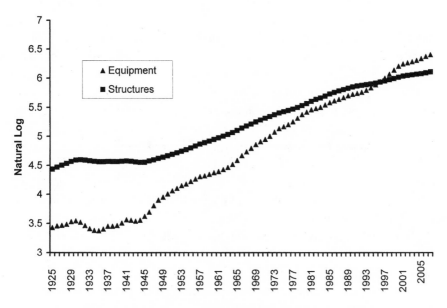

Figure 8.2: Natural Log of Real Net Nonresidential Equipment
and Structures Stocks, 1925–2007.
Source: BEA, Fixed Asset Tables 2.1 and 2.2, http://www.bea.gov.

tal was sold off to the private sector, more slowly through 1962, more rapidly through 1980, somewhat more slowly through 1992, somewhat more rapidly again through 2001, and then again at a slower pace through 2007. These accelerations and decelerations are minor, however, compared with the main feature of this series: the absence of a clear trend between 1925 and 1944, followed by a relatively steady rise at a rate of 4.47 percent per year thereafter. Figure 8.2 establishes that the accelerated growth of the equipment stock, both absolutely and as a share of private fixed capital, was not a new development in the 1990s but rather represented continuation of a trend that began as the Second World War came to an end.

The real net stock of structures series traces out a similar pattern, although postwar growth is less rapid: 2.49 percent per year between 1945 and 2007. The real net stock of private nonresidential structures rose between 1925 and 1931 and then trended downward slightly through 1945 before also embarking on its relatively steady growth path after the war, albeit one that was more moderate in comparison with that exhibited by equipment. These different growth rates are, of course, the cause of the rise in the ratio of equipment to structures in the postwar period.

Using the data included in table 8.1, we can explore the two propositions that lie at the core of the equipment hypothesis. The first is the claim of a positive relationship between the growth of the real net equipment stock and the growth of total factor productivity.[7] The second claim, related though distinct, involves an alleged asymmetry in the productivity effects of investment in structures as opposed to equipment. This will be discussed in the following section.

Figure 8.3 is a scatter plot of the data in columns 1 and 2 of table 8.1 (for the 1919–1929 period, I can calculate the annual rate of growth of the equipment stock only from 1925 onward). The highest rate of TFP growth (1929–1941) coincides with a slight downward trend in the real equipment stock. The period exhibiting the highest rate of growth of the real equipment stock, 1941–1948 — the consequence of a huge government-financed infusion of machine tools and other equipment[8] — shows substantially lower TFP growth than the interwar period in its entirety and much lower growth than the twelve-year period immediately preceding. What ultimately underlies the lack of a positive relationship in the scatter plot is the fact that the upward movement in real equipment investment, which began after the Second World War and is evident in figure 8.2, coincided with the downward drift in TFP growth for the private nonfarm economy evident in figure 8.1.

The absence of a positive relationship in figure 8.3 — and indeed the presence of a negative one — is confirmed econometrically. Since the units of analysis here are periods and since the data points reflect growth rates over these

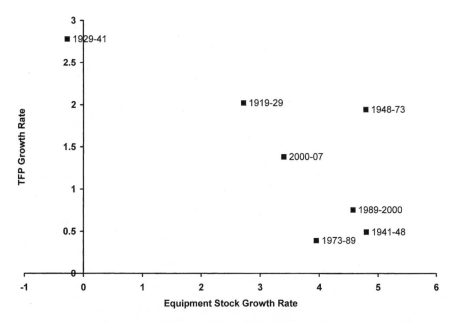

Figure 8.3: TFP Growth vs. Growth of Equipment Stock, United States,
Private Nonfarm Economy, 1919–2007
Source: Table 8.1, columns 1 and 2.

periods, there are only seven observations for each of these scatter plots. If one
regresses TFP growth on the growth of the real equipment stock, the coefficient
on growth of the equipment stock is negative and significantly different from
zero. When growth in the net equipment stock was fast, TFP growth tended to
be slow, and vice versa.

$$\Delta \ln \text{TFP} = \quad 2.68 \quad -.378 * \Delta \ln \text{EQUIPMENT}$$
$$R^2 = .58; n = 7 \ (4.90) \ (-2.64) \ (\text{t stats in parentheses})$$

Another interpretation of the equipment hypothesis would suggest the need
to correct for growth in the overall size of the economy. According to this interpretation, TFP growth should advance more rapidly when high levels of equipment investment cause the growth of the net stock to exceed the growth of
real output. Column 4 of table 8.2 shows the results of subtracting the growth
rate of PNE output (column 3) from the growth rate of the real net equipment
stock (column 2), which yields the growth rate of the equipment-output ratio.
Figure 8.4 plots the relationship of this measure to TFP growth.

The data reflect the fact that the interwar years, and particularly 1929–1941,
were years in which the capital-output ratio fell, and this was true for equipment capital as well as the fixed capital aggregate (another way of looking at it is

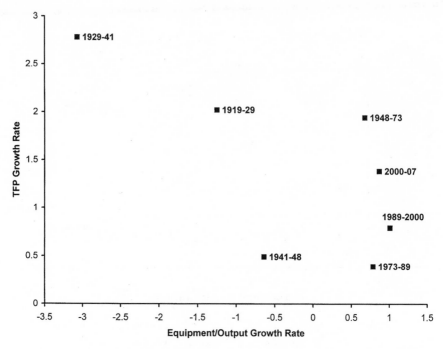

Figure 8.4: TFP Growth vs. Growth in Equipment/Output Ratio,
United States, Private Nonfarm Economy, 1919–2007
Source: Table 8.1, columns 1 and 4.

that these were years of sharp increases in capital productivity). The absence of
a positive relationship between this measure of equipment investment and TFP
growth continues to be apparent. Regressing the TFP growth rate on the rate of
growth of the equipment-output ratio yields a negative coefficient on the right-
hand variable, although, with six degrees of freedom, it is not quite statistically
significant.[9] As in the previous regression, however, the sign of the coefficient
on the equipment variable is negative, whereas if DeLong and Summers were
right, we might have expected it to be positive.

$$\Delta \ln \text{TFP} = \quad 1.29 \quad -.402 * \Delta \ln(\text{EQUIPMENT/OUTPUT})$$
$$R^2 = .47; n = 7 \ (4.72) \ (-2.09) \ (\text{t stats in parentheses})$$

THE ASYMMETRY CLAIM

The second key element of the equipment hypothesis is the asserted asymmetry between the respective abilities of growth in the equipment and the struc-

tures capital stock to stimulate TFP growth. Column 5 of table 8.1 reports, for each of the seven periods in question, the average ratio of equipment to structures over the period. These are calculated using the series on real net stocks of equipment and structures whose generation is described above. Figure 8.5 is a scatter plot of these data. Again, there is an absence of a positive relationship between the average equipment-structures ratio and TFP growth in the private nonfarm economy:

$$\Delta lnTFP = \quad 2.06 \quad -.104 * EQ/STRUCTAVG.$$
$$R^2 = .18; n = 7 \ (2.80) \ (-1.03) \ (t \text{ stats in parentheses})$$

The 2000–2007 datapoint weakens what is otherwise a fairly robust negative relationship. Still, the lowest ratio of equipment to structures occurs during the period of highest TFP growth (1929–1941).

As indicated above, DeLong and Summers "see no reason to expect that investments in structures should carry with them the same external effects as

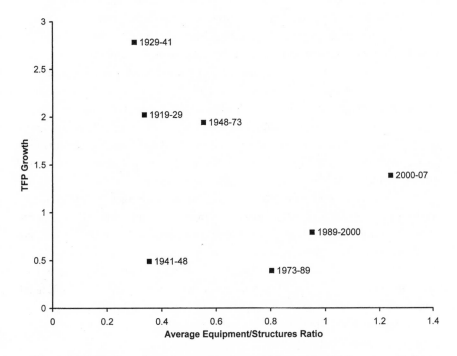

Figure 8.5: TFP Growth vs. Average Equipment/Nonresidential Structures Ratio,
United States, Private Nonfarm Economy, 1919–2007
Source: Table 8.1, columns 1 and 5.

plausibly attach to investments in equipment" (1991, p. 480). But they don't provide evidence in support of this assertion—it is assumed to be so obvious as not to require any. Innovations in building design can, however, have significant impacts on within-plant productivity, perhaps most notably in the United States during the 1920s in manufacturing.

During that period the net stock of private nonresidential structures was more than three times that of private equipment, and the revolution in factory design associated with the extraordinary TFP gains within manufacturing depended upon investments in new single-story factory structures. Although some of the contemporaneous TFP gains could be indirectly linked to prior advances in electric-power-generating machinery, much was the result of learning by doing and discovery of improved factory layout once the straightjacket of mechanical internal distribution of power was removed and the new plants constructed (chapter 2).

And for the economy as a whole, large-scale investment in government structures such as streets and highways can stimulate TFP growth in using sectors, as was likely true during the Depression years, and as Aschauer (1989) has argued for the postwar period. It is interesting to contrast the effects of the boom in street and highway and other infrastructure construction during the 1930s with the rather different government-financed capital formation boom that took place during the 1940s. The latter effort poured more than $10 billion of taxpayer money into GOPO plants. Almost all of this infusion was in manufacturing, and a large part of it went for equipment, particularly machine tools, in such strategic sectors as aluminum, synthetic rubber, aircraft engines, and aviation fuel refining (Gordon 1969).[10] The immediate consequence was that TFP growth in manufacturing became negative, retarding TFP advance for the private nonfarm economy as a whole.[11]

To be fair to the equipment hypothesis, one might object that it implicitly requires that the machinery be allocated by private markets, rather than government central planners. Higgs (1992) has argued that output growth in the war years was overstated,[12] and he would probably attribute the poor TFP showing in manufacturing between 1941 and 1948 to the fact that it was *public* equipment investment rather than that it was public *equipment* investment. The beneficial impact of street and highway construction in the 1930s should, however, caution us against dismissing on a priori grounds the potential growth-enhancing benefits of infrastructure spending.

The generality of the equipment hypothesis, repeatedly reaffirmed by DeLong and Summers, is therefore in doubt. Taking a broad overview of nine decades of twentieth- and twenty-first-century U.S. economic growth, we see absence of evidence of a systematic positive relationship between rates of equipment investment and TFP growth. The end-of-century surge in equipment investment, much of it related to information technology, did coincide with an accelerated growth in output per hour, above and beyond what one would have expected from the capital deepening alone (chapter 5). In a longer historical view, however, the IT productivity boom is less striking. The acceleration, though marked, produced a growth rate of the residual dwarfed by what took place during the Depression years, when there was a substantial increase in public infrastructure but declines in the net stocks of equipment, or during the 1920s, when the ratio of structures to equipment was several times what it is today (see figure 8.2).

To the degree that the mechanism identified in the equipment hypothesis is operative, its importance must vary across particular sectors and particular epochs or else be swamped by the effect of other influences. The problem for policymakers in favoring one type of investment over another is that it is quite difficult to determine ex ante, at any specific historical moment, which type (private structures, public infrastructure, private equipment) will have the biggest long-term impact on TFP. The economic history of the United States suggests that that there is nothing inherent in the category of equipment investment warranting a presumptive bias in its favor. To assume or conclude otherwise and to base policy on this presumption, either in developing countries or in those aspiring to become so, entails the same type of risks as adopting industrial policies favoring particular sectors.

9

General-Purpose Technologies

In the last decade one of the more successful memes in economic history has been the concept of a general-purpose technology. Timothy Bresnahan and Manuel Trajtenberg published the seminal article in 1995, and the list of publications building upon, amplifying, and drawing from the concept includes Helpman (1998), Rosenberg (1998), Caselli (1999), Crafts (2004), Crafts and Mills (2004), David and Wright (2003), Gordon (2004), Goldfarb (2005), Lipsey, Carlaw, and Bekar (2005), Jovanovic and Rousseau (2005), and Rousseau (2006, 2008).

Bresnahan and Trajtenberg built on earlier work by David (1990, 1991), and David and Wright's 2003 paper, "General Purpose Technologies and Surges in Productivity: Historical Reflections on the Future of the ICT Revolution," is widely cited. In a review of Helpman (1998), Wright defined GPTs as "deep new ideas or techniques that have the potential for important impacts on many sectors of the economy" (2000, p. 161). Although the argument of their 2003 paper—and its title—reflected an implied acceptance of the usefulness of what has become a widely used concept, David and Wright also observed the following after noting the broad range of technical and organizational advances for which the GPT appellation has been proposed: "One has only to consider the length of such proposed lists of GPTs to begin to worry that the concept may be getting out of hand. History may not have been long enough to contain this many separate and distinct revolutionary changes" (2003, p. 145).

My intent in this chapter is to ask whether, when the concept of a GPT and the ways it has been used are critically examined, we may conclude that its value for research in economic history—and economics more generally—is limited. This is not to take issue with the historical analysis of David and Wright or those of others, such as Rosenberg (1998) or Crafts (2004), which have influenced our thinking about the impact of technical change and the sources of TFP growth. It is rather to question the extent to which these, and other analyses within this tradition, depend in any essential way on the concept of a general-purpose technology.

WHAT GPTS PROMISE

The appeal of the GPT research program has been twofold. First, it captures the reality that technological change is unbalanced — occurring at widely different speeds in different industries or sectors. Over the last century and a half, TFP in the United States has grown at an average of roughly 1.5 percent per year. Across different shorter macrohistorical epochs, however, this rate has differed substantially, with the highest rates registered during the interwar period. Even more important, within any given epoch, TFP growth has been the result of highly differential rates of advance among different sectors of the economy. Arnold Harberger (1998) emphasized this when he argued that economic growth was typically driven by "mushrooms," which grow very rapidly here and there in a pattern that is tough to predict, as opposed to by "yeast," which causes different parts of a loaf of bread to rise at approximately the same rate.

David and Wright (1999) pointed out that growth within manufacturing in the 1920s was yeast- rather than mushroom-like, the result of a broadly diffused replacement of mechanical means for distributing power within the factory by wires and electric motors. Their empirical claim about manufacturing is supported by data at the two-digit level. But whereas growth looks yeast-like within manufacturing, if we step back and consider the economy as a whole, manufacturing sticks out in the 1920s like a giant mushroom on an otherwise placid and slow-growing lawn. Almost all of the roughly 2 percent per year growth in TFP in the private nonfarm economy between 1919 and 1929 was due to the extraordinary 5 percent per year advance within manufacturing (Kendrick 1961; see also chapter 2).

Viewed from this broader perspective, then, the experience of the 1920s can be seen as consistent with rather than at variance with Harberger's characterization of economic growth. Throughout history sectors (and often industries) experiencing high TFP growth and revolutionary cost reductions have coexisted with sectors experiencing evolutionary change or in some cases downright stagnation.

But GPTs and the criteria for identifying them have promised to do more than just remind us of the unbalanced nature of economic advance. They have aspired to offer a means of identifying and characterizing the most important "engines of growth" that underlie the dynamic sectors or industries within an economy. From the standpoint of technological history, therefore, the idea of a GPT, a technology leading to revolutionary change, also resonates with the obvious reality that some innovations are more important and have more long-lasting significance than others. Economic historians and historians of technology develop narratives that identify and distinguish those that are consequential from those that are not.[1] Does the concept of a GPT help in doing this? To answer, we need to apply GPT criteria consistently and study the technologies thus identified. We can then judge whether these screens deliver what they promise.

GPT CRITERIA

Much thought has gone into specifying GPT characteristics. Bresnahan and Trajtenberg (1995) and Lipsey, Carlaw, and Bekar (2005) identified several defining features of a GPT: (1) that it have potential for *rapid improvement* and elaboration; (2) that it have *broad applicability* across many sectors of the economy; and (3) that it *foster spillovers* by stimulating improvements in other products and processes, and in turn be stimulated by these complementary advances. Jovanovic and Rousseau (2005) used different words but said essentially the same thing: a GPT should be (1) *pervasive* — spreading to most sectors, (2) *improving over time*, and (3) *able to spawn new innovations*. They also stated that GPTs "transform both household life and the ways in which firms conduct business" (2005, pp. 1184–1185), a criterion enunciated as well by Gordon (2004). It's not entirely clear whether this is a clarification of the pervasiveness criterion or is intended as a separate test.

Where did these criteria come from? They have been distilled from a few canonical histories, most especially from information technology broadly defined. The criteria have subsequently been used to identify other technologies that might have similar features. The GPT concept, then, in the hands of theorists, took on a life of its own. Theoretically minded economists embraced the GPT because it appeared to be a powerful abstraction with interesting implications, for example, about the time pattern of productivity improvement associated with revolutionary technological change. In particular, because of the physical capital and complementary training and R and D requirements often associated with GPTs, one can argue that they might retard the rate of TFP growth before they advance it by diverting resources on the input side prior to the reaping of a bonus on the output side. Several of the more widely cited articles in the GPT tradition study relationships between upstream and downstream innovators and identify externalities in the R and D process that might produce coordination problems or deficient or excessive levels of innovative effort. Based simply on a page count or a study of its reference list, the seminal Bresnahan and Trajtenberg contribution was in fact more theoretical than historical in its focus.

Nevertheless, the literature has always anchored itself and seen itself as building upon research in economic history, and the prospects for cross-fertilization between history and theory partly explain the success of the meme. The usefulness of that cross-fertilization and the empirical validity of the theoretical implications deduced depend, however, on the soundness of the historical foundations upon which the basic category rests.

PROBLEMS WITH THE GPT CONCEPT

There are several difficulties with the derivation of the GPT concept from, and its application to, economic history. The first, noted by David and Wright (2003), is the expanding list of innovations to which various authors have attached this designation. If the criteria are to identify "engines of growth" that have given their character to entire epochs, there must be relatively few of them. In addressing why we may have ended up with too many and, more generally, in evaluating the usefulness of the concept for research in economic history, we must ask difficult questions. In the development of lists of GPTs, has a stable set of criteria been consistently applied? Have authors been clear about precisely what technologies they were discussing? Is it true that all of these were similarly revolutionary? And, perhaps most important as an evaluative test, has the filter represented by the GPT criteria done a good job in separating innovations that were consequential from those that were not? That is, can we point to innovations that economic historians and historians of technology agree are important in terms of their contributions to what Harberger called real cost reductions that nevertheless do not appear on GPT lists because they do not satisfy one or more of the GPT criteria? If that is so and if the main purpose of the GPT is to help us identify revolutionary innovations, have these criteria been of real value?

TOO MANY GPTS?

A number of economic historians have embraced the GPT as a useful way of framing studies of individual innovations, sectors, or industries (see, for example, David and Wright 2003 or Crafts 2004). But the most systematic effort to motivate the concept through examination of the historical record is to be found in Lipsey, Carlaw, and Bekar (2005), who also worked hard to try and refine the criteria for a GPT.

Chapters 5 and 6 of the Lipsey, Carlaw, and Bekar book survey the economic history of the world from the Neolithic revolution to the present, with lots of concrete discussion of specific advances, both technological and organizational. One of the central themes in the history of technology focuses on the sources and uses of power (Buchanan 1991), and this is reflected in the lists compiled by these authors. Prime movers, such as waterwheels, windmills, steam (external combustion) engines, and the internal combustion engine figure prominently, as do electric power systems, which enable prime movers to produce energy that can be moved across substantial distances, as well as applications of prime movers to transportation such as railroads and motor vehicles. More recently (and most commonly), of course, the GPT of note has been information technology or the Internet (IT or ICT).[2] Organizational innovations such as the factory system are also mentioned.

Lipsey, Carlaw, and Bekar identified roughly twenty innovations that they divided into six main categories:

Agricultural/biological engineering (domestication of plants and animals)
Mechanical/chemical engineering (bronze and iron)
Power generators (waterwheel, steam engine, dynamo, internal combustion engine)
Transport equipment (wheel, three-masted sailing ship, iron steamship, railways)
Data storage and communication (writing, printing, computers, Internet)
Organizational technologies (factory system, mass production, lean manufacturing)

Other authors, though less liberal with the designation, called attention to many of the same technologies. In his review of Helpman, Wright (2000) placed a big emphasis on prime movers (waterwheel, steam engine, electricity, and the internal combustion engine); transport equipment that used them (railways, motor vehicles); and data storage and communication (writing, printing, and IT). He also mentioned, in the materials category, bronze. Gordon (2004) mentioned steam, electricity, and the internal combustion engine, as well as the Internet. Rousseau (2008) limited attention to power generators (steam engine, "electricity," internal combustion engine) and data storage and communication (writing, printing, and IT). Rosenberg (1998) saw the principles underlying chemical engineering as a GPT; using similar logic and based on some of his earlier work, he might have argued that machine tools were also a GPT.

Bresnahan and Trajtenberg (1995) mentioned five technologies. In the category of agricultural or biological engineering, they referenced Griliches's work on hybrid corn (1958). Among power generators, they tagged the steam engine as well as the dynamo, although here the key innovation was alternatively described as electricity. They also mentioned the factory system. Finally, in IT, the principal focus of their study, they focused on semiconductors rather than the computer or the Internet per se.

Table 9.1 summarizes GPTs identified in these and other articles. We can draw three conclusions. First, a rather broad range of technologies have indeed been identified as GPTs. Second, three arenas—steam, electric power, and IT—appear on almost all lists. Third, even within the areas of greatest agreement, there are differences in exactly what is identified as the GPT. This is particularly so within the categories of electric power and IT. Sometimes "electricity" is simply referred to generically (Wright 2000; Gordon 2004; Crafts 2004; Jovanovic and Rousseau 2005; Rousseau 2008). Sometimes the reference is to the dynamo (a direct current generator, also sometimes called a magneto; Caselli 1999; Lipsey, Carlaw, and Bekar 2005) or to the electric motor (Bresnahan and Trajtenberg 1995). And sometimes what is described is the use of all three in factory electrification (David and Wright 2003).

In fact the electrification of the factory, often described as replacing steam power, depended critically on advancements in the steam engine, in particular the steam turbine. The turbine used steam to produce direct rotary motion, which in turn, using a magneto or dynamo mounted inline, produced electricity. It is true that the engines in Edison's Pearl Street station in 1882 used steam engines with pistons generating reciprocating motion that was then converted to rotary. Charles Parsons did not perfect the dynamo until two years later. But the latter, which directly produced steady, high-speed rotary motion without the efficiency losses associated with the reciprocating-to-rotary conversion, was particularly well suited to making electricity, where loads are stable and lack the variability common in other applications. The steam turbine was critical for the subsequent reductions in cost per kilowatt hour, which helped make the electrification of the factory economically feasible.

The GPT literature sometimes presumes that the technologies it identifies as such are as distinctly revolutionary as, for example, was the cotton gin. In part because the alleged impact of the GPT unfolds over what may be long periods of time, exactly what we are talking about can be elusive, as the above discussion reveals. But if an "engine of growth" is truly to be understood as informing the character of an entire epoch, we need to know specifically what it is.

A similar lack of clarity bedevils treatments of IT or ICT. It is sometimes referred to generically. Sometimes there are more specific references to

Table 9.1. General-Purpose Technologies

	Lipsey, Carlaw, Bekar 2005	Bresnahan & Trajtenberg 1995	Rosenberg 1998	Caselli 1999	Wright 2000	Basu et al 2003	Gordon 2004	Crafts 2004	Jovanovic and Rousseau 2005	Rousseau 2008	Wikipedia (2008)	TOTALS
Agriculture/biological engineering												
Domestication of plants	1											1
Hybrid corn		1										1
Domestication of animals	1											1
Materials/chemical engineering												
Bronze	1				1							2
Iron	1											1
Chemical engineering			1									1
Prime movers: mechanical/electrical engineering												
Waterwheel	1				1							2
Steam or steam engine	1	1		1	1		1	1	1	1	1	9

Technology	Count
Electricity	
Electric motor	6
Dynamo	1
Electronics	2
Internal combustion engine	5
Transport equipment/mechanical engineering	
Wheel	1
Three-masted sailing ship	1
Iron steamship	1
Railways or railroad	4
Motor vehicles or automobile	2
Data storage and communication	
Writing	2
Printing	2
IT or ICT	6
Semiconductors	1
Computer	2
Internet	3
Organizational technologies	
Factory system	3
Mass production	1
Lean manufacturing	1

Note: Lipsey, Carlaw, and Bekar (2005) refer separately to the computer and the Internet. Bresnahan and Trajtenberg (1995) refer to the electric motor, electricity, and hybrid corn on pages 83, 84, and 86 respectively. Caselli (1999, p. 78) refers to technological revolutions, not GPTs, but it is clear his paper is motivated by the GPT literature. Caselli notes that whereas capital-skill complementarity probably characterized steam, the dynamo, and IT, the reverse was true for the factory system.

semiconductors (Bresnahan and Trajtenberg 1995), computers (David 1990, 1991), or the Internet (Gordon 2004). Even these identifications, if one probes, can be problematic. When we speak of the "Internet," for example, what is paramount? Is it the hardware and software protocols such as TC/ICP, the http protocol, html markup language? Or is it the switches and routers or the innovations that permitted multiplexing hundreds of bitstreams over a single fiber optic cable? Economic history or the history of technology requires the opposite of vagueness on this score.

HAVE GPT CRITERIA BEEN CONSISTENTLY APPLIED?

If pervasiveness simply means that "a lot" of a technology is used, then most of the technologies on table 9.1 appear to qualify. But if broad applicability means that the technology is used across many sectors, the situation becomes murkier. It's hard to see, for example, how a sailing ship with three masts measures up, unless we mean simply that vessels using this design carried many types of raw materials and manufactured goods. If we adopt such a broad interpretation, however, and say that Technology A is used by Sector B if Sector B purchases a good or service whose production is enabled by Technology A (in this case Technology A is the sailing ship producing transport services), we will quickly get to a point where it is very difficult to distinguish between single-use and general-purpose technology, given the nature of input-output matrices. On the other hand, if we adopt the narrower approach, insisting on direct use of the technology in the sector or industry, the measure of pervasiveness is to a certain extent hostage to industrial organization, particularly the degree of vertical integration.

These ambiguities may help explain why only some authors refer to railways as a GPT, even though clearly "a lot" of them were used, they carried many different types of freight, and they led to spillovers, at least in the United States, by enabling, for example, Chandler's modern business enterprise (Field 1987). The use of steam power by railways helps make the case that the steam engine was pervasive (used in many sectors). But should railways themselves be considered as pervasive in the same way and therefore a GPT? The answer is no if we adopt the narrower definition of use, as I think we should.

Even with the "big three" (steam, electricity, IT) one needs to ask how consistently the criteria have been applied, particularly if we include the Jovanovic and Rousseau requirement (also suggested by Gordon) that the technology "transform both household life and the ways in which firms conduct business". Whereas "electricity" (or the electric motor) measures up, as does IT (semiconductors, computers, the Internet), it is questionable whether steam, or at least the steam engine, "transformed household life." It is true that steam can be used to facilitate central heating, for ironing clothes, and for certain types of cooking, but households simply did not make direct use of steam *engines* in any significant way, with the exception of the limited experience in the first part of the twentieth century with steam-powered automobiles or the eighteenth-century use of Savery engines in Britain to raise water for use in indoor plumbing.

DO THE GPT CRITERIA SEPARATE THE
CONSEQUENTIAL FROM THE INCONSEQUENTIAL?

Do all consequential innovations satisfy the GPT criteria? And does it matter if they do not? Imagine an innovation with limited impact on a larger number of sectors—perhaps the felt-tipped pen. It is clearly general purpose in the sense that it is pervasive—used in many different sectors of the economy. It has improved somewhat over time but probably has not generated many spillovers. Should we necessarily pay more attention to it than an innovation that had a large and revolutionary direct impact on only one or a few sectors?

Although the GPT criteria are several, the category label does emphasize pervasiveness—which implies use in many different sectors. That's what "general purpose" means. Arguably, improvement over time or the generation of spillovers are the more important features of technologies identified as GPTs, but my point here is that those features are not limited to general-purpose technologies but are often aspects of single-purpose technologies used in only one sector. Such innovations can be as consequential as, or perhaps even more consequential than, those identified using the GPT filter.

Table 9.2 presents a list of innovations that have typically been absent from lists of GPTs. Most will be well known to those who have taught or taken a course on the industrial revolution or European or U.S. economic history. To leaven the cake, I've added a few developments from the twentieth century. Enthusiasts might argue that a few of these (perhaps modern business enterprise) should be considered GPTs. But for most, it is hard to make the case because the technologies are single as opposed to general purpose. Because they are single purpose, there is little ambiguity about how they might usefully be employed. They offered relatively complete, immediately usable solutions to a readily apparent problem. It is hard to imagine that it might take two or three decades for entrepreneurs to see how they could be used to most productive effect, or that it would take expensive R and D efforts to figure this out, or that they would require large complementary investments in training before their

Table 9.2. Single- or Limited-Purpose Technologies

Agricultural/husbandry innovations
        3-field crop rotation
Textile innovations
        Cotton gin
        Flying shuttle
        Spinning jenny
        Water frame
        Mule
        Power loom
Iron- and steelmaking innovations
        Coke smelting
        Puddling
        Hot blast
        Gilchrist Thomas process
        Bessemer process
        Siemens-Martin open hearth process
        Basic oxygen furnace
Transport innovations
        Horse collar
        Horse shoe
        Pneumatic tire
        Jet engine
Miscellaneous
        Haber-Bosch process
        Gunpowder/explosives
        Elevator
        Containerization
Information communication, storage and retrieval
        Reading glasses
        Vertical file cabinet
        Carbon paper
        Xerox machine
        Telegraph
        Telephone
        Radio
        Television
Organizational technologies
        Modern business enterprise
        Interchangeable parts

benefits could be realized. And in most cases it is quite implausible that the appearance of these blueprints would have caused a significant initial productivity slowdown. Consider, for example, the innovations typically associated with the industrial revolution. Standard texts emphasize the steam engine, which is on most lists of GPTs.

The other oft-emphasized developments include complexes of innovations in textiles, on the one hand, and iron making on the other. Take textile inventions such as the cotton gin, the spinning jenny, the water frame, Crompton's mule, or the power loom. These innovations were improvable, and there was mutual interaction between the technical advances in downstream and upstream processes.

But they were not general purpose. They remained single or limited purpose. The cotton gin was used to clean short staple cotton. That's it. It was of no use in the preparation of wool, flax, silk, or even long staple cotton fibers. Was it important and consequential? Undoubtedly, since by dramatically reducing the cost of removing seeds, it shifted out the supply schedule for cleaned cotton, resulting in a major positive supply shock to the cotton textile industry. Many have argued that it gave a new lease to the peculiar institution—slavery—and thus might be held indirectly responsible for the American Civil War. But there is no way we can call the cotton gin a GPT. And the same is true for the spinning jenny, water frame, mule, or many of the innovations underlying the advance of the British iron industry, such as Darby's coke smelting, Cort's puddling, or Nielsen's hot blast, or the steel innovations of the second half of the nineteenth century (Bessemer converter, Gilchrist-Thomas process, or Siemens-Martin open hearth furnace).

The Bessemer and Siemens-Martin processes, for example, were industry- (and indeed material-) specific and would clearly not pass muster as GPTs. People grasped immediately how these innovations could simplify and cheapen a product that had been known for centuries. What was not so immediately obvious were the potential uses for cheap steel. Does that make steel a GPT? It took Andrew Carnegie and others time to persuade users they should make skyscrapers, plate ships, and replace iron rails with it. Cheap steel in turn encouraged complementary innovations such as (in the case of taller buildings) elevators. If bronze was a GPT, why not cheap steel? Again, my intent here is not to argue for an expansion of the list of GPTs but to determine how valuable it is as a filter.

If one follows the impact of product and process innovations far enough through the input-output table, one will eventually find products or technological complexes used as inputs in many other sectors, improving over time and with the potential to generate spillover effects in using sectors. These processes, products, or complexes, are the consequence of many separate breakthroughs as well as learning by doing, much of which has been sector-specific. Personal computers, for example, have required advances in software, sector-specific semiconductor manufacturing, and the thin film technology and mechanical engineering that underlies mass storage technologies.

Finally, consider the Haber-Bosch process for synthesizing ammonia. This is a single-purpose chemical process that permitted huge increases in world agricultural output through reduction in the cost of making fertilizer (Smil 2001). Without careful calculations it is hard to say definitively that the social savings or contributions to TFP growth of the Haber-Bosch process are lower or higher than those of, say, the steam engine or the Internet. The point here is that there is no necessary connection between pervasiveness, or use in both households and firms, and economic importance. A single-purpose innovation can have a larger economic impact than an innovation widely adopted in different sectors and thus pervasive but one that results in a relatively small move forward. If the purpose of the GPT concept is to provide a filter that reliably identifies technologies with large economic impact, we must question how well it succeeds.

Economic history already has language and methodology for addressing the economic importance of an innovation. Ultimately, in terms of distinguishing between important innovations and those that are relatively inconsequential, we want to differentiate between those that, counterfactually, add a lot to TFP growth and those that add only a little. Classic works in economic history (Fogel 1964; Fishlow 1965) attempted to estimate the social saving of an innovation, in this case railroads. Crafts (2004) and Field (2006b) have independently noted the close relationship between social saving calculations and estimates of the contribution of a new technology to TFP growth.

The method is not by any means perfect—there is a large literature on the challenges of applying it—but does the GPT approach and its associated criteria offer a better alternative? There are many single-purpose innovations (for example, the cotton gin) with arguably large implications for TFP (and all sorts of other outcomes), and there can be "general-purpose" innovations that represent relatively marginal improvements over previously existing technology and have low social saving/contribution to TFP (for example, the felt-tipped pen).

The originators of the GPT concept intended it to help separate the wheat from the chaff. Evidence that the concept and its associated criteria were intended to catch "big," "important," "revolutionary" innovations abounds in the title, abstract, and text of Bresnahan and Trajtenberg. "Whole eras of technical progress and growth appear to be driven by a few 'General Purpose Technolo-gies' (GPT's), such as the steam engine, the electric motor, and semiconduc-tors," reads the abstract, and the title refers to GPTs as "Engines of Growth." The intent to provide a filter differentiating the important from the inconse-quential is also reflected in the following passage: "Anecdotal evidence aside, are there such things as 'technological prime movers'? Could it be that a hand-ful of technologies had a dramatic impact on growth over extended periods of time? What is there in the nature of the steam engine, the electric motor, or the silicon wafer, that make them prime 'suspects' of having played such a role?" (1995, p. 84). And in their concluding remarks, the authors speak of the inter-play between "'key' technologies and the industrial organization and firms that spring up around them" (1995, p. 102).

One might try and defend the approach by arguing that the real value of the GPT concept is that it helps us to identify a subset among "engines of growth" in which there is a substantial lag between initial innovation and the reaping of productivity benefits due to the need to make complementary investments in training and R and D, as well as spillover interactions between downstream and upstream processes. There is undoubtedly merit in technological history and assessment in focusing on the incremental and ongoing process of technologi-cal change and in particular on the spillover dynamic.

The problem is that this dynamic is not unique to GPTs. Consider again the classic histories of the textile innovations, with bottlenecks created in weaving, then spinning, and then weaving again. David Landes (1969) described these as sequences of challenge and response. Similarly in iron making, with break-throughs first in smelting and then in refining. The need to make complemen-tary investments pertains to single- as well as general-purpose technologies. Or consider containerization, arguably one of the most consequential innovations of the twentieth century. It is hard to argue that containerization is a GPT, but it most certainly required large complementary investments in ship, truck, and railroad design, as well as port and other transshipment facilities. And these systems had spillovers in marketing and distribution; the success of companies such as IKEA is hard to imagine without it.

It is difficult to assess whether GPTs are more likely than other engines of growth to exhibit long delays before their full productivity benefits are reaped and (arguably) short-term retardation in the period when complementary in-vestments are required. A principal reason is the aforementioned lack of clarity in the literature about what the exact innovations are. If the steam engine is a GPT, is the railroad, which uses a steam engine to provide motive power, also a separate and distinguishable GPT? The muddiness of labeling makes it possible, using different choices about what is called the revolutionary technology, to claim that benefits were more or less immediately realized or that they were long delayed.

Much of Bresnahan and Trajtenberg (1995) is involved with modeling the interactions between GPT producing and using sectors and the ways in which industrial organization may provide appropriate incentives for R and D investment or result in too little of it. The authors are motivated by the assumption that the history of semiconductors and their uses is an illustration of a more general phenomenon, and they speak of future research in which they will conduct historical inquiry to explore how slow-to-change institutions might have influenced the size and trajectory of the contributions of engines of growth (1995, p. 103). But their discussion of motivation begs the question of whether what they are focused on is an episode worthy of study in its own right but one that does not generalize.

IS THE EXPERIENCE OF IT REALLY GENERALIZABLE TO ELECTRIC POWER AND STEAM?

Sticking with the "big three" and assuming we resolve ambiguities about exactly which technologies we are talking about, we must ask whether their histories share enough similarities to justify the distillation of their experiences into a common category with presumably broader applicability. In making this assessment, one must be cautious about the use of stylized facts.

Bresnahan and Trajtenberg's understanding of steam power relies, for example, on some questionable claims. Continuous rotary motion is not a "central defining feature" or "generic function" of a steam engine (1995, p. 86). No steam engine (or internal combustion engine, with the exception of the Wankel) produces rotary motion directly. Only with Parsons's work on the steam turbine in the 1880s did this become possible. Until the turbine, the reciprocating motion of eighteenth-century steam engines such as those of Newcomen or Watt, desirable in many applications (such as pumping water, fulling wool, or refining iron), could be converted to rotary motion only through such "downstream" innovations as the crankshaft or sun- and planet-gearing systems. Reciprocating engines remained the norm throughout the nineteenth century, even as fuel efficiency improved dramatically with high-pressure and compound engines. They remain the norm today, except in electric power generation. Powered by external or internal combustion engines, most automobile and ship transport continues to be driven by reciprocating engines. And again, it is not at all clear what they mean when they write that continuous rotary motion makes sewing cheaper (Bresnahan and Trajtenberg 1995, p. 86). One of Isaac Singer's key innovations was the use of a foot-operated treadle connected to a crankshaft that converted reciprocating into rotary motion (previous machines had used a hand crank). Rotary motion was then reconverted to the up-and-down reciprocating action required in the actual process of sewing. In almost all instances sewing machines were human-powered and involved at least one conversion between rotary and reciprocating motion. Few sewing machines were ever driven by steam power.

Calling attention to these details might be dismissed as missing the larger picture if the history of steam power and its application indeed turned out to have strong analogies to what has been experienced in IT. But the suggestion that its history is isomorphic, central to much of the GPT literature, turns out to be questionable. Crafts (2004) carefully reexamined steam and its application in Britain and concluded, first, that its overall contribution to TFP growth was modest and, second, that its greatest impact was not until the last part of the nineteenth century—almost a century after Watt's innovations—and depended on the cost reductions and performance improvements associated with the development of high-pressure engines.

Within manufacturing, entrepreneurs understood quickly how steam might be valuable. It was another prime mover, providing more flexibility in location than water power; the choice between steam and water was based on a comparison of costs and benefits. Unlike systems of electric power, which eventually comprised installations to generate and transmit power over long distances to drive electric motors, the minimum efficient scale of a steam engine was too large to permit any fundamental redesign of manufacturing facilities.[3] And there is relatively little evidence of spillovers influencing the design or use of other equipment within steam-powered factories. Most of the fundamental textile innovations, for example, were designed to be driven by other types of power, in particular water (see Crafts 2004, p. 348; von Tunzelmann 1978).

Within the transportation sector, at least within Britain, the evidence of major spillovers as the result of the use of steam-powered vehicles is also weak. Railroads had relatively little impact on location decisions on an island covered with rivers and canals and featuring a heavily indented coastline. And Britain did not rush to embrace the new organizational form known as the modern business enterprise (for the United States, see Field 1987). Over water, wind-powered sailing ships remained effective competitors to steamships for decades. Steamships were not economic for longer journeys until coal consumption fell sufficiently such that the space and weight requirements of carrying fuel crowded out a smaller portion of payload capacity (Harley 1988).

While Crafts worked within the framework of the GPT tradition and interpreted his research as reinforcing the point that it might take a long time (forty years in the case of electricity, eighty years in the case of steam) for a GPT to have its full impact on TFP growth, his analysis of steam power in fact raises doubts that the history of IT can be distilled and reified as an instantiation of a more general phenomenon. And indeed, his final comments reinforce this interpretation (2004, pp. 348, 349).

What about electric power? It was of course the analogies between the electrification of the manufacturing sector and the productivity trajectory of IT described by David (1990) that Bresnahan and Trajtenberg built upon in developing their concept of a general-purpose technology. The computer age is still very much upon us, and most of us are sympathetic to the idea that the diversity of uses to which these new devices might be put was not immediately apparent when they developed. This goes all the way back to Kenneth Olsen, the head of Digital Equipment Corporation, whose skepticism about the potential market for computers in homes was famous. It clearly did take some time for both consumers and producers to figure out how most effectively to make use of what advances in semiconductor manufacture, mass storage technologies, and software had made possible; productivity improvements resulting from better supply-chain management would be an example.

This is the analogy to which David (1990, 1991) and David and Wright (2003) appealed in looking back to electrification. But it is important to note their discussion of other developments that helped precipitate factory electrification: "It did not acquire real momentum until after 1914–1917, when the rates charged consumers by state-regulated regional utilities fell substantially in real terms, and central station generating capacity came to predominate over generating capacity in *isolated* industrial plants. Rapid efficiency gains in electricity generation during 1910–1920 derived from major direct investments in large central power plants, but also from the scale economies realized through integration and extension of power transmission over expanded territories" (David and Wright 2003, p. 6).

This suggests, to a greater degree than is often emphasized in the GPT literature, that the timing of factory electrification was the consequence of a sharp fall of electric power rates, not simply the initial failure of imagination on the part of factory designers and operators, or the need to develop a skilled cadre of engineers and technicians who understood the potential for productivity gains in an electrified factory, or the need to figure out how to make smaller electric motors. While this is not an either/or choice, to the degree that the timing of electrification is attributed to a more mundane matter of costs rather than imagination, the similarities to the narrative frequently told about IT become weaker.

A second historical point emerging from this reconsideration is that whatever the key revolutionary technology we focus on here—the GPT literature refers inconsistently to electricity, the electric motor, or the dynamo—the dynamo is probably the least appropriate candidate. The dynamo, or magneto or direct current generator, had been around for decades. What was needed to make the commercial electric power industry truly viable was a steam engine that could directly produce rotary power. This Parsons supplied with the steam turbine, patented in 1884.

The scale economies to which the above passage refers also depended on advances in high-voltage transmission of electricity across long distances, including, most would argue, the switch to alternating current. Finally, there is the small electric motor. Perhaps this is what David meant by the dynamo since the device in principle can convert electricity into rotary motion as well as the reverse. This is not, however, common usage: a dynamo refers usually to a device, using principles discovered by Faraday in the 1820s, in which a magnetic enclosure induces a current within a rotating coil of wires.[4]

It matters that we get the history right. The critical innovation in making commercial electric power a possibility was not the magneto or the dynamo, which had been under development for decades, but the steam turbine. In part because of the scale issues identified in the above passage, however, it took several decades for electric rates to fall sufficiently to warrant the wholesale reorganization and redesign of American factures that was such a distinctive feature of the productivity history of the 1920s.

In his earlier work David (1990, 1991) identified the steam engine and the electric motor as general-purpose *engines*. By this he meant that these power sources were used in many sectors and industries (this is the origin of the pervasiveness criterion). The reciprocating steam engine, for example, pumped water out of deep mines. In manufacturing, it powered trip hammers to refine iron, drove bellows in blast furnaces, fulled cloth, or (converted to rotary motion) drove spindles and looms in textile factories. And in transportation, of course, steam engines powered both railroads and steamships (which most do not consider GPTs in their own right, although some do).

The electric motor, in turn, found wide application throughout transport (streetcars and urban subways, submarines), industry, and in the home. David also emphasized the long delay between the first commercial power installation (the Pearl Street Station in New York in 1882) and the electrification of factories in the 1920s and suggested that the productivity benefits of computers might be delayed, possibly for similar reasons. Even though computers are not themselves engines, they find a broad range of applications in various sectors of the economy and in the home and thus can legitimately be viewed as general purpose in the sense that they satisfy the pervasiveness test.

Bresnahan and Trajtenberg built on David's work and ideas, although they emphasized semiconductors rather than computers. Are the isomorphisms in fact sufficient to justify moving from two general-purpose engines to three general-purpose technologies and then beyond?

Countering one of the foundational assumptions of the GPT approach, one can argue that the history of IT should be treated sui generis. Unlike electric power, which enabled a different means of producing, for example, rotary motion in a factory, IT involved products that were sufficiently distinct from their antecedents that they could be considered genuinely new. The isomorphisms between IT and electricity are not exact, and this is even less the case with steam. When one goes beyond this, the analogies become even weaker. The more one probes the underpinnings of the idea of a general-purpose technology, the more one concludes that there is less here than meets the eye.

WHAT GPT GAVE THE GREAT DEPRESSION ITS CHARACTER?

Economic theory evolves in part as a result of an independent scholarly dynamic, but it also responds to the spirit of the times. With some distance from the 1990s, we can see the GPT concept, along with changes in the presentation in government statistics (the BEA's Fixed Asset Tables, for example, now give pride of place to IT capital goods) and efforts to provide a rationale for tax advantaging equipment investment (DeLong and Summers 1991), as each in its way a response to the Solow paradox (see chapters 5 and 8). More prosaically, each was a response to the felt imperative to provide theoretical, statistical, and policy support for high and rising stock valuations. These valuations and optimistic forecasts of the growth potential of the "New Economy" were largely driven by hope and faith. The promise of delayed productivity benefits offered by GPT analysis provided an encouraging rationale for that growth potential.

The stock market was central to the zeitgeist of the second half of the 1990s in the United States. The NASDAQ index quintupled in value between July 1995 and March 2000 before falling back by September 2002 almost to its 1995 value.[5] During the upswing there was at times an almost theological character to discussion, as economists, along with stock analysts and investors, described conversion experiences, acknowledging how they "got religion," surrendering to the conviction that this time it really was different, and embracing some of the wilder tenets of New Economy thinking. This was the intellectual environment into which the GPT concept was launched.

There was merit in the underlying notion that advances in IT were generating or would generate productivity growth that would ultimately be reflected in higher returns to capital as well as labor. But the size of the likely impacts was exaggerated. A similar type of thinking emerged as stock market valuations rose in the second half of the 1920s, particularly 1928 and 1929.

The GPT concept crystallized the essential features of the IT dynamic, but its analytic value is limited by the historical experience from which it was distilled. The IT productivity boom, which had its biggest impact between 1995 and 2005, was distinguished, particularly before 2000, by its narrow locus of advance (chapter 5). Between 1989 and 2000, a third of TFP advance came from within manufacturing, almost all of it from within durables, and within durables, from within the old SIC 35 and 36 (now NAICS 334: Computer and Electronic Products). The remainder was largely attributable to three IT equipment-intensive sectors: retail trade, wholesale trade, and securities transactions. After 2000, advance spread somewhat more broadly within manufacturing and outside of it to sectors associated with real estate and health care (chapter 5).

One could say that this history, particularly the higher post-2000 rates of productivity increase, validated the predictive usefulness of the GPT concept. But the highly concentrated nature of advance between 1995 and 2005 was quite unusual and indeed unlike that in other dynamic periods of U.S. economic growth. For that reason, the GPT concept, which tries to capture the essential features of the economic history emerging from these data, turns out to be of more limited usefulness in understanding the contribution of technological progress to growth in other periods.

The Depression years, in particular, experienced TFP advance that was much faster and occurred across a much broader frontier than was the case in 1995–2005. But there is no individual innovation or complex of innovations that gave its character to that earlier epoch. While steam, electricity, and automobiles all played a role in the economic history of the period, none of these, nor any other "general-purpose technology," defined it. The substantially faster and broader-based TFP advance during the 1930s simply does not fit any of the standard GPT narratives. Nor is there a GPT that we can view as having given its character to the golden age, during which PNE TFP growth was almost as high as it had been during the 1920s.

The experience of the 1920s, the decade during which the internal distribution of power within manufacturing was largely electrified, provided historical inspiration for the GPT work. There were, nevertheless, important differences in comparison with the IT experience. Aside from a rate of TFP advance within the manufacturing sector that was more than three times as high as it was between 1989 and 2007, what was striking was the across-the-board nature of the improvement within the sector. One sees high rates of advance across every single two-digit industry within manufacturing, within both durables and non-durables. As noted above, TFP advance within this sector in the 1920s was, to use Harberger's (1998) metaphors, yeast-rather than mushroom-like.

There is a tension in the concept of a GPT between the criterion of pervasiveness and the idea that there is a delay in diffusion and the reaping of productivity gains. The latter dynamic is more applicable to IT in the 1990s and early 2000s than it was to factory electrification in the 1920s. Adoption then did not start in one industry and then slowly spread to a few others after additional learning and complementary investments had been made. It may have taken some time to work out the principles of factory electrification and to advance the electric-power-generating business to the point that it was cheap enough for this to be profitable. But once these conditions were in place, adoption of an essentially similar blueprint throughout the manufacturing sector was rapid and widespread. The factory electrification dynamic was largely spent by 1929, with electricity already driving close to four-fifths of U.S. manufacturing capacity (Devine 1983, p. 349).

In August 2006, Joel Mokyr wrote of the GPT concept in the past tense, as "a theme that briefly rose to prominence a decade ago in the literature of the economics of technological change." But, with apologies to Mark Twain, the rumors of the death or exhaustion of the GPT concept are exaggerated. There has perhaps been some cooling of enthusiasm for the concept within economic history. The idea, nevertheless, because of its appeal, continues to crop up in new papers, particularly outside economic history narrowly defined.[6] Since the usefulness of the concept stands or falls on how well it is both grounded in and illuminates the record of economic history, it is important that economic historians, in dialogue with other economists, participate actively in discussions of its merits.

Why be critical of the GPT enterprise if it generates useful collaboration between economic historians and theorists and if the models developed lead to interesting implications? Because if the concept is best applied to the economic history of the period from which it was derived, the use of models based upon it to analyze other periods may well encourage unproductive lines of inquiry as scholars try to demonstrate that what works in theory works in history. A case in point is Jovanovic and Rousseau's (2005) suggestion that the productivity slow-down beginning in 1973 could be attributed to the need to make training and

R and D investments to complement the first stage of computerization, which they dated from Intel's invention of the 4004 single chip microprocessor in 1971. The authors were careful not exactly to say that computers caused the post-1973 slowdown, although in a roundabout way they implied this.[7] If IT is a GPT (and if it is not, what is?) and if GPTs require complementary investments with sometimes long gestation periods before returns are enjoyed, then productivity growth rates might well decline before they increase. No one has a completely satisfactory explanation for the deceleration of TFP advance during the dark ages of U.S. productivity growth (1973–1989), and so we are open to alternate and novel accounts.

But an explanation's novelty does not necessarily mean that it is right. There are at least two reasons why we should be skeptical. First, IT capital was a very small fraction of the fixed-asset stock in the 1970s. In 1971 the current cost net stock of computers and peripheral equipment ($5.3 billion) and software ($4.6 billion) was together less than .5 percent of a total fixed-asset stock of over $2.3 trillion.[8] Furthermore, the data on R and D investments cast doubt on the idea that this initial era of computerization stimulated a large surge of complementary spending in this area. R and D spending as a share of GDP peaked in 1964 at 2.88 percent, fell gradually to the end of the decade (2.53 percent), and then plummeted in the 1970s, reaching a nadir in 1978 at 2.12 percent.[9] In the light of these trends, it requires a considerable stretch of the imagination to believe that the introduction of computers could have been responsible for much of the productivity slowdown.

The technological and organizational improvements that contribute to growing TFP are much more interconnected than the GPT concept leads us to imagine. Even if we limit our discussion to the big three, violence is done to the historical record when we speak of "steam," "electricity" or "IT" as separate and distinct "engines of growth." As noted, the factory electrification of the 1920s was part of the historical inspiration for the GPT. But the developments that made this possible represented a closely intertwined set of advances in both electricity generation and the use of steam power.

The last two decades of the nineteenth century witnessed a remarkable series of innovations in the area of power generation. These included Parsons's and de Laval's work on the steam turbine in the 1880s; Edison's, Siemens's, and Ferranti's advances in the production and transmission of electricity; and Daimler's, Benz's, and Diesel's advances on the internal combustion engine (see Buchanan 1991; Smil 2005). These technologies have been subject to evolutionary improvement, but the twentieth century in fact produced few new advances in inanimate power generation. Nuclear power could be viewed as an exception, but from the standpoint of the technology of power generation, it represents the simple development of an alternate fuel to generate the heat to produce the steam for a steam turbine. Most of our electricity is still produced by steam turbines, and most of our vehicles and ships are still driven by reciprocating internal combustion engines. These innovations all date from the late nineteenth century (Buchanan 1991, p. 76). The productivity history of the twentieth century, particularly the very strong performance in the second quarter of the century, could be understood partially as the working out of the implications of the steam turbine, cheaper electric power, and the internal combustion engine.

A parallel line of development drove advance in the area of information transmission, storage, and retrieval. We can trace this thread from the telegraph and telephone through tabulating machines, the vertical filing cabinet, and radio and television to the modern computer and Internet.

These themes and the histories of the big three are tightly woven together. Just as the development of the commercial electricity industry depended critically on advances in steam power, advances in computing depended on moves forward in electrical engineering and semiconductors. In each of these cases, a detailed understanding of technological history is a critical ingredient in deciphering the causes of fluctuations in TFP growth rates over time. Whether the GPT concept adds anything essential to these explorations remains an open question.

Part Three

Historical Perspectives
on 2007–2010

10

FINANCIAL FRAGILITY AND RECOVERY

This book has been built around a reinterpretation of the economic history of the Great Depression that, if accepted, leads us to rethink many aspects of the growth narrative for the United States since the Civil War. The traditional historiography of 1929–1941 focused almost exclusively on cyclical issues. The emphasis in chapters 1 and 2 and elsewhere in part I, in contrast, has been on a Depression-era growth of economic capacity obscured by the large output gaps that characterized the period. But obviously, both growth and cycle matter, in particular, as chapter 12 suggests, because there may be some connections between them.

This chapter considers the financial fragility that laid the groundwork for the near collapse of the U.S. economy in 2008–2009, with an eye to sharpening our understanding of the origin and depth of the Great Depression. It then examines aspects of Depression-era recovery from 1933 onward, as preparation for thinking about prospects for the revival of private sector physical capital accumulation in the second decade of the twenty-first century.

During 2007–2009, the U.S. economy weathered its worst economic downturn since 1929–1933. Massive monetary and fiscal interventions undertaken by the Federal Reserve and Treasury arrested what otherwise could have been a terrifying free fall, but a substantial gap between actual and potential output remains a realistic possibility for several years into the future (this is written in November 2010). In each of the last three months of 2009, unemployment exceeded 10 percent, approaching the record post-Depression rate of 10.8 percent in November and December 1982, and unemployment remained at 9.5 percent or above throughout the first ten months of 2010. Commercial real estate loans persisted as a continuing threat to the banking system's fragile balance sheets, which still had not fully recognized the damage from securitized lending to the residential sector.[1]

Although recoveries in equity and bond prices from their troughs in March 2009 dulled the memories of some investors and policymakers, macroeconomists, economic historians, and other scholars cannot so easily forget the intellectual challenges posed by what came to be called the Great Recession. The economic history of 2007–2009 requires us to reconsider what were widely held beliefs about the inherent stability of the economy and the unmitigated benefits of financial innovation and deregulation. This process of rethinking will almost certainly influence the future direction of macroeconomic and historical research.

A complete reckoning of the import of what has transpired awaits its historical dénouement. But it is evident that in a number of respects the precursors, challenges, and opportunities faced as the economy entered the 2010s bore similarities to those confronted at the start of the 1930s. First, although both episodes had important international dimensions, the epicenter of each was in the United States. And in that country, most obviously, both economic downturns were preceded by a speculative real estate boom characterized by rising land and house prices and a rising share of GDP devoted to construction.

The 1920s boom was in part a response to the personal automobile, which opened up prospects for suburban commuting in areas beyond those previously accessible by streetcar. Farmland values declined from their peak after the First World War, but prices in and around every major and most minor American cities and towns soared as developers bought greenfield land from farmers, slapped nineteenth-century urban city plats on them, and sold off the pieces to buyers, many of whom were often intent on earning a quick buck by flipping them. The residential boom, whose most egregious features were chronicled in Galbraith (1955), peaked in 1926, when a hurricane swept through Florida—a center then as now in real estate speculation—revealing that much of the land changing hands was literally under water, and some had been so even before the storm. But what Galbraith described in Florida had in fact been occurring across the country. Before the end of the decade the boom in single-family housing had been followed by a boom in apartment construction and then one in downtown central business district building. It took more than a quarter century for construction in the United States to recover fully from these enthusiasms.

In 1924, 1925, 1926, and 1927, housing construction comprised more than 8 percent of GDP, a figure subsequently approached but never again exceeded. In the 2001–2005 boom, the share of residential construction rose from 4.6 percent of GDP in 2000 to 6.2 percent in 2005 (the year that housing prices peaked nationally) before falling to 3.4 percent in 2008 and 2.5 percent in 2009 (NIPA table 1.1.5).[2] In absolute terms, real investment in residential structures bottomed out in 2009:2 at 44 percent of its 2005:4 peak before beginning to recover very slowly in the second half of 2009.

In both the 1920s and the 2000s, the residential housing peak led the financial crisis by several years, and in both instances a residential boom was followed by an upswing in the building of commercial structures. Nonresidential construction, which comprised 3.2 percent of GDP in 2000, fell to 2.6 percent in 2004 but then rose steadily before peaking at 4.0 percent in 2008. By 2009:3 it was down to 3.1 percent, in 2009:4 to 2.8 percent, and in 2010:1 to 2.6 percent. In absolute terms nonresidential construction continued to decline in the second half of 2009. In 2009:4, real spending on nonresidential construction had fallen to 71 percent of its 2008:2 peak (these numbers are based on the July 30, 2010, release of NIPA tables 1.1.3 and 1.1.5).

A second similarity is that in both instances—and in contrast with the decades following the Second World War—the periods preceding the crises featured absent or diminished governmental regulation of the financial sector, along with a relaxed attitude toward enforcement of existing rules. The boom periods were marked by financial innovation associated with new instruments, a greater appetite for risk taking on the part of both borrowers and lenders, and rising debt-to-equity ratios (leverage) within households, nonfinancial businesses, and banking institutions.[3] The mutual fund (invented in 1924), the investment trust (essentially a closed-end mutual fund), the extension and development of the call money market (which enabled purchasers of stocks to buy with as little as 10 percent down), the issuance of collateralized debt instruments secured by mortgages on commercial real estate (Goetzmann and Newman 2010), and the innovation of installment sales for consumer durables (Olney 1991) are examples from the 1920s. Collateralized debt obligations, which moved beyond simple pass-through mortgage-backed securities, and the vast growth in the market for credit default swaps are instances from the more recent episode. Prior to both crises the relative size of the financial sector and the remuneration and skill-intensity of its employees rose (Philippon and Reshef 2009). In contrast, the U.S. financial sector shrank during the Depression and remained relatively small into the 1980s.

The bust part of the financial cycle in both cases saw significant and sometimes frightening disruptions in credit markets, with many bankruptcies or near bankruptcies of financial institutions and big declines in the price of equities, with high stock market volatility—large upswings and larger downswings.

Most of the largest one-day stock price *increases* in the twentieth century took place between 1929 and 1932, as the Dow Jones Industrial Average lost a total of 89 percent of its value, and stock market volatility in 2008 and 2009 rivaled that of the early 1930s. In both cases during the upswing that preceded crisis, households and firms borrowed, lent, and spent with abandon. And in both instances, the challenge facing policymakers, at least in the short run, was to cajole, incentivize, and otherwise encourage households and firms to borrow, lend, and spend—just what had gotten them into difficulty in the first place.[4]

There were, of course, differences. In the 1920s a major stock market boom followed the residential portion of the real estate boom, whereas the tech stock boom of the second half of the 1990s preceded a real estate boom, which took off only after the equity bubble had deflated. In the 1920s there were low "down payment" requirements for buying stock (margin requirements as low as 10 percent), whereas retail home buyers typically had to put down 50 percent of the purchase price. The situation was largely reversed in the 2000s. The collapse of the tech bubble after 2001 had a smaller impact on household spending than the stock market crash after 1929, in part because collapsing stock prices after 2001 were mostly paper losses and did not, to the same degree as had been true in 1929, trigger margin calls. Similarly, the residential real estate collapse after 1926 had less severe immediate effects on the real economy than did the end of the housing boom in 2006 and after. A comparison of the two episodes suggests that the benefit of higher margin requirements in each case was not so much that they provided obstacles to the collapsing price of assets (or their prior inflation) but that they weakened the effect of these wealth changes on consumer spending.

A second difference was that during the 1920s the United States ran current account surpluses and capital account deficits—exporting financial capital to the rest of the world—whereas during the 2000s (and indeed since the mid-1980s) the reverse was true. While capital flows were initially "pulled" into the country in response to high real interest rates, reflecting the collision of fiscal deficits with tight money in the first half of the 1980s, by the late 1990s inflows contributed to low interest rates rather than responding to high ones, reflecting what some economists, including Bernanke (2005), referred to as a global saving glut.

The willingness of creditors outside the country to lend enabled the United States to fund residential and nonresidential construction booms in the 2000s while at the same time running substantial government deficits. But one must be cautious in attributing the asset price bubbles to these inflows. The history of the 1920s reminds us that capital inflows are not necessary conditions for the development of speculative asset bubbles in either real estate or stocks.

Despite differences in the timing and impact of equity and real estate bubbles and their deflation, there were important similarities between the 1920s and the more recent period. Speculative booms in real estate and/or equities coincided with a relaxed attitude toward risk, creating economies that became increasingly financially fragile. A financially fragile economy will experience a more dramatic reduction in real activity in the face of a given shock than one that is more robust. The simple truth is that rising debt-to-income or debt-to-equity ratios within households, nonfinancial businesses, and financial businesses (banks or bank-like intermediaries) make an economy more vulnerable. The increasingly complex web of contractual obligations involving debt and other credit market instruments makes interchange among counterparties more susceptible to precautionary and legal gridlock in the event of an asset bubble deflation.

A number of economists, in particular John Taylor (2009), argued that the 2007–2010 recession was precipitated by a policy of low interest rates between 2001 and 2004.[5] As Bernanke (2010) pointed out, however, in defending the record of the Fed, other countries with less expansionary monetary policies also experienced an asset price bubble and construction boom. And although Austrian economists such as Murray Rothbard (1963) argued that credit creation was too liberal during much of the 1920s, it is widely accepted that one of the immediate triggers of the Great Depression was *high* rather than low nominal and real interest rates in 1928 and 1929 (Field 1984; Hamilton 1987).[6]

A similarity between the interwar years and the 2000s is that excessively expansionary monetary policy has been alleged in the run-up to both the Depression and the more recent downturn. A difference is that, in contrast to what has been written about 1928–1929, no one has blamed the 2007–2009 recession on monetary policy that was too restrictive in the years immediately preceding. It is not impossible that monetary policy that was first too loose and then too tight might, in sequence, be implicated in laying the foundation for the collapse that began in 1929. Still, it is worth remarking that monetary economists have been willing to identify policy that was too tight in the 1920s and too loose in the 2000s (both periods of low or nonexistent goods and services price inflation) as the proximate cause of recession. This is, I will suggest, indicative of a focus on an excessively narrow range of central bank actions or inactions that may contribute to boom and bust.

Prior to the Great Recession the consensus in the Fed and elsewhere was that using tight monetary policy to prick an asset bubble was less advisable than using loose money to clean up the mess afterward, mitigating spillovers of an asset price deflation on the real economy. The experience with the tech bubble seemed to reinforce the merits of this view, which can trace its origins to lessons learned (rightly or wrongly) from the experiments with selective credit controls in the late 1920s. Discussion of the policy actions and inactions contributing to the growing fragility of the economy in the 2000s needs, however, to go beyond what the Fed did about the federal funds rate or other monetary indicators in different periods.

Indeed, the consensus that the role of a central bank in avoiding recessions and depressions is largely limited to interest rate policy should be one of the casualties of 2007–2009. It is clear now that reducing the risk of major depression over the longer run depends at least as much on the regulation of borrowing and lending and the prudential supervision of systemically important financial entities as it does on monetary policy narrowly understood. The idea that these responsibilities can be treated as an afterthought in instruction or in practice is no longer sustainable, if it ever was.

Whether or not higher interest rates between 2001 and 2004 would have prevented a boom and subsequent crash, the Fed's response to the crisis, which probably prevented a world financial crisis and depression, was to flood the economy with liquidity, pushing short-term rates close to zero. Still, the critical issue is less the direct influence of interest rates on the dimensions and timing of the asset price boom but rather why the rise and decline in real estate prices, and the slowing of construction spending, had such a devastating effect on the financial system and posed such a threat to the real economy. Again, interest rate policy may have contributed to fragility, but it was far from the only—or even the most important—policy factor contributing to it. The largely reversed role of margin requirements for buying stocks and real estate in the 1920s, as compared with 1995–2005, for example, is illustrative of policies affecting the extent of leverage in different asset markets, policies distinct from monetary policy per se that nevertheless played an important role in influencing the response of the real economy to different types of financial shocks.

Prior to the Great Recession, most economists believed that the U.S. saving rate, close to zero or even negative, was too low and that neither the high share of consumption in GDP (over 70 percent in 2002–2004 and again in 2007, 2008, and 2009) nor the very high debt-to-household income ratios could be sustained. And yet most who could remember an older style of macroeconomics agreed that in the short run, individual efforts by households to increase their saving, reduce their consumption, and reduce their debt-to-income ratios would worsen the recession. Whereas many economists from across the political spectrum bemoaned the fiscal deficits incurred by the Reagan and Bush presidencies because of concerns about the crowding out of private capital formation, most economists agreed, at least initially, that the immediate response to economic downturn had to be to allow the deficit and debt to increase further (there were differences about how much fiscal stimulus was needed and therefore how much the deficit should be allowed to widen).

These are some of the ironies of recession economics, first identified by John Maynard Keynes, and they underlay the rationale for the countercyclical fiscal stimulus initiated by the Obama administration in 2009. The reality, with which many students have struggled and indeed with which many economists continue to experience discomfort, is that policies and behavior likely to foster long-term growth are often the opposite of those needed to counteract a serious recession.

Finally and most important, within the United States and other countries, the downturns resulted in falling output and employment. In each instance, while the upswing of the financial cycle supercharged the accumulation of physical capital, particularly structures, its aftermath retarded it. The upswing of the financial cycle laid the groundwork for a subsequent contraction in physical accumulation, which, amplified by multiplier effects and only partially counteracted by fiscal and monetary policy, contributed in both cases to the decline in aggregate demand that induced recession. Whether economic downturns can have a silver lining, in the form of a boost to the long-term rate of productivity growth, is a question considered in chapter 12.

THE ORIGINS OF FINANCIAL FRAGILITY

The events of 2007–2009, in light of our past history, including that of the interwar period and the savings and loan crisis of the late 1980s, force us to ask why capitalist economies such as the United States continue to experience financial crises and a boom/bust cycle of physical capital accumulation. These are not matters of concern only to economic historians. If we are fully to understand the trajectory of and prospects for future U.S. growth, we need to better understand the causes and consequences of financial instability. This is particularly so because much research on recessions and depressions seeks to locate the source for the onset and persistence of downturns in labor markets. Arguments are often made that recessions result because wages are too high or because they are downwardly inflexible due to unions or ill-considered government supply-side policies.

It is nearly impossible, however, to blame the Great Recession on dysfunctional or distorted labor markets, and indeed it is notable that no one on either side of the political spectrum has seriously tried to do so.[7] Unionization in the United States, outside of the public sector, declined steadily in the last decades of the twentieth century. Real wages stagnated, as labor failed to share in the gains from lower productivity growth, which accrued mostly to owners of capital and, more generally, to the top quintile or decile of U.S. households. This was in contrast with the golden age, in which the gains from substantially higher productivity growth were enjoyed relatively equally across the quintiles of the income distribution, with perhaps a slight bias toward the bottom. Skill-biased technical change interacted with assortative mating in marriage markets, tax policies favoring upper-income groups, and the ballooning share of profits accruing in the financial sector to produce a worsening of both wealth and income inequality from the 1970s onward. Trends or interventions tilting the income distribution toward the bottom cannot have been responsible for 2007–2009. The conclusion that the origins of the Great Recession are to be found primarily in financial as opposed to labor markets has implications as well for our understanding of the Great Depression.

Financial instability accelerates and then curtails the accumulation of physical capital. It does this because periods of confidence, rising risk tolerance, and higher leverage increase the availability of finance and reduce its costs in ways only partially reflected in the interest rates controlled by the central bank. In contrast, periods of uncertainty, fear, and deleveraging do the reverse. Most students of intermediate macroeconomics confront historical time series demonstrating the much higher volatility of investment spending for equipment and structures (both residential and nonresidential), as compared, for example, with consumption spending.[8] Working through the Hicks-Hansen interpretation of Keynes as instantiated in the workhorse IS/LM system permits an exploration of the consequences of private sector instability as well as fiscal and monetary interventions by the government. Most of the emphasis on private sector instability, however, is typically on the IS side of the system.[9]

Students learn that the IS curve is potentially volatile primarily because of the fact that fixed investment decisions involve long-term commitments, and businessmen can know the future state of industry and macroeconomic conditions only with uncertainty. Thus the prospective stream of returns that might be associated with investing, for example, in a $4 billion wafer fabrication plant reflects educated guesses, and these prospective values might fluctuate suddenly and wildly in the face of waves of pessimism or optimism (there are typically references here to Keynesian "animal spirits"). Because of the interaction of a relatively more stable consumption function and a volatile private sector component of autonomous planned spending through the multiplier, the inherent volatility of planned investment in a laissez-faire economy allows what is after all a relatively small part of aggregate demand (typically about a sixth of gross domestic expenditure) to be a tail wagging the larger economic dog. And students learn that the volatility can in principle be tamed by some combination of countercyclical fiscal or monetary policy.

From a purely accounting standpoint, the precipitous decline in spending on real investment between 1929 and 1933 can, along with multiplier effects, "explain" the drop in real output and rise in unemployment over those years. NIPA table 1.1.6A shows real components of GDP in chained 1937 dollars.[10] Gross Private Domestic Investment (GPDI) alone fell from $12.2 billion in 1929 to $2.3 billion in 1933 for a delta of $9.9 billion (there is an even larger decline, from $12.2 to $1.5 billion, measuring to 1932). GDP dropped from $87.3 billion in 1929 to $64.0 billion in 1933 for a delta of $23.3 billion. A crude calculation implies a multiplier of 2.35.

A more complete calculation includes the deltas for other components of autonomous planned spending. Keynesian analysis drew a distinction between induced and autonomous spending, with induced spending the consequence of receipts of current income and autonomous spending determined "exogenously" by other factors. The multiplier was defined as $\Delta Y/\Delta A_p$, where Y is GDP and A_p is autonomous planned spending. $A_p = I_p + a + G - cT + NX$, where I_p is planned spending, which we can approximate by gross private domestic investment; a is autonomous consumption, proxied by spending on consumer durables; G is government spending on goods and services; $-cT$ is the negative of the marginal propensity to consume (c) times autonomous taxes (which we can proxy by property and motor vehicle taxes); and NX is the autonomous portion of net exports. Because imports are sensitive to income, there is an induced influence on net exports, although it is swamped during the Depression years by tariff changes, exchange rate changes associated with abandonment of the gold standard, and the general disruption of world trade. Net exports deteriorated from .8 billion in 1929 to −.1 billion in 1933 (delta of −.9 billion), the opposite of what one would have expected if the effect of income on imports were the only influence. I've treated it as autonomous (see table 10.1).

Spending on consumer durables dropped from $7.8 billion to $4.2 billion (delta of −$3.6 billion). Government spending increased from $9.2 to $9.9 billion (delta of $ +.7 billion). Autonomous tax collections (property and motor vehicle taxes) declined from $5.3 to $4.4 billion; with the adjustment for the saving leakage (see note to table 10.1), this is a positive offset to the declines in other components of A_p of $.8 billion. Summing the five deltas, we have real autonomous spending changing by −$12.9 billion. Real GDP dropped $23.3 billion, which implies a multiplier of about 1.81.

Table 10.1. Multipliers during the Depression

Deltas (billions of 1937 $)	1929–1933	1933–1937	1937–1941
GDP	−23.3	27.9	30.2
GPDI	−9.9	9.9	5.4
Government	0.7	2.6	12.8
Taxes (see note)	0.8	−0.2	−1.1
Net exports	−0.9	0.2	0.7
Consumer durables	−3.6	3.2	2.2
Change in A_p	−12.9	15.7	20.0
Multiplier	1.81	1.78	1.51

Source: With the exception of taxes, all data are from BEA, http://www.bea.gov, NIPA table 1.1.6A.
Note: All data are in billions of 1937 dollars. Autonomous taxes are calculated by summing property and motor vehicle taxes (nominal) from NIPA table 3.5 and converting to 1937 dollars based on the ratio of government expenditures (real) from NIPA table 1.1.6A to government expenditure (nominal) from NIPA table 3.1. The change in real autonomous taxes is then multiplied by an estimate of the marginal propensity to consume, proxied by 1 minus the average of the gross saving rate for the two years (NIPA table 5.1). The multiplier is the ratio of the change in real output to the change in real autonomous planned spending (A_p). Data accessed on November 3, 2010.

A similar calculation from 1933 to 1937 yields a multiplier of 1.78. Calculating from 1937 to 1941 yields a multiplier of 1.51 (see table 10.1), comparable to what the Council of Economic Advisors used in forecasting the impact of the 2009 stimulus package. The estimates for 1929–1933 and 1933–1937 are higher. Why? One explanation is that when labor income and particularly income to capital dropped in the trough, average and marginal propensities to save became very low, which increased the size of the multiplier. Depression reduced income, but it also reduced inequality, and this reduced saving both in the aggregate and as a share of GDP. Gross saving as a share of GDP was 18.6 percent of GDP in 1929 but fell to 5.6 percent in 1932. It recovered to 17.5 percent in 1937 and had risen to 23.5 percent in 1941 (NIPA tables 5.1 and 1.1.5).[11]

Practitioners of "modern" macroeconomics may find such calculations antediluvian, but when the economy headed south in 2008, it was precisely a well-worn and sometimes derided Keynesian tool kit to which policymakers turned in attempting to calculate the appropriate size of an economic stimulus. Nevertheless, something important is missing from this style of analysis, particularly in respect to what underlay the boom and bust in physical accumulation. Some of the elevated private sector autonomous planned spending in the 1920s, and its depressed value in the 1930s, can be treated as exogenous, the result of a wave of optimism among borrowers followed by pessimism, aggravated in the late 1920s by tight money (Field 1984). What is lacking, however, is a deeper acknowledgement that the evolving contractual web of financial obligations is not just a transparent veil. The volatility of investment spending, and of the economy as a whole, was also the consequence of the evolution of the financial sector, a process that made the system differentially vulnerable over time to external shocks of similar magnitude. This dynamic is a process to which memory (which affects expectations and attitudes toward risk), government regulation or its absence, and the pursuit of profit by private sector actors all contribute.

The events of 2007–2009 demonstrated that the picture of finance acquired by most students had become too simplified, too much of a caricature of the real world. The financial sector had been too often treated as a largely passive conduit of loanable funds made available on terms largely controlled by the Federal Reserve. Students learned that through open-market operations, and to a lesser degree the discount window, the central bank controlled the growth of monetary aggregates and, through this means, the overall availability of credit. The banking and finance system itself—I use the term here broadly to include commercial banks, savings and loans, investment banks, insurance companies, hedge funds, private equity groups, and various other financial intermediaries— was a black box

All analysis has to simplify, to leave out details in order to focus on what is viewed as essential. There are always tradeoffs involved, and, from an explanatory perspective, a balancing of costs and benefits. The financial meltdown of 2007–2009 showed that these simplifications had come to involve an increasingly poor bargain. Too much had been sacrificed on the altar of simplicity. The Fed, of course, did and does exercise some control over the terms upon which finance is offered, but this control was and is blunt and imprecise. Financial innovation, the growth of nonbank institutions, the increased importance of foreign bank branches, and the development of near monies all meant that domestic credit could expand elastically for a considerable time even when the Fed was passive or even attempting to apply the brakes using traditional tools of monetary policy. The income velocity of money was procyclical and influenced over the longer run by financial innovation, changes in transactions technology, and a variety of factors perturbing the demand to hold cash.

The instability of velocity is the main reason why attempts to apply a constant growth rate of the money supply rule, advocated by monetarists in the 1970s and early 1980s, did not and could not stabilize an economy and were eventually abandoned by most central banks. With some exceptions, inflation targeting supplanted constant growth rate rules as an organizing principle for policy. But, as noted, a central bank with this focus lacks clear guidance when confronted with a situation in which asset prices are rising rapidly but output prices are not. These conditions prevailed in the run-up to the Great Depression (1922–1929), as well as in the years preceding 2007–2009. In the case of both the equity bubble of the late 1990s and the real estate bubble of 2001–2005, the Fed avoided intervening out of fear that in attempting to deflate a bubble, it would end up inducing a recession in the real economy. As noted, some, such as John Taylor, believe the crisis could have been avoided if the Fed had practiced a tighter monetary policy between 2001 and 2004. This was, of course, a criticism of policies undertaken by Alan Greenspan and subsequently endorsed by Bernanke.

In his 1996 comments about irrational exuberance, Greenspan acknowledged the possibility of an equity bubble, but he asserted in the early 2000s that there could not in fact be a real estate bubble.[12] Ultimately and in the face of events, his stance evolved to the position that perhaps there was one, but if so, the Fed wasn't responsible for it. His argument turned first on the claim that the Fed controlled only short rates, while long rates, which influenced mortgage lending, were governed by a global savings glut. The claim that the Fed couldn't influence long rates was embedded in a more long-standing argument for inaction—one that had certainly been voiced in the 1920s—that it was simply hard for a central bank to identify an asset bubble in advance and deflate it without adversely affecting the real economy.

Monetary policy is indeed a blunt instrument. But monetary policy alone cannot control nor can it be held principally responsible for the increasing fragility of a financial system. The systemic risks posed by the evolution toward fragility involved two distinct but related dynamics affecting the healthiness and resistance to stress of balance sheets. The first, which affected the assets (left-hand) side, involved an increased willingness to hold riskier assets. The second, which affected the liabilities (right-hand) side, was an evolution toward greater leverage: higher ratios of debt to equity. Although the two tended to go hand in hand (particularly because one entity's assets could be another's liabilities), it is conceptually possible to have one without the other. Indeed, one can now look back and say that the bursting of the tech bubble in 2001 did relatively little lasting damage to the U.S. economy because although the lead-up to it involved households holding progressively riskier equities, margin requirements on stock purchases restrained the evolution of household leverage from this source. This meant that come the crash, households were spared some of the downside losses they might otherwise have experienced had their stock holdings been more highly levered. The effects on household spending (consumption) were therefore milder than they might have been. It also meant that banks and other financial institutions weren't heavily exposed to loans secured by stocks that had plummeted in value and could not be repaid. Credit markets were consequently not seriously impaired.

The overarching policy/regulatory problem prior to 2007 was the failure to control the growth of leverage; the relaxation (and in some cases elimination) of "margin" requirements on real estate reflected this but was part of a larger dynamic. That's not to say that low short-term interest rates made no contribution to the bubble, but rather that we should not have expected or relied upon open-market policy alone to "manage" the economy or moderate the financial/business cycle. Responsibility for control of leverage lay not just with the Federal Reserve (or at least not just with its control of interest rates), but also with a variety of other agencies, including the Securities and Exchange Commission (SEC), the Office of Thrift Supervision, the Commodity Futures Trading Commission (CFTC), the Office of the Comptroller of the Currency, the Federal Deposit Insurance Corporation (FDIC), and various state banking and insurance commissioners. In retrospect it was a multifaceted failure involving rules governing down payment; income and documentation requirements for mortgages; the subcontracting of what perhaps should have been a governmental responsibility to ratings agencies (state governments regulated what qualities of securities certain entities could hold, but the federal government certified private companies to rate the securities); the unwillingness to rein in credit default swaps; and, most important, the failure of the regulatory regime to ensure that the financial system as a whole held sufficient capital to protect against the various risks to which its lending activities exposed it. This was a failure of regulatory and supervisory responsibility, not just of interest rate policy.

This failure of regulatory oversight did not happen overnight. Nor am I suggesting that government was principally to blame for the catastrophe. That is like saying that when a thief burgles your house, it is all the fault of the local police force for failing to prevent it. Surely the burglar deserves some of the credit. The evolution toward greater risk taking and higher leverage in the private sector that made the financial system fragile reflected natural human proclivities whose consequences have been periodically evident for centuries.

The key point is that if we accept an important government responsibility for the moderation of business cycles—one enshrined in law in the Employment Act of 1946—this includes responsibility for the prevention or moderation of financial crises, and we cannot expect this to be executed through interest rate policy alone. The control of leverage through financial supervision and regulation needs to be the focus of any policy regime hoping to reduce the probabilities of recurrence. This lesson was learned and then gradually un-learned during and after the Great Depression. What needs to be done to re-duce the likelihood that the U.S. and world economy will again be threatened by 1930s-style depression is in principle straightforward.

Rethinking the fragmented nature of our supervisory and regulatory struc-ture is obviously necessary. The main problem has been that financial institu-tions held too little capital given the risks to which they were exposed, which is simply the flip side of the explosion of leverage. Higher capital adequacy re-quirements; restrictions on the use of off-balance sheet special-purpose vehicles whose intent and effect is to circumvent them; requirements that regulations apply to institutions that are banks in everything but name only—the need for all of this is evident. The Basel II standards, which gave banks considerable dis-cretion in how much capital they held, need revision because the flexibility that was their hallmark gave banks too many opportunities to do end runs around them. FDIC chair Sheila Bair issued prescient warnings about the dangers that Basel II would allow banks to hold too little capital, increasing their profit po-tential on the upside but leaving taxpayers increasingly vulnerable to downside risk (Bair 2007).

These standards were, however, only part of the problem since much of the shadow banking system was not subject to them. Economic historians are well aware of George Santayana's dictum that those who don't know their history are compelled to repeat it. The lessons of history were available, but many of us chose to ignore them, or not inform ourselves of them, or deny their ap-plicability, or otherwise stick our heads in the sand with the view that what we didn't know couldn't hurt us. What a closer reading of history could have told us was that long periods of relatively stable economic growth breed financial in-novation, pressure for lighter regulatory oversight, greater risk tolerance among lenders and borrowers, and resort to higher leverage in efforts to boost returns. A financial system becomes highly vulnerable when the evolution of holding riskier assets and the pursuit of greater leverage simultaneously characterize household, nonfinancial, and financial business balance sheets. This was the state reached by the U.S. economy in 2007 and 2008.

In some, although not all, respects this was similar to what happened to the U.S. economy in 1928 and 1929.[13] Just as a closer reading of history could have helped us avoid the largely self-inflicted wounds of 2007–2009, recognizing the origins of the more recent downturn in an increasingly complex web of finan-cial relationships can sharpen our understanding of the Great Depression and its persistence. Economists have given greater emphasis in recent years to legal and institutional structures in comparative studies of economic growth in different countries. The transactions costs associated with litigation and other legal processes also influence the depth and duration of recessions. In extreme cases a financial system will effectively cease to function under the weight of a sea of suits, countersuits, and bankruptcy filings resulting from broken promises: the inability or unwillingness to fulfill past contractual obligations. This is the practical meaning of the overused term "financial meltdown."

Misreadings of the Coase theorem have sometimes encouraged economists to treat law and rights as a veil, with little effect on outcomes. This is a mistake. We know, based on the experience of Eastern Europe after the collapse of communism, that the absence of a transparent system of land registration, leading to insecurity of land title, can prove an obstacle to economic development. So too, in a different way, can the legal detritus of a prior boom hinder recovery. Greater attention to legal and regulatory issues is warranted as we think about policies to mitigate the effects of the 2007–2009 experience and reduce the likelihood of recurrence and as we ponder how its lessons may lead us to rethink our interpretation of the Depression.

Left unchecked by effective regulation, profit-seeking behavior rendered a financial system progressively more fragile so that a shock that, in an earlier period characterized by less risky lending and less levered balance sheets, might have been absorbed without a large impact on output and employment, now had the potential to wreak havoc on the real economy. At that point, the only thing preventing a cataclysm was massive intervention by both the fiscal and monetary authorities. All of this was abundantly clear from the vantage point of 2010. Why wasn't it so earlier?

MINSKY AND FINANCIAL FRAGILITY

One macroeconomist whose posthumous reputation deserved and experienced a large boost was Hyman Minsky. Those who knew Minsky could recall that he made a strong impression in person, trying with great intensity to help those who would listen to understand his point of view. Reading his work (1975, 1986) in light of 2007–2009, one cannot help but be impressed by his insights and prescience. To be sure, his analysis of inflation might have acknowledged the possible influence of supply shocks in the 1974 and 1979 episodes. And the low course of inflation over the last quarter century does not accord with his view that the periodic government responses to financial crises necessarily imparted an inflationary bias to the economy. But when it comes to understanding what transpired in the financial sector starting in 2007—or for that matter what happened in the buildup to the Great Depression—his analysis of the evolution of financial fragility provides an excellent starting point. Partly in response to the gathering crisis, some theoretically minded economists (for example, Geanakoplos 2009; Shin 2009) began investigating the systemic effects of higher leverage, but their work has been almost entirely ahistorical. Minsky effectively placed the financial cycle of boom and bust within a larger historical context. Charles Kindleberger's (1978) popular history of manias and panics drew on Minsky's insights.[14]

Minsky's thinking was original. Although he bore the onus in some circles of being considered heterodox, he was not out to bash capitalism, and indeed he argued that a free market economy might do a pretty good job of allocating the goods produced in a year. But he distinguished between what he called allocation efficiency and stabilization efficiency. His identification of the key economic problem was not so much the static allocation of given resources among competing resources as it was what he called the capital development of the economy through time (Minsky 1986, p. 114). Although some expansion projects could be financed through retained earnings, an important feature of an advanced economy was and always would be external finance. To the degree that this was debt finance, always more significant in magnitude than equity finance, firms sold IOUs and received cash now in return for a promise of cash later. Debt contracts linked cash flows in the present with those in the future. The provision of finance was critical in influencing the amount of investment spending undertaken.

As, over time, riskier projects were undertaken with higher leverage, the potential for a financial panic increased. When borrowers were unable to meet maturing obligations out of current receipts, either because their assets were illiquid or not performing or because their short-term liabilities weren't being rolled over, they sold assets, and when this became endemic, particularly when the selling was done by financial intermediaries, the economy underwent a financial panic.

Minsky allowed that a laissez-faire approach might do a better job with allocation efficiency. But big government could more successfully avert large financial crises. The relative magnitudes of the potential losses had to be kept in mind. Because the likely damage from "stabilization inefficiency" was far greater than whatever efficiency losses might be introduced by big government "interference" in the short run, a regulatory state was both necessary and desirable. Unless well-designed and executed rules governing the financial sector were in place, profit-seeking behavior would eventually produce a financial crisis with negative consequences for the real economy. The question was not if but when. Even if regulations were effective, the most that could be hoped for was an amelioration in its depth and duration. When the crisis hit, the real economy would experience a prolonged decline in output and employment unless the problem was addressed on an emergency basis with sufficient fiscal and monetary stimulus. The federal government was too small during the Depression years to provide this, although the Second World War demonstrated the merits of the prescription.

Capitalist economies, said Minsky, endogenously produce financial crises. These crises were periodic features of economic history and not simply the result of external shocks, be they technological, fiscal, or monetary. The financial buccaneering of the years prior to the Great Depression led to a regulatory response, a central legacy of the New Deal. In late 2010 it remained to be seen whether the response to the Great Recession would be as effective.

After the Second World War households and businesses held low-risk liquid assets with low leverage. The forced saving during the war—the result of full employment, saving bond drives, rationing, and the simple unavailability of certain goods—meant that the asset side of household portfolios consisted primarily of insured demand deposits and directly held government bonds. The asset sides of bank balance sheets were dominated by safe government debt. Interest rate restrictions (Regulation Q) controlled what banks paid for their funds, and households confidently held deposits in banks because of federal deposit insurance instituted during the New Deal. Banking was boring, and the relative skills and remuneration of its labor force declined relative to the pre-Depression years.

As economic growth and inflation whittled away at the burden of debt repayment, the ratio of government debt to GDP shrank, and banks replaced government bonds with loans to the private sector that were riskier but paid higher returns. As the economy moved into the 1970s, attention shifted from the assets to the liabilities side of balance sheets. Firms expanded their liabilities beyond simply equity and demand deposits to include Certificates of Deposit, overnight repurchase agreements, and borrowing in the Federal Funds market. These latter categories of debt did not require that reserves be held against them and allowed an increase in debt-to-equity ratios, which, everything else equal, boosted bank profits.[15]

Again, in combination, these strategies—increasing the riskiness of lending, which showed up in the assets held on the left-hand side of the balance sheet, and increasing bank leverage, as reflected in the debt-to-equity ratio on the liability (right-hand) side—were the twin engines, along with the political dynamic of deregulation and other private sector financial innovation, that permitted a huge growth in finance sector profits, as well as big increases in the skill, education, and remuneration levels of those working in the sector. The financial sector of the U.S. economy booked less than 9 percent of domestic corporate profits in 1948. That share rose moderately in the 1950s and 1960s, breaking 20 percent for the first time in 1970. During the 1970s and 1980s it averaged 18.3 percent. In the 1990s, the share notched up, averaging 25.3 percent (NIPA tables 6.16A, 6.16B, and 6.16C).

The finance sector soared in the new millennium, with the spread of increasingly complex derivatives, facilitated by the removal of any trading restrictions as a consequence of the Commodity Futures Modernization Act in December 2000. In the years 2001–2003 inclusive, the finance sector booked over 40 percent of domestic corporate profits and approximately a third of domestic corporate profits in 2004–2007 inclusive—this from a sector that employed a little over 6 percent of FTE workers in the country.[16] The finance sector's share of domestic corporate profits dropped to 28 percent in 2008 (NIPA table 6.16D, lines 2 and 3) before recovering sharply.[17] The housing boom was not unrelated to this derivatives explosion since the fees to be earned from apparently turning dross into gold generated an almost insatiable appetite for more risky assets (such as subprime and alt-A mortgages) that could be securitized. The swollen share of financial sector profits, besides influencing the career plans of many Ivy League graduates, played an important role in worsening income inequality in the United States.

Minsky's writings pointed out that investment volatility was not simply the result of waves of enthusiasm and pessimism among entrepreneurs and corporations. It also reflected self-generating cycles of increasingly aggressive risk taking among lenders, including commercial banks and other financial institutions, with influences on both sides of their balance sheets.

The Modigliani-Miller theorem states that under certain conditions debt-equity ratios should be irrelevant in determining the value of a firm. But for the economy as a whole, leverage matters for both nonfinancial firms (typically borrowers) and financial firms (both lenders and borrowers). It matters for the obvious reason that it makes units more vulnerable to insolvency in the face of a downturn. It matters for the more technical reason that it impairs the ability of the banking system to judge the credit worthiness of borrowers, arguably its most important function. Asymmetric information means in this instance that potential borrowers know more about their projects, in particular their riskiness, than do lenders. Lenders would like to advance money to borrowers who will agree to pay high interest rates and undertake (or invest in) low-risk projects that will yield enough to allow them to repay the loan. Similarly, health insurance companies would like to write policies on individuals who will pay high premiums and not get sick. In both types of markets adverse selection is a problem. Those most eager for health insurance are those who think it most likely they will get sick, although they won't necessarily reveal this to the insurance company. And borrowers most eager to take money from a lender on given terms are likely to be those who plan to undertake riskier projects. If a risky project pays off, a borrower will profit handsomely. If it doesn't, the lender will own a good part of the downside. Credit markets allow people to gamble with other people's money.

Ideally, banks use their resources to evaluate independently the likely success of projects and thus overcome the adverse selection that otherwise results. Applicants with riskier projects will be charged higher interest rates to compensate for their greater probability of default or in the limit will be denied credit entirely. But the process of judging credit worthiness and rationing credit operates increasingly poorly when financial institutions become highly levered, as they become borrowing as much as lending institutions.

Moral hazard emerges in situations where individuals or institutions bear risk without taking full account of or bearing the full prospective burdens of a bad outcome. Once a loan is made, for example, borrowers may be tempted to use the money for a riskier project than the one they described in their loan application. The temptation exists, again, because the borrower owns the upside but the lender owns much of the downside. As a financial system becomes more fragile, moral hazard comes to afflict not just traditional borrowers—households and nonfinancial corporations—but financial corporations as well, because they also are big borrowers.

Managers and executives in banking face temptations to make risky bets with other people's money—since if realizations are good, they get huge bonuses, but they are unlikely to suffer proportionally if things go bad, although taxpayers, bank stockholders, and other uninsured creditors might. Principals (in this case bank creditors) face challenges in getting agents (in this case bank loan officers) to act in the principals' interest. This reality underpins the case for government-enforced changes in financial sector compensation policies.

These types of problems are much reduced if a firm invests its own retained earnings, and, in the case of external finance, they are mitigated when there is sizable firm equity at risk. The borrower has more skin in the game and therefore shares more of the downside risk. Similarly, the greater the down payment a house buyer makes, the less the lender has to worry about the temptation to engage in risky gambling with other people's money. Just as banks face temptations to juice their returns by holding riskier assets and pursuing higher leverage, so too do firms and households, particularly when the loans (as is the case in most real estate lending in the United States) are nonrecourse.[18]

With a very few exceptions, those within the financial sector were, in the run-up to the Great Recession, too busy making money to worry about the future—and the same was true of many of the borrowers.[19] Economists and other policymakers who should have known better suffered from the human impairment of fickle memory. Periods of relatively steady economic growth and financial stability such as that between 1946 and 1966 bred a misplaced complacency and a lack of interest in those warning of impending crisis. There is, after all, rarely a shortage of doomsayers—most of the time they are wrong, and there are costs to trying to mitigate what may be overblown threats. So it was natural that whistle-blowers had a hard time getting our attention. This was surely the case for Minsky, who died in 1996.

And it was true for Brooksley Born, then head of the CFTC, who in 1998 tried to bring the trading of credit default swaps under the purview of that regulatory agency. She was effectively—and apparently almost literally—shouted down by Alan Greenspan (chairman of the Fed), Arthur Levitt (head of the SEC), Robert Rubin (secretary of the Treasury), and Larry Summers (then his deputy and ultimately his successor).[20] Summers told Congress that "the parties to these kinds of contract are largely sophisticated financial institutions that would appear to be eminently capable of protecting themselves from fraud and counterparty insolvencies."[21] The issue, as it turned out, however, was not simply a question of consumer or investor protection. It was a question of protecting the larger population either from a devastating depression or from substantial liens on future incomes in the form of higher taxes. Greenspan, Rubin, Levitt, and Summers, to a greater or lesser degree, subsequently admitted that they had been wrong to dismiss Born's concerns.[22]

Having successfully defeated legislative initiatives in 1994 (Tett, 2009, ch. 2), and dodged Born's bullet in 1998, an organized group of financial sector lobbyists determined in 2010 to forestall any government oversight of derivatives or, failing that, carve out large areas of exemption.[23] Financial crisis and the recession that followed strongly suggest that the opportunities for private profit in writing these contracts (and presumably the gains to those who buy them) are far outweighed by the threat to the real economy and the public purse they present.

There was and is less consensus about the damage done by the repeal of the Depression-era Glass-Steagall Act by the Gramm-Leach-Bliley Act in 1999. Other countries, such as Germany, integrated commercial and investment banking without necessarily increasing systemic risk (Glass-Steagall had separated them). For a long time repeal was defended by those who said that the larger, more diversified financial firms made possible by Gramm-Leach-Bliley proved to be less vulnerable to the housing shock. But this argument is not consistent with evidence that behemoths such as Citigroup and Bank of America were among the most seriously impaired. Citigroup, in particular, went furthest down the road of becoming a financial supermarket and remained, in the fall of 2009, "effectively a ward of the state, kept alive through multiple infusions of taxpayer funds" (Morgenstern and Martin 2009; Sorkin 2009, p. 530). In the fourth quarter of 2009, Citigroup continued to lose money. And the same was true of Bank of America, which suffered massive losses on its mortgage loan and consumer-lending portfolios. If these companies did not technically fail, unlike the more than one hundred smaller banks shut down by the FDIC in 2009, it was because the FDIC lacked the power and capability to deal with such large organizations, a lacuna that the Dodd-Frank Act (2010) tried to remedy.

Within the U.S. context, Gramm-Leach-Bliley can now be seen as another milestone on the road to allowing the development of huge diversified financial supermarkets whose size, complexity, and interconnectedness—particularly through issuance and ownership of structured debt securities and credit default swaps—were key aspects of the growing financial fragility of the U.S. economy. But the damage the repeal of Glass-Steagall may have done to the economy resulted from its interaction with other regulatory decisions.

In interviews reported on in a May 2009 *New York Times* article, former President Bill Clinton took responsibility for accepting the arguments of Greenspan and others against the regulation of credit default swaps, viewing this as the worst economic error of his presidency. Clinton summarized the indictment against his administration in the area of financial policy as threefold. First, that he used the Community Reinvestment Act to pressure banks to make loans to borrowers who were unlikely to repay. This he rejected as a political canard: he did not see much evidence that this was an important cause of the crisis (see also Posner 2009, p. 242, and McLean 2009, who reach similar conclusions). The second strike against him, he argued, was that he signed Gramm-Leach-Bliley in 1999. He acknowledged that this might have allowed some banking institutions to get bigger, which contributed to the difficulty of unwinding them, but he also repeated the familiar claim that more diversified institutions did better and that allowing commercial banks to perform investment banking functions was not an important source of the problem. He also said, however, that he did not anticipate eight years of a largely neutered SEC.

Clinton's uncertainty about how much responsibility to attribute to the repeal of Glass-Steagall mirrors that within the economic profession itself. It is clear that the effects of repeal cannot be analyzed in a vacuum. These effects were in part a function of changes in other aspects of the regulatory environment. Mervyn King, governor of the Bank of England; former Federal Reserve chairman Paul Volcker; and other economists, such as Simon Johnson and Joseph Stiglitz, called for a reintroduction of the separation of commercial and investment banking because of their conviction that the alternative—better regulation—simply wouldn't work. Columbia economist Charles Calomiris argued that the economies of scale and scope enabled by large, diversified financial organizations ultimately redounded to the benefit of customers, but such assurances faced a more skeptical audience than was true before the financial crisis.[24]

On the third count against him, however, his failure to heed Born's call to regulate derivatives, Clinton was unequivocal. He accepted responsibility for not backing her proposals that derivatives be regulated and exchange traded and for signing the Commodity Futures Modernization Act, the last legislative act of his presidency. He made no attempt to defend these decisions, any more than he tried to defend his decision not to intervene in Rwanda to stop genocide, which he saw as one of his major foreign policy mistakes (Baker 2009). And in a speech and question and answer session on May 29, 2009, former president George W. Bush said that "a big culprit in the nation's economic crisis was the lack of responsible regulation," although, in contrast with Clinton, he did not acknowledge any personal responsibility for this outcome.[25]

It may seem peculiar in a book about economics and economic history to cite interviews with policymakers, to descend into what is sometimes derided as "the blame game." This matters, however, because there is a widespread inclination, particularly among financial market insiders, to view the crisis as an act of God, something nobody could have foreseen or done anything to prevent. Therefore no one can or should be held responsible, and therefore, it is argued, attempts at strengthened regulation will impose costs without appreciably reducing the probability of recurrence.

Economic forces in a competitive market economy diffuse responsibility. They are impersonal—you can't attribute the amount of wheat produced worldwide or its price to any one or a small group of individuals. No farmer can control, or be held responsible for, these outcomes. The situation is different in the political processes that structure the legal or regulatory environment or when one is talking about decisions within large business or financial organizations with some market power. In these realms the methodologies of the economist, the historian, and the journalist complement each other. Identifiable individuals can and do influence outcomes. It makes sense to award credit, assign blame or responsibility, and more generally hold individuals accountable for their actions. Policy decisions—and these go beyond Federal Reserve decisions about interest rates—can have large consequences, just as can a decision to go to war in Iraq or to refrain from launching a nuclear strike. Identifying policy errors—

those of omission and those of commission — is a necessary and desirable part of figuring out how we got to where we are and trying to avoid these outcomes in the future. The financial fragility of the U.S. and world economies — their increasing vulnerability to a shock of a given magnitude — was only partly the outcome of the impersonal forces of the market. It was also a function of identifiable decisions that shaped the legal and regulatory environment in the public sector and of innovations, financial strategies, and incentives within the private sector.

A few economists, such as Nouriel Roubini, predicted the crisis, and Robert Shiller warned repeatedly that the rise in housing prices was unsustainable. Both were generally ignored. Raghuran Rajan flagged the growing riskiness of the financial structure at an August 2005 conference in Jackson Hole, Wyoming, honoring Alan Greenspan. Larry Summers suggested that Rajan was a Luddite (Lahart 2009). It is of course true that there will always be those who predict disaster, and now and then, like a stopped clock, they will be right. But it is too facile to dismiss all who raised warnings in this fashion (as does John Cochrane in his September 2009 reply to Paul Krugman's article on the state of macroeconomics). Where the evidence and reasoning behind the prediction had substance, it behooves us to examine why some individuals were able to get it more or less right.

From the vantage point of 2010, it is evident that a series of postwar financial crises, of generally increasing severity, afflicted the U.S. economy, starting arguably as early as 1966 (this was Minsky's position). Each of these crises was effectively contained by government interventions, which addressed the immediate problems. But these interventions themselves helped lay the foundations for subsequent problems by reinforcing more relaxed attitudes toward risk — since market participants viewed themselves as protected on the downside by the Federal Reserve and the U.S. Treasury. All of this was potentiated by well-organized political efforts to loosen some of the regulatory "straightjackets" that represented the legacy of New Deal reforms, which constrained the growth of bank and financial sector profits.

Landmarks along this road included the Garn-St. Germain Depository Institutions Act of 1982, which led directly to the savings and loan crisis less than a decade later; the 1994 Reigle-Neal Interstate Banking and Branching Efficiency Act; repeal of the Depression-era Glass-Steagall Act in 1999 by the Gramm-Leach-Bliley Act;[26] and the 2004 decisions by the SEC under William R. Donaldson to remove controls (the 1973 net capital rule) that limited leverage of investment banks to the eleven to twelve range. This regulatory relaxation allowed what were then the five large investment banks (Bear Stearns, Goldman Sachs, J. P. Morgan Chase, Merrill Lynch, and Lehman Brothers) to enter a

"Consolidated Supervised Entity" program permitting them to escape the traditional debt-to-equity limitations, substituting an "alternative net capital rule" (Coffee 2008). The consequence was that leverage in these firms soared to thirty-three or thirty-five to one, with generally disastrous results, once house prices ceased to appreciate at the same rate. After the crash, financial firms, many of them receiving federal bailout assistance, spent millions successfully lobbying the Financial Accounting Standards Board (FASB) and Congress for a relaxation of fair value, or mark-to-market accounting rules, in spite of the fact that existing rules already contained exceptions for assets that traded infrequently (Pullian and McGinty 2009).

The exuberant phase of a financial cycle involves financial innovation, and that was certainly the case in preparing the ground for 2007–2009. Mortgage-backed securities (MBSs) were innovated by government-sponsored enterprises, including the Government National Mortgage Association (Ginnie Mae), the Federal National Mortgage Association (Fannie Mae or FNMA), and the Federal Home Loan Mortgage Corporation (Freddie Mac). The first MBSs were issued in 1970. They were what are now called plain vanilla, or pass-through securities, bonds that gave their holders a right to a pro rata share of the interest and principal payments from the underlying pool. A pass-through derivative could not turn junk into gold. It couldn't alter the expected return from the underlying mortgages, although the diversification resulting from securitization could reduce the variance of the payout compared to what one might have obtained had one loaned to an individual mortgagee.

Collateralized debt obligations (CDOs) were a private sector innovation dating from the 1980s, and they could perform that alchemy. Starting with a pool of risky mortgages, CDO engineers created different grades or tranches of derivative securities. Senior tranches paid lower interest rates but were safer. More junior tranches paid higher interest rates but took the first hit if some of the underlying mortgages went bad. Ratings agencies (the most important were Moodys, Standard and Poors, and Fitch) stamped the senior tranches AAA, with the result that insurance companies and pension funds with fiduciary responsibilities could legally hold them. These senior tranches were now considered investment grade, even if all of the underlying mortgages were subprime. Dross had apparently been turned into precious metal. Still, some holders of these bonds were not entirely convinced and worried about how safe they were or wished to bet that they weren't.

Enter credit default swaps (CDSs). For a small "premium," institutions could insure themselves against the risk the bonds might default. And unlike home or life insurance, one could buy insurance against the default of assets one didn't hold. Since swaps were not technically insurance, they were largely beyond the reach of state regulators, and American International Group (AIG) and other issuers did not maintain adequate reserves to meet collateral calls when the likelihood of default rose or when their own credit rating was downgraded. In a sense, they simply pocketed the premiums without providing the insurance.[27]

Did it make sense to have government regulators require that certain institutions hold investment-grade securities but then allow private companies (given a stamp of approval by the government but paid by the issuers of the securities) to determine whether particular bonds measured up? Ratings agencies faced a conflict of interest because they were being paid by the "sell side" rather than the "buy side." At the same time, it should be acknowledged that most of the acquirers were sophisticated institutions that in many instances wanted the high-yielding AAA tranches as much as did the entities issuing them and the agencies rating them. It was win-win-win for all concerned, except, as it will likely turn out, the taxpayer and the unemployed.

The securitization of mortgages and the evolution of an originate-and-distribute model for mortgage lending were part of a growing and dangerous belief that the wonders of diversification and the construction of complex derivatives could make it unnecessary for the originators of loans to either scrutinize individual loans or seriously assess whether they were in fact likely to be repaid. Thus one of the central functions of a system of financial intermediation fell by the wayside. The developing system allowed the originators not to care because a loan could be sold into a larger pool, and other institutions were eager to hold securities derived from it, particularly if they could also hold insurance on it, which other institutions were eager to provide. So down payments became optional, and traditional verification of income or requirements for income were, in many cases, no longer deemed necessary. The securitization of mortgages in CDOs rather than plain vanilla pass-through bonds introduced an additional layer of complexity and opacity separating the derivatives from the underlying mortgages, which further reduced possible market discipline on the originators.

Indeed, a feature of both the 1920s and the 2000s was a growing opacity of financial instruments, with CDOs squared, for example, consisting of derivatives whose underlying securities were CDOs, whose underlying securities were ultimately individual mortgages. Like nesting matrushka dolls, it became difficult to know what was of value at the core, and in the manic phase of a financial boom, people stopped caring. The investment trusts of the 1920s—essentially closed-end mutual funds (White 2000)—shared some of these features. Such innovations are usually touted for their diversification or risk allocation features, but one cannot help thinking that the opacity is, at some level, not a bug but a design feature, as is said in Silicon Valley when people complain about software glitches.

For those skeptical of the safety of CDOs and other complex derivatives, CDSs provided cheap insurance against the risk that they might go bad. AIG, a major seller, saw the "premiums" as essentially free money since it thought massive defaults to be unlikely, and it failed to carry adequate reserves against these liabilities (indeed the company held many senior tranches of these CDOs itself). Technically, the CDS contracts were not considered insurance and were thus largely exempt from the oversight of state insurance regulators. Following the defeat of Brooksley Born's 1998 proposal, the Commodity Futures Modernization Act guaranteed that these contracts, including many sold to entities that did not hold the underlying asset being insured, would escape all regulation.

Throughout the economy, profit-seeking actors in households, nonfinancial corporations, commercial banks, investment banks, private equity firms, and hedge funds were pursuing the double magic of holding riskier assets and attempting to supercharge returns through higher leverage. A skeptical attitude toward the merits of financial sector regulation under both Presidents Clinton and Bush completed the sunny picture. But the consequence was a fragile system that can now only be sustained through liens on future taxpayer incomes in the context of a significant reduction in the wealth of American households and in the face of what will, even with successful containment, be a long recession. These facts are stubborn.

The huge profits earned in the latter part of 2009 by Goldman Sachs and J. P. Morgan Chase and the ability of these and other companies to repay Troubled Asset Relief Program (TARP) funds does not alter this reality. Most of the taxpayer losses will likely be booked at non-banks such as AIG, Fannie Mae, Freddie Mac, the FHA, and the General Motors Acceptance Corporation (GMAC). The effective guaranteeing of the liabilities of these entities is one reason part of the banking system was able to return to profitability by the end of 2009.[28] Thus responsibility for the crisis should not necessarily be allocated according to where the largest taxpayer costs are finally incurred, nor should entities ultimately able to pay off their TARP funds necessarily be let off the hook. The liabilities of these non-banks served as assets of other financial institutions, and in guaranteeing or making good on these liabilities, the government strengthened the balance sheets of counterparties.

Prior to the Great Depression, lightly regulated financial institutions financed waves of infrastructure and other physical capital accumulation. This period ended with the failures of thousands of banks in the early 1930s, a catastrophic decline in output and employment, and a regulatory response that accompanied recovery. This was followed after the war by two decades of financial tranquility, which was in turn succeeded by periods of generally slower economic growth marked by financial crises of increasing severity, culminating in 2007–2009.[29] How much this will disrupt the accumulation of physical capital remains a big question. What is not in doubt is that financial cycles, which are, as Minsky argued, endogenous to a capitalist economy, affect the accumulation rates of structures and equipment, and that the resulting instability affects productivity growth, certainly in the short run but possibly also in the longer run. As noted, the course of recent events bears similarities to what happened during the worst years of the Depression.

Both Alan Greesnpan and Ben Bernanke argued that there was little the Fed could have done to prevent the housing bubble because the United States was overwhelmed by a wave of global saving that drove down long-term interest rates over which the central bank had little control. This tidal wave washing on to American shores was partly the result of reactions to the 1998 financial crisis (Asian central banks wanted a buffer of U.S.-denominated reserves to protect themselves in future crises from the ministrations of the International Monetary Fund), as well as recycled petrodollars generated by the run-up in the price of oil between 1998 and mid-2008. These inflows of saving financed not only the U.S. government deficits but also the boom in residential capital formation. They made it possible for the country to have large government deficits along with relatively full employment without much private sector crowding out.

There are reasons, however, to be skeptical that this is the whole story. As Bernanke argues as evidence against Taylor's view, asset price bubbles also developed in a number of other countries that were not pursuing accommodative monetary policies. On the other hand, the history of our international economic relations casts doubt on the view that a global saving glut was at the root of our problems. In the 1920s we were exporting financial capital to finance a current account surplus, whereas from the mid-1980s onward we were importing financial capital to finance a current account deficit. As noted, this stark difference suggests that the financial cycle evolves according to a dynamic that is to a large degree independent of the state of the balance of payments or current account/capital account.

The regulatory or policy failure was not simply or primarily a matter of interest rate policy. Rather it was a failure to control, or really to be interested in controlling, the growth of leverage. This is understandable from a political-economic perspective. In the boom period, higher leverage combined with riskier lending engendered vastly increased financial sector profits and compensation and both the means and motivation to lobby effectively against government regulation, which stood in the way of the continued operation of this money train. That is how we got to where we are.

There is thus a strong case that lax regulatory environments contributed to the onset of both the Great Depression and the recession of 2007–2009 and that well-designed rules are necessary to reduce the likelihood of future crises. In part it is a matter of fairness. Citizens should not be faced with the choice of either saving the creditors and employees of financial institutions that are too big or too interconnected to fail from the consequences of their risky behavior or enduring serious declines across the economy in output or employment.

Once the economy goes into recession, of course, it is too late. The question then becomes what can be done to mitigate the severity of the downturn. Whereas the probability of future crisis will be influenced by the nature of reforms in financial regulation, the cumulative output loss from the Great Recession will depend on current fiscal and monetary policies, as well as the ability and willingness of the banking sector as a whole to clean up its balance sheets. The economic history of the 1930s provides object lessons on the importance of certain kinds of spending, particularly on private and public capital accumulation, in contributing to recovery, as well as the consequences of persisting weakness in components of private sector accumulation, in part due to earlier excesses, in prolonging duration.

CAPITAL ACCUMULATION AND INCOME TO CAPITAL DURING THE DEPRESSION

Financial crisis disrupts the accumulation of structures and equipment, and economic recovery depends in part on the revival of private spending on such assets. The broad contours of what happened to capital accumulation during the Depression are well known. Gross private domestic investment, which had been at historically high levels between 1923 and 1928, plummeted between 1929 and 1933. Aggregate investment then recovered through 1937, fell off in 1938, and surged again through 1941. This boom and bust was in part the reflection of a financial cycle of leveraging and a relaxed attitude toward risk, followed by deleveraging and a greatly increased fear of risk, in many respects similar to what happened in the 2000s.

Although the disruption to the accumulation of equipment (producer durables) during the Depression was transitory, the retardation in the accumulation of longer-lived structures persisted until after the war. The raw data show that it was most prolonged for nonresidential structures, particularly commercial and office structures, as well as manufacturing structures, structures associated with the generation of electric power, and railroad structures. Residential structures recovered somewhat more rapidly, but it was really only after the war that the economy was able to move beyond the legacies of the 1920s boom. Some of the slowed recovery in manufacturing and railroad structures, however, should be interpreted as the consequence of capital-saving innovation, which reduced the need and demand for new structures. For housing, it is harder to make this argument, and retardation can be more closely linked to the legacy of the prior expansion.

In the 1920s as well as the 2000s, the credit boom resulted from the enthusiasms of lenders, not just borrowers. During the early 1930s, some of the slowed flow of credit to finance longer-lived structures reflected lender reluctance, not just lack of interest on the part of borrowers. This was especially so prior to 1934, as thousands of banks failed, information capital on the credit-worthiness of borrowers was destroyed (Bernanke 1983), and both lending and accumulation plummeted. By the second half of the decade, access to loanable funds was less of a constraint. With the exception of railroads, retardation in accumulation appears to have been principally the result of factors on the demand side that varied by asset category.

The slower recovery of investment in structures reflected in part the fact that, in an environment of uncertainty and heightened risk aversion, lenders were, everything else equal, more likely to lend for equipment acquisition than the construction of buildings. Both types of loans could be collateralized, but resale markets for equipment were thicker and transactions costs lower in the event of repossession because equipment categories are more homogenous. Equipment is shorter lived, so the loans made for its acquisition were likely to be paid back sooner. Thus even in railroads, the sector most credit-constrained in the second half of the 1930s, the revival of equipment spending was substantially stronger than it was for structures.

Figure 10.1 plots the three main components of fixed investment in the United States from 1919 to 1941, measured in 1929 dollars. The series are constructed by taking the chain-type quantity indexes for investment in fixed assets from table 2.7 of the BEA's fixed asset data and translating them into 1929 dollars based on the values for that year in current dollars from Fixed Asset Table 2.8. These constant dollar numbers show investment in residential housing peaking in 1925–1926, staying relatively high through 1928, and then, already in 1929, beginning a steep downward slide. At its nadir in 1933, real investment in residential construction had fallen 85 percent from its 1925–1926 high point. And while recovering substantially after 1933, it did not reattain its already reduced 1929 level until just prior to the war in 1941.

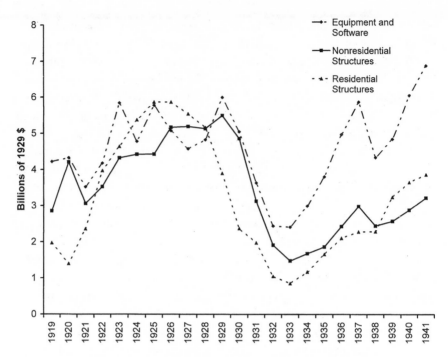

Figure 10.1: Gross Investment, Major Categories, 1919–1941
Source: BEA, Fixed Asset Tables 2.7 and 2.8, http://www.bea.gov.

Although gross investment in housing remained positive throughout the Depression years, net investment became negative in 1932, 1933, and 1934, for a total decumulation over the three-year period of $1.2 billion (current prices) (see table 10.2). Because houses are long lived, however, annual depreciation is a relatively small portion of the stock, so these deficiencies resulted in only small declines in the stock. Average prices of houses over those three years were about 77 percent of prices in 1929 (see Fixed Asset Table 5.5.4A), so we can translate this $1.2 billion nominal into roughly $1.6 billion in 1929 dollars on a net fixed residential housing stock in 1931 of $120.61 billion in 1929 dollars. In spite of plummeting investment, therefore, the decline in the value of the real net stock of housing was small, as can be seen in figure 10.4. As positive accumulation resumed, the net stock recovered and grew modestly after 1934 so that by 1941 it was about 5 percent higher than its 1931 peak. The growth during the 1931–1941 decade was, nevertheless, much slower than between 1925 and 1928, when the stock advanced 12 percent in just three years. The average age of the residential housing stock, which reached a low point in 1928 of 23.6 years, had increased to 30 years in 1941 (Fixed Asset Table 5.9).

Table 10.2. Gross and Net Investment, 1929–1941 (billions of current dollars)

Investment Type	1929	1930	1931	1932	1933	1934	1935	1936	1937	1938	1939	1940	1941
Equipment and software (gross)	5.5	4.2	2.6	1.5	1.4	2.1	2.8	3.9	4.8	3.4	3.9	5.2	6.4
Capital consumption	4.4	4.4	4.1	3.7	3.3	3.4	3.3	3.4	3.7	3.9	3.9	4.1	4.6
Equipment and software (net)	1.1	-0.2	-1.4	-2.2	-1.9	-1.3	-0.5	0.5	1.1	-0.5	0.0	1.1	1.9
Nonresidential structures (gross)	5.5	4.4	2.6	1.4	1.1	1.2	1.4	1.9	2.7	2.1	2.2	2.6	3.3
Capital consumption Nonresidential	2.4	2.4	2.2	1.9	1.9	1.9	1.9	2	2.2	2.2	2.1	2.2	2.4
Nonresidential structures (net)	3.0	2.1	0.4	-0.5	-0.8	-0.7	-0.5	-0.1	0.5	-0.1	0.1	0.4	0.8
Residential structures (gross)	4.0	2.4	1.8	0.8	0.6	0.9	1.3	1.7	2.1	2.1	3.0	3.5	4.1
Capital consumption Residential	1.6	1.6	1.4	1.2	1.1	1.3	1.2	1.3	1.5	1.5	1.5	1.6	1.8
Residential structures (net)	2.4	0.8	0.4	-0.4	-0.5	-0.3	0.1	0.4	0.6	0.6	1.5	1.9	2.3

Source: BEA, http://www.bea.gov, NIPA table 5.25, "Gross and Net Domestic Investment by Major Type."

The series for investment in nonresidential construction peaked later (1929) and stayed relatively high through 1930, the consequence of a central business district building boom that followed the previous waves of apartment and single-family housing construction and involved projects (such as the Empire State Building) that were only partially complete when the aggregate economy began heading south in 1929. Figure 10.2 shows a breakdown of some of the components of nonresidential construction. The construction of commercial space peaked in 1927, but office and hospital construction peaked in 1930. Figure 10.3 plots investment in railroad and manufacturing structures. Investment in railroad structures peaked in 1926, in manufacturing structures in 1929. Other than its later peak, the series for real investment in nonresidential construction traces out a pattern similar to that for residential construction, except that nonresidential construction did not fall quite as far or recover quite as much during the Depression.

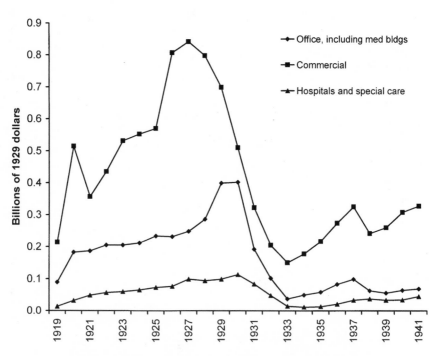

Figure 10.2: Gross Investment in Commercial, Office,
and Hospital Structures, 1919–1941
Source: BEA, Fixed Asset Tables 2.7 and 2.8, http://www.bea.gov.

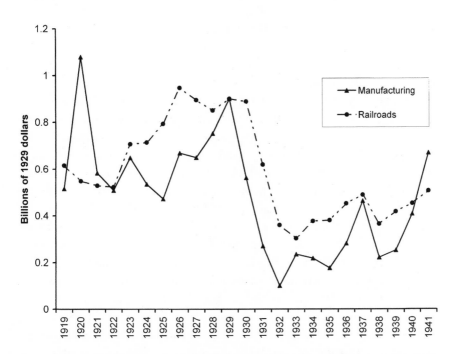

Figure 10.3: Gross Investment in Railroad and Manufacturing Structures, 1919–1941
Source: BEA, Fixed Asset Tables 2.7 and 2.8, http://www.bea.gov.

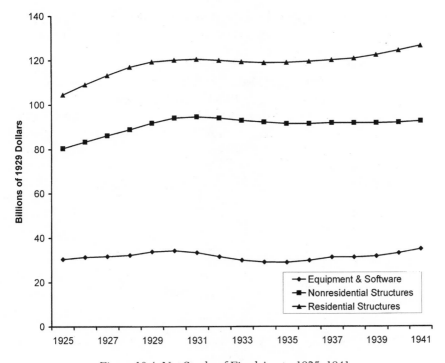

Figure 10.4: Net Stocks of Fixed Assets, 1925–1941
Source: BEA, Fixed Asset Tables 2.1 and 2.2, http://www.bea.gov.

The net stock of nonresidential structures (figure 10.4) reflects these investment trends. After rising sharply between 1925 and 1930 (a total of 17 percent
over five years) and then decelerating to a peak in 1931, the real net stock declined 3.4 percent to a trough in 1936, reflecting net decumulation over the
years 1932–1936 inclusive (see table 10.2). Decumulation resulted in a decline
in the net stock of $3.19 billion on a 1931 base of $94.62 billion (in 1929 dollars).
In contrast with the 15 percent decline in the net stock of equipment (see below), which was entirely made up by 1941, and the 1.3 percent drop in the net
stock of housing, which was made up and then exceeded by 1941, the decline
in the net stock of nonresidential structures persisted: the 1941 stock was barely
above the 1936 trough. The average age of nonresidential structures rose from
14.6 years in 1929 to 18.8 years in 1941 (Fixed Asset Table 1.7, line 7).

The decline in the net stock of nonresidential structures was largely driven by
a decline in railroad structures and to a lesser degree manufacturing structures,
along with modest declines in commercial and office structures. In contrast,
the net stock of structures in communications and petroleum and natural gas
rose, but they had smaller weights in the aggregates. Table 10.3 analyzes the
contributors to the decline in nonresidential structures. Railroads remained at
this time a very important part of the economy, accounting for more than a
quarter of the net stock of nonresidential private structures.

For equipment (producer durables), the pattern is different (figure 10.1).
Like the two construction series, accumulation fell precipitously during the

Table 10.3. Contributions to Decline in Real Net Stock of Nonresidential
Structures, 1931–1941 (billions of 1929 dollars)

	1931	1941	Change
Nonresidential structures, total	94.62	92.64	−1.98
Major decliners:			
Railroad	27.20	25.50	−1.70
Manufacturing	11.60	11.00	−0.60
Commercial	11.25	10.91	−0.34
Major increasers:			
Petroleum and natural gas	3.83	4.88	1.05
Communications	3.18	3.45	0.27
Education	1.29	1.45	0.16

Source: BEA, http://www.bea.gov, Fixed Asset Tables 2.7 and 2.8; see text.

1929–1933 downturn. But in contrast, the series for real equipment investment recovered smartly in Roosevelt's first term, almost reattaining its 1929 level by 1937 and surpassing it in 1940.

Another way of looking at these trends is that from 1923 through 1928, each of the three components of gross fixed investment was of about the same magnitude, ranging in value from $4.3 to $6.0 billion in 1929 dollars. And the plunge between 1929 and 1933 also saw their magnitudes remain relatively close together. After 1933, however, real investment in equipment grew much more rapidly so that by 1937, its value was more than twice that of residential investment and almost twice that of nonresidential investment.

There are key differences between structures and equipment in terms of the time it takes to build them, how long they last and thus depreciation's share of gross investment, the institutional mechanisms for financing their construction, the thickness of their secondary markets, their susceptibility to "overbuilding," and their attractiveness as vehicles for asset price speculation. Equipment is shorter lived, and a large proportion of annual gross investment represents the replacement of assets wearing out that year.

Because depreciation exceeded gross investment in equipment during the years 1930–1935 inclusive (the worst decumulation took place between 1931 and 1934, as table 10.2 shows)—and by a fairly substantial amount—the real net stock of producer durables in the United States declined 15 percent between 1930 and 1935 (about $5.28 billion on a 1930 base of $34.38 billion, measured in 1929 dollars). Due to the rapid growth of gross equipment investment after 1935, this decline was entirely reversed by 1941. Net equipment accumulation was negligible across the Depression years, with the real net stock in 1941 value barely above that registered in 1929 or 1930 (see figure 10.2).

Still, it is a mixed picture with respect to equipment accumulation across the Depression. On the one hand, because such a large fraction of gross equipment investment represented depreciation each year and because of the shortfall represented by the excess of depreciation over gross investment between 1930 and 1935 inclusive, the net stock was barely higher in 1941 than it had been in 1929–1930. On the other hand—and this is the point I wish to emphasize— gross equipment investment recovered much more strongly than investment in structures after 1933. Although there was little net private sector equipment accumulation or capital deepening across this period, the U.S. economy succeeded across the Depression years in maintaining its equipment capital stock and making good on the effects of depreciation. Some narrative accounts might suggest the contrary, but 1941 was not saddled with a stock of old, deteriorated equipment.

In 1929 the net stock of equipment was $33.8 billion, and depreciation was $4.4 billion. In a no-growth steady state the entire stock of equipment would have turned over in less than eight years. Twelve years elapsed between 1929 and 1941. The net stock at the end of this period was about the same, so we can conclude that most of the private sector equipment stock at the time the country entered the Second World War was less than a decade old. Data support this conclusion. The average age of equipment at year end was 7.3 years in 1929. It rose to a peak of 9.8 in 1935 but had fallen back to 8.7 by 1941 (Fixed Asset Table 1.7, Current Cost Average Age at Year End of Fixed Assets). Whatever uncertainty and risk aversion may have affected the willingness of businessmen to borrow or invest or the willingness of banks to lend in the New Deal, particularly after 1935, these did not pose an obstacle to sustaining the nation's stock of equipment. The nation replaced what wore out, and the stock in 1941 was only marginally older than it had been in 1929. And if the real value of the stock hadn't changed much, its composition had, in subtle ways. It contained, for example, more trucks, agricultural machinery, communications equipment, and metalworking machines and somewhat less railroad rolling stock.

Bank failures, deflation, and deleveraging under President Herbert Hoover arrested the accumulation of all three of the components of gross private fixed investment. But in comparison with structures, the impact on producer durables was more transitory. These data suggest that after 1933 access to finance posed few obstacles to equipment accumulation. Lending to finance equipment acquisition involves something more substantial than a "self-extinguishing" commercial loan to finance the holding of inventories. But the asset lives of equipment are shorter than those for structures, and the quasi-rents that will provide the cash flows to service the loan are anticipatable within a much shorter time frame than is the case with buildings.

Particularly striking on the equipment side is the rapid acceleration of investment in communication equipment after 1935 and agricultural machinery after 1933 (figures 10.5 and 10.6). Another notable feature is the large percentage increase — sustained through the 1929–1933 period as well as thereafter — in investment in nonmedical instruments. Although this investment was relatively small in total dollar value, it played an important role in subsequent productivity gains in a variety of sectors (see chapter 2). And in figure 10.7, we can see the revival of accumulation of certain types of manufacturing machinery. Note especially the sharp rise in metalworking machinery, as the economy began to gear up for war. Figure 10.8 shows that both truck and railroad equipment investment recovered after 1933–1934, but truck investment surpassed its levels from the 1920s, whereas railroad equipment investment never reattained these

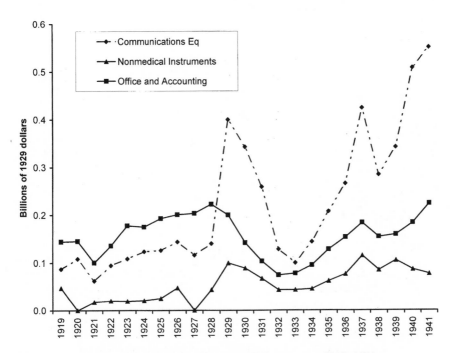

Figure 10.5: Gross Investment in IT Equipment, 1919–1941
Source: BEA, Fixed Asset Tables 2.7 and 2.8, http://www.bea.gov.

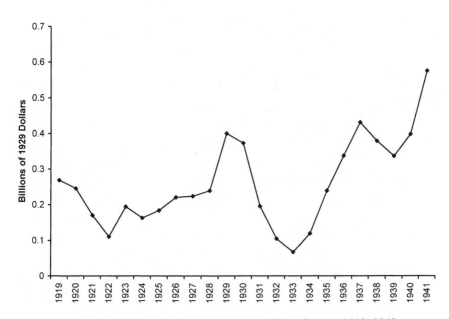

Figure 10.6: Gross Investment in Agricultural Machinery, 1919–1941
Source: BEA, Fixed Asset Tables 2.7 and 2.8, http://www.bea.gov.

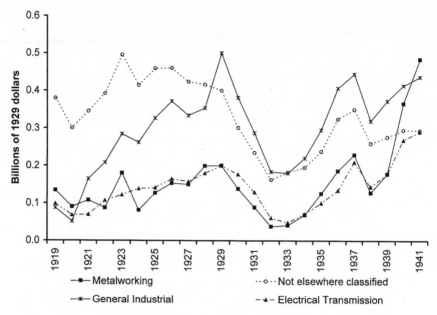

Figure 10.7: Gross Investment in Industrial Machinery, 1919–1941
Source: BEA, Fixed Asset Tables 2.7 and 2.8, http://www.bea.gov.

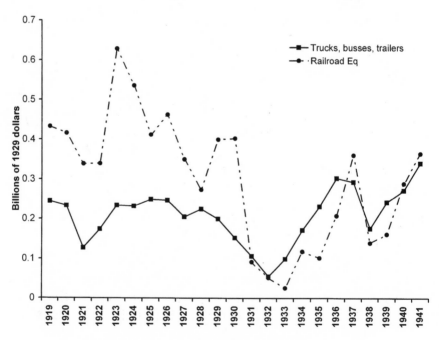

Figure 10.8: Gross Investment in Transport Equipment, 1919–1941
Source: BEA, Fixed Asset Tables 2.7 and 2.8, http://www.bea.gov.

levels. These data reflect both the expansion of trucking in the 1930s and the growing complementarity between trucking and rails.

The message of these series is that with the exception of railroad equipment (a special case discussed below), when technical innovation promised significant gains in labor or capital productivity through investment in new equipment, the financial sector, especially after 1935, did not pose an obstacle to such accumulation.

Overall, the argument that "regime uncertainty," as Robert Higgs (1997) characterized the supposed unwillingness of the moneyed classes to invest in America's future under Roosevelt, does not stand up well. Undoubtedly many wealthy Americans disliked Roosevelt—even hated him. But that didn't stop them from making money during his presidency. Figure 10.9 is perhaps the most damaging to Higgs's thesis. It shows trends in real capital income across the Depression. The series reflect nominal data from NIPA table 1.1.2 deflated by the Consumer Price Index, 1982–1984 = 100.

The data show that with one exception, recipients of capital income did terribly under Hoover. The one exception was bondholders. This is very similar

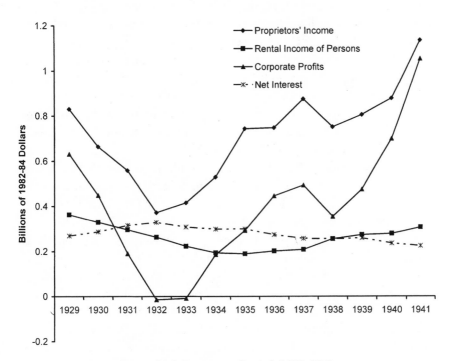

Figure 10.9: Income to Capital, 1929–1941
Source: BEA, NIPA Table 1.12, http://www.bea.gov.

to what happened through early March 2009: all asset categories with the exception of fixed income performed poorly. Obviously, there were defaults, but many debtors remained current on their payments, and given that the economy was deflating, the real value of net interest payments went up almost 22 percent between 1929 and 1932.[30] For all other types of capital income, particularly proprietors' income and corporate profits, Hoover's administration was a disaster. Proprietors' income fell 56 percent, and corporate profits fell more than 100 percent—they were negative in 1932 and 1933. Hoover's presidency was not great for employee compensation either (not shown on figure 10.9), which declined 24 percent in real terms between 1929 and 1932. But it was even worse, in the aggregate, for those receiving capital income.

Proprietors' income and corporate profits recovered sharply after 1933 and surpassed their 1929 levels by 1940. By 1937, the Dow index was almost five times the level of its 1932 trough, reflecting the sharp upswing in corporate profits and more optimistic expectations for the future (the stock market's performance was weaker between 1937 and the end of the war). This was a period of rapid TFP growth, which must show up on the income side as rising returns to capital or labor or both (see appendix). Recipients of labor income and most types of capital income did well after 1933, as TFP began to climb sharply, reflecting recovery from the depths of the recession and a high trend growth rate.

Bondholders did not do as well under Roosevelt as under Hoover, but their losses were trivial compared to the huge increases in other types of capital income. The one bleak spot for capital income recipients across both administrations was rental income of persons, which declined through 1935 and recovered only modestly thereafter. These statistics are consistent with the generally slower recovery of construction during the Depression.

Perhaps under some different state of the world, political or otherwise, physical accumulation might have been even more rapid. At the same time, we cannot avoid the conclusion that the economy, and most people in it, did much better under Roosevelt than under Hoover. Recovery from 1933 onward, particularly up through 1937, whether measured by income to capital, income to labor, GDP, GPDI, or employment, was extraordinarily rapid—not enough, to be sure, to get us back to potential output, but extraordinarily rapid nonetheless.

The abandonment of the gold standard and the modest reflation this facilitated, along with the restoration of confidence that accompanied the ascendancy of Roosevelt to the presidency, took the economy a long way toward recovery. A substantial output gap still remained, of course, even at the local peak in 1937. Much of this was the unfortunate temporary byproduct of the rapid rate of technological and organizational change, which made it possible to produce more output with no increases or even decreases in labor and capital inputs. Part reflected the continuing weaknesses in aggregate demand. The recovery of gross investment in equipment and spending on consumer durables (which by 1937 was within 5 percent of its 1929 level) was not enough, particularly in the context of continued depressed levels of construction spending, as well as deterioration in net exports.

Throughout the 1920s, gross investment in equipment, residential structures, and nonresidential structures was roughly the same magnitude for each category (figure 10.1). In 1937, real residential construction fell short of investment in equipment by $3.6 billion. The shortfall in nonresidential construction was about $2.9 billion (1929 dollars), for a total construction shortfall of approximately $6.5 billion relative to a 1920s baseline in which each of these three magnitudes was roughly equal. Converting to 1937 dollars, using the ratio of real (1937 dollars) to nominal value of investment in structures for 1929 (NIPA tables 1.1.6A and 1.1.5), we have a net shortfall in construction spending relative to the 1920s of approximately $5.8 billion in 1937 dollars. If we assume a multiplier of 1.78 (see table 10.1), real GDP might have been $10.3 billion ($5.66 × 1.78) higher if the two components of construction had maintained the rough equality with spending on equipment evident in the 1920s. In other words GDP would have been $102.2 billion rather than its actual value of $91.9 billion.

In order for real GDP to have grown 3 percent per year from 1929 to 1937, however, GDP would have had to have grown from $87.2 billion in 1929 to $110.9 billion in 1937 (1937 dollars). Still, this calculation suggests that from an aggregate demand standpoint, the shortfall in construction spending was responsible for more than half of the remaining output gap in 1937. Had net exports and consumer durables in 1937 been at their 1929 levels (they fell short of them by $.7 billion and $.4 billion respectively), GDP might have been another $2 billion higher, getting us to $104.2 billion. The remaining output gap ($6.7 billion) would have required additional injections of $3.8 billion (6.7/1.78) of autonomous spending in 1937, from either the government or the private sector—probably more, since the multiplier seems to have been declining with rising saving rates as we approached the war.[31]

Over the entire period 1929–1941, the accumulation of equipment across the Depression years was affected relatively modestly. Again, as noted, it's a mixed picture with respect to producer durables. Gross investment in equipment could have been higher, but it had made a very strong recovery from the depths of the Depression. The net stock did not grow across the Depression years, but neither did it shrink. Much bigger deficiencies lay in the area of structures. One can make a case, especially for railroads, that uncertainty biased the flow of loanable funds toward less risky loans on equipment. At the same time and with the important exception of railroads, conditions specific to particular asset categories placed special restraints on the demand for loans to build structures. With respect to housing, the obstacles to revival were largely to be found in the legacy of the 1920s boom, not in any unease that Roosevelt may have sowed in the minds of corporate leaders about the security of their property rights. Much legal and structural detritus, the legacy of uncontrolled land development in the 1920s, remained on the ground in the 1930s, hindering the revival of house construction (chapter 11).

Housing capital is often termed unproductive, in contrast with, say, factory buildings, machinery, or transportation equipment. But this is not really a justifiable position if we view economic activity as concerned ultimately with the satisfaction of human wants. Housing typically generates upward of 10 percent of GDP. The productivity problem in the sector involves translating investment in buildings and residential infrastructure into market-validated rental service flows. Residential construction was much more effective in doing this after World War II, but this was in part due to zoning, land use regulations, and innovations in the design of residential subdivisions pioneered during the Depression but not having their full effect until after the war. The diffusion of new principles of subdivision design required governmental leadership if it was to influence any but high-end developments. The success of the Federal Housing Authority (FHA), which laid the foundation for potential output growth in the sector after the war, represents another positive legacy of the New Deal. On the aggregate demand side, the retardation of investment in structures is an important reason why the Depression lasted so long. Decisions on investments in housing construction were largely local.

For nonresidential structures, overbuilding in the 1920s aggravated the demand/supply imbalance for commercial office space. Other types of nonresidential structures showing weak investment recovery in the 1930s included manufacturing structures, structures associated with electricity generation, and railroad structures (figures 10.3 and 10.9).

Investment in structures associated with the generation and transmission of electric power soared after the First World War, peaking in 1924, as the housing boom went into full swing. These investments were instrumental in lowering the cost of electric power, one of the preconditions for the shift from shafts to wires in manufacturing that led to such high-productivity growth in that sector in the 1920s (chapter 2). Investment in electric power structures declined during the remainder of the 1920s, fell precipitously between 1929 and 1933, and recovered only gradually during the remainder of the Depression. On the other hand, because of the long-lived nature of these structures, their net private stock fluctuated little over the Depression years. And of course the public sector was making major additions to hydroelectric facilities and facilitating rural electrification.

Investment in manufacturing structures hit a peak just after the First World War in 1920 and then a lower peak in 1929 before collapsing between 1929 and 1932. It then recovered through the remainder of the Depression, although until 1941 it remained below its level during any year of the 192cs. The data do not suggest, however, that after 1935, lack of access to financing was the problem. First, such spending was growing rapidly after 1933, with a small hiccup in the 1938 recession. Second, much of the productivity improvement across the Great Depression was capital saving. The continuation of the electrification of internal power distribution within factories and other innovations enabled capital productivity and output to continue to rise, and as a consequence, output expansion could take place without necessarily requiring the building of new manufacturing structures. Electrification enabled much more efficient use of factory floor space and obviated the need for multistory structures to reduce the friction losses associated with the mechanical distribution of power.

Just as labor-saving technical improvement can produce a jobless recovery, so too can capital-saving innovation retard the rate of accumulation of structures.

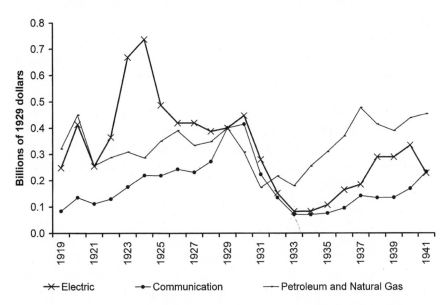

Figure 10.10: Gross Investment in Electric Generation, Communication, and Oil and Gas Structures, 1919–1941

Sources: BEA, Fixed Asset Tables 2.7 and 2.8, http://www.bea.gov.

A similar dynamic may have affected the communication sector, where structures investment peaked in 1930 and recovered only slowly after the trough in 1933 (figure 10.10). Investment in communication equipment was very strong in the latter part of the 1930s (see figure 10.5). Much of this consisted of investment in improved automatic switching technology, which saved both the labor of phone operators and the floor space required for telephone exchange offices.

This chapter has compared the run-ups to the Great Depression and the Great Recession and studied the degree to which the lingering effects of the financial crisis impeded the revival of physical capital accumulation in the 1930s. Differences between the 1920s and 1995–2005 include the sequence of asset price booms, the mirror image margin requirements for real estate and equities in the two periods, and the possible role of capital inflows in fueling asset price booms in the more recent period. There are also many similarities. In both cases a sequence of asset bubbles in the context of low inflation and light financial sector regulation preceded financial crisis and downturn in the real economy. In both instances an endogenous process of growing financial fragility rendered the economy increasingly vulnerable to shocks of a given magnitude.

Real estate was implicated in the onset of both episodes, and while the acquisition and replacement of equipment proceeded relatively smoothly after 1935, this was less true for private structures. In some cases, such as manufacturing, capital-saving innovation reduced the demand for new structures. In other areas, particularly housing, slow recovery reflected the legacy of financial crisis and the physical excesses of the building booms of the 1920s (see chapter 11). If Depression-era experience is a guide, then the 2007–2009 downturn is likely to have associated with it serious but relatively short-lived effects on the accumulation of equipment. The consequences for investment in structures may be more persistent, both because of overbuilding and because of the possibility of obstacles presented by legal and physical detritus from the prior boom (although the latter was a bigger problem in the 1930s).

The 2007–2009 downturn can also usefully be contrasted with the 1982 episode, which used to hold title as the worst recession since the Great Depression. That recession was caused by deliberate Federal Reserve policies aimed at disinflation. The policy achieved its objective, with an assist from collapsing oil prices, but at the cost of high unemployment and a large amount of foregone output. Unlike 2007–2009, the 1982 recession did not coincide with a financial crisis and was associated with—indeed caused by—tight money. Fiscal stimuli associated with the Reagan tax cuts and an unprecedented peacetime military buildup helped bring the economy out of it. Those policies—tax cuts and increased military spending—were motivated by supply-side and foreign policy considerations, although, as was true for the Bush tax cuts of 2001 and 2003, when the economy went into recession, they were rebranded as Keynesian stimulus.

Between 1929 and 1933, financial crisis aggravated what would have otherwise been a serious downturn by constricting the supply of loanable funds at the same time the demand for them was weak. After 1934, constraints on the supply of lending were less binding, with the exception of the railroad sector, and of course with the acknowledgement that the monetary tightening in 1937–1938—an ill-advised Federal Reserve response to the fear of inflation and excess reserves held by the banking system—discouraged investment and the acquisition of consumer durables through normal interest rate channels. But the very fact that central bank decision makers could think about tightening— could even worry that the economy might overheat—is in a sense testimony to the rapid recovery of the economy during Roosevelt's first term.[32]

The idea that the New Deal hindered recovery by leading to a capital strike, advanced by Higgs (1997) and (referencing somewhat different mechanisms) by Cole and Ohanian (2004), is questionable given the evidence of strong revival in equipment accumulation and large increases in income to capital. The major problem was in construction, and it's implausible that uncertainty about the security of property rights or the National Industrial Recovery Act or the Wagner Act had much to do with the slow rate of structures accumulation. Nevertheless, it's in that sector, not in manufacturing, that these hypotheses have to do the heavy lifting if they are to be affirmed.

By the beginning of 2010, it appeared that the U.S. and world economies had avoided a potentially catastrophic economic meltdown, although pessimists cautioned against the conclusion that we were out of the woods. For the second quarter of 2009 the annualized rate of real gross private domestic investment was, overall, down a third from its peak in 2007:2. Real investment in residential structures was less than half its peak rate in 2005:4. Gross investment in equipment and software was down 20 percent from its peak in 2007:4. Nonresidential construction was down 20 percent from its peak in 2008:1 and declined further before bottoming out in 2009:4. GDP had fallen 4.1 percent below its peak in 2007:4. Given growth in capacity, the output gap as a percent of GDP was at least twice that. Unemployment continued to increase in the second half of 2009, although GDP began to recover from its trough in 2009:3, and by the second quarter of 2010, real gross private domestic investment had recovered to 80 percent of its 2006:1 peak (all of these numbers are based on the July 30, 2010, release of NIPA table 1.1.3).

In 2010, income to capital revived strongly. J. P. Morgan Chase and Goldman Sachs reported strong profits, and Google announced its best quarter ever. But unemployment remained stubbornly at 9.5 percent or above.

Recovery from the Great Depression required fiscal and monetary stimuli—not fully adequate until 1942—and was accompanied by banking and financial market reform that laid the groundwork for the resumption of a relatively smooth process of physical capital accumulation for several decades following the Second World War. If the output loss from 2007–2010 ends up in the range of the 1982 downturn, it will be because Congress and the Federal Reserve moved more quickly and effectively with immediate remedies than was true in the 1930s. If an even more serious crisis occurs within the next decade, it will be because the regulatory response ended up being less effective than that which was summoned during the New Deal.

——————————●●●——————————

UNCONTROLLED LAND DEVELOPMENT AND THE DURATION OF THE DEPRESSION

In the four years following the Depression's trough in 1933, recovery was rapid and dramatic, with striking revivals in equipment investment, manufacturing output, and income to both capital and labor (chapter 10). But the fact remains that at the local peak in 1937, unemployment was still 14.3 percent, and the economy ended up experiencing double-digit unemployment for the entire decade, from 1931 through 1940. Some of this was due to the high rates of TFP advance characterizing the Depression years, which allowed output to grow with only modest increments to employment or hours.

But part also was due to continuing weakness in construction. Aggregate economic activity was heavily influenced by the construction sector's expansion, collapse, and failure to revive during the interwar years. The 1920s building boom was the first to respond to the potential of the automobile and the last to be almost entirely unplanned. Its uncoordinated character slowed the growth of full employment output toward the end of the 1920s. And the physical and legal detritus of unregulated land development posed continuing obstacles to recovery during the second half of the 1930s. Obstacles to revived building, particularly of residential houses, were partly physical and partly legal. In restraining the growth of construction spending, they contributed to persisting weakness in aggregate demand that was not entirely overcome until the Second World War.

Regulations and policies affecting zoning, land subdivision, house construction, and real estate finance were, with the partial exception of finance, either absent or less restrictive in the 1920s than they were in the 1980s or the 2000s. The problems faced by construction in the second decade of the twenty-first century will not replicate exactly those encountered in the 1930s. But the interwar period is a reminder that real estate booms, which played a role in the 1920s as well as the 1980s and the 2000s, leave an infrastructural and transactions cost footprint with the potential to influence the character and pace of future recovery.

This chapter is concerned principally with understanding how the legacy of the 1920s construction boom influenced the depth and duration of the Depression, but it has more general implications. The story is as much about the 1920s and the 1950s as it is about the 1930s, and the narrative has relevance for understanding land development and financial intermediation in the 1980s, the growth retardation of the early 1990s, and the real estate boom of the early 2000s and its aftermath.

Traditional Keynesian macroeconomics placed heavy emphasis on the volatility of investment spending in explaining fluctuations in aggregate activity. During the 1920s, infrastructural investment, much of it complementary to the automobile, dominated net capital formation, even more so than it has in other peacetime expansions. The enormous amount of building during that decade stands in sharp contrast to the depressed levels of such activity in the 1930s (see chapter 10). As noted, residential construction alone exceeded 8 percent of GNP in each of the four years 1924–1927, and the subsequent downturn was severe (Gordon and Wilcox 1981, p. 78). Real spending on new private nonfarm housing fell 89 percent from its peak in 1926 to the trough in 1933; over the same period total real spending on new construction fell 71 percent.[1] These declines can be closely linked through multiplier effects to the depth of the initial downturn.[2] The failure of construction to revive, in at least a mechanical sense, provides part of the explanation for the Depression's unprecedented duration.[3]

The argument developed in this chapter builds on several key postulates. First, no coherent account of the depth and duration of the Depression can ignore the causes of fluctuations in investment spending. Second, such spending was so heavily dominated by structural investment in the 1920s that accounts focusing principally on fluctuations in producer durables or consumer durables are at best incomplete.[4] Third, structural investments differed from producer durables investment or consumer durables purchases in several important respects, most particularly in the degree to which their productivity depended on platting decisions reversible only at great cost.

This chapter develops the implications of these points and explores the relationship between the legacy of the construction boom and the sector's failure to revive. An emphasis on the sheer volume of construction during the expansion would not in itself be novel. A number of authors have stressed "overbuilding" or "overinvestment," and the link between construction collapse and failure to revive remains an important part of the traditional account of the Depression.[5] The argument here goes beyond issues of mere quantitative excess. Because of the uncontrolled character of development in the prior decade, the Depression-era developer faced transactions and site redevelopment costs that presented formidable obstacles to renewed operations. Construction's collapse and failure to revive in the 1930s can therefore be linked to the institutional and regulatory environment within which subdivision and construction took place in the 1920s and to the encumbering of locationally choice acreage with the physical and legal debris of an unplanned, uncoordinated development boom.

PHYSICAL AND LEGAL OBSTACLES TO CONSTRUCTION RECOVERY

The construction boom of the 1920s involved an upsurge in subdivision and detached dwelling construction that peaked in 1925, a smaller orgy of apartment building peaking in 1927, and a surge in private corporate spending on nonresidential structures that continued through 1929.[6] Aggregate real spending on construction peaked in 1926 but in 1929 was still at 88 percent of its 1926 peak. Twenty-one years would elapse before real spending on residential construction surpassed its 1926 peak, and twenty-two years before nonresidential private building reattained its 1929 level (BEA Fixed Asset Table 6.1, lines 4 and 7). For central business district construction, which rose from the ashes in the early 1960s under the aegis of urban redevelopment agencies, recovery would take almost three decades.[7]

Although many of the arguments of this chapter apply with equal force to construction in general, the emphasis here is on nonfarm housing, particularly detached dwellings. Housing was and is the largest single component of the nation's capital stock. White elephant apartment buildings, poorly located and with low occupancy rates, figure prominently in journalistic accounts of the boom and were certainly a feature of the late 1920s, but between 1922 and 1929 less than a fifth of the spending on new residential housing was devoted to apartments.[8] The remainder went for detached one-to-four family units.

The hypothesis that uncontrolled development in the 1920s left obstacles to revival of construction is consistent with trends in the components of output and spending in the latter part of the 1930s. By 1937 long-term interest rates had fallen almost a third. Real consumption was higher than in 1929, as was manufacturing employment. Passenger vehicle production had risen to within 12 percent and producer durables to within 5 percent of their 1929 highs. Yet real spending on nonresidential construction was 54 percent of its 1929 peak; real spending on new housing was less than 39 percent of its 1926 peak (BEA Fixed Asset Table 6.1, lines 4 and 7). What idiosyncratic factors differentiated construction from other components of capital formation, making it less responsive to monetary ease and reviving aggregate demand? Why did construction behave so differently in comparison with the post–World War II period, when it typically led upturns in aggregate activity?[9]

Of the three major categories of reproducible tangible assets (RTA), structures are the least forgiving of errors in design, manufacture, or location. Alternatives available ex ante quickly become more expensive ex post. Structures are difficult to move once built; in comparison with durables or inventories, they take years to wear out. And it is generally much more expensive to reassemble than to subdivide land.

Uncontrolled development in the 1920s left a legacy of site assembly encumbrances on locationally choice acreage that raised the cost to developers of exploiting the economies of building multiple units within a subdivision. These encumbrances included legal and transactions costs associated with land reassembly and, where poorly planned improvements had been made, the choice between demolition, removal, and site restoration costs and development within platting constraints that were uneconomic and in many respects dysfunctional.[10] Rural land under single ownership was available, but it was less favorably situated, farther from employment opportunities or transport nodes (Muth 1959, pp. 5–6). While the technology of building profitable neighborhoods through coordinated large-scale development was more widely understood by the late 1930s, recovery relied disproportionately on owners of individual plots contracting directly with builders.[11] Only after the Second World War, when the better roads built during the Depression years were available, aggregate demand had revived more strongly, and public institutional mechanisms for overcoming the transactions costs of land reassembly had been innovated, did private construction revive fully.

Many abandoned subdivisions were located so far from the immediate course of metropolitan development that, even under different institutional arrangements, they would not have been profitably developed during the 1930s. Others were more favorably situated, but a variety of obstacles hindered their redevelopment. Sometimes these took the form of the costs of removing infrastructure and restoring the site to a buildable state. When street layouts and utility hookups were unusable because their layout or capacity did not match desired new configurations, the choice was to abandon the land or to tear them out and start fresh (Colean 1944, p. 20). Although the dollar value of unutilized public improvements was substantial, the share of prematurely subdivided lots with a full complement of utilities was small, revealing the scale on which premature subdivision had occurred during the post–World War I expansion (Ratcliff 1949, p. 309).

With or without leftover infrastructure, systematic and profitable redevelopment required land reassembly, an enterprise made problematic by the extensive subdivision of the 1920s. It was first of all not easy to track down owners of record and bargain with them. One overreaching individual could effectively block reassembly by holding out for a larger share of the developer's anticipated profit (Muth 1959, p. 97.) Many owners of record had simply walked away from their tax (and mortgage) obligations in a declining land market, and under such circumstances, lenders (some themselves bankrupt) had often not bothered to foreclose.

Deflation increased the real value of property tax liens, making even more urgent the rapid recycling of real estate to make it attractive to new private holders. In fact, the process moved very slowly in the 1930s (Cornick 1938, pp. 157, 166–167; Michigan State Planning Commission 1939, p. 4). Municipalities had the power (and responsibility) to rejuvenate dead land through sale of tax liens or through seizure and sale at public auction. But the initiation of such proceedings required expenditures at a time when municipalities were strapped for cash and when the payoff was highly uncertain. Moreover, an aggressive sales program threatened to further depress land prices, thus weakening what remained of the existing tax base.

The impact of fractionated ownership on the costs of land reassembly was further aggravated by uncertainties of ownership. Title insurance was not common in the 1920s. Purchasers were sometimes unaware that the underlying land in a development had been pledged as collateral elsewhere. All the units in a subdivision could be affected by default on the mortgage whereby the original undivided parcel had been purchased, even where the holders of individual lots were current in mortgage and property tax payments. Pending lawsuits — or in the case of bankrupt development companies, the absence of an active owner-agent — had sometimes prevented or delayed conveyance of title to buyers purchasing through a land contract or contract for deed (Colean 1944, pp. 22, 215).

Is it surprising that developers preferred "clean" land — unencumbered, with clear title, and under single ownership? The costs of raw land and professional fees associated with purchase and subdivision of a unitary parcel were almost invariably lower than those associated with reassembly.[12] A 1946 document that was forward-looking in its outline of strategies to be used in redevelopment also provided an excellent retrospective on the legacy of the 1920s:

It seems clear that the first wave of post war home building will be on the outskirts of cities. . . . In their eagerness to find tracts of land in single large ownership, unhampered by fixed arrangements of streets and utilities, developers . . . will pass by hundreds of thousands of plots already equipped with paved streets, curbs, sidewalks, water and other utility mains into which millions of dollars have been sunk — enough, indeed, to have bankrupted many townships and villages. . . .

Many of the millions of lots still shown on assessors' books are entirely unimproved and never represented more than some stakes set out in a field. . . .

Even those that are improved and ready for use are sterilized because the ownerships are dispersed in the hands of nonresidents who cannot be located and who have long since ceased to pay taxes. . . . To unsnarl the legal and financial tangles that have resulted from a generation of neglect and abandonment is beyond the resources of the private developer. . . . The problem here is . . . eliminating legal costs that are often as much as the lot is worth as a building site. . . .

No sound estimates have been developed of the total amount of abandoned subdivisions, either in area or cost. Studies have been made in California, New Jersey, Michigan, Illinois, New York, and other states which suggest that there may be from twenty to thirty million vacant subdivided lots of record in the whole country. (National Housing Agency 1945, pp. 36–37)

The maintenance of land records was and remains the province of county and municipal governments in the United States, one reason why we do not have a complete accounting of the number of prematurely subdivided lots in the nation as a whole. Six studies at the local level, covering metropolitan areas in two eastern, two midwestern, and a western state, provide the basis for the above extrapolation. These studies, summarized in table 11.1, show the widespread prevalence of premature subdivision.[13]

In New Jersey alone, the one state for which we have a complete survey, researchers found enough prematurely subdivided acreage in 1936 to supply over a million six-thousand-square-foot lots, one for every family then resident in the state (New Jersey State Planning Board 1941, p. 8). Even more striking is the statistic for metropolitan Detroit. In the area surrounding Motor City the potential impact of the automobile on suburban development had been so enthusiastically embraced that subdivided land extended to Pontiac and Flint, 20–50 miles from downtown Detroit. More than 95 percent of recorded lots in four townships in suburban Detroit were vacant in 1938. The magnitude of the estimate of 20–30 million vacant lots of record nationally is brought into perspective when it is compared with the 1930 housing stock, which contained

Table 11.1. Regional Estimates of Undeveloped Lots, 1928–1938

Place	Year	Percent Undeveloped[a]
New York		
Westchester County		
(suburban New York City)	1934	.59
Monroe Country		
(suburban Rochester)	1934	.63
Suburban Buffalo	1934	.81
New Jersey (state)[b]	1936	.40
Michigan		
Four townships		
(suburban Detroit)	1938	.95
Grand Rapids	1931	.44
Illinois		
Chicago	1928	.30
Cook County		
(excluding Chicago)	1928	.69
California		
Los Angeles County		
(urban area)	1937	.40

Sources: New York: Cornick 1938, tables B.2, M.2, W.2, pp. 40–41, 55, 68–69; New Jersey: New Jersey State Planning Board 1941, table 1, p. 21; Michigan: Michigan State Planning Commission 1939, table 8, p. 24; E. Fisher and Smith 1932, table 1, p. 471; Illinois: Simpson and Burton 1931, p. 12; California: Los Angeles Regional Planning Commission 1938, table VIIA.
[a]The denominator is platted acreage in New Jersey and California; elsewhere it is recorded lots.
[b]The New Jersey study, the only statewide estimate available, divided platted acreage into unoccupied, semi-occupied (1–5 houses per block), and occupied (more than 5 houses per block) areas. The statistic reported is the ratio of the sum of unoccupied (108,894) and semi-occupied (74,885) to platted (459,153) acreage, which in turn represented 9.5 percent of New Jersey's total land area in 1936. See also Colean 1944, pp. 14–16.

approximately 30 million occupied housing units (U.S. Bureau of the Census 1975, II, Series N-238–241, p. 646).

Redevelopment agencies broke the transactions cost logjam by combining the power of eminent domain with access to cheap public credit. On the eve of the postwar housing expansion in 1947, the American Municipal Association reported that "foreclosure and forfeiture action since 1930 has in most places reduced the problem of tax delinquent vacant land to minor proportions."[14]

Issued more than two decades after the peak of premature subdivision in the 1920s, this report marked the concluding stages of lengthy, costly, and drawn-out legal processes necessitated by the prior boom and deflation. In the interim, particularly during the 1930s, the revival of construction was hindered by land encumbrances, both physical and legal. How did all of this come about?

LAND DEVELOPMENT AND THE
REGULATORY ENVIRONMENT

Housing services can be generated only after structures and other improvements are incorporated onto raw land. This process begins with street layout and subdivision and continues through the construction of residences and the provision of utilities, parks, schools, and other amenities, not always necessarily in this order. The residential subdivision based on the private automobile was new in the 1920s, and the value-creating relationships among improvements were imperfectly understood. The design, provision, and use of shared infra-structure critically affect characteristics of neighborhoods and communities, which influence the economic value of housing services to a degree that cannot fully be accounted for with reference to the features of individual structures alone.

The diffusion of the automobile and electric power had a powerful impact on land use in the 1920s. As farmland fell and urban/suburban land rose in value, fortunes could be made simply from the subdivision, sale, and resale of land, particularly where the city contacted the countryside.[15] The gains to be made from such activity deflected the attention of real estate marketers and developers away from issues relating to the design, location, and interrelation of infrastructual improvements. Nevertheless, an enormous boom in real capital formation accompanied the speculative activity. Billions of dollars of capital, both public and private, were invested in a relatively short time.

Decisions made in the 1920s committed land and structures to particular uses and configurations and in some cases foreclosed developmental options that might have been more appropriate, and productive, over the longer term. The modal pattern of land distribution militated against anything more than the minimal planning associated with the imposition of a rectilinear grid on farm land. Individual lots were typically sold in an undeveloped state for buyers to hold for appreciation or to develop, as they chose (Weiss 1987, p. 4).

Although the 1920s saw principles of planned residential development re-fined and systematized by a small group of builder-developers, these principles did not inform the bulk of subdivided acreage (Weiss 1987, pp. 141–142). Real estate activity was dominated by subdivider-marketers.[16] Millions of lots—certainly the majority of those prematurely subdivided—remained entirely undeveloped. Infrequently, subdividers provided streets and utilities; in other instances municipalities stepped in to provide what marketers had not, burdening lots with special tax assessments to pay for roads, sewers, and utility hookups.[17]

Here and there buyers erected houses, producing an uncoordinated patchwork quilt of developed and undeveloped properties. In the absence of zoning or restrictive covenants, purchasers could do what they wanted with their land.[18] Prior to the internal combustion engine, urbanization had already increased the frequency of conflicts between residential and noxious or noisy commercial or industrial uses. Municipalities found themselves saddled with expenditures that could have been avoided through better coordination of private investment projects.[19] The automobile, even more so than the electric streetcar, made economically feasible the physical separation of residential and commercial/industrial use. It accelerated the pace and extent of land subdivision, exacerbating conflicts in land use but also, through the mobility it gave to individuals, made more feasible their partial resolution.

In the aftermath of World War I, the ideological climate, particularly at the federal level, was not favorable to expanded regulation. The decade of the 1920s was one of experimentation at the local level, but controls were weak, poorly understood by their implementers, and limited in their geographic coverage.[20] As metropolitan areas continued to expand, the potential of the automobile came to be better understood, and, most important, the consequences of the unregulated boom of the 1920s became more apparent. A political consensus in favor of increased regulation of housing and land use began to emerge among a variety of interest groups and levels of government.[21] The new regulatory environment would involve a federal role, which was novel, along with the strengthened application by localities of the common-law police power, which was not.[22] Gradually, principles of improved subdivision design for the automobile age, perfected in the 1920s by private builder-developers, became, in a sense, public property (Federal Housing Administration 1940b, p. 23).

In 1934, a coalition of bankers, builder-developers, and academics midwifed the birth of the FHA. After working with some success to reopen the flow of credit to housing, the agency in 1938 and 1939 experimented with encouraging improved subdivision and construction standards by making FHA-provided mortgage insurance conditional on conformance of underlying properties to these standards. During these years the agency worked with developers to recycle several hundred of the failed 1920s subdivisions and with purchasers to encourage acceptance of low-down-payment long-term financing.[23] It also encouraged local jurisdictions to adopt zoning and planning ordinances and to cooperate in regional planning with unincorporated areas and counties. Although the institutional experimentation and innovation would be of lasting importance, FHA activity in the 1930s had a comparatively modest immediate or direct influence on the housing industry. Like so much of the New Deal, its real significance would be experienced after the war.

SLOWED GROWTH IN HOUSING SERVICES
AND THE OVERSUPPLY HYPOTHESIS

The automobile persisted after World War II, but institutional and regulatory influences on land development had changed. Evidence that the absence of these conditions earlier mattered quantitatively is found in the productivity of the 1920s housing boom in comparison with the boom of comparable magnitude that began in 1947.

Between 1922 and 1929 the stock of reproducible tangible assets in the United States (in 1929 prices) rose approximately one-third, from $238 billion to $319 billion.[24] Over 65 percent of the increment consisted of new structures (over 80 percent if consumer durables are excluded from the denominator). By far the largest portion ($29.8 billion) was new nonfarm housing, whose real value increased 49 percent, from $60.8 billion to $90.6 billion.[25]

The values of both marketed and imputed housing services can be measured by the "rental" portion of personal consumption, where that spending is understood to include the consumption by owner-occupiers of the output of their own structures. Over the years 1922–1929, during which the stock of houses in the United States rose 49 percent in real value,[26] real output of housing services rose only 16.6 percent (see table 11.2).[27] As a consequence of this slow growth, the share of housing services in GNP declined from 13.3 percent in 1922 to 11.1 percent in 1929.[28] The process of generating housing services is unusual, in that inputs to the production function are dominated by capital. The decline in the output-capital ratio in housing from .174 in 1922 to .127 in 1929 reflected a decline in the sector's marginal and average productivity.

The contrast with the post–World War II housing boom is informative. In both episodes the real housing stock went up by roughly a half, but after the Second World War, real services increased by a substantially higher percentage than the percent increase in the stock. Regional planning, improved subdivision design, and architectural and construction changes reduced the incremental capital-output ratio in housing. The virtual absence of undeveloped or incompleted subdivisions in the postwar period is further testimony to the fact

Table 11.2. Residential Capital Stock and Service Flow, 1922–1929, 1947–1958

	1	2	3	4
	Real Stock of Residential Structures	*Spending on Housing Services (Nominal)*	*CPI Rent (1967=100)*	*Real Flow of Housing Services (1967 Prices)*
1922	60.8	9.87	76.7	12.87
1929	90.6	11.42	76.0	5.03
% chg.	+49.0	+15.7	−1.0	+16.8
1947	241.5	15.66	61.1	25.64
1958	379.0	41.13	89.1	46.16
% chg.	+56.9	+162.5	+45.8	+80.0

Sources: U.S. Bureau of the Census 1975, I and II, series F-449 (for column 1, 1922 and 1929), F-478 (for column 1, 1947 and 1958), G-477 (for column 2, 1922 and 1929), G-429 (for column 2, 1947 and 1958), and E-150 (for column 3). The 1922 figure for column 2 was interpolated from the 1921 and 1923 series F-449 data, based on the relationships among annual data on consumption of housing services reported in Barger 1942. For each of those three years, Barger's estimate of spending on housing services was taken as the sum of lines 2a, 2b, and 2c in his appendix 22, p. 226. *Notes*: Values in columns 1, 2, and 4 are in billions of dollars. Values in columns 1 and 2 are in 1929 prices for 1922 and 1929, in 1958 prices for 1947 and 1958. Column 2 includes the imputed rental value of the owner-occupied portion of the stock. The values in column 4 are equal to (column 2 divided by column 3) times 100.

that the housing industry had undergone major changes in its ways of doing business (Grebler, Blank, and Winnick 1956, pp. 5–8).

Occupancy data confirm the success of the postwar boom in contrast to that of the 1920s. Denison's (1974) calculations show the ratio of actual to potential housing sector output at 92.5 in 1929 and still at 93.6 as late as 1940.[29] One interpretation of these statistics is that they are evidence of oversupply. A different interpretation is that they reflect "mismatch," the essence of which is that people are not willing to pay for what has been offered and would like to pay for what has not. In the several decades after World War II, mismatch was substantially reduced through effective regional and local planning and the coordinated influence of the FHA on the character, location, and intensity of housing demand and supply.

The equation of overbuilding in the 1920s with oversupply—widespread in the literature—assumes that the large increase in the housing stock generated a comparably large increase in service flow. Housing services, according to this view, expanded more rapidly than demand, which grew more slowly than earlier because of restrictions on immigration and other demographic factors.[30] But the hypothesized effect of such forces is not evident in the CPI for housing services (rent), which was virtually unchanged from 1922 to 1929.[31] Since the price of structural services had not collapsed in 1929, one must conclude that housing supply had not outrun the growth of demand.

The principal problem with the oversupply analyses is the presumption that service flow expanded pari passu with the stock. This assumption may overestimate the increase in the effective supply of services when the investment occurs, as it did in the 1920s, in an institutional environment characterized by poor planning and subdivision design, and the absence of effective land-use controls. The flow of housing services, which is produced by capital units heterogeneous in their design, location, and relation to each other, cannot always be well proxied by unit totals or stock estimates built up from construction data.[32]

Nor is it likely that the relatively low increase in the real flow of services between 1922 and 1929 can be attributed to deficiencies in aggregate demand during the latter year. The unemployment rate averaged 3.2 percent in 1929, a full percentage point below what it had been in 1928 and less than half what it had been in 1922 (U.S. Bureau of the Census, 1975, I, Series D-86, p. 135). Additional aggregate demand stimulus would not significantly have altered either the low occupancy rates or the observed disproportion between the growth in the residential capital stock and the growth in its service flow.

Understanding the causes of the disappointing outcomes of the 1920s construction boom requires a focus not only on the structures built, but also on the platting within which they were situated or intended to be situated. The deficiencies of 1920s platting were many, but the most significant was the dominance of short blocks.[33] Short blocks decreased the acreage available for building and, by raising the total length and acreage taken up by streets, substantially increased the cost per dwelling of public improvements: street paving and lighting, sidewalks, sewers, storm drains, water mains, and gas and electric hookups. Performance was also impaired; contoured platting with longer blocks simultaneously reduced through-traffic in residential areas and the time required by residents for ingress and egress.

Information contained in a 1939 *Architectural Forum* article ("Arithmetic of Land Development" 1939) permits a micro-level perspective on the impact of subdivision design on housing unit costs. According to this article, public improvements per lot historically cost more than twice what the structure did itself (40 percent vs. 18 percent of wholesale cost).[34] These percent shares are reflected in column 1 of table 11.3. The differences between columns 1 and 2 of this table are based on the article's provision of two proposed layouts for a new thirty-three acre subdivision, using in each case lots averaging five thousand square feet. Platting with longer blocks (as compared with the traditional alternative) reduced total street length and the (closely related) costs of public improvements by 31 percent and increased the number of usable lots by 8 percent (from 156 to 169). As a result, public improvement costs per lot fell 34 percent (line 4). Costs of the structure on each lot remain by assumption unchanged (line 3). Total costs of raw acreage and professional fees also remain unchanged, but because the number of lots increases, their contribution to per-lot cost drops slightly (lines 1 and 2).

Redesigning subdivisions along "modern" standards had the potential to reduce unit cost by approximately 20 percent without shrinking average lot size.

Table 11.3. Effect on Unit Costs of Improved Platting
within a Residential Subdivision

	1920s Gridiron Platting Cost in Dollars		Contoured Long Block Platting Cost in Dollars	
	Per Lot	*%*	*Per Lot*	*%*
(1) Raw land	127	(17)	118	(20)
(2) Professional fees	38	(5)	35	(6)
(3) Structure	135	(18)	135	(23)
(4) Public improvements	300	(40)	192	(32)
(5) Carrying charges (interest)[a]	150	(20)	120	(20)
(6) Total unit cost	750	(100)	600	(100)

Source: "Arithmetic of Land Development" 1939.
Note: Under the gridiron plat, 5,850 feet of street serviced 156 lots. The $300 cost of public improvement per lot is based on the assumption that total costs in this category ran $8 per street foot. The remaining dollar values in gridiron platting are derived assuming that $300 represented 40 percent of unit costs (see text). Platting with longer blocks reduced total street length to 4,050 feet (a 31 percent decline) and increased the number of usable lots to 169 (an 8 percent increase). Consequently, public improvement costs per unit (line 4) drop to $192 (a 34 percent decline), and overall unit costs (line 6) are lower by approximately 20 percent. Reductions in lines 1 and 2 are strictly due to the 8 percent increase in usable lots. A raw acreage cost of approximately $600 is implied by this analysis.
[a]Line 5 is equal to 25 percent of lines 1 through 4.

Economically advantageous platting also improved performance on other dimensions, including those of safety and aesthetics.[35]

FIDUCIARY RESPONSIBILITY, BANKRUPTCY, AND DISRUPTED INTERMEDIATION

In the absence of effective zoning or subdivision regulation, the inexperience of developers in the 1920s in designing subdivisions for automobiles, combined with the marketing emphasis on sales of undeveloped lots, was an explosive mixture. The conflicts of interest in developer-dominated financial intermediaries added fuel to the tinder. Real estate loans occupied a prominent place on the asset side of the financial sector's balance sheet.[36] In the absence of effective governmental regulation of land use, a system of private financial intermediation bereft of conflicts of interest might have exercised more control on land development in the 1920s, in a manner benefiting depositors and the economy in the long run.

With enormous speculative gains to be made, however, lending institutions paid little attention to the long-range productivity of the platting and infrastructural investments accompanying land development. This would have been a serious problem even had arms' length relationships obtained throughout, which they did not. Savings and loans were the most important source of funds for real estate development, and local realtors and developers often sat on their boards or were otherwise intimately involved with their establishment and operation.[37] The problem extended beyond savings and loans, and it permeated the financial system in a manner bearing some analogies to the conflicts of interest that characterized financial intermediation in the 1980s and again in the 2000s. This is not altogether surprising since regulations weakened in the 1980s had been written in the 1930s to prevent the reoccurrence of problems manifested in the 1920s.[38] As the boom continued, overoptimism and developer influence led lenders increasingly to make loans of higher yield, greater risk, and poorer quality.[39]

As housing service flows experienced a growth retardation in the 1920s and land values ceased accelerating, bankruptcy rates rose.[40] Bankruptcy data show, as one would expect, a sharp rise in filings during the first three years of the 1930s, when the economy in the aggregate turned downward. What is more surprising initially are the high levels and steady increase in filings from 1921 onward.[41] These data become more understandable when one recognizes that the incidence of default increases not only with decelerations in the growth (or actual declines) of income, but also with an expansion in the fraction of economic units vulnerable to such declines. Real estate lending, the mortgage debt to which it gave rise, and the poor economic payoffs associated with it played a major role in bankruptcy and lending institution failure throughout the interwar period.

The acceleration in filings in the early 1920s was centered in agricultural states, the immediate consequence of the sharp drop in the value of agricultural land (and its outputs) after the wartime boom. As the decade continued, the debt-financed accumulation of structural capital exposed a growing fraction of American households, businesses, and municipalities to increased risk of bankruptcy. The disappointing growth of structural service flow (and income) associated with uncoordinated investment and, together with it, the much larger share of indebted (and therefore vulnerable) entities were two sides of a financial pincer squeezing units in the late 1920s.[42] These relationships are clearly evident at the disaggregated level, for example, in the more than quadrupling of bankruptcy filings for the southern judicial district of Florida between 1926 and 1927 (Field 2001a). Through its roles both in diffusing debt and in hampering its ability to be repaid, the boom in uncoordinated structural investment contributed, with a lag, to the continuing upsurge in bankruptcy and bank failures, which by the early 1930s seriously disrupted intermediation by obstructing or shutting down credit channels.

Postwar research on the causes of the downturn in 1929, and its subsequent depth and duration, has, until recently, been overwhelmingly demand-side in its orientation.[43] In emphasizing the collapse of and failure to revive of construction spending as central to any explanation of the Depression's depth and duration, this chapter remains within that tradition. It goes beyond the traditional account of duration, however, in emphasizing micro-level supply-side elements—the legacy of the unplanned 1920s development—that stood in the way of construction recovery.

An older tradition, against which Keynes rebelled, was also more supply-side in its orientation (Haberler 1937). That tradition viewed the duration of the Depression as at least in part the consequence of the "excesses" of the 1920s (see also Rothbard 1963 and Eichengreen and Mitchener 2004 for more recent exemplars of this style of thinking). In its concern with linking the problems of the 1930s with the boom of the 1920s, this chapter's analysis has some affinity with these writers. But the emphasis here is not so much on excessive investment in the aggregate as on the consequences of the unplanned fashion in which the bulk of it was effectuated in the context of a radically new means of personal transportation.

The initial contribution to the downturn came through the disappointing productivity of new additions to the capital stock. Poorly planned structural investment resulted in slowed growth in housing service flow, contributing, on the supply side, to a deceleration in the growth rate of potential output and income toward the end of the 1920s. On the demand side, although construction fell moderately toward the end of the 1920s, aggregate spending remained robust due to exports and the strength of consumption, particularly durables spending.[44] When, following the stock market crash, spending on durables also began to drop while construction continued to collapse, the economy developed a serious deficiency in aggregate demand, to which the decline in exports from 1929 to 1932 also contributed.[45]

The rate of return to land development, particularly in residential housing, had already begun to drop in 1926 and 1927. High real interest rates in 1928 and 1929 accelerated the decline in construction spending and capital formation and contributed to rising bankruptcy rates. Finally, and perhaps most significant, the subdivision and construction activity of the 1920s created physical and legal residues that hindered recovery in that sector (and perforce the economy as a whole) during the second half of the 1930s.

The consequences of fluctuations in construction investment, and the institutional factors influencing them, need to be addressed in any complete account of the Depression experience.[46] Poorly planned development meant that the output of housing services (and perforce output as a whole) grew more slowly than it might otherwise have in the 1920s. By encumbering locationally choice areas with poorly planned neighborhoods, partially complete developments, and diffuse and uncertain ownership, the uncoordinated boom laid the groundwork for a collapse in construction spending, disrupted intermediation, and a prolonged depression. Had developers not been forced to choose between the often prohibitive costs of overcoming the legal and physical debris of past subdivisions and working with undeveloped rural land further from the city center, revived building on a larger scale could have begun earlier.

Housing and construction remained highly cyclical in the post–World War II period, vulnerable to periodic and unpredictable credit crunches. When credit conditions relaxed, construction generally resumed quickly, partly because prior capital had been laid down within design and planning constraints enforced by local and regional commissions and the FHA. During the 1950s large developments were opened in sections, and virtually all units in a section were sold before a new section opened. Planning and land-use controls, whatever their other defects, facilitated recovery at the conclusion of a credit crunch and may have contributed to the postwar moderation of the business cycle as much as the much vaunted role of fiscal and monetary policy. Land-use control escaped the brunt of the deregulatory fervor of the first Reagan administration, which was perhaps not to be lamented.[47]

Starting in the 1980s, financial liberalization loosened or dismantled the federal and state regulatory structure governing mortgage market intermediation. This was not matched at the local level by a dismantling of land-use controls, which appear to have survived largely intact, as they did the 1980s savings and loan boom. If this impression is wrong, then the economy is in for far more serious difficulty. But if it is correct, the legacy of the construction boom of the 2000s, like that of the 1980s but unlike that of the 1920s, will largely be limited to an overhang of excess residential units and commercial office space that can be worked off over a period of several years. Legal transactions costs associated with defaults, foreclosures, and mortgage renegotiations will still hinder recovery. But we will be spared the severe consequences of the physical detritus of poorly planned and incomplete subdivisions that were a common feature of the Depression years. Such an eventuality will provide more evidence of the constructive role that government regulation, both federal and local, can play in moderating the duration and severity of recessions.

DO ECONOMIC DOWNTURNS
HAVE A SILVER LINING?

Chapters 1–6 and 8–9 of this book are primarily about growth. Chapters 7 and 10–11 have a greater focus on cyclical issues. It is natural, in this concluding chapter, to ask about their possible interaction. In particular, do economic downturns somehow on balance provide a long-term boost to the growth of potential output? It would be comforting to answer in the affirmative. The Depression-era experience suggests that although there can be positive consequences, the effects are mixed, and the answer we give must be nuanced.

What long-run effects, if any, does the financial cycle, and the cycle of physical accumulation to which it helps give rise, have on productivity growth and thus the growth of potential output? This requires consideration of beneficial and adverse consequences of both boom and bust. The most obvious influences are clearly negative. In the later stages of a credit boom, as lending standards deteriorate and as financial institutions push credit on borrowers rather than just responding to their demands for it, it becomes increasingly less likely that physical capital will be allocated to its best uses. The wrong types of capital goods may be produced, and they may be sold or leased to the wrong firms or installed or built in the wrong places. These problems are more easily remedied for equipment because producer durables are physically moveable and, in any event, are relatively short-lived.

Structures are longer lived and generally immobile, and in their case a configuration decided upon in haste in the upswing may foreclose other infrastructural developmental paths. As is evident from the 1920s, it is not always simply a problem of overbuilding, with an overhang that can be worked off in a few years. Some decisions about structural investment are irreversible or reversible only at great cost. The 1920s building booms left a legacy of physical and legal detritus that hindered revival of construction in the 1930s (chapter 11). In growth models, more physical capital accumulation is generally better than less, but the reality is that in some cases the economy would have been better off (because of disposal and remediation costs) had poorly thought-out prior investment not occurred at all.

Zoning and other types of planning and land-use regulation can partially mitigate these effects. These were largely absent in the 1920s, so the adverse effects on the revival of accumulation were more acute in the interwar period than they were in the 1980s or will likely be today. During and after the Depression and partly in response to it, and alongside the more well-known apparatus of financial sector control, municipalities developed a locally administered system regulating the physical accumulation of structures (both government- and privately owned). The regulation of land use and construction survived the deregulatory enthusiasms of the last three decades more successfully than did the restraints on finance. Why this was so is an interesting story in itself. It had to do in part with the lower concentration of the real estate development industry, the fact that battles would have had to have been fought at the level of hundreds of local jurisdictions rather than primarily at the federal level, and the fact that land-use regulation and local building codes, although sometimes perceived as irritants, did not hinder the potential for private sector profit as much as did the legacies of New Deal regulation of the financial sector.

As noted, one of the consequences of the persistence of a regime of land-use and construction regulation was that the adverse effects of a prior building boom were less severe in the aftermath of the savings and loan debacle of the late 1980s and, for the most part, will probably be so for the current crisis as well. Still, the real estate collapse starting in 2006 was geographically specific in the severity of its impact, and it is possible some new construction may well end up evolving into blighted neighborhoods that will ultimately need to be razed.

The second adverse impact on potential output takes place during the downturn. In the bust phase of the cycle, as the financial crisis disrupts lending and other financial intermediation, physical accumulation slows down. Assuming that the speculative fever has broken, we can now expect the borrowing and lending that takes place to be more considered. But because both borrowers' and lenders' balance sheets are weaker, loans are perceived as riskier, and fewer of them are made. So the bust imposes a purely quantitative loss of potential output in the form of accumulation not undertaken. On the expenditure side, a recession represents foregone opportunities for investment as well as consumption. Stilled productive capacity could have been used to add to the nation's physical capital stock but wasn't. Idle productive capacity (representing the unused service flows of both labor and capital) is like an unsold airplane seat or hotel room. The dated service flows represent potential gone forever if not utilized. And so some houses, warehouses, apartment buildings, or producer durables are not acquired or built that could have been.

In sum, a financial boom-bust cycle misallocates physical capital in an upswing, in some cases with irreversible or expensively reversible adverse consequences. And the downswing deprives the economy of capital formation that might have taken place in the absence of the recession. In contrast with an imagined world in which accumulation took place at steadier rates, both of these effects on aggregate supply have to be entered on the negative side of the ledger in an accounting of the effect on the trend growth rate of productivity of the boom-bust financial cycle and the closely related cycle of physical capital accumulation.

The question I now pose is whether there is some compensatory effect during a recession—some positive impact on the long-run growth of potential output. In other words, is there a silver lining to depression? A subterranean theme in some economic commentary seems almost mystically to view depression as a purifying experience, not only purging balance sheets of bad investments and excessive leverage, but also refocusing economic energies on what is truly important and perhaps stimulating creative juices in a way that expands the supply of useful innovations. This style of argument is reflected in Richard Posner (2009) in a chapter entitled "A Silver Lining?" and it echoes Treasury Secretary Andrew Mellon's Depression-era encouragement to "Liquidate labor, liquidate stocks, liquidate the farmers, liquidate real estate. . . . It will purge the rottenness out of the system. . . . People will work harder, live a more moral life" (quoted in Hoover 1952, p. 30).[1]

TFP GROWTH IN THE DEPRESSION AND TODAY

Is it possible for a diet of feast then famine to toughen up the economic patient, ultimately allowing the economy to grow more rapidly, compensating for the effect on potential output of misallocated capital in the boom and foregone accumulation in the trough? The years of the Great Depression were the most prolonged period in U.S. economic history in which output remained substantially below potential. That period was also the most technologically progressive of any comparable period. It is natural to ask whether there was some connection and whether, because the Depression experienced such pronounced advance in this regard, we could expect some boost to longer-run growth as a direct consequence of the 2007–2009 recession.

We won't have much real evidence on the longer-run trajectory of TFP for some time since trend growth can only reliably be measured between business cycle peaks (but see chapter 7's conclusion for preliminary data). Thus we will need to await the closing of the output gap and the economy's return to potential output to get a good reading. Even then there will be a question—as there is in the case of the Depression—as to how much of the advance would have taken place anyway. Still, the issue of whether we can expect a "recession boost" to potential output is an obvious one to ask, and it is natural to turn to the Depression experience for possible indications as to whether this is likely. That long-run trajectory bears on many important issues, including the adequacy of Social Security funding, our ability to address escalating health costs, and the more general question of what will happen to our material standard of living.

I offer a nuanced answer to the question of whether 1929–1941 bred productivity improvements that might foreshadow what will happen over the next decade. The issue is best approached by thinking of TFP growth across the 1930s as resulting from the confluence of three tributaries. The first was the continuing high rate of TFP growth within manufacturing, the result of the maturing of a privately funded R and D system. The second was associated with spillovers from the buildout of the surface road network, which boosted private sector productivity, particularly in transportation and wholesale and retail distribution. The third influence, which I call the adversity/hysteresis effect, reflects the ways in which crisis sometimes leads to new and innovative solutions with persistent effects. It is another name for what adherents of the silver lining thesis describe, and it is a mechanism reflected in the folk wisdom that necessity is the mother of invention.

In the absence of the economic downturn, we would probably have gotten roughly the same contribution from the first two tributaries. That is, certain scientific and technological opportunities, perhaps an unusually high number of them, were ripe for development in the 1930s, and they would have been pursued at about the same rate even in circumstances of full employment. With or without the depression Wallace Carothers would have invented nylon. Similarly, by the end of the 1920s, automobile and truck production and registrations had outrun the capabilities of the surface road infrastructure. As noted in chapter 1, strong political alliances in favor of building more and improved roads had been formed, and issues regarding the layout of a national route system had been hashed out by 1927. It is highly probable that the buildout of the surface road network would have continued at roughly the same pace in the absence of the Depression. So it is the third effect, the kick in the rear of unemployment and financial meltdown, that is most relevant in terms of a possible causal association between depression and productivity advance.

The adversity/hysteresis mechanism is familiar to households unexpectedly faced with the loss of a wage earner or suddenly cut off from easy access to credit that had been formerly available. Under such circumstances, successful families inventory their assets and focus on how they can get more out of what they already have, not just how they can get more.

Adversity does cause some people to work harder, just as it causes some people to take more risks; these are people for whom the income or wealth effects of adversity dominate the substitution effects. For others, the substitution effect leads to withdrawal from the labor force or discouragement. In more severe forms this is evident in increases in a variety of mental and physical disorders that show up clearly in aggregate statistics on alcoholism, depression, suicide, and divorce. The overall effect on innovation, work effort, and risk taking is not easy to predict, given that in economic terms, both income and substitution effects are operative and that they pull in opposite directions.[2] There is merit in the adage that what doesn't kill you makes you stronger. It's just that sometimes it kills you. Not all families or firms are successful, and in some instances adversity destroys them. So I am skeptical overall that we can take an unqualified optimistic view of the effects of economic adversity on innovation and creativity.

THE ADVERSITY/HYSTERESIS EFFECT

The above ambiguities notwithstanding, there is nevertheless one important sector that appears to have benefited from the silver lining effect during the Depression, and that is railroads. Railroads confronted multiple challenges. They faced adverse demand conditions specific to the industry that would have continued to plague firms with or without the Depression. The automobile was already eroding passenger traffic in the 1920s, and trucking was changing the freight business by providing strong competition in the short-haul sector. For an industry faced with these challenges and characterized by heavy fixed costs, the downturn in aggregate economic activity was particularly devastating and pushed many railroads into receivership. Access to capital was disrupted, although some ailing roads received loans from the Reconstruction Finance Corporation, and, paradoxically, bankrupt rails, no longer required to meet obligations to their original creditors, could obtain credit, especially short-term financing for equipment purchases, with greater ease than lines that had not gone bankrupt. But access to cheap fifty-year-mortgage money—widely available in the 1920s—was pretty much gone (Schiffman 2003). Railroads responsible for roughly a third of U.S. track mileage were in receivership by the late 1930s and had their financing constraints somewhat relaxed. A corollary, however, is that railroads responsible for the remaining two-thirds were not in receivership. With generally weak balance sheets, they faced limited access to credit.

Confronted with these challenges, both labor and management took a hard look at what they had and worked to use their hours and capital resources more effectively. Both capital and labor inputs declined substantially. Underutilized sections of track, for example, were decommissioned, and the net stocks of both railroad structures and railroad equipment declined, as did the number of employees.[3] Rolling stock went down by a third, and the number of employees declined by almost that percentage (see figure 12.2 below).

Yet logistical innovation enabled railroads to record slightly more revenue ton-miles of freight and book almost as many passenger miles in 1941 as they had in 1929. Kendrick's (1961) series for sector output, drawn from Barger (1951), shows overall output (a weighted average of freight and passenger traffic) 5.5 percent higher in 1941 than it was in 1929. Given the big declines in inputs, this was an impressive achievement. Other factors, largely independent of the business cycle, certainly contributed to the strong productivity performance of railroads during the Depression. For example, the buildout of the surface road network facilitated a growing complementarity between trucking and rails. But some of the productivity improvement resulted from responses internal to organizations. And whereas in households it is sometimes argued that memories are short and there is little permanent carryover of behavioral changes when times improve, institutional learning and memory particular to the corporate form probably allowed some hysteresis. Beneficial logistical and organizational innovations when times were poor persisted when times improved and contributed to permanently higher levels of TFP, as well as the far superior performance of the U.S. rail system in the Second World War as compared with the First.

In exploring this question, we need to keep the larger context in mind. If we compare total GDP in 1929 and 1941 using the Bureau of Economic Analysis's chained index number methodology, we see from the latest revisions that the aggregate grew at a continuously compounded growth rate of 2.8 percent per year over that twelve-year period (BEA, NIPA table 1.1.6). This is close to the 3 percent per year often viewed as the long-run "speed limit" for the U.S. economy. GDP surpassed its 1929 level in 1936 and was 40 percent above its 1929 level by 1941. Because private sector labor and capital inputs increased hardly at all over that period (hours were flat and net fixed assets increased at only .3 percent per year [BEA, Fixed Asset Table 1.2]), virtually all of this was TFP growth (see chapter 3; table 3.6). We would like to have a sense of how much of this, if any, was the result of this adversity/hysteresis effect relative to the other two tributaries.

If the adversity/hysteresis mechanism has some empirical punch to it, then it is possible that the storm clouds of recession/depression can have something of a silver lining. The disruption of credit availability and an increase in the cost of equity finance were both central features of the 1930s, just as the easy accessibility and cheap cost of credit through most of the 1920s had been a feature of that decade. The boom-bust cycle was associated with declining physical capital accumulation and productivity, particularly between 1929 and 1933. At least in the case of railroads, however, there appear to have been longer-run benefits to the downswing phase of the financial cycle and the closely related cycle of physical accumulation in the form of technical innovation within the context of effective organizational responses.

RAILROADS AND THE SILVER LINING

In the last part of the nineteenth century, railroads dominated the U.S. economy in a way no other economic organization ever had or ever has again. They remained a formidable presence in the 1930s, although beset with challenges from several sides. What differentiated railroads from other parts of the private economy was the scale of their enterprise, particularly the size and value of the physical capital they owned, capital whose acquisition was financed largely by borrowing. Coming out of the 1920s, railroads had huge fixed nominal debt service obligations. They didn't necessarily have to worry about rolling over short-term debt since much of their borrowing was in the form of long-term mortgages, but they still had to meet mandated payments. In the face of an economic downturn and wrenching changes in market opportunities associated with the growth of trucking and the automobile, railroads were the poster child for Irving Fisher's debt-deflation thesis. By 1935, railroads responsible for more than 30 percent of first track mileage were in receivership (figure 12.1), and this remained so for the remainder of the Depression. But the problems for the sector as a whole were in a sense less those of the roads in receivership and more the challenges faced by those who weren't. The former were actually less cash strapped than the latter. Railroad organizations were under enormous stress during the Depression, so their productivity performance over this period is all the more remarkable.

If we ignore variations in income shares—which are relatively stable over time—a TFP growth rate calculation is basically a function of three numbers: the rate of growth of labor input, the rate of growth of capital input, and the rate of growth of output. As noted above, Kendrick (1961) shows output 5.5 percent higher in 1941 than it was in 1929. Kendrick's labor input series (also from

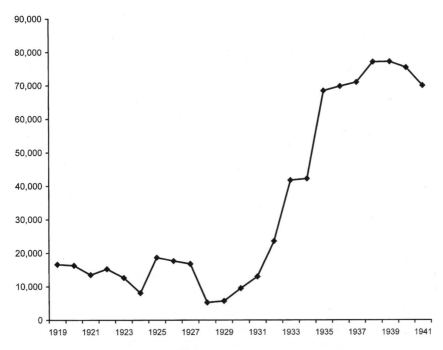

Figure 12.1: Miles of Railroads under Receivership, 1919–1941
Source: U.S. Bureau of the Census 1937, 1944, 1947.

Barger 1951) are identical to those that continue to be listed on the Bureau of Economic Analysis website (NIPA table 6.8A, line 39). Between 1929 and 1941, the number of employees declined 30.4 percent (see figure 12.2) and employee hours 31.4 percent. Kendrick's railway capital series is taken from Ulmer (1960) and shows a 1941 decline of 5.5 percent between 1929 and 1941. Putting these all together, Kendrick has railway TFP rising at 2.91 percent per year over the twelve years of the Depression.

It is not possible given currently available data to do better than Kendrick for output and labor input. But the BEA's revised Fixed Asset Tables do give us an opportunity to update capital input. Figure 12.3 brings together NIPA data on gross investment in railroad equipment and structures. Gross investment in railroad equipment peaked in 1923 and then moved fairly steadily downward to virtually nothing in 1933. It then revived somewhat, particularly after 1935 and the big increase in railroads in receivership. Investment in railroad structures peaked in 1926 but remained high through 1930 before declining to a trough in 1933 and then recovering modestly in the remainder of the Depression, although not as sharply as equipment investment. Using the data underlying these series, I calcu-

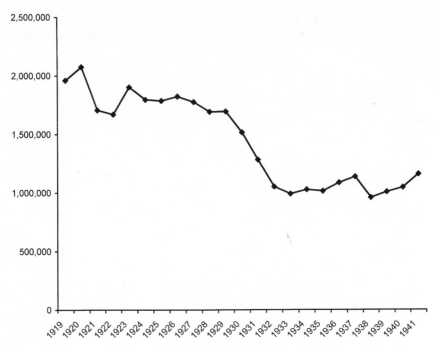

Figure 12.2: Railroad Employees, 1919–1941
Source: U.S. Bureau of the Census 1937, 1944, 1947.

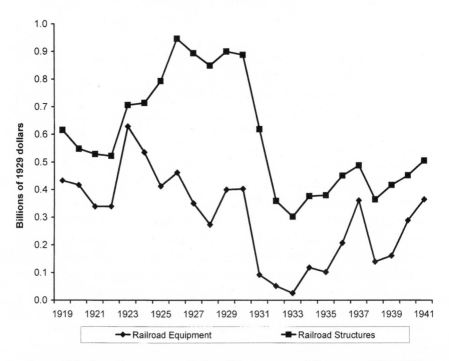

Figure 12.3: Gross Investment in Railroad Equipment and Structures, 1919–1941
Source: BEA, Fixed Asset Tables 2.7 and 2.8, http://www.bea.gov.

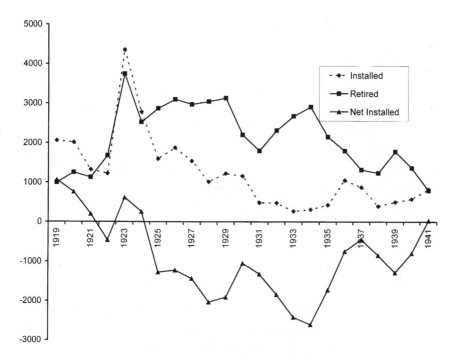

Figure 12.4: Locomotives Installed and Retired, 1919–1941
Source: U.S. Bureau of the Census 1937, 1944, 1947.

late that between 1929 and 1941, the real net stock of railroad structures declined
from $27 billion to $25.65 billion, and railroad equipment from $6.5 billion
to $4.77 billion. Overall, then, the real net capital stock declined 9.2 percent
over the twelve-year period, while Kendrick has it declining only 5.5 percent.
(Kendrick 1961, table G-III, p. 545). A more rapid decline in capital input
(.69 percent per year rather than .47 percent per year) would boost TFP growth
in railways between 1929 and 1941 from 2.91 to 2.97 percent per year.[4]

We can get further insight into trends in railroad accumulation by looking at
detailed numbers on rolling stock (figures 12.4–12.6; these data are in units, not
dollars). The locomotive numbers show decumulation in 1922 and then again
starting in 1925. The number of locomotives then shrinks continuously until
1941. Some of this reflects replacement of locomotives with larger, more powerful engines, but the overall trend is unmistakable. The total number of locomotives shrank from 61,257 in 1929 to 44,375 in 1941. A small but growing number
of replacement engines were diesel-electric; the count of such locomotives rose
from 621 in 1929 to 895 in 1941 (U.S. Bureau of the Census 1944, table 525,

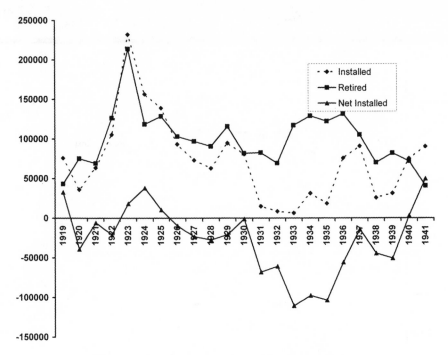

Figure 12.5: Freight Cars Installed and Retired, 1919–1941
Source: U.S. Bureau of the Census 1937, 1944, 1947.

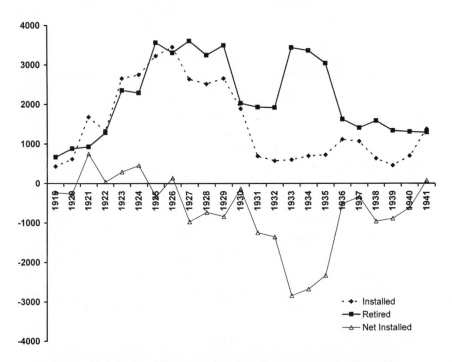

Figure 12.6: Railroad Passenger Cars Installed and Retired, 1919–1941
Source: U.S. Bureau of the Census 1937, 1944, 1947.

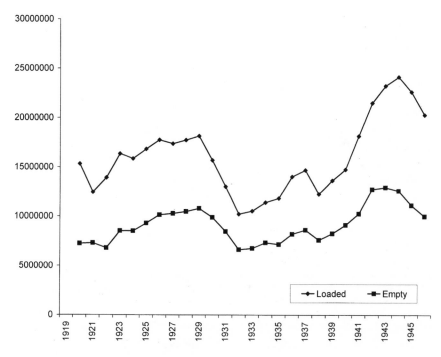

Figure 12.7: Railroad Freight Car Miles, 1920–1946
Source: U.S. Bureau of the Census 1937, 1944, 1947.

p. 473), while the average tractive power of the remaining steam engines increased from 44,801 to 51,217 pounds.

Annual freight car data show continuous decumulation from 1920 through 1939, with the exception of 1924–1926 (figure 12.5). Over the same period, aggregate freight car capacity in kilotons shrank from 105,411 to 85,682 (U.S. Bureau of the Census: 1937, table 427, p. 372; 1944, table 523, p. 472). But the replacement cars were bigger; average capacity rose from 46.3 to 50.3 tons between 1929 and 1941. Passenger car decumulation was modest through 1930, then increased dramatically through 1933. There is some recovery to lower rates of decumulation, particularly after 1935, but the number of passenger cars did not grow again until 1941 (figure 12.6). Numbers fell from 53,838 in 1929 to 38,344 in 1941. Bringing together all of the data on labor and capital inputs, we have a system undergoing wrenching rationalization midwifed by the economic downturn and the threat or actuality of receivership.

Figures 12.7 and 12.8 provide data on freight car miles and ton-mile revenues. Despite a net stock of structures that had fallen 6 percent since its peak in 1931, a labor force that was 31 percent smaller than it had been in 1929, and a real

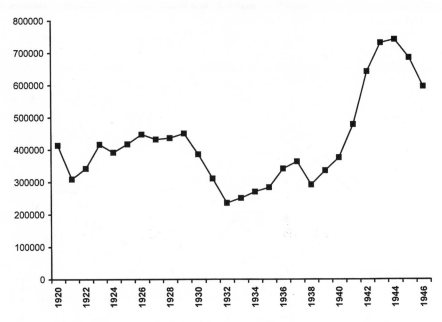

Figure 12.8: Revenue Freight Ton-Miles (millions), 1920–1946
Source: U.S. Bureau of the Census 1937, 1944, 1947.

stock of railroad capital that was a full one-third lower than it had been in 1929, revenue ton-miles were 6 percent greater in 1941 than in 1929.

The data on passenger miles (figure 12.9) show steadily declining output by this measure throughout the 1920s—testimony to the growing threat to passenger traffic posed by the automobile and bus—and a sharp drop to 1933. But 1941 passenger miles were within 6 percent of carriage in 1929. It is clear that since more freight was carried with many fewer freight cars, a substantial portion of the railway sector's productivity gains came from increases in freight car capacity utilization rates, which generated big increases in capital productivity. The ability to carry more freight and about the same number of passengers with much reduced numbers of locomotives, freight cars, and passenger cars also reduced the demand for railway structures (maintenance sheds, sidings, roundhouses, etc.), which was serendipitous since the financing for expanding the stock of structures was not readily available. The U.S. railroad system was able in 1941 to carry more freight and almost as many passengers as it did in 1929 with substantially reduced inputs of labor and capital. That meant big increases in both labor productivity and TFP. By the end of the Depression, the U.S.

rail system was in much better shape than it had been at the start of the First World War and was able to cope well with huge increases in both passenger and freight traffic during the Second World War. Figures 12.7 and 12.9 include data on output over the war years. If one measures from 1929 through 1942 using Kendrick's data, TFP in the sector grows by 4.48 percent per year.

Table 12.1 allows a closer examination of trends in and contributors to productivity increase. It calculates the percent change in a variety of input, output, and physical productivity measures between 1919 and 1929, 1929 and 1941, and 1929 and 1942. It also reports the underlying data, as well as aggregate economic data, for 1929, 1941, and 1942. The first year of full-scale war mobilization is 1942, and one can see in the aggregate data the partial crowding out of consumption and investment as a result of the doubling of government expenditure. Still, civilian unemployment averaged 4.7 percent for the year, and the distortions for the economy were not as extreme as in 1943 and 1944. Therefore, there is some merit in calculating productivity growth in railroads between 1929 and 1942 as well as 1941 since the output gap in 1942 is closer to what it was in percentage

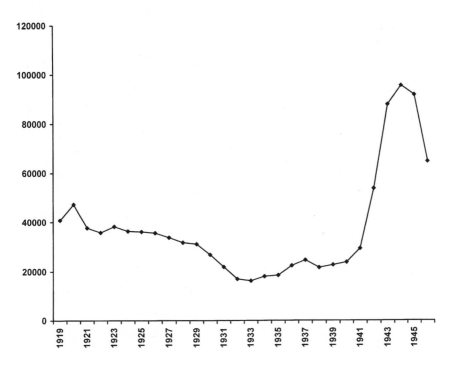

Figure 12.9: Railroad Passenger Miles (millions), 1919–1946
Source: U.S. Bureau of the Census 1937, 1944, 1947.

Table 12.1. Inputs, Outputs, and Productivity in the U.S. Railroad Sector, 1919–1942: Levels and Percent Change

	1919	1929	1941	1942	Percent Change		
					1919–1929	1929–1941	1929–1942
Inputs							
Employees	1,960,439	1,694,042	1,159,025	1,291,000	-13.6	-31.6	-24.8
Locomotives	68,977	61,257	44,375	44,671	-11.2	-27.6	-27.1
Freight cars	2,426,889	2,323,683	1,732,673	1,773,735	-4.3	-25.5	-23.7
Passenger cars	56,920	53,888	38,334	38,445	-5.3	-28.9	-28.7
Miles of first track	263,707	262,546	245,240	242,744	-0.4	-6.6	-7.5
Outputs							
Revenue ton-miles (millions)	367,161	450,189	477,576	640,992	22.6	6.1	42.4
Freight car miles (loaded) (thousands)	14,273,422	18,169,012	18,171,979	21,535,673	27.3	0.0	18.5
Freight car miles (unloaded) (thousands)	6,531,570	10,805,302	10,251,079	12,755,362	65.4	-5.1	18.0
Passenger miles (millions)	40,838	31,165	29,406	53,747	-23.7	-5.6	72.5
Physical productivity measures							
Ton-miles per freight car	0.151	0.194	0.276	0.361	28.1	42.3	86.5
Tons of revenue freight per loaded car	25.72	24.78	26.28	29.76	-3.7	6.1	20.1

Average miles per car per day	23.0	32.3	40.6	46.3	40.4	25.7	43.3
Average freight car capacity (tons)	41.9	46.3	50.3	50.5	10.5	8.6	9.1
Average freight car speed (mph)	0.979	1.459	1.920	2.263	49.1	31.6	55.0
Number of freight car loadings (thousands)	41,832	52,828	42,352	42,771	26.3	−19.8	−19.0
Average haul, revenue freight (miles)	309	317	369	428	2.8	16.2	34.9
Ton-miles per mile of first track	1.392	1.715	1.947	2.641	23.2	13.6	54.0
Passenger miles per passenger car	0.717	0.578	0.767	1.398	−19.4	32.6	141.7
Ton-miles per employee	0.187	0.266	0.412	0.497	41.9	55.1	86.8
Passenger miles per employee	0.021	0.018	0.025	0.042	−11.7	37.9	126.3
Aggregate economic indicators							
Unemployment rate		3.2	9.9	4.7			
Real GDP (billions of chained 1937 dollars)		87.3	122.1	144.6		39.8	65.6
Real gross private domestic investment		12.2	17.6	9.3		44.3	−23.8
Real government consumption and investment		9.2	25.6	60.3		178.3	555.4
Real consumption		63.1	78.2	76.4		23.9	21.1

Source: U.S. Bureau of the Census 1937, 1944, 1947; BEA, http://www.bea.gov, NIPA table 1.1.6A.

terms in 1929. Also, since we are examining physical productivity measures, the distortions in pricing and valuation associated with wartime are somewhat less of a concern.

What these data show is that overall, in spite of or perhaps in part because of the trying times, railroad productivity growth was significantly stronger across the Depression years than it had been in the 1920s. The most important measure of physical productivity is revenue ton-miles per freight car, which grew 28.1 percent between 1919 and 1929, 42.3 percent from 1929 to 1941, and 86.5 percent between 1929 and 1942. Let's look more closely at what underlay the Depression-era increases. The total number of miles traversed by loaded freight cars in 1941 was approximately the same as it had been in 1929. The big driver of productivity improvement was that the number of cars had declined 25.6 percent. The average capacity of each car was somewhat greater—it had grown from 46.3 to 50.3 tons, making it easier to achieve a 6.1 percent increase in tons of revenue freight per loaded car. Overall, we can deduce that the average speed of each freight car (a function of average time stopped and average speed while in motion) had increased, since had it remained the same as it had been in 1929, the 25.6 percent decline in the number of cars would have reduced total freight car miles by a comparable percentage. We also know that the number of freight car loadings in thousands declined from 52,828 in 1929 to 42,352 in 1941; freight traveled on average a longer distance, reflecting the inroads of trucking in shorter hauls.

In contrast, between 1919 and 1929, the number of freight cars remained about the same, but total miles traversed rose. Note, however, that miles booked by empty cars increased much faster than loaded miles during the 1920s, whereas between 1929 and 1941, while the total number of loaded miles remained unchanged, unloaded miles dropped. This is another reflection of logistical improvement, in part made possible by improvements in freight interchange and growth of western states as centers of consumption as well as production.

An alternate measure of the physical productivity of freight haulage is ton-miles per mile of first track. This grows more strongly in the 1920s than during the Depression years, although if one measures to 1942, the reverse is true. Ton-miles per employee, a rough measure of labor productivity in freight haulage, grew 41.9 percent during the 1920s but 55.1 percent during the Depression and 86.8 percent if one measures to 1942.

Passenger miles per passenger car declined 19.6 percent during the 1920s but rose sharply across the Depression years—32.6 percent if we measure to 1941, 141.7 percent if we measure to 1942. Finally, passenger miles per employee, which declined almost 12 percent during the 1920s, rose 37.9 percent across the Depression years and 126.3 percent through 1942.

The Depression-era history of the U.S. rail system provides a compelling example of the operation of the adversity/hysteresis effect. Faced with tough times in the form of radically changing demand conditions, crushing debt burdens, and lack of access to more capital, railroad organizations changed their operating procedures, introduced new technologies, and reduced their trackage, rolling stock, and employees, in most cases dramatically. In the face of these cuts, output nonetheless grew modestly to the beginning of the war and rapidly thereafter. It is true that the sector faced tough times in the quarter century following World War II as it struggled with the continued erosion of its passenger business and the reality that trucking also threatened its long-haul freight revenues. But it emerged by the last decades of the twentieth century in relatively good shape, once again displaying rapid productivity growth.

Should we be sanguine about recessions on the grounds that they are likely to provide a boost to long-run productivity growth—indeed, perhaps even welcome them as analogous to the fires that keep healthy forests of sequoias? Unfortunately, the answer on balance is probably no. Overall, welfare and economic growth benefit from moderation of the business cycle. Recessions impose an irrecoverable burden of lost output, income, and expenditure. They disrupt the process of the physical accumulation of capital, imposing costs on the long-run growth of potential output. And unemployment is associated with rising measures of social anomie and reductions in labor market attachment that may have longer-run consequences for labor supply. All of that said, there will be areas of the economy whose response to adversity generates persisting beneficial consequences. For the Depression period, railroads were one of these.

The experience of U.S. railroads during the Depression provides some support for the silver lining hypothesis, the view that recession may sometimes provide a longer-term boost to the growth of potential output. It is possible that something like this could happen in what remains of the U.S. automobile industry. Certainly the combination of adverse demand conditions, crushing debt burdens, and a drying up of access to more capital absent a bankruptcy proceeding are familiar. Even with some silver lining effect, however, we must still conclude that the growth of potential output would likely be higher in the presence of a smoother path of capital accumulation—that is, without either the boom or the bust. We cannot comfort unemployed workers with the thought that their sacrifices pave the way for a better tomorrow.

        •●►

Epilogue

The 1939–1940 New York World's Fair took place within the shadow of the Second World War, but it was a paean to modernism, a hopeful celebration of technological and human potential as the United States emerged from a decade of double-digit unemployment. The most popular exhibit was General Motors' Futurama, designed by Norman Bel Geddes, the patron saint of modernism's aerodynamic aesthetic. Visitors lined up for hours for an opportunity to gaze at vistas of modern infrastructure with cars moving along fourteen-lane freeways. From everything we can tell, it appears that Americans contemplated these vistas with a complete lack of any kind of distancing or ironic sensibility. They had seen enough on the ground already to understand that Bel Geddes's vision of the United States in 1960 would not, by and large, be science fiction.

A quarter century later, at the 1964–1965 New World's Fair at the same site in Flushing Meadows, General Motors tried to replicate its earlier success with a new Futurama, looking forward another quarter century and beyond, to human colonies living on the moon, in Antarctica, the jungle, the desert, and the ocean floor. It was unable to capture the popular imagination, and its forecasts of the future have proved far off the mark. The contrasting receptions of these two similarly titled exhibits are consistent with what the aggregate and sectoral data are trying to tell us.

A final piece of popular history is relevant to placing the information technology boom in perspective. When Disneyland opened in 1955, it attempted to carry forward in one of its themed sections the spirit of the 1939–1940 fair: "You will actually experience what many of America's foremost men of science and industry predict for the world of tomorrow," wrote a guidebook from the late 1950s (Handy 2000, p. 115). Tomorrowland was initially the most popular of Disneyland's four areas and had as its centerpiece a rocket poised to transport visitors to the moon and beyond. Fourteen years later American astronauts did in fact go to the moon, albeit in a three-stage rocket. But by the 1990s, Tomorrowland had begun to look a bit down at the heels. Disney's Imagineers apparently pulled out their hair trying to develop a new and compelling vision of the future that their audience, with its more jaded and ironic attitude toward new technology, would accept.

They were unable to do so and in this instance did not try. Instead, in the updated area that opened in 1998, they aimed at recapturing the visual imagery of 1930s (and earlier) visions of the future. Disney felt compelled to develop a *retro* Tomorrowland, replete with Buck Rodgers and other vintage imagery. The one remnant of the earlier vision was an exhibit called Innoventions, a display area for new products soon to be launched commercially. It represented an island of technological futurism within a sea of nostalgia. What used to be front and center had become almost a side show. Audiences were no longer so easily gripped by the vision of a bigger, better tomorrow that had so enthralled visitors to Bel Geddes's exhibit.

Is it entirely accidental that what is generally acknowledged to have been the greatest international exposition of the twentieth century took place in New York in 1939 and 1940, as the United States neared the end of its most technologically dynamic epoch, having opened up a substantial productivity gap between itself and Europe and the rest of the world? After the 1964–1965 New York fair, the fairs in Montreal in 1967 and Osaka in 1970 can claim some measure of critical if not always financial success. But who now speaks of or will long remember those in Spokane (1974), Knoxville (1982), New Orleans (1984), Vancouver (1986), or Seville (1992)?

This book has traversed much ground. It has moved from qualitative to quantitative economic history and back again; from macro to micro data and back again; from growth to cycles and back again. Specialist readers want to know about trees, and I've tried to describe them carefully. Periodically, though, I've pulled back the camera, making the forest visible for all, including the lay reader. This epilogue considers our great leap forward, that extraordinary expansion of potential output across the Depression years, from the standpoint of its impact on the cultural imagination.

One may be skeptical of such an approach, dismissing these stories as anecdotes. It is when read in the light of the aggregate data on labor and TFP growth that they take on real significance. During the years when Alvin Hansen (1938) and others were expounding a theory of secular stagnation, the U.S.

economy was, in fact, experiencing a period of technological and organizational creativity that, in the aggregate, remains as yet unmatched. Hansen's colleague at Harvard, Joseph Schumpeter, had a better fix on what was going on. He developed his homage to the power of creative destruction (1942) against the backdrop of what turned out to be the most technologically dynamic epoch of the twentieth century. Schumpeter may have misjudged the terrain on the road to socialism, but his theories more successfully reflected the technological spirit of the age in which he wrote.

Appendix: A Brief Description of Growth Accounting Methods

Taking upper-case letters as levels and lower-case letters as continuously compounded rates of growth, the following definitions apply:

Y = real output

N = labor hours

K = capital input

Y/N = labor productivity.

The growth rate of labor productivity is the difference between the growth rate of output and the growth rate of labor hours:

$y - n$ = labor productivity growth.

To calculate the level of total factor productivity and its rate of growth, we introduce the concept of a production function. We assume that output is produced using inputs of capital and labor services, combined according to a functional form known as Cobb-Douglas:

(1) $Y = A K^{\beta} N^{1-\beta}$ = production function (Cobb-Douglas).

Because the coefficients on the two inputs (β and $1-\beta$) sum to one, we are assuming that the aggregate production function exhibits constant returns to scale. Doubling all inputs will double output. The term A refers to the efficiency with which inputs can be combined to produce output, or total factor productivity. We expect its long-term trend growth rate to be positive, reflecting the advance of scientific, technological, and organizational knowledge. If the rate of advance of such knowledge is slow or nonexistent, A will not grow through time.

(2) $A = Y/(K^{\beta} N^{1-\beta})$ = total factor productivity.

We can also show that under the assumption that competition results in factors getting paid their marginal product, the coefficients on the inputs (β and $1-\beta$) correspond to the

Appendix

shares of these two factors in national income, with labor typically claiming a two-thirds to three-quarters share and capital the remainder.

To show this, note that the marginal product of labor will be

$$dY/dN = (1-\beta) A K^\beta N^{-\beta} = \text{wage rate.}$$

If we accept the marginal productivity theory of income distribution, labor's share will be the wage rate (the above expression) multiplied by N (the number of hours)

$$= (1-\beta) A K^\beta N^{-\beta} N$$

$$= (1-\beta) A K^\beta N^{1-\beta}$$

$$= (1-\beta)Y \text{ (from (1)).}$$

The same argument applies to capital, and thus its share will be βY.

If we now take natural logs of both sides of equation (2) and differentiate both sides with respect to time (denoted by $\dot{A}$ for A and so on), we obtain the following expression, with lower-case letters corresponding to continuously compounded growth rates:

$$a = y - \beta k - (1-\beta)n = \text{growth rate of TFP,}$$

where $a = \dot{A}/A$, $y = \dot{Y}/Y$, $k = \dot{K}/K$, and $n = \dot{N}/N$

or

$$(3)\ y = a + \beta k + (1-\beta)n,$$

which is the fundamental growth accounting equation.

Multiplying out, subtracting n from both sides of the equation, and consolidating terms, we obtain the very useful expression showing that growth in output per hour can be decomposed into the effect of TFP growth (a) and of capital deepening $\beta(k-n)$

$$y - n = a + \beta(k-n) = \text{growth rate of labor productivity.}$$

This is exactly the decomposition to which the Solow growth model calls our attention, and these formulae are the basis for Solow's original (1957) empirical work on growth accounting.

The rate of growth of TFP can also be shown to be arithmetically equivalent to a weighted average of the growth rates of capital productivity and labor productivity, the weights corresponding again to the respective shares of these factors in national income.

To demonstrate this, start with the expression in (3),

$$y - n = a + \beta(k-n),$$

which is our now familiar equation decomposing labor productivity growth into the influences of technological change and capital deepening. Rearranging, we have

$$a = y - n - \beta(k-n).$$

Multiplying out,

$$a = y - n - \beta k + \beta n.$$

Adding βy and −βy to the right-hand-side of this equation and rearranging, we have

$$a = βy − βk + y − n − βy + βn.$$

Factoring out yields

$$a = β(y−k) + (1−β)(y−n),$$

which puts into mathematics what the previous paragraph says in words: $(y−k)$ is the growth of capital productivity (Y/K), and $y−n$ is the growth of labor productivity (Y/N); TFP growth (a) is a weighted average of the two. Note that capital productivity (Y/K) is the inverse of the more familiar capital-output ratio.

A final restatement: the growth of the residual must, on the factor income side, resolve itself into growth of the real wage (the return to labor) and growth in the return to capital. Let

W = wage rate (return to labor)
R = return to capital.

The equality of gross output and income tells us that

$$(4)\ Y = RK + WN.$$

Note then that

$$RK/(RK+WN) = RK/Y = \text{capital's share } (β), \text{ and}$$
$$WN/(RK+WN) = WN/Y = \text{labor's share } (1−β).$$

Differentiating (4) with respect to time and rearranging, we have (again, lower-case letters refer to continuously compounded growth rates)

$$y = β (r + k) + (1−β) (w + n).$$

To see why this is so, first take the discrete approximation:

$$ΔY = R\ ΔK + K\ ΔR + W\ ΔN + N\ ΔW.$$

Divide by Y on the left side and its equivalent (RK + WN) for each of the right-hand-side (RHS) terms. Consider the first RHS term. We have (R ΔK)/(RK + WN). Multiply the numerator of this expression by K/K, yielding (RK(ΔK/K))/(RK + WN)) which equals (RK/(RK + WN))(ΔK/K). This is just βk—capital's share times the rate of growth of the capital stock. Similar logic applies to each of the other three terms. Multiplying out, we have

$$y = βr + βk + (1−β)w + (1−β)n.$$

Subtracting the second and fourth right-hand-side terms from both sides of the equation, we have

$$y − βk − (1−β)n = a = βr + (1−β)w.$$

This alternate expression for the residual (the dual) tells us that because of the equality of gross output and gross income, any growth in the residual must resolve itself into a growth in the return to labor and the return to capital. In a period of very rapid advance in TFP, such as from 1933 through 1937, we should expect both the real wage and the return to capital to increase sharply, the division of gains between the two reflecting institutional and political factors as well as the bias of technical change (see below). The dual reminds us that in a period of strong TFP growth, such as in 1929–1941, we should anticipate significant gains in both wages and income to capital. Even though the quantities of these inputs did not increase very much, the return to each unit of input should have risen. And this is in fact what happened.

To summarize, the basic procedure for calculating the rate of growth of TFP is to subtract from the rate of growth of real output a weighted average of the growth rates for key inputs, in particular labor and capital. The weights sum to 1, reflecting the assumption of constant returns to scale, and reflect shares of the factors in national income. Any difference in the growth of output reflects the influence of factors not captured in inputs conventionally measured. The dual tells us that this TFP growth must show up in increases in the return to labor or to capital or to both.

BIAS OF TECHNOLOGICAL CHANGE

The "a" term in the above equations is a measure of what John Hicks called neutral technological change. For a given capital-labor ratio, such change will increase the marginal product of both labor and capital proportionately, leaving their ratio unchanged. Harrod neutral, or labor-augmenting technological change, raises labor productivity but leaves capital productivity unchanged. Harrod neutral technological change is calculated based on a production function written as $Y = K^\beta(AN)^{1-\beta}$ rather than $Y = A K^\beta N^{1-\beta}$.

To the degree that technological change is Hicks neutral, or indeed has any form that raises the return to capital (purely capital-augmenting technological change is sometimes called Solow neutral), and to the degree that economy-wide saving behavior has a positive elasticity with respect to the real interest rate, the clean distinction that Solow tried to make between the forces of thrift and those of invention is at risk. That is because, in a consideration of the growth of output per hour, some of the capital deepening might be responsive to the rise in the return to saving and investment produced by technological change and not reflect some autonomous shift in the saving propensities of the population. In this case the measure of "a" would underestimate the total contribution to growth in output per hour of technological change.

A more complex possibility is that technological change might shift a higher proportion of income to capital, which would result in a larger share of income going to higher-income households, who might have higher saving propensities. In this case, even though the saving propensities of no individual household would have changed, the redistribution could result in an increase in the aggregate saving rate, which again would ultimately have been caused by technical change.

Whereas these scenarios are of potential interest for some periods, neither is particularly relevant for the 1930s because there was so little growth of the private capital stock. But the issues do arise in discussions of the IT productivity boom between 1995 and 2005 (chapter 5), as well as treatments of late-nineteenth-century growth (chapter 6).

NOTES

INTRODUCTION

1. TFP is the ratio of output to a combined measure reflecting inputs of both capital and labor. The concepts of TFP and its closely related cousin, labor productivity, are discussed in more detail below.

2. In growth rate calculations, both output and capital are "real" magnitudes: the effects of inflation have been removed. Some of the tables in the book also report trends in capital productivity, which is the ratio of output to capital input (the inverse of the capital-output ratio). As the appendix shows, total factor productivity growth, mathematically, is a weighted average of the growth of labor and capital productivity growth.

3. The higher estimate results from the use of new chained index methods of calculating the growth of real outputs. The problem chain index methods address is that real output growth calculated using beginning year prices will generally not be the same as if it is calculated using end-period prices. This is the famous index number problem. The chain index method involves for each year calculating growth using initial year prices and then using end-year prices and then taking a geometric average of the two. A geometric average multiplies the two growth rates together and takes the square root of the product.

4. The main exceptions to the requirement that goods or services be sold on the market are government services, such as publicly provided education, which are valued at their cost of acquisition, as well as the imputation for the value of the owner-occupied portion of the housing stock. GNP is a citizenship-based category while GDP is a geographical concept. GNP includes product and income accruing to U.S. labor and capital outside of the country; it does not include product and income accruing to foreign labor or foreign-owned capital in the United States. GDP records products generated within the geographical confines of the United States, regardless of the citizenship or ownership of inputs.

5. The output of nonprofit institutions and paid household workers and the rental value of owner-occupied housing is also excluded from the numerator of this measure. On the denominator (input side) of the TFP calculation, hours worked by household employees and employees of nonprofit institutions, as well as nonprofit sector physical capital and owner-occupied residential housing capital are excluded. See U.S. Department of Labor 1997, ch. 10, p. 90.

6. The labor force is a subset of the population that includes those working and those actively seeking work

7. Most of the raw material for Kendrick 1961 came from government census summary volumes, industry trade association publications, and other reports.

8. Capital account surpluses are the mirror image of current account deficits. When imports exceed exports, an economy taps into saving flows from outside the country. A country's sum of consumption, investment, and government spending can then exceed what it produces. Note that "investment" as a term used by macroeconomists means actual spending by firms on new plant or equipment (or the buildup of inventories). The term is used differently in a personal finance class—to represent, for example, the acquisition by an individual of stock in a particular company. Since that stock was most likely previously issued, such a transaction is of little macroeconomic consequence, aside from the commission generated for the broker.

9. Criticism of Bernanke and his predecessor, Alan Greenspan, for failing, prior to the crisis, to take more aggressive steps to control the growth of leverage, or even to acknowledge that there might be a problem, has merit (see chapter 10). That said, the country benefited from Bernanke's historically informed response to near catastrophe.

CHAPTER 1: THE MOST TECHNOLOGICALLY
PROGRESSIVE DECADE OF THE CENTURY

1. The reference in the chapter title to a decade reflects poetic license: my interest here is in a twelve-year period. See Mitchell (1947) for precedent. Some scholars refer to the years 1929–1933 as the Depression (Friedman and Schwartz 1963 called it the Great Contraction). As a terminological matter, I treat the Depression as having extended over the twelve years 1929–1941; during these years output was persistently depressed below its potential.

2. Abramovitz (personal conversation) used the metaphor of larder stocking to distinguish between technological advances that were more or less immediately exploited and those that provided a foundation for what could be developed in subsequent periods. A larder was (literally) a pantry or cellar in which household food supplies were stored.

3. "Before allowing for the vintage effect, the rate of refined TFP growth from 1948 to 1966 stands higher than that from 1929 to 1948. Allowing for the vintage effect, the reverse seems to have been true" (Abramovitz and David 2000, p. 29). The "vintage effect" is an adjustment to capital input made by the authors to take account of the asserted (unmeasured) improvement in the quality of capital goods, particularly equip-

ment. The adjustment will reduce calculated TFP growth rates in periods of more rapid physical capital accumulation, such as the golden age, because it causes the (adjusted) capital input series to rise more rapidly. Abramovitz and David's principal interpretive emphasis was on a contrast between economic growth based on the accumulation of physical capital in the nineteenth century and the knowledge-based growth of the twentieth.

4. Multifactor productivity, a term used principally by the BLS, is a synonym for total factor productivity. For its calculations of productivity growth for aggregates such as the private nonfarm economy, the BLS adheres to the methodology described in the introduction. For sectoral measures, however, instead of calculating the growth of value added not explained by the growth of labor and capital, the BLS calculates the growth of gross revenues not explained by the growth of capital, labor, and purchased inputs other than wage and salaried labor, including in particular energy, materials, and services. These sectoral calculations are known as KLEMS estimates, with the acronym standing for the multiple inputs (capital, labor, energy, materials, and services). KLEMS estimates are further described below in note 8 of chapter 5.

5. Capital per hour will grow more slowly than capital per worker when hours per worker are rising.

6. The physical capital stock has three components: structures, equipment, and inventories. The sum of structures (which can be divided into residential and nonresidential) and equipment (also known as producer durables and including machinery and other moveable capital such as locomotives or aircraft) is the fixed capital stock. Physical capital accumulation can take place when an economy devotes part of its current output (known as gross investment) to replace worn out buildings and equipment and add to the stock. So long as gross investment is greater than depreciation, the physical capital stock will grow.

7. Chapter 6 shows that TFP growth was in fact substantially higher between 1873 and 1906 than it was between 1973 and 1995 or even 2007.

8. The C-47 was the military version of the DC-3. Over ten thousand of these aircraft were produced during the Second World War, and the labor hours required to assemble them declined steadily with cumulated output.

9. William Baumol wrote that "except in wartime, *for the better part of a century,* U.S. productivity growth rates have been low." (1986, p. 1073; emphasis added). His comment, although within the context of an international comparison, reflects a widespread belief that twentieth-century wars, and particularly the Second World War, have been relatively favorable influences on U.S. productivity growth.

10. The influence of atomic power on productivity in the electric-power-generating sector proved eventually a mixed blessing, although a full discussion of the case is beyond the scope of this work. The crash program for the development of techniques for the mass production of penicillin obviously had persisting benefits from the standpoint of public health (Mowery and Rosenberg 2000, p. 819).

11. Cole and Ohanian (1999) examined Kendrick's data over the interval 1929–1939, noted the sharp decline through 1933 and rapid recovery thereafter, and observed that TFP

growth overall over the decade they examined was "about normal." But 1939, with its 17.2 percent unemployment, is even less desirable than 1937 as a benchmark in a period characterized by strongly procyclical productivity movements (see chapters 2 and 7).

12. Annual BLS data on multifactor (total factor) productivity are available beginning only in 1948; see http://www.bls.gov. In contrast with Solow (1957), neither Abramovitz and David (1999) nor Gordon (2000b) includes the type of detailed annual data available in Kendrick, although both acknowledge their debt to him.

13. One of the differences between the Gordon and the Abramovitz and David chronology is that Gordon uses 1950 as a reference peak, as opposed to 1948. It's not clear why. Unemployment in 1948 was 3.8 percent, vs. 5.2 percent in 1950. Output peaked in 1948:4 (quarter 4), and the year remains a peak in labor productivity, even after series are cyclically adjusted (P. Clark 1978). On a variety of dimensions 1948 appears to be a superior year for a peacetime peak-to-peak comparison, and I follow Abramovitz and David in using it. Gordon's reasons for preferring 1928 to 1929 are similarly unclear: both the output peak and the unemployment trough occur in the latter year, although 1928 unemployment, at 4.2 percent, was closer to the 3.8 percent of 1948 than was the 3.2 percent of 1929. The most likely explanation is that Gordon viewed the economy as above potential in 1929. There is little indication in 1929, however (in contrast, for example, to the war years), of upward pressure on the prices of goods and services. As subsequent chapters demonstrate, I believe that the Kendrick data actually paint too conservative a picture of the growth of potential output across the Depression. The inclusion of a cyclical adjustment for 1941 (chapter 2) and/or the use of newer chained index methods for calculating the growth of real output substantially increase the estimated growth rate of TFP. The Kendrick numbers are, however, an appropriate starting point for the analysis.

14. Keep in mind that any upward adjustment in input growth rates—those of either labor or capital—will reduce the growth rate of the residual.

15. There are some inconsistencies between tables 5 and 6 in Gordon 2000b. The numbers reported above are based on the sum of columns 5, 6, and 7 in table 5 for the two respective time intervals. For 1928–1950, this is very close to what one gets by subtracting column 5 from column 6 in table 6, although there is a considerable difference (−.27 vs. −.45) when one attempts this for 1950–1964. I rely on table 5 because it presents a more detailed breakdown of the components of the capital quantity adjustment.

16. This is reflected in Gordon 2000b, table 5, column 7.

17. Gordon's GOPO adjustment is apparently based on the data on line 28 of table 7.2 of the Bureau of Economic Analysis (BEA) Fixed Asset Tables (the source notes in Gordon 2000b in this instance are opaque). It is not clear, however, whether the BEA's valuations for the postwar period reflect the cost of replacement for the original use or for the use to which the assets may have been put following demobilization. There remains an unresolved dispute over the usefulness for civilian production of this capital after the war. Some have criticized the transfers to the private sector as sweetheart deals; the valuations reflected in the sales, however, have been defended

on the grounds that substantial retrofitting was often required to make them suitable for civilian production. To the degree that defenders of the postwar sales have a point, the adjustment for GOPO capital that Gordon has included may be somewhat too large and may artificially inflate capital input for 1950.

18. Gordon's adjustment for variable lifetimes depends on the assumption that annual service flow remains uniform throughout the life of an asset. If structures and equipment were retained in service longer than normal during the Depression and war years, service flow could well have declined as the assets aged, with the consequent equivalent of chewing gum and baling wire allowing the continued operation of assets that had not just depreciated but deteriorated. There are still 1959 Chevrolets operating on the streets of Havana. The question is whether the equipment is providing the same service flow it did four decades ago.

19. Using an entirely different data source—technical publications in the Library of Congress catalogue—Alexopoulos and Cohen (2009) reached broadly similar conclusions about the technological progressivity of the Depression era.

20. The George Washington, Golden Gate, and Oakland Bay Bridges; the Lincoln Tunnel; the Hoover Dam; and the Pennsylvania Turnpike, Merritt Parkway, and Pasadena Freeway are notable achievements in civil engineering in the 1929–1941 period. Exhibits highlighting these achievements, in particular the General Motors exhibit and Democracity, were the standout attractions at the 1939–1940 New York World's Fair. See Gelertner (1995). The last major suspension bridge built in the United States was the Verrazano Narrows, completed in 1964.

21. Thus the famous quote: "Fiscal policy . . . seems to have been an unsuccessful recovery device in the 'thirties—not because it did not work, but because it was not tried" (Brown 1956, pp. 863–866).

22. Its labor policies, including encouragement of the right to organize, they see as persisting through the instrumentality of the Wagner Act. Encouragement of firms to cartelize they see persisting, at least through the first Franklin Roosevelt administration, through lax antitrust enforcement. In both cases, the putative negative supply shock comes in the form of higher nominal wages or product prices than would otherwise have prevailed.

23. Cole and Ohanian argue that the legacy effects of the National Industrial Recovery Act combined with the Wagner Act meant that recovery and employment growth were lower than they might have been. Yet high rates of unionization and strong real wage growth coexisted with employment growth and a decent capacity utilization record during the golden age. My current view that, for the United States, the main causes of recession and delayed recovery are typically to be found in financial rather than labor markets has been influenced and reinforced by the events of 2008–2009 (see chapter 10).

24. See, e.g., Margo 1993, p. 43, or Goldin 2000. In her 2000 survey article, Goldin noted that nonfarm hourly labor productivity "grew during the 1930s at a rate greater than that for the 1920s". She attributed this to Depression-era cuts in hours per worker and the probability that those unemployed were less educated and "probably less skilled" than those retained (pp. 566–567).

25. But note the very sharp increase in man hours per unit of output for the automobile industry reported for 1930, 1931, and 1932 in Weintraub (1938, p. 161) and the drop in output per hour between 1929 and 1933 evident in Kendrick. The Weintraub data raise questions about the relative empirical importance of selective retention and provide some support for labor hoarding, at least in manufacturing, during the worst phase of the downturn.

26. The drop in weekly hours per worker explains why total hours inputted remained about the same.

27. Hysteresis refers here to the possibility of persisting negative effects from the downturn, even after the economy has apparently recovered. The decline in hours per worker could, however, have contributed something to a rising trend in output per hour, as Goldin (2000) suggested. Empirically, when an employee's hours of work go down, output per hour in the remaining hours generally rises.

28. Denison's education quality index for civilian employment shows 4.8 percent increase for males and 4.5 percent improvement for females between 1929 and 1941 (1974, table I-18, p. 252). This is consistent with positive but modest improvement in labor force quality over these years.

29. I refer here to a statistical distribution.

CHAPTER 2: THE INTERWAR YEARS

1. The transportation sector includes railroads, trucking and warehousing companies, firms engaged in air or water transportation, and those running pipelines except for natural gas. It does not include the output of firms making cars, aircraft, barges, locomotives, etc., which is part of manufacturing. Public utilities consists mostly of electricity and gas companies. These are typically natural monopolies and thus regulated; that is why, though often privately owned, they are called public utilities. Until the early 1930s, 90 percent of the electric power industry was privately owned (Kendrick 1961, p. 565).

2. "Greenfield" in the sense that they were built on sites that were not previously industrial or urban.

3. The Standard Industrial Classification (SIC) system was officially used for the study of manufacturing in the United States until 1997. Two-digit codes delimited the broad industry groups listed in table 2.2. Within each industry, narrower subcategories at the three- or even four-digit level reflected an extremely fine-grained statistical apparatus. The SIC has now been supplanted by the North American Industrial Classification System (NAICS; see chapter 5), but SIC codes are still commonly used in historical work.

4. TFP growth fell in the sector because output didn't grow as fast as a weighted measure of input growth.

5. Stated alternately, the share of services increased. Transportation, distribution, and other important contributors to GDP such as law and medicine generate services that perish in the instant of their creation. In contrast, goods-producing sectors sell a tangible product to a final user.

6. Data are from http://www.bea.gov, Industry Economic Accounts, Gross Domestic Product by Industry; accessed July 21, 2009. These percentages reflect the BEA's revised statistical framework; manufacturing shares are now reduced by the removal of value added in printing and publishing to a new category of "Information." If one adds printing and publishing back into manufacturing in 1948, its share of value added is about 26.3 percent.

7. The distinction between durables and nondurables concerns whether the expected life of the product is greater or less than one year.

8. The average rate of advance within manufacturing between 1929 and 1941 was even higher because, as table 2.3 shows, TFP growth in manufacturing was negative between 1941 and 1948.

9. The Fixed Asset Tables are contained in the portion of the BEA's Web site that gives access to annual data on the value of the physical capital stock going back to 1925. Starting at http://www.bea.gov, click on Fixed Assets; then click on "Interactive Tables: Fixed Asset Tables," and then on "Choose a Table from the Standard Fixed Asset Tables." The use of a net rather than gross capital stock measure as proxy for capital service flow is consistent with Kendrick's practice (for arguments as to why this is appropriate and preferable to using a gross measure, see Kendrick 1961, pp. 34–36). Measuring from peak to peak largely controls for the variations in capacity utilization that occur over the business cycle.

10. Only SIC 35 and 36 turned in stronger performances over eight decades, and textiles is the only two-digit industry to register higher TFP growth in the 1929–1948 period as compared with 1919–1929. And it did so while ranking toward the bottom of industries in terms of the educational attainments of its workers (Goldin and Katz 1998, p. 709). The main source of productivity advance in textiles in the interwar period appears to have involved changes in plant layout, with the shift to linear arrangements of machines and improved speed of material work flow (see Weintraub 1939). Gavin Wright has suggested a role for New Deal minimum-wage mandates in encouraging this (personal communication). Other industries, however, had already benefited in the 1920s from such reorganization (see David and Wright 2003). Cole and Ohanian (2004) can also be read as suggesting a possible link between New Deal wage policy and productivity advance, although their main concern is with the effect of wage policy on employment.

11. See http://www.bea.gov, Fixed Asset Table 4.2, line 19; accessed July 21, 2009; Kendrick 1961, appendix table D-II.

12. To say that there is capital-skill complementarity is to say that new physical capital required highly skilled workers in order to get the most out of it, and vice versa. A more familiar example: left and right shoes are considered to be economic complements.

13. Keep in mind that the productivity growth rates in question are measured from 1929 to 1941.

14. This calculation is based on index numbers for manufacturing output and hours from Kendrick (1961, appendix table D-2, p. 466) and index numbers for fixed capital in manufacturing from the BEA's Fixed Asset Table 4.2, line 19. A capital share of .31 is

assumed. The sum of proprietors' income, rental income, and corporate profits as a share of national income was .313 in 1929 and .314 in 1941. See National Income and Product Accounts table 1.12, lines 2, 9, 12, and 13; http://.www.bea.gov, Gross Domestic Product Data; accessed January 4, 2010.

15. BEA Fixed Asset Table 7.1A, footnote 5.

16. See note 6 above.

17. Most of the government infrastructural addition is streets and highways, 89 percent of it in 1929 and 86 percent of it in 1941.

18. See the introduction or appendix for explication of the rationale for this calculation.

19. Because of the larger size of high schools in comparison with elementary schools and the need to assemble students together from a much larger area, surface road improvement may also have played a role in the acceleration of high school graduation rates across the country during the 1930s (see Goldin 1998, p. 368).

20. Productivity trends in housing services are distinct from those in construction, which are discussed below. Construction builds houses. Once houses are built, they are part of the nation's capital stock, "producing" housing services.

21. Since housing services are largely generated using housing capital alone (in principle the residential stock emits housing services without a direct assist from humans), TFP growth in the sector can be taken as proxied for by the growth in output per unit of capital.

22. Manufacturing's share of value added in 1948 was .26. The private nonfarm economy, which excludes agriculture, government, nonfarm housing services, health services, private education services, social services, and membership organizations, was 73 percent of value added. Thus manufacturing's share of the PNE was .36. Its estimated TFP growth rate between 1941 and 1948 was −.35 (see table 2.3), and it therefore contributed −.13 percentage points per year (.36 x −.35) to the PNE's TFP growth rate of 1.29 percent. This implies that TFP growth outside of manufacturing must have been over 2.2 percent per year. That figure, 2.2 percent, times the share of nonmanufacturing in the PNE (.64) yields a contribution of 1.41 percentage points, enough to compensate for the negative contribution of manufacturing and yield an overall PNE growth rate of 1.29 percent per year. For consideration of implications for the equipment hypothesis, see chapter 8.

23. Output in construction only began to reapproach levels typical in the 1920s after 1938 (see chapter 11).

24. Ideally, we would use an average of sectoral shares in 1919 and 1929; data availability forces this compromise.

25. The figures in brackets are the capital growth rate less the labor growth rate multiplied by the capital share—yielding the contribution to labor productivity growth of capital deepening. See the appendix for the derivation of the equation apportioning labor productivity growth into the contribution of total factor productivity growth and capital deepening.

26. In 1915 Emily Post, contemplating a cross-country car trip across the United States, asked a friend who had done it many times what the best route was across the United

States. "The Union Pacific," the friend replied without hesitation. See http://www
.fhwa.dot.gov/infrastructure/not2.pdf; accessed January 4, 2010.

27. In other words, with an emphasis on the putative contribution of spending to the
increase of potential output, rather than simply its benefits in giving unemployed
individuals work.

28. U.S. routes were, of course, built to substantially lower standards, with lower average
speeds and capacities, than were the interstates, controlled-access divided highways
that eschewed stop lights. But the 1941 system, essentially what the country had in
1956, represented an enormous improvement over what was in place in 1929.

29. Public infrastructural investment during the 1930s affected all four modes. The U.S.
internal water transportation system, for example, also received substantial upgrades.
The Tennessee Valley Authority built dams that controlled floods and generated
hydropower but also improved river navigation. Elsewhere in the country, the U.S.
Army Corps of Engineers improved navigation channels. The Nine-Foot Channel
navigation project, for example, benefited river transport on 284 miles of the Upper
Mississippi. Barge transport also benefited from the switch from tow to push barges.
But in contrast with trucking and warehousing or railroads, TFP growth within water
transport was very low across the Depression years (see table 2.6).

30. A steam-powered automobile won the first Los Angeles to Phoenix race in 1908 with
an average speed of 17.5 mph. See http://www.fhwa.dot.gov/infrastructure/not2c.cfm;
accessed January 4, 2010.

31. The Federal Motor Carrier Act (1935) introduced regulation for trucking.

CHAPTER 3: THE SECOND WORLD WAR

1. Details of the magnitude of the fiscal and monetary stimulus can be found in Edelstein 2000; these aggregate demand shocks are not the main focus of this chapter. The
supply-side story is sometimes more implicit but encountered frequently. Optimism
about the supply-side effects of war is reflected, for example, in Baumol 1986, p. 1073.
For a more recent illustration, see Ruttan (2006). Presumptions about the long-term
economic benefits of war have, perhaps understandably, been somewhat less preva-
lent in Europe.

2. This demand shock was sufficient to end the Depression, in the sense that it drove
unemployment from 9.9 percent in 1941 to under 2 percent within two years. But
was it necessary? By the end of the 1930s (and certainly by 1941) the private economy
was on the road to recovery and might have continued in that direction, even in the
absence of the growing stimulus from the government sector. Of all components of
autonomous spending, residential construction took the longest to reapproach levels
experienced during the 1920s (see chapter 11). Nevertheless, after reaching a nadir in
1933, it climbed back steadily, and by 1941, before the war curtailed private house construction, it was approaching 1929 levels (see figure 3.6; housing had actually peaked
in 1926). Some of the recovery after 1939 was in response to the stimulus provided
by anticipatory rearmament spending. But as I show below, only a small fraction

of cumulative war spending had actually taken place at the time Pearl Harbor was attacked.

3. Although the United States did not resort to an industrial draft, as did Britain, where workers could be commanded (rather than enticed) to work in a war industry, the United States did effectively socialize investment flows and direct them in ways dictated by the imperatives of war (see Higgs 2004). As figures 3.5, 3.6, and 3.7 show, private domestic investment, as well as non-war-related public investment, such as the construction of streets and highways, was crowded out during the conflict, and vast amounts of taxed or borrowed money were used by the government, through the instrument of the Defense Plant Corporation, to purchase new machine tools and construct plants in strategic sectors. Civilian automobile and appliance production was shut down, and critical raw material flows were allocated essentially by fiat, with some dual-use inputs (gasoline and tires, for example) subject to rationing.

4. Simon Kuznets was probably the first fully to appreciate the magnitude of the expansion in capacity that had taken place. As part of the war-planning process, he was tasked with estimating the potential output of the U.S. economy in order to allow the setting of war production goals consistent with planned force levels and civilian consumption. His estimates turned out to be considerably higher than most had expected, leading military leaders to multiply their production targets and forcing Kuznets and others to fight a rear-guard action to bring them down to realistic levels (Edelstein 2000; Fogel 2001, pp. 213–214). The outward shift of the production possibility frontier during the Depression years was the principal reason potential output in 1942 was so much higher than had been anticipated.

5. Military spending and manpower tripled between 1940 and 1941, but they did so from a very low base, and only a small fraction of cumulative war expenditure had actually taken place at the time of the Japanese attack. As a consequence, war-related spillovers and learning by doing cannot have had much to do with achieved 1941 productivity levels.

6. Data for the Lend-Lease program itself show a similar pattern. The legislation was passed on March 11, 1941, and shipments did take place prior to Pearl Harbor. Their rate of growth starting from a base of zero was of course astronomical. But 1941 shipments comprised only about 3.2 percent of the cumulative total for the program between 1941 and 1945; more than 96 percent occurred after 1941 (see U.S. Bureau of the Budget 1946, chart 49, p. 412).

7. Although many of the institutional foundations for war and postwar military procurement were established between May 1940 and the declaration of war in December 1941 (U.S. Bureau of the Budget 1946; Higgs 1993), the actual impact of government regulation and control on the economy was relatively minor prior to 1942. Effective control of retail prices, for example, did not begin until the General Maximum Price Regulation of May 1942 (Harris 1945, p. 9).

8. See U.S. Bureau of the Census 1951, p. 740. Corroborative evidence for a peak in industrial production in late 1943 comes from data from the War Production Board that show production of munitions alone peaking in the fourth quarter of 1943 (U.S. War Production Board 1945). Production of aluminum, magnesium, zinc, and chemicals

all peaked in 1943, as did new merchant marine tonnage (U.S. Bureau of the Budget 1946, chart 15, p. 137; chart 38, p. 300; chart 41, p. 319).

9. A somewhat analogous treatment of the disruptive effects of the war on capital accumulation (investment flows) can be found in Higgs 2004.

10. "Crowding out" refers to the process, in an economy at or close to capacity, whereby increases in government spending reduce private consumption or investment spending. In a peacetime economy, which component gets hit harder depends on the method by which the government spending is financed. If taxes rise, consumption will tend to drop. In an economy near capacity, if the spending is financed by borrowing, the upward pressure on interest rates as the needs of government financing collide with those of the private sector will reduce investment spending (spending on new plant and equipment; this includes housing). During a war direct controls supplement these reallocative mechanisms. Unilateral transfers are included in the current account because they represent in a sense purchases by the United States of good will or other behaviors from recipient countries.

11. The evidence for this can be found in the very high rates of TFP growth in trucking and railroads and, to a lesser extent, in wholesale and retail distribution (see chapter 2). The buildout of the surface road network created substantial spillover effects in both trucking and railroads. Trucking successfully substituted for railroads for certain routes and commodities. But the two modes were also highly complementary, and trucking's flexibility contributed to improved productivity in the railroad sector even in the presence of capital shallowing. One important mechanism was the smoothing of seasonal fluctuations in the demand for freight cars (see chapter 2).

12. For more extensive discussion of the motivation for this regression specification and its interpretation, see chapter 7.

13. The 2.78 percent compound annual growth resulting from this exercise is very close to the 2.83 percent implied by the intercept term on the regression using 1929–1941 data.

14. On the other hand, the physical capital stock was used intensively during the war, and the depreciation allowances applied by government statisticians may not adequately have accounted for the effects of wear and tear and deferred maintenance. This consideration could counterbalance an underestimate of the value of GOPO capital transferred to the private sector. See Higgs 2004, pp. 515–517.

15. Although there is no way of knowing if peacetime advance would have continued at the same rate throughout the 1940s in the absence of the war, had TFP advance between 1941 and 1948 persisted at the rate of 2.78 percent per year rather than .49 percent, TFP in 1948 would have been 17.4 percent higher than it actually was.

16. See http://www.bea.gov/NIPA Table 1.1.6, Real Gross Value Added by Sector, line 3; accessed January 5, 2010.

17. Chained index methods "solve" the index number problem in calculating real magnitudes through time, but they do so at a price: the sum of the growth of components when calculated using these methods may exceed or fall short of the growth of the aggregate as one proceeds through time. As a consequence they are not well suited for exercises calculating the share that various sectors of the economy contributed to

TFP growth, such as those conducted in chapter 2. That analysis, therefore, remains within the context of the statistical framework developed by Kendrick. There is another technical point about Kendrick's methods. Kendrick used a weighted arithmetic average of labor and capital input to create levels of his total factor input index, rather than the multiplicative index suggested by the assumption of a Cobb-Douglas production function ($Y = AK^\beta N^{1-\beta}$, where β is capital's share; see the appendix and Domar 1962). Because private sector labor and capital input growth was negligible between 1929 and 1941, even with a modest upward adjustment for capital input, this issue is nevertheless irrelevant for the Depression-period TFP growth calculations. If the two main inputs are essentially at the same level at the beginning and end points, it doesn't matter how one weights them in creating a combined input measure

18. "In World War II, no combat plane that had not been substantially designed before the outbreak of hostilities saw major service" (Galbraith 1971, p. 18).

19. See Searle 1945 or Alchian 1963 for detailed discussion.

20. Even with respect to general human capital formation, one must keep in mind that many of the war-production workers, particularly women, left the labor force after the war.

21. See especially the series of articles by Higgs already referenced, as well as work by Edelstein and Rockoff.

CHAPTER 4: THE GOLDEN AGE AND BEYOND

1. The shares are calculated from a 2004 spreadsheet from the Bureau of Economic Analysis: "GDP by Ind_VA_SIC.xls." Subsequently, the BEA moved printing and publishing out of manufacturing, combining it with the old communications category and some other subsectors previously in services to form a new grouping known as "information." I prefer the earlier categorization for historical work, so in this instance I have not used the most recent numbers from the BEA Web site, which are available at http://www.bea.gov, Industry Economic Accounts, Gross Domestic Product by Industry.

2. Http://www.bea.gov, NIPA Table 6.8B, Persons Engaged in Production by Industry; accessed July 22, 2009.

3. U.S. Department of Labor 2004.

CHAPTER 5: THE INFORMATION TECHNOLOGY BOOM

1. The reference is to Glassman and Hasset (1999).

2. On October 14, 2009, the Dow index crossed 10,000, an impressive achievement. But the Dow first reached this level ten years earlier, in March 1999. Neither of these comparisons factors in the effects of inflation.

3. As noted above, the SIC codes have been largely replaced in post-1997 reporting with NAICS codes, but I retain the older vocabulary in this chapter.

4. See http://www.bls.gov/mfp; accessed July 24, 2009.

5. The availability of new types of office and communication equipment in an IT-using sector might stimulate innovations in work organization or lead to other improvements in the sector's own technological processes. These "spillovers" would be measured as increased TFP in the using industry and would result in an additional boost to labor productivity.

6. The private nonfarm economy excludes government (12.3 percent of value added in 2000); agriculture, forestry, and fisheries (1 percent in 2000); private household activity including roughly two-thirds of real estate, which in 2000 would be 11.0 × .66 = 7.3 percent; and nonprofit businesses (mostly in education, health, and social services). Private household activity is excluded because of lack of information on hours of household labor expended in home maintenance and operation. Sectoral growth rates in real estate, health, and education are based on data from the commercial (profit-making) portions of these sectors.

7. If one puts the manufacturing surge in its best light, by measuring from 1992 through 2004, its sectoral rate of advance was 2.04 percent per year.

8. The disaggregated sectors use the KLEMS methodology. The rate of increase of the gross value in the sector is compared with a weighted average of inputs, including capital, labor, energy, materials, and services, with the weights corresponding to the share of gross income in the sector going to each of these inputs. For the private nonfarm economy, the rate of increase of value added is compared with growth of a weighted average of inputs of capital and labor, the weights corresponding to the shares of these factors in national income. The KLEMS data outside of manufacturing are unpublished; my thanks to Steven Rosenthal at the Bureau of Labor Statistics for making them available to me.

9. The story told here is not sensitive to using 1990 rather than 1989 (the level of TFP in the private nonfarm economy was identical, so the annual rates calculated would rise a little if we measured from 1990), although choosing 2001 rather than 2000 would reduce the calculated growth rates since TFP grew only modestly between 2000 and 2001.

10. For early takes on the contributors to labor productivity growth between 1995 and the end of the century, see McKinsey Global Institute 2002 or Nordhaus 2002.

11. It opens up questions as well about the nature of business cycles and how they should be defined—whether their principal determinants should be viewed as technology or aggregate demand shocks and whether they should be demarcated by changes in unemployment and an output gap. For more on this, see chapter 7.

12. For more detailed analysis of the end-of-century boom, see chapter 6.

13. For example, the rising share of equipment to structures in investment flows and the capital stock, which began after the Second World War, coincided with a long term *downward* trend in TFP. On the other hand, the interpretation of 2000–2007 PNE TFP acceleration as due to spillovers in IT-using sectors might be viewed as consistent with this view.

14. The introduction of hedonic prices has been politically controversial because it reduces measures of consumer price inflation and therefore the amount of legally

mandated payouts, such as those associated with Social Security, which are tied to increases in the cost of living.

15. How much growth in output per hour and its acceleration should be credited to the enabling technologies of the IT revolution was a burning question during the IT productivity boom. With the collapse of tech stocks after March 2000, disenchantment with the "New Economy" idea, and preoccupation with the real estate boom and its aftermath, it has since been eclipsed by other concerns.

16. The "dual" approach to estimating TFP advance looks at relative price changes across sectors as an alternate means of inferring its incidence (see appendix). Again, however, as noted in the previous section, hedonic methods may overshoot in putting downward pressure on these deflators.

17. Assertions or assumptions of such a link are easy to find: "Ongoing technological advances in these [IT-producing] industries have been a direct source of improvement in TFP growth, as well as an indirect source of more-rapid capital deepening" (Jorgenson and Stiroh 2000, p. 128); "The spread of information technology throughout the economy has been a major factor in the acceleration of productivity through capital deepening" (U.S. Council of Economic Advisors 2001, p. 33).

18. David is clear that the nineteenth-century traverse was "set in motion by Thrift, that is, by a pronounced rise in the proportion of output saved" (1977, p. 197). In some passages he appears to treat it as exogenous, as opposed to a response to an upward movement in the real interest rate. In Abramovitz and David, the authors speak of "technologically induced traverses" (1973, p. 429). The implied argument seems to be that new blueprints led to an increase in real returns to investment, which induced an upsurge in the saving rate, propelling one to a different steady state involving higher output per hour. In Abramovitz and David (1999) the authors suggest that the bias in technical change led to an increase in capital's share, which redistributed income to households with higher propensities to save, and this is the mechanism that led to the upsurge in the saving rate. Williamson more explicitly bases his findings on an analysis of the consequences of an upward shift in saving propensities: "For still unknown reasons the saving rate rose markedly during the Civil War decade" (1973, p. 593).

19. This analysis is driven by the basic accounting identity $S = I + G - T + NX$, where S is gross private domestic saving, I is gross private domestic investment, $G - T$ is gross government dissaving (the gross government deficit), and NX is net exports (exports less imports, or the current account surplus, or the negative of the capital account surplus). In this instance depreciation has been netted out of both domestic saving flows and domestic investment, the investment numbers include government investment, and the government deficit is the negative of net government saving (current receipts less current expenditures).

20. In this respect as well the railroad/infrastructure investment boom of the late nineteenth century was analogous to the IT boom of the late twentieth century: both triggered and were associated with foreign borrowing.

21. Estimates of the amount of this capital formation surge have been augmented by the Bureau of Labor Statistics' 1999 reclassification of business software acquisition

as capital formation (as opposed to its previous treatment of it as an intermediate good).

22. A runner-up would probably be improvements in medical procedures.

CHAPTER 6: FIN DE SIÈCLE

1. Abramovitz was famous for characterizing TFP growth as a "measure of our ignorance" (Abramovitz 1956, p. 11), but he also clearly felt that measures of the rate of advance of the residual bore some relationship to the growth of (useful) knowledge. Those who devote time to refining these estimates must believe that they tell us something of interest about the sources of economic growth. Arithmetically, the residual captures growth in output not attributable to growth in inputs conventionally measured. TFP advance is interpreted (sometimes apologetically) as a measure of disembodied technological change. This can be the consequence of organizational as well as more narrowly technological innovation. It can also reflect shifts in the economy from sectors with lower productivity to those with higher productivity, as well as quality improvements in inputs not otherwise accounted for. As discussed in the introduction, TFP growth may overestimate the total effect on output per hour of technological change, but it can also underestimate it to the degree the latter raises the return to capital, inducing higher saving, or skews income to households with higher income and higher propensities to save, in either case leading to rises in capital-labor ratios. Whether or not TFP advance underestimates the total effect of technological change, as Abramovitz and David (1973) argued, the point here is that TFP growth during this period was not low by the standards of the late twentieth century.

2. Calculations of output growth were, for example, based on unpublished worksheets from Robert Gallman. See Rhode (2002).

3. Editing by Cambridge University Press eliminated the detailed appendix tables that would have included the subperiod calculations (personal communication from Paul David). My point, however, is as much about narrative as it is about data. It remains true that the view into an alternate interpretation of the nineteenth-century data, which one finds in Abramovitz (1993), is absent in Abramovitz and David (2000).

4. See chapter 3 for the case of World War II, but for an alternate view see Ruttan 2006.

5. Abramovitz (1993, p. 228) reported TFP growth of 1 percent per year between 1871 and 1890 and .91 percent per year for the PDE between 1890 and 1905.

6. There are, as the text notes, a set of issues about whether 1892 and 1906 are to be preferred to 1890 and 1905 as business cycle peaks. Another set of issues involves the five-year averaging method. This is sensible if the most important problem is simply noise in the data. But it is more difficult to defend in the presence of strong cyclical effects. Consider comparing a sharp business cycle peak, with steep drop-offs on either side, with a rounded one (close to potential output on either side). In such an environment, measuring between five-year averages centered on the peaks may give a less meaningful estimate of TFP advance than simply measuring between peaks. The averaging method would, in the above instance, give a result that is biased upward

in the presence of procyclical TFP because the initial-period level would be brought down by the lower TFP on either side of the peak more than would the end-period level. These issues of method and dating are, however, probably minor in terms of the larger argument of this chapter. Whether TFP growth averaged closer to 1 percent or closer to 1.2 percent a year over the gilded age is in some sense beside the point since both numbers reflect robust advance relative, to growth at the end of the twentieth century.

7. The identification of a peak can differ depending on the frequency of data examined. For monthly data, one would say May 1907; for quarterly data, 1907:2; but for annual data, 1906 because this is the year for which the estimates of the annual unemployment rate bottom out.

8. TFP in agriculture grew at a rate of 1.57 percent per year between 1892 and 1906 as compared with .56 percent per year between 1869 and 1892 (Kendrick 1961, table B-1).

9. Fishlow (1966) is critical of Ulmer's (1960) data, which underlie Kendrick's railroad capital stock indices. But even Fishlow's data indicate declines in the capital-labor ratio in railroads, although not to the same degree. Between 1870 and 1910, Fishlow has persons engaged growing at 5 percent per year, while capital grew at 4.5 percent per year (1966, table 10, p. 626).

10. For the private nonfarm economy, capital grew at 4.99 percent per year and man-hours at 3.46 percent between 1873.5 and 1906, so capital deepened at more than 1.5 percent per year (Kendrick 1961, table A-XXIII).

CHAPTER 7: PROCYCLICAL TFP

1. These conclusions are robust to substituting the pre-1948 unemployment series generated by Weir (1992) for the Lebergott (1964) numbers, which continue to be used by most researchers.

2. Manufacturing's share of national income averaged 30.6 percent between 1941 and 1960. The share declined modestly in the 1960s and then more rapidly beginning in the 1970s (Carter et al. 2006, series Ca35 and Ca41).

3. The coefficients on the change in the unemployment rate all fall within a narrow range bounded by −.83 for the post–World War II era (regression 1.8) and −1.03 for the entire period from 1890 to 2004 (regression 1.10).

4. "But even brief consideration of the most important deficiencies of the estimates in Appendix D suggests that the margins of error in the annual series in the comparison are such that it would be unwise to use the annual data and study the annual differences between the national product totals and those of capital formation" (Kuznets 1937, p. 46).

5. Kehoe and Prescott "view the increase in the stock of useful knowledge . . . as exogenous. Our view is that this stock increases smoothly over time." They "hypothesize that the growth rate [in the stock of knowledge] is two percent per year" (2008, pp. 9–10). Their estimate is roughly half a percentage point higher than the estimate of 1.5 percent per year suggested for the years 1890–2004 by the constant terms in regressions 1.9–1.11 in table 7.1.

6. A JSTOR search (http://www.jstor.org) shows almost all articles referencing the phenomenon appearing after 1995. JSTOR is an online archive containing many of the most widely referenced journal titles in economics.

7. Basu and Fernald, for example, take it as a given that both TFP and labor productivity are procyclical. "Productivity is procyclical. That is, whether measured as labor productivity or total factor productivity, productivity rises in booms and falls in recessions" (2000, p. 1). The more robust empirical regularity, as tables 7.1 and 7.2 show, is the procyclicality of TFP.

8. The simple correlation between the unemployment rate and the BEA's chain-type quantity index for investment in private fixed assets (table 6.8 in the Fixed Asset Tables, available at http://www.bea.gov; accessed August 16, 2009) is –.14.

9. Capital shallowing, the opposite of deepening, refers to situations in which the capital-labor ratio declines.

10. I ignore here any cyclical influences on capital's share.

11. This second effect applies equally to variable capital: the holding costs of a stock of wholesale or retail inventory are invariant to how frequently it turns over. For a similar analysis, which places more emphasis on the market power that is the logical concomitant of large fixed-capital installations, see Hall 1988. See also Field 1987.

12. Basu and Fernald 2000, p. 35, also make utilization adjustments that reduce the procyclicality of TFP. Their adjustments, designed to correct for utilization of both labor and capital, are based on sectoral data on changes in hours worked per worker, combined with the assumption that these data proxy both for unmeasured changes in the intensity of work and for the "workweek of capital" (flow of capital services). The adjustment applicable to capital is, however, too large. The capital stock is dominated by structures, and the service flow contributed by a warehouse or hotel is largely invariant to how full or empty it is, let alone to how many hours employees within it work.

13. In spite of a rise in the share of equipment, structures remain dominant today within the U.S. private fixed-asset stock, as they were throughout the twentieth century. In 2007, total private fixed assets comprised $33.4 trillion, with equipment and software totaling only $5.3 trillion. Nonresidential structures accounted for $10.2 trillion; the remainder were residential structures. BEA, Fixed Asset Table 2.1, http://www.bea .gov; accessed June 22, 2009. For historical data, see Field 1985.

14. Hall 1988, p. 923, makes a similar assumption about depreciation. The rate of deterioration (depreciation) of a tar and gravel roof on a warehouse, for example, is independent of how much is stored inside it.

15. The quest for a unified theory of both growth and fluctuations, as well as dissatisfaction with received terminology, is expressed by Prescott: "The use of the expression *business cycle* is unfortunate. . . . It leads people to think in terms of a time series' business cycle component which is to be explained independently of a growth component; our research has instead one unifying theory of both of these" (1986, p. 2). RBC pioneers such as Lucas and Prescott initially granted that their approach was not applicable to major macroeconomic disruptions such as the Great Depression. Lucas, for example, wrote that "the Great Depression . . . remains a formidable barrier to a completely unbending application of the view that business cycles are all alike"

(1980, p. 273). While Lucas maintained this position, Prescott relaxed the disclaimer, attributing his change of view to the work of Cole and Ohanian (see de Vroey and Pensieroso 2006).

16. If there is a unifying feature of the broader DSGE program, it is the insistence on providing strong microeconomic foundations for macroeconomic relationships. This has always seemed to me as much an aesthetic preference as a scientific imperative.

17. De Córdoba and Kehoe summarize the contributions of Kehoe and Prescott (2007): "The authors of each of the studies . . . start by decomposing the decline in output during the depression into declines in inputs of labor and capital and a decline in the efficiency with which these factors are employed, measured as productivity. They find that a large drop in productivity always plays a large role in accounting for the depression" (2009, p. 2). "Accounting for" means here more than simply "contributing to" in an arithmetical sense. It means causing. Most economists are comfortable with this interpretation for long-term analysis. The differences involve its applicability to short-term cyclical fluctuations.

18. The rationale is the close and systematic relationship between the unemployment rate and the output gap, first identified by Arthur Okun and known colloquially as Okun's Law (Okun 1962).

19. In "The NBER's Business Cycle Dating Procedures," Hall et al. note the following: "While the NBER has traditionally placed substantial weight on output measures, one could instead define expansions and recessions in terms of whether the fraction of the economy's productive resources that is being used is rising or falling (in which case the behavior of the unemployment rate would be a critical guide to whether the economy was in expansion or recession), or in terms of whether the quantity of productive resources being used was rising or falling (in which case employment would be a critical indicator). Either of these alternative definitions is defensible." In response to a frequently asked question about the 2001 recession and why more emphasis was not placed on trends in the unemployment rate and employment in determining its end, the document simply states that to have dated it in this fashion would have been "inconsistent with the procedures it had used to date earlier recessions" (2003, p. 7).

20. As Sergio Rebelo has written, "Macroeconomists generally agree that expansions in output, at least in the medium to long run, are driven by TFP increases that derive from technical progress. In contrast, the notion that recessions are caused by TFP declines meets with substantial skepticism because, interpreted literally, it means that recessions are times of technological regress" (2005, p. 9).

21. The literature is voluminous; these references are illustrative.

22. In nominal terms investment in producer durables dropped by more than half between 1929 and 1931 ($5.5 to $2.6 billion). Consumption spending on durables dropped 40 percent, from $9.8 to $5.5 billion. Spending on nondurables dropped less than a quarter and on services less than 15 percent. BEA, NIPA Table 1.1.5, http://www.bea.gov; accessed October 25, 2009.

23. For other examples of negative TFP growth, see Baier, Dwyer, and Tamura (2006).

24. Whereas interest rate and unemployment data are available at relatively high frequency (the former on a daily basis, the latter monthly), TFP estimates are available only annually.

25. The discount rate remained in double digits from July 1979 through August 1982. See http://www.newyorkfed.org/markets/statistics/dlyrates/fedrate.html; accessed December 14, 2009.

26. The argument here is about positive external effects. As aggregate output approaches and then exceeds natural output, negative external effects, in the form of scarcities and higher real costs of inputs such as labor, may also be felt.

27. Note that I am calling this short-term economies of scale, not short-term increasing returns to scale. These are not necessarily the same. Increasing returns are commonly defined as a situation in which a given percentage increase in all inputs leads to a larger percentage increase in output. That is not what happens as one comes out of recession because output increases first without much increase in either labor or capital inputs, and subsequently as the result of a more rapid increase of hours than of capital input.

28. As has been the case at least since the writings of Alfred Marshall, the short run is understood as referring to a period of time during which it is not easy to alter the level or rate of growth of the firm's capital stock. To say that a firm is optimized for a particular output level is to say that there is some output at which the firm's minimum average cost is attained.

29. Another factor predisposing to skepticism is the substantial variability in trend growth rates over the past century, which seems much more likely to have been the result of differential rates of arrival of new technological and organizational products and processes. In endogenous growth theory, the proximate cause of TFP improvement would still be the growth of useful knowledge—useful knowledge presumably not available in the initial period. In theoretical models such as Paul Romer's, however, the rate of growth of such knowledge, rather than being taken as exogenous, is assumed to be positively influenced by an economy's scale.

CHAPTER 8: THE EQUIPMENT HYPOTHESIS

1. "We interpret our results as suggesting that the social return to equipment investment in well functioning market economies is on the order of 30 percent per year" (DeLong and Summers 1991, p. 446).

2. "We see no reason to expect that investments in structures should carry with them the same external effects as plausibly attach to investments in equipment" (DeLong and Summers 1991, p. 480).

3. "Growth—measured by labor or by TFP—is as tied to high equipment investment for rich countries as it is for newly industrializing ones. . . . Equipment investment appears to have a very high net social return—in the range of 20 percent per year; more than half of this comes from increased TFP. We conclude that the macroeconomic data give no evidence that poorer countries benefit more from high rates of

equipment investment than do richer countries. This suggests, significantly, large external benefits from equipment investment, even in rich economies. We conclude that policies that tilt the playing field against equipment investment are likely to be disastrous and that a strong case exists for at least a modest bias in favor of equipment investment" (DeLong and Summers 1992, p. 159).

4. A ten percentage point decline in one year in the estimated social return to equipment investment is quite remarkable in itself. Note that DeLong interpreted his longitudinal cross-sectional analysis of advanced economy growth as suggesting a rate of return to machinery investment of over 50 percent per year or more, returns that "dwarf the profits that investors in the capital goods are able to appropriate directly" (1992, p. 322). He acknowledged, however, that this estimate might be too high.

5. The time series are series of growth rates over specified business cycle intervals.

6. For the United States 1948 is a more appropriate peak; unemployment was 3.8 percent, as compared with 5.3 percent in 1950.

7. DeLong and Summers (1991) state that the hypothesis involves rates of gross equipment investment and growth in output per hour, but it is impossible to have an increase in the real net stock without persisting flows of gross investment. Changes in the stock will obviously be closely related to levels of the flows.

8. This equipment was initially in GOPO plants. But by 1948 it was largely under private ownership, the major exception being synthetic rubber capacity, which was kept in government hands until the mid-1950s.

9. One might argue that it takes substantial time for equipment investment to affect TFP growth rates. But the relationship between TFP growth and growth rates of the equipment capital stock (figure 8.3) or the equipment-structures ratio (figure 8.4) and one period later are no more favorable to the equipment hypothesis.

10. Most of this was then sold off to the private sector after the war, the main reason that 1941–1948 shows the highest growth of the real net equipment stock.

11. TFP growth in manufacturing declined from the 2.76 percent per year experienced between 1929 and 1941 to −.35 percent per year registered between 1941 and 1948 (see table 2.3).

12. This overstatement, to the degree that it took place, should not, however, affect calculations over the 1941–1948 interval.

CHAPTER 9: GENERAL-PURPOSE TECHNOLOGIES

1. "Consequential" in the sense that they add significantly to the growth of TFP and thus the growth of output and output per hour. A related way of putting this is to ask what their contributions were to social savings (Fogel 1964; Fishlow 1965). A third way is to ask how much they contributed to what Harberger (1998) called real cost reductions.

2. The acronym in Europe tends to be ICT: Information and Computer Technology.

3. Electric power also provides two other areas of functionality not matched by water or steam: the direct production of light or heat.

4. David's title was intended to play off the title of a chapter (25) in Henry Adams's autobiography.

5. The NASDAQ index, which first broke 1000 in July 1995, quintupled between then and its peak in March 2000. It then collapsed precipitously to a low of 1100 in September 2002. Although the Dow index hit its peak in the first decade of the 2000s after the tech crash, in inflation-adjusted terms, its peak was higher in the second half of the 1990s.

6. For examples, see Basu and Fernald 2006; Guerrieri and Padoan 2007; and Thoma 2009. An online search will reveal others.

7. Choosing words carefully, they write that "the arrival of IT . . . did not reverse the decline in productivity growth that had begun more than a decade earlier" (2005, p. 1184).

8. BEA, Fixed Asset Table 2.1, http://www.bea.gov; accessed July 23, 2008.

9. Http://www.nsf.gov/statistics/nsf07331/tables/tab13.xls; accessed July 24, 2008.

CHAPTER 10: FINANCIAL FRAGILITY AND RECOVERY

1. This is particularly so for smaller banks, 25 of which failed in 2008 and 140 of which failed in 2009. The 2008 failures included Washington Mutual, which was the country's largest savings and loan and became its largest bank failure. Total assets of failed banks were $374 billion in 2008 and $171 billion in 2009. As of November 19, 147 banks in the United States had already failed in 2010. This is one reason why there is ambiguity about whether we should describe the downturn as ending in 2009. The NBER has dated the beginning of the recession in December 2007 and identified its end as occurring in June 2009. Output began to rise in the third quarter of 2009, which appears consistent with this determination. The persistence of high unemployment, a large output gap, and continuing problems in real estate and banking, however, give one pause.

2. In this as in earlier chapters I make frequent reference to two sets of data tables maintained by the Bureau of Economic Analysis at http://www.bea.gov. The first provide details from the National Income and Product Accounts (as noted, referred to as NIPA). The second are the Fixed Asset Tables (referred to as FAT), which describe the accumulation and stocks of structures and equipment (reproducible tangible assets) in the U.S. economy.

3. The debt-to-income ratio for U.S. households, which stood at .17 in 1945, had risen to .64 by 1965, remaining in this range for roughly two decades. Starting in the mid-1980s it increased rapidly. By 2006 it had risen to 1.27, having almost doubled in a quarter century, and reached an all-time high of 1.33 in 2007. Source: http://www.bea.gov and https://www.federalreserve.gov, as summarized in https://www.invescoaim.com/pdf/ConRec.pdf.

4. Examples of incentives included the Cash for Clunkers program, which encouraged automobile sales, and the $8,000 tax credit for first-time home buyers.

5. Taylor may have been right then, but he also opposed a policy of low interest rates as late as February 2008, a month before the investment firm of Bear Stearns collapsed. See Posner 2009, p. 254; Taylor 2009a.

6. Most economists have been skeptical of Rothbard's reasoning due to the absence of any evidence of inflation in the prices of goods and services between 1922 and

1929. There is a similarity between the 1920s and the 1990s and 2000s in that asset price bubbles developed in environments of low inflation as that term is traditionally understood.

7. After writing this, I encountered an article in which Casey Mulligan (2009) suggested that "three rises" in the nominal federal minimum wage had something to do with the 2007–2009 recession. Even with these increases, the real minimum wage remained below where it had been in 1986 and substantially below where we were in 1968.

8. I emphasize intermediate macroeconomics because what is taught there has proved to be more useful in understanding both economic history and our current plight than much of what has come to dominate the graduate curriculum. Gordon (2009) argues along similar lines, referring to Keynesian economics melded to an expectations-augmented Philips curve and more explicit treatment of aggregate supply as "1978-era Macro."

9. For more information on the IS (investment-saving)/ LM (liquidity-money) system, see any intermediate macroeconomics textbook. On its origins, see Keynes 1936, Hicks 1937, and Hansen 1951. In the 1970s and 1980s, monetarists argued that the private sector determinants of both the IS schedule and the demand for money schedule were stable. Instability in investment was attributed almost entirely to misguided policy interventions by the central bank.

10. All of the expenditure data that follow in this section are in 1937 dollars. Because of the peculiarities of chained index measurement, the BEA provides tables with five different base years: 1937, 1952, 1972, 1982, and 2000 (NIPA tables 1.1.6, 1.1.6A–D). For this exercise we use 1937 dollars because that base year is most appropriate for studying changes during the Depression.

11. Fishback and Kachanovskaya (2009) have estimated state-level expenditure multipliers, but, as they recognize, these will be lower because of import leakages or "small country" effects: spending in Rhode Island will leak into stimulus to production in neighboring Massachusetts or Connecticut.

12. In October 2005, as housing prices reached their peak, Bernanke also denied there was a housing bubble (see Henderson 2005). In May 2007 he saw "no serious broader spillover to banks or thrift institutions from the problems in the subprime market" (Bernanke 2007).

13. Obviously, the run-up to the current crisis is not identical to what happened in 1928–1929. The current situation is greatly complicated by the counterparty risk associated with the widespread holding of derivative securities, particularly credit default swaps. A number of economists and economic historians distinguish between the Great Depression, which they see as fundamentally a liquidity problem that could easily have been solved by massive open-market operations, and the Great Recession, which involved insolvent banks whose balance sheets were so impaired that their problems could not be remedied in this fashion. I see the diagnoses as less distinct. Much of the fragility of the banking system in the 1930s was due to ill-considered loans made in the 1920s (see chapter 11). In this respect there are parallels to the current situation.

14. The influence of Minsky's thinking, although not always acknowledged, is increasing. See, for example, Posner: "So it is not really the initial shock to a robust system that is the culprit in a depression; it is the vulnerability of the process by which the system adjusts to a shock. This makes the adequacy of the institutional response to that vulnerability critical" (2009, p. 7).

15. These are the two conceptually distinct routes to supercharged profits in finance: on the asset side, hold riskier assets that on average yield higher returns, and on the liability side, finance these positions with higher ratios of debt to equity. The distinction can be understood by considering a household evaluating a purchase of one of two investment properties. One property is likely to appreciate in value slowly but with relatively little variance in annual gains. A second property has the potential for much higher increments, but its annual appreciation (or depreciation) is also likely to exhibit higher variance. Investing in the second property, the riskier asset, will increase expected return. If the household then leverages the purchase by borrowing 90 percent of the sales price from a bank, it can supercharge its gains. If a million dollar property financed with 10 percent down rises in value to $1.1 million, the rate of return to the owner is not 10 percent but 100 percent. Of course, leverage can also supercharge losses. With a modest decline in the property value, the household, having borrowed money to buy the house, may quickly find itself under water, owing more on the property than it is worth.

16. In 2008, finance, insurance, and real estate employed about 8 million FTE workers, out of total U.S. employment of about 130 million FTEs (NIPA table 6.5, lines 2, 57, and 62). Note that the rise in the finance sector's share of corporate profits starting in the 1980s coincided with a period in which TFP in the economy as a whole was, from a longer-run historical perspective, declining (see chapter 8).

17. Quarterly data showed the share dropping to 10 percent in 2008:4 but recovering to 25 percent in 2009:3, 36 percent in 2009:4. A slight decline in share in 2010:1 (to 34 percent) was due not to a decline in the absolute level of financial sector profits but rather growth in the denominator (total domestic corporate profits).

18. If a collateralized loan is nonrecourse, a borrower can walk away from the loan obligation, surrendering the collateral to the creditor, and the creditor cannot go after the borrower's other assets or income.

19. This is known informally in the banking business as IBG-YBG: I'll be gone and you'll be gone (so don't worry).

20. Leising and Runnigen 2008. On May 7, 1998, the CFTC issued a "concept release" seeking comments on the possible regulation of over-the-counter derivatives. On May 11, 2009, Secretary of the Treasury Timothy Geithner announced a legislative initiative similar to what Born had had in mind years earlier, but with a large loophole for custom-designed derivatives. Provisions similar to this proposal were included in the financial regulation legislation passed by Congress in July 2010.

21. See Summers 1998. Summers's testimony, which criticized Born for even raising questions about possible regulation by releasing a concept memo on the subject, is worth reviewing in its entirety for a clear picture of how the leaders of the Fed, Treasury,

and SEC squelched her initiative. See also the excellent PBS *Frontline* program "The Warning," available at http://video.pbs.org/video/1302794657/.

22. Greenspan's admission or mea culpa was the most public and had the most pathos. See reports on his October 23, 2008 congressional testimony (Andrews 2008).

23. Large banks, recipients of federal bailout money, launched a coordinated lobbying effort to reprise their success in the late 1990s in avoiding regulation. See Morgenstern and Van Natta 2009. In this instance they did not entirely succeed. Although some exceptions remained for the treatment of customized derivative contracts, comprehensive regulation of the over-the-counter derivatives market and the companies engaging in these trades was included in the Dodd-Frank Wall Street Reform and Consumer Protection Act signed into law on July 22, 2010.

24. The main function of investment banks, as understood in section 21 of the 1933 Banking Act, was underwriting: serving as intermediaries between nonfinancial corporations issuing equity or debt and bank clients who purchased these securities. Today, this is a small part of what investment banks (or those that used to be) do; the bulk of their income comes from fees associated with securitizations and the writing of derivative contracts and from trading assets on their own account. Of the five large broker dealers prior to the crisis, Bear Stearns was bought by JP Morgan and Merrill by Bank of America. Lehman failed and Morgan Stanley and Goldman Sachs almost failed even after the rescue of AIG and takeover of Fannie Mae and Freddie Mac (Sorkin 2009, pp. 417–464). Without capital infusions and regulatory forbearance, Bank of America and Citigroup would almost certainly have failed, joining Washington Mutual and Wachovia and a host of smaller banks and shadow banks, including General Electric. A version of the so-called Volcker rule, restricting proprietary trading by banks, was included in the Dodd-Frank legislation passed in July of 2010. The details of how this will be implemented, however, remain unresolved.

25. As reported by National Public Radio. See Dwyer 2009.

26. Canada has historically allowed integrated investment and commercial banking without adverse consequences. The different outcome suggests that a more rigorous framework of supervision and regulation might have mitigated some of the resulting problems. That said, in the United States, it is not so evident what the benefits associated with the repeal of Glass-Steagall have been. Proponents argue that getting rid of this regulation allowed financial institutions to realize economies of scale and scope. Repeal was associated with major new private profit opportunities and clearly complicated and rendered less effective the Fed's supervision of bank holding companies. Whether benefits ultimately devolved to consumers and taxpayers is unclear.

27. The contracts AIG wrote required the company to post collateral to its counterparties in the event its (AIG's) credit rating was downgraded.

28. See Wigmore 2010 for discussion of financial remediation in the 1930s as compared with 2008–2009. One of the difficulties in reckoning the magnitudes of taxpayer bailouts is that guarantees, although measured in dollars, are often not commensurate. Promising to make good on a trillion dollars' worth of liabilities that are unlikely to and in fact do not default is different from guaranteeing a similar amount of liabilities

that are expected to and in fact do default. It is often difficult to know ex ante what these probabilities are, and they are not independent of guarantees, in the sense that they are likely to be influenced by the overall size and structure of the remediation effort itself.

29. Economic policy succeeded for a quarter century after 1982 in moderating the inflation rate and the variance of GDP growth rates. These successes, however, contributed to complacency about the growing dangers of private sector innovation and profit seeking in the context of a relaxed and increasingly laissez-faire regulatory environment.

30. As Irving Fisher (1933, p. 346) wrote, the more debtors attempted to pay off or liquidate their debts, the more they owed, due to the deflation that was partly the consequence. Fisher noted, contra Mellon, that "liquidation does not really liquidate but aggravates the debts" (p. 349). What was disastrous for debtors benefited bondholders.

31. Because of exceptionally rapid TFP growth, the speed limit for the economy during the 1930s was probably higher, perhaps closer to 3.5 percent per year. Three percent per year continuously compounded amounts to $125 billion in 1941 (1937 dollars). The actual figure was $122.1 billion. The 9.9 percent unemployment that year implies, however, a higher growth rate of potential output.

32. The idea that, on the fiscal policy front, Roosevelt cut back on spending because of the belief that the Depression was over is not, however, supported by data on government investment, which increased from $3.7 billion in 1937 to $4.1 billion in 1938 (most of it on structures). The big hit in the 1938 recession was to spending on consumer durables, which dropped from $6.6 to $5.4 billion, and on gross private fixed investment, which declined from $13.8 to $12.5 billion. The fiscal situation was aggravated by the onset of the payroll taxes associated with the initiation of the Social Security system (BEA, Fixed Asset Table 1.5).

CHAPTER 11: UNCONTROLLED LAND DEVELOPMENT AND THE DURATION OF THE DEPRESSION

1. The more moderate drop in public construction, 85 percent of which was state and local in 1929, provided a slight counterbalance (U.S. Bureau of the Census 1975, II, Series N 71–77, p. 623; F 67, 70, p. 230).

2. Backward linkages to supplier industries as well as multiplier effects were important. See discussion in Soulé 1947, pp. 170–174.

3. Temin's argument (1976, p. 67) that an unexplained drop in consumption caused the Depression, and his argument that had such spending not collapsed in 1930, and with it aggregate demand, the decline in construction spending would have been arrested, represented an inversion of traditional Keynesian causal orderings. See also Gordon and Wilcox, who note that Temin "abruptly dismissed" the construction hypothesis (1981, p. 75).

4. As figure 10.1 showed, gross investment in structures during the 1920s was typically twice that in equipment. On the tendency to underrate the share of structures in the capital stock and net investment flows, see Field 1985 and chapter 8.

5. R. A. Gordon 1951; Gordon and Wilcox 1981, p. 78.

6. Goldsmith 1955, I, table R-28, p. 620.

7. U.S. Bureau of the Census 1975, II, Series N-71,73, p. 623.

8. Allen 1931, p. 287; Goldsmith 1955, I, table R-28, p. 620; Blank 1954, table 17, p. 68. See also Hickman 1960, pp. 319–320; Federal Housing Administration 1940a, pp. 3–8. The long-term legacy of the apartment boom may have been less damaging than that associated with uncontrolled subdivision. Less acreage was involved, and even where the apartment was poorly located, the builder was forced to address the orientation of units to each other, as well as the coordinated provision of water, sewers, and utilities.

9. U.S. Bureau of the Census 1975, I, Series D-725, p. 164; F-48, p. 229; II, Series Q-148, p. 716; N-71, 73, p. 623; X-491, p. 1004. These data do not support Temin's suggestion that consumption recovery was all that stood in the way of construction revival. While real producer durables spending fell a third during the 1938 recession, residential construction actually rose, highly anomalous behavior from the perspective of the post–World War II period (see figure 3.5).

10. Colean 1944, p. 20. Where anticipated service flows from a different use exceeded those from current use, plus interest on legal, demolition, disposal, and site conversion costs, tear-down and redevelopment did occur in the 1930s. See Muth 1959, p. 9; also discussion in Federal Housing Administration 1939, pp. 16–17.

11. In 1938 more than half the houses constructed in the United States were not built in multiple-unit subdivisions. "Arithmetic of Land Development" 1939, p. 367.

12. "For hundreds of years . . . cities have been developed and their areas subdivided. All the customs and legal procedures facilitated the breaking up processes, and did nothing to facilitate the regrouping of parcels in larger tracts" (Federal Housing Administration 1941, p. 1). The obstacles to development posed by land fractionation were not limited to central business districts.

13. On the extent of subdivision activity, see also E. Fisher 1933, pp. 157–158. South Florida was simply the most egregious expression of what had in fact been a national phenomenon. Writing in *The Nation* in 1928, Henry Villard described the approach to Miami by road: "Dead subdivisions line the highway, their pompous names half obliterated on crumbling stucco gates. Lonely white-way lights stand guard over miles of cement sidewalks, where grass and palmetto take the place of homes that were to be. . . . Whole sections of outlying subdivisions are composed of unoccupied houses, past which one speeds on broad thoroughfares as if traversing a city in the grip of death" (cited in Allen 1931, p. 281). Speculative development reached almost unimaginable levels in Florida, in terms of both the amount of land subdivided (enough of it, by some estimates, to house the entire U.S. population) and the amplitude of the cycle. See Blank 1954, table 26, p. 95. But as Allen also noted, "There was a boom in suburban lands outside virtually every American city" (1931, p. 285). See also Simpson 1933, p. 169; Galbraith 1955, pp. 8–13; Hoyt 1933, ch. 5.

14. Los Angeles and Chicago remained "outstanding exceptions." Cited in Colean 1953, pp. 77–78.

15. See E. Fisher 1933, p. 162. Between 1920 and 1926, U.S. farmland dropped in value from $55 billion to $37 billion. During the same years, urban land in cities with popu-

lations greater than thirty thousand grew in value from $25 billion to $50 billion. See Hoyt 1933, p. 234. Hoyt estimated that urban land values in Chicago subsequently dropped 60 percent between 1928 and 1933 (pp. 272–273).

16. These individuals were referred to by their rivals as "curbstoners," because of the purported location of their offices, or the "free ride and barbecue" type of developer (Weiss 1987, pp. 17–18; Colean 1944, p. 3). Subdividers made money by buying wholesale and selling retail; through the appreciation of their inventory during the interval spanning purchase, subdivision, and sale; and by brokering repeat sales of undeveloped property.

17. Municipalities could access private capital markets on somewhat more favorable terms than could private developers. Public borrowing to construct subdivision infrastructure was a major contributor to municipal bankruptcy in the 1930s. See New Jersey State Planning Board 1941; Cornick 1938.

18. Signatures of traditional platting include deep, narrow lots with minimal front and side setbacks and short blocks. Planned developments included Roland Parks in Baltimore, River Oaks in Houston, Palos Verdes Estates in California, the Country Club District in Kansas City, Lake Forest in Chicago, and Radburn in New Jersey (Weiss 1987, ch. 2).

19. Streets improperly aligned with each other, or insufficiently wide to accommodate anticipatable improvements, were examples of such burdens.

20. These mechanisms fall into three general categories: zoning (the public designation of separate residential, industrial, and commercial districts); subdivision regulation (requirements that a subdivision plan meet minimum design standards prior to the commencement of lot sales); and comprehensive regional or major thoroughfare (street) planning (Weiss 1987, chs. 4–5). Early zoning regulations designated too much land for commercial purposes or were riddled with variances granted through political pressure.

21. On the changing views of academics, representatives of the developer community, and local politicians, see Simpson 1933, p. 168.

22. See Reps 1969; Cornick 1938, p. 223. State-level regulatory initiatives focused on reducing marketing abuses through the licensing of brokers. Public law was not the only means to ensure coordination within a subdivision. Developers in the 1920s, and even earlier, had controlled externalities through the use of restrictive covenants in deeds. Such covenants were also used, less attractively, for purposes of racial exclusion. These covenants had their limits, however: although amenities could be regulated within a subdivision, land use in adjoining or nearby parcels could not (Weiss 1987, pp. 71–72; Michigan State Planning Commission 1939, p. 23).

23. Mortgages in the 1920s were not self-amortizing, typically required 50 percent down payment, and had to be refinanced after five or fewer years. The establishment in 1937 of the Federal National Mortgage Association (Fannie Mae or FNMA) helped on the demand side by increasing the liquidity of mortgages, thereby making intermediaries more willing to hold them.

24. U.S. Bureau of the Census 1975, I, Series F-449, p. 256. The macrodynamics of the Depression cannot be understood if one limits the study of investment to producer

durables (only $7.3 billion of the 1922–1929 increment), let alone producer durables in manufacturing—a very small portion of overall capital formation.

25. The increase expressed in current prices was comparable: from $56.6 to $89.5 billion. The current dollar statistic doesn't match the constant dollar value for the 1929 base year because of the treatment of depreciation allowances. For the current dollar series, Goldsmith (1955) valued construction expenditures in a year—as well as depreciation allowances on all prior construction—in the prices of that year, whereas for the constant dollar series, both construction expenditures and depreciation flows for each year were valued in 1929 prices. With these methods, the current dollar value of a stock can differ from its constant dollar value even in the base year.

26. Goldsmith's estimates of the stock differ from the Grebler, Blank, and Winnick estimates, which show a rise in the constant dollar (1929 prices) value of structures from $58.3 billion in 1922 to $80.6 billion in 1929 (U.S. Bureau of the Census 1975, II, Series N-196–199, p. 642; Grebler, Blank, and Winnick 1956, table D-1, pp. 360–361). Part of the $10 billion end-period discrepancy is due to Grebler, Blank, and Winnick's non-inclusion of $2.175 billion of nonhousekeeping (hotel and motel) investments (1956, tables B-5, B-8, and D-1, footnote 1). Their data underlie the residential investment series in Gordon and Veitch 1986, p. 328.

27. Housing consumption rose less than half as fast as real personal consumption—up 35 percent in real terms between 1922 and 1929 (U.S. Bureau of the Census 1975, I, Series G-470, p. 320). The 1922 figure is interpolated from 1921 and 1923 data, based on the relationship among data for the three dates reported in Barger 1942, table 9, column 5 (total consumption), p. 93.

28. GNP rose from $74.1 billion in 1922 to $103.1 billion in 1929 (U.S. Bureau of the Census 1975, I, Series F-1, p. 224).

29. Ratios this low are absent from the immediate postwar data (Denison 1974, table 3.6, p. 28).

30. R. A. Gordon (1956) stressed the slowdown of population growth in the second half of the 1920s. Hickman (1960, pp. 319–320) reached similar conclusions, as did Campbell (1961, pp. 255–258). See also Hickman 1974.

31. It did rise and then decline over the seven-year period (U.S. Bureau of the Census 1975, I, Series E-150). The rent index in U.S. Bureau of the Census 1975 is based on data collected by the Retail Price Division of the Bureau of Labor Statistics beginning in 1913 and conducted as part of Bureau efforts systematically to measure changes in the cost of living. A 1941 bulletin describes the procedures used (U.S. Department of Labor 1941, p. 19). I am grateful to staff members of the Bureau of Economic Analysis (John Gorman and Frank deLeeuw) and the Bureau of Labor Statistics (Richard Bahr, Dan Ginsburg, and Steve Henderson) for elucidating (to the extent possible) past and present government data-collection procedures.

32. Campbell's (1961) analysis also embodies a simplified and inflexible view of household demand behavior, called into question by his analysis of the post–World War II expansion. For booms prior to 1947–1958 his methodology tracks occupied units reasonably well. But it fails to predict the 1947–1958 episode, which was, in his terms,

driven by a historically unprecedented increase in headship rates, apparently related to rapidly rising incomes. Hickman 1974 is not subject to this criticism.

33. These blocks were typically 650 feet × 200 feet, as opposed to the longer (up to 1,300 feet) blocks recommended by the FHA. See Colean 1944, p. 19; Adams 1934.

34. The source for these cost shares was an existing two-hundred-acre, 1,300-unit development.

35. Principles of coordinated residential development—and their advantages—were set forth in a variety of FHA publications, including a pamphlet entitled *Planning Profitable Neighborhoods* (Federal Housing Authority 1940c). This publication codified good practice and through its graphic illustrations provided, indirectly, a catalogue of the "mistakes" of the 1920s. The text provided specific advice on internal street layout, lot size and orientation, and integration with existing topography and transport networks.

36. Nonfarm mortgages accounted for 39 percent of the private long-term debt of nonfinancial corporations in 1929 (E. Clark 1933, p. 10). See also Wigmore 2010.

37. For a general treatment of the problem see Herman 1969. The regulatory rule introduced in the 1930s requiring that savings and loans have a minimum of four hundred shareholders was a response to the experience of the 1920s, during which developers sometimes exercised disproportionate and self-serving influence on lending policies. The rule was abandoned in the deregulatory fervor of the 1980s.

38. See Simpson 1933, p. 164. Savings and loans held 23 percent of the residential mortgage debt in 1925. The traditional rules of commercial banking made illiquid real estate loans anathema, and for national banks such loans were effectively proscribed by the National Banking Act between 1864 and 1913. The Federal Reserve Act relaxed these constraints, and mortgage lending by commercial banks grew in the 1920s, although their role in infrastructual investment remained relatively small (Grebler, Blank, and Winnick 1956, pp. 201–203).

39. On domestic lending, see Edwards 1933, p. 6, and Saulnier 1950. On international lending, see Mintz 1951.

40. Simpson (1933, p. 165) and Friedman and Schwartz (1963, p. 355) do not reject the possibility of a deterioration in the quality of domestic lending, although they are skeptical about its likelihood. Temin (1976, p. 85; 1989, p. 50) stresses the excesses and poor real estate loans of the Bank of the United States, whose failure figures prominently in the Friedman and Schwartz story (1963, p. 355).

41. Beginning in 1921 at 13,588, annual filings rose steadily, topping 40,000 in 1923 and 50,000 in 1928 and peaking at 70,049 in 1932 (U.S. Department of Justice, 1920–1940; see also Field 2001a).

42. Nonfarm residential mortgage debt grew from $8 billion in 1919 to $30 billion in 1930, after which it began to decline in nominal terms. Wealth declined even faster so that the ratio of such debt to nonfarm residential wealth, 11.1 percent in 1919, continued to climb through 1932, when it peaked at 34.1 percent (Grebler, Blank, and Winnick 1956, table L-6, p. 451).

43. This is true of research emphasizing declines in investment as well as work focusing on (autonomous) drops in consumption (see Temin 1976 or C. Romer 1990). It is also

true of work emphasizing a contractionary monetary shock as the proximate cause of the economic downturn in 1929. Field (1984) emphasized an unrecognized and unaccommodated increase in the transactions demand for money. Hamilton (1987) reached similar conclusions regarding the stringency of monetary policy in 1928–1929 but interpreted monetary tightness as the consequence of conscious Federal Reserve actions to stem a gold outflow. See chapter 7 for discussion of real business cycle approaches.

44. The overall decline in real construction spending was initially moderate because the surge in spending on private nonresidential and public building compensated for much of the drop-off in residential spending.

45. The collapse in construction, which continued through the 1929–1933 period, was both larger in volume and more precipitous than that of durables (U.S. Bureau of the Census 1975, I, Series F-47–90, p. 229). Some of the decline in durables, particularly appliances, furniture, carpets, and home furnishings, is directly related to the drop in new construction. See Mishkin 1978 for analysis of the linkages between deteriorations in household net wealth and spending flows.

46. The impact on aggregate demand of construction's collapse and failure to revive is also significantly larger than can be attributed to the drop in net exports resulting from international economic policies. Both the German and British economies recovered better than that of the United States in the mid- and later 1930s; both experienced housing and infrastructural booms during these years (Temin 1989, pp. 117, 126). Although this is certainly not the only explanation for their more successful recoveries, the differences among developed countries in the institutional contexts in which building took place in the interwar years, particularly the greater European reliance on municipal and regional planning, deserve more emphasis in an understanding of the variations in their macroeconomic histories. As E. Fisher and Smith noted, "One of the most striking differences between American and European cities is found in this connection. European cities are compact, the American sprawling. European cities are closely built up; the American are loosely strung together with vacant lots scattered throughout the area" (1932, p. 457).

47. For arguments that such controls should have been eliminated, see Siegan 1976. Siegan holds up Houston, lacking a zoning ordinance, as an example to be emulated. For a balanced appraisal of the impact of local land-use regulation, see Haar and Kayden 1989, particularly the contributions by Robert H. Nelson and William C. Wheaton.

CHAPTER 12: DO ECONOMIC DOWNTURNS HAVE A SILVER LINING?

1. Posner captures the essence of the silver lining hypothesis insofar as it applies to productivity: "A depression increases the efficiency with which both labor and capital inputs are used by businesses, because it creates an occasion and an imperative for reducing slack. . . . When a depression ends, a firm motivated by the recession to reduce slack in its operations will have lower average costs than before" (2009, pp. 222–223).

2. The same can be said for the effect of increases in the after-tax wage rate on labor supply or the effect of increases in after-tax returns on saving.

3. First track mileage operated was roughly unchanged from 1919 to 1929 (263,707, declining to 262,546). But between 1929 and 1941, it dropped 5.9 percent (262,546 to 245,240) (U.S. Bureau of the Census 1945, table 521, p. 470).

4. The difference between Kendrick's (1961) capital input decline rate of .47 and the rate of decline based on the latest BEA data (.69) is .22 percent per year, which, with a .31 weight on capital in the growth accounting equation, would add .068 percent per year to the sector's TFP growth rate.

BIBLIOGRAPHY

Abramovitz, Moses. 1956. "Resource and Output Trends in the United States since 1870." *American Economic Review* 46 (May): 5–23.

———. 1986. "Catching Up, Forging Ahead, and Falling Behind." *Journal of Economic History* 46 (June): 385–406.

———. 1993. "The Search for the Sources of Growth: Areas of Ignorance, Old and New." *Journal of Economic History* 53 (June): 217–243.

Abramovitz, Moses, and Paul David. 1973. "Reinterpreting Economic Growth: Parables and Realities." *American Economic Review* 63 (May): 428–439.

———. 1999. "American Macroeconomic Growth in the Era of Knowledge-Based Progress: The Long Run Perspective." SIEPR Discussion Paper No. 99–3. Stanford, California (unpublished).

———. 2000. "American Macroeconomic Growth in the Era of Knowledge-Based Progress: The Long Run Perspective." In Engerman and Gallman, *The Cambridge Economic History of the United States*, vol. 3, pp. 1–92.

Ackley, Gardner. 1961. *Macroeconomic Theory.* New York: Macmillan.

Adams, Thomas. 1934. *The Design of Residential Areas.* Cambridge, MA: Harvard University Press.

Alchian, Armen. 1963. "Reliability of Progress Curves in Airframe Production." *Econometrica* 31 (October): 679–693.

Alexopoulos, Michelle, and Jon S. Cohen. 2009. "Measuring Our Ignorance, One Book at a Time: New Indicators of Technical Change." *Journal of Monetary Economics* 56:450–470.

Allen, Frederick Lewis. 1931. *Only Yesterday.* New York: Harper and Row.

Andrews, Edmund L. 2008. "Greenspan Concedes Error on Regulation." *New York Times,* October 23. Available at http://www.nytimes.com/2008/10/24/business/economy/24panel.html.

"Arithmetic of Land Development." 1939. *Architectural Forum* 70 (May): 367–370.

Arrow, Kenneth. 1962. "The Economic Implications of Learning by Doing." *Review of Economic Studies* 29 (June): 155–173.

Arthur, Brian. 1989. "Competing Technologies, Increasing Returns, and Lock-In by Historical Events." *Economic Journal* 89 (March): 116–131.

Aschauer, David A. 1989. "Is Public Expenditure Productive?" *Journal of Monetary Economics* (March): 177–200.

Atack, Jeremy, Fred Bateman, and Thomas Weiss. 1980. "The Regional Diffusion and Adoption of the Steam Engine in American Manufacturing." *Journal of Economic History* 40 (June): 281–308.

Auerbach, Alan A., Kevin Hasset, and Steven Oliner. 1994. "Reassessing the Social Returns to Equipment Investment." *Quarterly Journal of Economics* 109 (August): 789–802.

Backman, Jules, and Martin R. Gainsbrugh. 1949. "Productivity and Living Standards." *Industrial and Labor Relations Review* 2 (January): 163–194.

Baier, S., G. Dwyer, and R. Tamura. 2006. "How Important Are Capital and Total Factor Productivity for Economic Growth?" *Economic Inquiry* 44:23–49.

Baily, Martin Neil. 1983. "The Labor Market in the 1930s." In *Macroeconomics, Prices, and Quantities*, ed. James Tobin. Washington, D.C.: Brookings Institution.

Baily, Martin Neil, and Robert J. Gordon. 1988. "The Productivity Slowdown, Measurement Issues, and the Explosion of Computer Power." *Brookings Paper on Economic Activity* 19:347–432.

Bair, Sheila. 2007. "Remarks at 2007 Risk Management and Allocation Conference, Paris, France." Available at http://www.fdic.gov/news/news/speeches/archives/2007/chairman/spjun2507.html.

Baker, Peter. 2009. "It's Not about Bill." *New York Times*, May 26. Available at http://www.nytimes.com/2009/05/31/magazine/31clinton-t.html?pagewanted=1&hp.

Barger, Harold. 1942. *Outlay and Income in the United States: 1921–1938*. New York: National Bureau of Economic Research.

———. 1951. *The Transportation Industries, 1899–1946*. New York: National Bureau of Economic Research.

Barro, Robert J., and Xavier Sala-i-Martin. 1995. *Economic Growth*. New York: McGraw Hill.

Basu, Susanto, and John Fernald. 1995. "Are Apparent Productive Spillovers a Figment of Specification Error?" *Journal of Monetary Economics* 36 (August): 165–188.

———. 2000. "Why Is Productivity Procyclical? Why Do We Care?" Federal Reserve Bank of Chicago Working Paper No. 2000–11.

———. 2006. "Information and Communications Technology as a General-Purpose Technology: Evidence from U.S. Industry Data." Federal Reserve Bank of San Francisco Working Paper No. 2006–29 (December).

Basu, Susanto, John Fernald, Nicholas Oulton, and Sylaja Srinivasan. 2003. "The Case of the Missing Productivity Growth: Or Does Information Technology Explain Why Productivity Accelerated in the U.S. but Not the U.K.?" NBER Working Paper No. 10010.

Baumol, William J. 1986. "Productivity Growth, Convergence, and Welfare: What the Long Run Data Show." *American Economic Review* 76:1072–1085.

Bell, Spurgeon. 1940. *Productivity, Wages and National Income*. Washington, D.C.: Brookings Institution.

Bernanke, Ben. 1983. "Nonmonetary Effects of the Financial Crisis in the Propagation of the Great Depression." *American Economic Review* 73 (June): 257–276.

——. 2005. "The Global Saving Glut and the U.S. Current Account Deficit." Available at http://www.federalreserve.gov/boarddocs/speeches/2005/200503102/.

——. 2007. "The Subprime Mortgage Market." Speech given at the Federal Reserve Bank of Chicago's 43rd Annual Conference on Bank Structure and Competition, Chicago, May 17. Available at http://www.federalreserve.gov/newsevents/speech/bernanke 20070517a.htm.

——. 2010. "Monetary Policy and the Housing Bubble." Speech given at the annual meeting of the American Economic Association, Atlanta, Georgia, January 3. Available at http://www.federalreserve.gov/newsevents/speech/bernanke20100103a.pdf.

Bernanke, Ben, and Martin Parkinson. 1991. "Procyclical Labor Productivity and Competing Theories of the Business Cycle: Some Evidence from Interwar U.S. Manufacturing Industries." *Journal of Political Economy* 99:439–459.

Berndt, Ernst R., and Melvyn Fuss. 1986. "Productivity Measurement with Adjustments for Variations in Capacity Utilization and Other Forms of Temporary Equilibrium." *Journal of Econometrics* 33 (October/November): 7–29

Berndt, Ernst R., and Catherine J. Morrison. 1981. "Capacity Utilization Measures: Underlying Economic Theory and an Alternate Approach." *American Economic Review* 71 (May): 48–52.

Berndt, Ernst R., Ellen R. Dulberger, and Neal J. Rappaport. 2000. "Price and Quality of Desktop and Mobile Personal Computers: A Quarter Century of History." Unpublished working paper, MIT.

Bernstein, Michael. 1987. *The Great Depression: Delayed Recovery and Economic Change in America, 1929–1939.* New York: Cambridge University Press.

Bix, Amy Sue. 2000. *Inventing Ourselves out of Jobs? America's Debate over Technological Unemployment, 1929–1981.* Baltimore: Johns Hopkins University Press.

Blank, David M. 1954. *The Volume of Residential Construction, 1889–1950.* New York: National Bureau of Economic Research.

Bodfish, H. Morton. 1929. "The Free Lot Subdivider: His Method of Operation and the Available Methods of Control." *Journal of Land and Public Utility Economics* 5 (May/August): 187–198, 285–292.

Bresnahan, Timothy F., and Daniel M. G. Raff. 1991. "Intra-Industry Heterogeneity and the Great Depression: The American Motor Vehicles Industry, 1929–1935." *Journal of Economic History* 51 (June): 317–331.

Bresnahan, Timothy F., and Manuel Trajtenberg. 1995. "General Purpose Technologies: Engines of Growth?" *Journal of Econometrics* 65 (January): 83–108.

Brown, E. Cary. 1956. "Fiscal Policy in the 'Thirties: A Reappraisal." *American Economic Review* 46 (December): 857–879.

Buchanan, R. A. 1991. *The Power of the Machine: The Impact of Technology from 1700 to the Present.* New York: Viking.

Burnside, Craig, and Martin Eichenbaum. 1996. "Factor Hoarding and the Propagation of Business Cycle Shocks." *American Economic Review* 86 (December): 1154–1174.

Byrn, Edward W. 1900. *The Progress of Invention in the Nineteenth Century*. New York: Munn.

Caballero, R. J., and R. K. Lyons. 1990. "Internal versus External Economies in European Industry." *European Economic Review* 34:805–826.

Campbell, Burnham O. 1961. "The Housing Life Cycle and Long Swings in Residential Construction: A Statistical and Theoretical Analysis." Ph.D. diss., Stanford University.

Carter, Susan B., Scott Sigmund Gartner, Michael R. Haines, Alan L. Olmstead, Richard Sutch, and Gavin Wright, eds. 2006. *Historical Statistics of the United States, Millennial Edition*. New York: Cambridge University Press.

Caselli, Francesco. 1999. "Technological Revolutions." *American Economic Review* 89 (March): 79–102.

Chandler, Alfred. 1977. *The Visible Hand: The Managerial Revolution in American Business*. Cambridge, MA: Harvard University Press.

Ciccone, Antonio, and Robert E. Hall. 1996. "Productivity and the Density of Economic Activity." *American Economic Review* 86:54–70.

Civilian Production Administration. 1947. *Industrial Mobilization for War*, vol. 1: *Program and Administration*. Washington, D.C.: Government Printing Office.

Clark, Evans. 1933. *The Internal Debts of the United States*. New York: Macmillan Press for the Twentieth Century Fund.

Clark, Peter. 1978. "Capital Formation and the Recent Productivity Slowdown." *Journal of Finance* 33 (June): 965–975.

Cochrane, John H. 2009. "How Did Paul Krugman Get It So Wrong?" http://faculty .chicagobooth.edu/john.cochrane/research/Papers/krugman_response.doc. Accessed September 22, 2009.

Coffee, John C., Jr. 2008. "Analyzing the Credit Crisis: Was the SEC Missing in Action?" *New York Law Journal*, December 5. Available at http://www.law.com/jsp/PubArticle .jsp?id=1202426495544.

Cole, Harold, and Lee Ohanian. 1999. "The Great Depression in the United States from a Neoclassical Perspective." *Federal Reserve Bank of Minneapolis Quarterly Review* 23 (Winter): 2–24.

——. 2004. "New Deal Policies and the Persistence of the Great Depression: A General Equilibrium Analysis." *Journal of Political Economy* 4 (August): 779–816.

Colean, Miles. 1944. *American Housing: Problems and Prospects*. New York: Twentieth Century Fund.

——. 1953. *Renewing Our Cities*. New York: Twentieth Century Fund.

Cornick, Philip H. 1938. *Premature Subdivision and Its Consequences*. New York: Institute of Public Administration, Columbia University.

Crafts, N. F. R. 2004. "Steam as a General Purpose Technology: A Growth Accounting Perspective." *Economic Journal* 114:338–351.

Crafts, N. F. R., and Terence Mills. 2004. "Was 19th Century British Growth Steam-Powered? The Climacteric Revisited." *Explorations in Economic History* 41 (April): 156–171.

Dash, Eric. 2009. "Failures of Small Banks Grow, Straining F.D.I.C." *New York Times,* October 11. Available at http://www.nytimes.com/2009/10/11/business/economy/11banks .html?em.

David, Paul A. 1977. "Invention and Accumulation in America's Economic Growth: A Nineteenth Century Parable." In *Carnegie-Rochester Conference Series on Public Policy,* vol. 6, ed. Karl Brunner and Allan Meltzer, pp. 179–228. New York: North-Holland.

———. 1990. "The Dynamo and the Computer: An Historical Perspective on the Modern Productivity Paradox." *American Economic Review* 80 (May): 355–361.

———. 1991. "The Computer and the Dynamo: The Modern Productivity Paradox in a Not-Too-Distant Mirror." In *Technology and Productivity: The Challenge for Economic Policy,* pp. 315–347. Paris: OECD.

———. 2004. "The Tale of Two Traverses: Innovation and Accumulation in the First Two Centuries of U.S. Economic Growth." Gallman Lecture presented at Conference on Understanding the 1990s: The Economy in Long Run Perspective, Duke University, March 26–27, 2004.

David, Paul A., and Gavin Wright. 1997. "Increasing Returns and the Genesis of American Resource Abundance." *Industrial and Corporate Change* 6 (March): 203–245.

———. 1999. "Early Twentieth Century Productivity Growth Dynamics: An Inquiry into the Economic History of 'Our Ignorance.'" Working paper, All Souls College, Oxford University.

———. 2003. "General Purpose Technologies and Surges in Productivity: Historical Reflections on the Future of the ICT Revolution." In *The Economic Future in Historical Perspective,* ed. Paul A. David and Mark Thomas, pp. 135–166. Oxford: Oxford University Press.

de Córdoba, Gonzalo Fernández, and Timothy J. Kehoe. 2009. "The Current Financial Crisis: What Should We Learn from the Great Depressions of the Twentieth Century?" Federal Reserve Bank of Minnesota, Research Department Staff Report 421 (February).

DeLong, J. Bradford. 1992. "Productivity Growth and Machinery Investment: A Long Term Look, 1870–1980." *Journal of Economic History* 52 (June): 307–324.

DeLong, J. Bradford, and Lawrence H. Summers. 1991. "Equipment Investment and Economic Growth." *Quarterly Journal of Economics* 106, no. 2 (May): 445–502.

———. 1992. "Equipment Investment and Economic Growth: How Strong Is the Nexus?" *Brookings Papers on Economic Activity* 22:157–211.

Denison, Edward. 1974. *Accounting for United States Economic Growth, 1929–1969.* Washington, D.C.: Brookings Institution.

Devine, Warren. 1983. "From Shafts to Wires: Historical Perspective on Electrification." *Journal of Economic History* 43:347–372.

De Vroey, Michel R., and Luca Pensieroso. 2006. "Real Business Cycle Theory and the Great Depression: The Abandonment of the Abstentionist Viewpoint." *B. E. Journal of Macroeconomics* 6, Article 13.

Domar, Evsey. 1962. "On Total Productivity and All That." *Journal of Political Economy* 70 (December): 597–608.

Duke, John, Diane Litz, and Lisa Usher. 1992. "Multifactor Productivity in Railroad Transportation." *Monthly Labor Review* (August): 49–58.

Dwyer, Dustin. 2009. "George W. Bush Speaks in Benton Harbor." May 29. Available at http://www.publicbroadcasting.net/michigan/news.newsmain/article/1/0/1511524/ Michigan.News/George.W..Bush.Speaks.In.Benton.Harbor.

Dyer, Frank L., and Thomas C. Martin. 1929. *Edison: His Life and Inventions*. New York: Harper and Brothers.

Eckstein, Otto, and Thomas Wilson. 1964. "Short Run Productivity Behavior in U.S. Manufacturing." *Review of Economics and Statistics* 46 (February): 41–54.

Edelstein, Michael. 2000. "War and the American Economy in the Twentieth Century." In Engerman and Gallman, *The Cambridge Economic History of the United States*, vol. 3, pp. 329–406.

Edquist, Harald, and Magnus Henrekson. 2006. "Technological Breakthroughs and Economic Growth." *Research in Economic History* 24:1–53.

Edwards, George W. 1933. "The Control of the Security Investment System." *Harvard Business Review* 12 (October): 1–11.

Eichengreen, Barry. 1992. *Golden Fetters: The Gold Standard and the Great Depression, 1919–1939*. New York: Oxford University Press.

Eichengreen, Barry, and Kris J. Mitchener. 2004. "The Great Depression as a Credit Boom Gone Wrong." *Research in Economic History* 22: 183–237.

Elmendorf, Douglas. 1996. "The Effect of Interest Rates on Household Saving and Consumption." Washington, D.C.: Federal Reserve Board.

Engerman, Stanley, and Robert Gallman, eds. 2000. *The Cambridge Economic History of the United States*, vol. 3. Cambridge: Cambridge University Press.

Evans, W. D. 1947. "Recent Productivity Trends and Their Implications." *Journal of the American Statistical Association* 42 (June): 211–223.

Fabricant, Solomon. 1952. "Armament Production Potential." In *War and Defense Economics*, ed. Jules Backman, pp. 19–45. New York: Rinehart.

Fano, Esther. 1987. "Technical Progress as a Destabilizing Factor and as an Agent of Recovery in the United States between the Two World Wars." *History and Technology* 3:249–274.

Federal Housing Administration. 1939. *Sixth Annual Report*. Washington, D.C.: Government Printing Office.

———. 1940a. *Low Rental Housing for Private Investment*. Washington, D.C.: Government Printing Office.

———. 1940b. *Seventh Annual Report*. Washington, D.C.: Government Printing Office.

———. 1940c. *Planning Profitable Neighborhoods*. Washington, D.C.: Government Printing Office.

———. 1941. *A Handbook on Urban Redevelopment for Cities in the United States*. Washington, D.C.: Government Printing Office.

Federal Reserve System, Board of Governors. 1976a. *Banking and Monetary Statistics, 1914–1941*. Washington, D.C.: Publications Services, Board of Governors of the Federal Reserve System.

———. 1976b. *Industrial Production, 1976 Revision*. Washington, D.C.: Publications Services, Board of Governors of the Federal Reserve System.

Fenichel, Stephen. 1996. *Plastics: The Making of a Synthetic Century*. New York: Harper Business.

Ferguson, Niall. 2004. *Colossus: The Price of America's Empire*. New York: Penguin Press.

Fernald, John. G. 1999. "Roads to Prosperity: Assessing the Links between Public Capital and Productivity." *American Economic Review* 89 (June): 619–638.

Field, Alexander J. 1984. "Asset Exchanges and the Transactions Demand for Money, 1919–1929." *American Economic Review* 74 (March): 43–59.

———. 1985. "On the Unimportance of Machinery." *Explorations in Economic History* 22 (October): 378–401.

———. 1987. "Modern Business Enterprise as a Capital Saving Innovation." *Journal of Economic History* 47 (June 1987): 473–485.

———. 1992a. "The Magnetic Telegraph, Price and Quantity Data, and the New Management of Capital." *Journal of Economic History* 52 (June): 401–413.

———. 1992b. "Uncontrolled Land Development and the Duration of the Depression in the United States." *Journal of Economic History* 52 (December): 785–805.

———. 1996. "The Relative Productivity of American Distribution, 1869–1992." *Research in Economic History* 16 (Greenwich: JAI Press): 1–37.

———. 1998. "The Telegraphic Transmission of Financial Asset Prices and Orders to Trade: Implications for Economic Growth." *Research in Economic History* 18 (Greenwich: JAI Press): 145–184.

———. 2001a. "Bankruptcy, Debt, and the Macroeconomy, 1919–1946." *Research in Economic History* 20 (Greenwich: JAI Press): 99–133.

———. 2001b. "Not What It Used to Be: *The Cambridge Economic History of the United States*, Volumes II and III." *Journal of Economic History* 61 (September): 806–818.

———. 2003. "The Most Technologically Progressive Decade of the Century." *American Economic Review* 93 (September): 1399–1413.

———. 2006a. "Technological Change and U.S. Economic Growth in the Interwar Years." *Journal of Economic History* 66 (March): 203–236.

———. 2006b. "Technical Change and U.S. Economic Growth: The Interwar Period and the 1990s." In Rhode and Toniolo, *The Global Economy in the 1990s*, pp. 89–117.

———. 2007a. "The Equipment Hypothesis and U.S. Economic Growth." *Explorations in Economic History* 43 (January): 43–58.

———. 2007b. "The Origins of U.S. Total Factor Productivity Growth in the Golden Age." *Cliometrica* 1 (April): 63–90.

———. 2008. "The Impact of the Second World War on U.S. Productivity Growth." *Economic History Review* 61 (August): 672–694.

———. 2009. "U.S. Economic Growth in the Gilded Age." *Journal of Macroeconomics* 31 (March): 173–190.

———. 2010a. "The Procyclical Behavior of Total Factor Productivity Growth in the United States, 1890–2004." *Journal of Economic History* 70 (June): 326–350.

———. 2010b. "Should Capital Input Receive a Utilization Adjustment?" Unpublished.

Finch, Christopher. 1992. *Highways to Heaven: The AUTObiography of America*. New York: Harper Collins.

Fishback, Price, and Valentina Kachanovskaya. 2009. "In Search of the Multiplier for Net Federal Spending in the States during the New Deal: A Preliminary Report." Working paper, University of Arizona, June.

Fisher, Ernest M. 1933. "Speculation in Urban Lands." *American Economic Review* 23 (March): 152–162.

Fisher, Ernest M., and Raymond F. Smith. 1932. "Land Subdividing and the Rate of Utilization." *Michigan Business Studies* 4 (Ann Arbor).

Fisher, Irving. 1911. *The Purchasing Power of Money: Its Determination and Relation to Credit, Interest, and Prices*. New York: Macmillan.

———. 1933. "The Debt Deflation Theory of Great Depressions." *Econometrica* 1 (October): 337–357.

Fishlow, Albert. 1965. *American Railroads and the Transformation of the Antebellum* Economy. Cambridge, MA: Harvard University Press.

———. 1966. "Productivity Change and Technological Change in the Railroad Sector, 1840–1910." In *Output, Employment, and Productivity in the United States after 1800*, pp. 583–646. National Bureau of Economic Research, Studies in Income and Wealth, vol. 30. New York: Columbia University Press.

Fogel, Robert. 1964. *Railroads and American Economic Growth: Essays in Econometric History*. Baltimore: Johns Hopkins University Press.

———. 2001. "Simon S. Kuznets, 1901–1985: A Biographical Memoir." Washington: National Academy of Sciences

Friedman, Milton, and Anna J. Schwartz. 1963. *A Monetary History of the United States, 1867–1960*. Princeton: Princeton University Press.

Galambos, Louis. 2000. "The U.S. Corporate Economy in the Twentieth Century." In Engerman and Gallman, *The Cambridge Economic History of the United States*, vol. 3, pp. 927–968.

Galbraith. John Kenneth. 1955. *The Great Crash 1929*. Boston: Houghton Mifflin.

———. 1971. *The New Industrial State*, 2nd ed. Boston: Houghton Mifflin.

Geanakoplos, John. 2009. "The Leverage Cycle." Paper presented at the Annual Conference on Macroeconomics of the National Bureau of Economic Research (April).

Gelernter, David. 1995. *1939: The Lost World of the Fair*. New York: Free Press.

Gemery, Henry A., and Jan S. Hogendorn. 1993. "The Microeconomic Bases of Short Run Learning Curves: Destroyer Production in World War II." In Mills and Rockoff, *The Sinews of War*, pp. 150–165.

Glassman, James, and Kevin Hasset. 1999. *Dow 36,000: The New Strategy for Profiting from the Coming Rise of the Stock Market*. New York: Times Business.

Goddard, Stephen B. 1994. *Getting There: The Epic Struggle between Road and Rail in the Twentieth Century*. New York: Harper Collins.

Goetzmann, William, and Frank Newman. 2010. "Securitization in the 1920s." NBER Working Paper no. 15650.

Goldfarb, Brent. 2005. "Diffusion of General-Purpose Technologies: Understanding Patterns in the Electrification of US Manufacturing 1880–1930." *Industrial and Corporate Change* 14:745–773.

Goldin, Claudia. 1998. "America's Graduation from High School: The Evolution and Spread of Secondary Schooling in the Twentieth Century." *Journal of Economic History* 58:347–374.

———. 2000. "Labor Markets in the Twentieth Century." In Engerman and Gallman, *The Cambridge Economic History of the United States*, vol. 3, pp. 549–623.

Goldin, Claudia, and Lawrence F. Katz. 1998. "The Origins of Technology-Skill Complementarity." *Quarterly Journal of Economics* 113:693–732.

Goldin, Claudia, and Frank Lewis. 1975. "The Economic Cost of the Civil War: Estimates and Implications." *Journal of Economic History* 35 (June): 299–326.

Goldin, Claudia, and Robert Margo. 1992. "The Great Compression: The Wage Structure of the United States at Mid-Century." *Quarterly Journal of Economics* 107 (February): 1–34.

Goldsmith, Raymond. 1955. *A Study of Saving in the United States*, 3 vols. Princeton: Princeton University Press.

Gordon, Robert A. 1951. "Cyclical Experience in the Interwar Period: The Investment Boom of the Twenties." In *Conference on Business Cycles*, pp. 163–214. New York: National Bureau of Economic Research.

———. 1956. "Population Growth and the Capital Coefficient." *American Economic Review* 46 (June): 307–322.

Gordon, Robert J. 1969. "$45 Billion of U.S. Private Investment Has Been Mislaid." *American Economic Review* 59 (June): 221–238.

———. 1979. "The "End-of-Expansion" Phenomenon in Short-Run Productivity Behavior." *Brookings Papers on Economic Activity* 2:447–461.

———. 1993. "The Jobless Recovery: Does It Signal a New Era of Productivity-Led Growth?" *Brookings Papers on Economic Activity* 1:271–316.

———. 1999. "U.S. Economic Growth since 1870: One Big Wave?" *American Economic Review* 89:123–128.

———. 2000a. *Macroeconomics*, 8th ed. Reading, MA: Addison-Wesley Longman.

———. 2000b. "Interpreting the "One Big Wave" in U.S. Long Term Productivity Growth." In *Productivity, Technology, and Economic Growth*, ed. Bart van Ark, Simon Kuipers, and Gerard Kuper, pp. 19–66. Boston: Kluwer.

———. 2000c. "Does the "New Economy" Measure up to the Great Inventions of the Past?" *Journal of Economic Perspectives* 14 (Fall): 49–74.

———. 2003. "Exploding Productivity Growth: Context, Causes, and Implications." *Brookings Papers on Economic Activity* 2:207–279.

———. 2004. "The 1920s and the 1990s in Mutual Reflection." Paper presented at Conference on Understanding the 1990s: The Economy in Long Run Perspective, Duke University, March 26–27, 2004.

———. 2009. "Is Modern Macro or 1978-Era Macro More Relevant to the Understanding of the Current Economic Crisis?" Unpublished paper, September.

———. 2010. "The Demise of Okun's Law and of Procyclical Fluctuations in Conventional and Unconventional Measures of Productivity." Paper delivered at the 2010 NBER Summer Institute meetings.

Gordon, Robert J., and John M. Veitch. 1986. "Fixed Investment in the American Business Cycle." In *The American Business Cycle: Continuity and Change*, ed. Robert J. Gordon, pp. 267–357. Chicago: University of Chicago Press.

Gramlich, Edward M. 1994. "Infrastructure Investment: A Review Essay." *Journal of Economic Literature* 32 (September): 1176–1196.

Grebler, Leo, David Blank, and Louis Winnick. 1956. *Capital Formation in Residential Real Estate: Trends and Prospects.* Princeton: Princeton University Press.

Greenspan, Alan. 1996. "The Challenge of Central Banking in a Democratic Society." Available at http://www.federalreserve.gov/boarddocs/speeches/1996/19961205.htm.

Griliches, Zvi. 1958. "Research Costs and Social Returns: Hybrid Corn and Related Innovations." *Journal of Political Economy* 66:419–431.

———. 2000. *R&D, Education, and Productivity: A Retrospective.* Cambridge, MA: Harvard University Press.

Guerrieri, Paolo, and Pier Carlo Padoan. 2007. "Modeling ICT as a General Purpose Technology: Overview and Summary." *Collegium* 35 (Spring): 6–21.

Haar, Charles M., and Jerold S. Kayden, eds. 1989. *Zoning and the American Dream: Promises Still to Keep.* Chicago: American Planning Association.

Haberler, Gottfried. 1937. *Prosperity and Depression: A Theoretical Analysis of Cyclical Movements.* Geneva: League of Nations.

Hacker, Louis M. 1947. *The Triumph of American Capitalism: The Development of Forces in American History to the End of the Nineteenth Century.* New York: Columbia University Press.

Hall, Robert E. 1988. "The Relation between Price and Marginal Cost in U.S. Industry." *Journal of Political Economy* 96 (October): 921–947.

———. 1990. "Invariance Properties of Solow's Productivity Residual." In *Growth/Productivity/Unemployment: Essays to Celebrate Bob Solow's Birthday,* ed. Peter Diamond, pp. 71–112. Cambridge, MA: MIT Press.

Hall, Robert E., Martin Feldstein, Jeffrey Frankel, Robert Gordon, Christina Romer, David Romer, and Victor Zarnowitz. 2003. "The NBER's Business Cycle Dating Procedures." Http://www.nber.org/cycles/recessions.pdf. Document dated October 21, 2003. Accessed March 8, 2007.

Hamilton, James D. 1987. "Monetary Factors in the Great Depression." *Journal of Monetary Economics* (19): 145–169.

Handy, Bruce. 2000. "Tomorrowland Never Dies." *Vanity Fair* (March): 114–126.

Hansen, Alvin. 1938. *Full Recovery or Stagnation?* New York: Norton.

———. 1951. *Business Cycles and National Income.* New York: Norton.

Harberger, Arnold. 1998. "A Vision of the Growth Process." *American Economic Review* 88 (March): 1–32.

Harley, C. Knick. 1988. "Ocean Freight Rates and Productivity, 1740–1913: The Primacy of Mechanical Invention Reaffirmed." *Journal of Economic History* 48:851–876.

Harris, Seymour E. 1933. *Twenty Years of Federal Reserve Policy, Including an Extended Discussion of the Monetary Crisis, 1927–1933,* vol. 2: *The Monetary Crisis.* Cambridge, MA: Harvard University Press.

———. 1945. *Price and Related Controls in the United States.* New York: McGraw Hill.

Hart, Robert A., and James R. Malley. 1999. "Procyclical Labour Productivity: A Closer Look at a Stylized Fact." *Economica* 66 (November): 533–550.

Helpman, Elhanan, ed. 1998. *General Purpose Technologies and Economic Growth.* Cambridge, MA: MIT Press.

Henderson, Nell. 2005. "Bernanke: There's No Housing Bubble to Go Bust." *Washington Post,* October 26. Available at http://www.washingtonpost.com/wp-dyn/content/article/2005/10/26/AR2005102602255.html.

Herman, Edward S. 1969. "Conflicts of Interest in the Savings and Loan Industry." In *Study of the Savings and Loan Industry,* vol. 2, ed. Irving Friend, Federal Home Loan Bank Board, pp. 763–969. Washington, D.C.: Government Printing Office.

Hickman, Bert. 1960. *Growth and Stability of the Postwar Economy.* Washington, D.C.: Brookings Institution.

———. 1974. "What Became of the Building Cycle?" In *Nations and Households in Economic Growth: Essays in Honor of Moses Abramovitz, ed.* Paul A. David and Melvin Reder, pp. 291–314. New York: Academic Press.

Hicks, John R. 1937. "Mr. Keynes and the Classics: A Suggested Reinterpretation." *Econometrica* 5 (April): 147–159.

Higgs, Robert. 1992. "Wartime Prosperity? A Reassessment of the U.S. Economy in the 1940s." *Journal of Economic History* 52 (March): 41–60.

———. 1993. "Private Profit, Public Risk: Institutional Antecedents of the Modern Military Procurement System in the Rearmament Program of 1940–41." In Mills and Rockoff, *The Sinews of War,* pp. 166–198.

———. 1997. "Regime Uncertainty: Why the Great Depression Lasted So Long and Why Prosperity Resumed after the War." *Independent Review* 1 (Spring): 561–590.

———. 1999. "From Central Planning to the Market: The American Transition, 1945–1947." *Journal of Economic History* 59 (September): 600–623.

———. 2004. "Wartime Socialization of Investment: A Reassessment of U.S. Capital Formation in the 1940s." *Journal of Economic History* 64 (June): 500–520.

Hilsenrath, Jon. 2003. "Behind Surging Productivity, the Service Sector Delivers." *Wall Street Journal,* November 7.

Hoover, Herbert. 1952. *The Memoirs of Herbert Hoover,* vol. 3: *The Great Depression 1929–1941.* New York: Macmillan.

Hoyt, Homer. 1933. *One Hundred Years of Land Values in Chicago: The Relationship of the Growth of Chicago to the Rise in Its Land Values.* Chicago: University of Chicago Press.

Hulten, Charles R. 2001. "TFP: A Short Biography." In *New Developments in Productivity Analysis, ed.* Charles Hulten, Edwin R. Dean, and Michael J. Harper. Chicago: University of Chicago Press for NBER.

Hultgren, Thor. 1960. "Changes in Labor Cost during Cycles in Production and Business." NBER Occasional Paper No. 74.

Johnson, Bradford C. 2002. "Retail: The Wal-Mart Effect." *McKinsey Quarterly* 1:40–43.

Jones, Charles I. 1995. "R and D Based Models of Economic Growth." *Journal of Political Economy* 103 (August): 759–784.

Jorgenson, Dale. 2001. "Information Technology and the U.S. Economy." *American Economic Review* 91 (March): 1–32.

Jorgenson, Dale, and Kevin Stiroh. 1999. "Information Technology and Growth." *American Economic Review* 89 (May): 109–115.

———. 2000. "Raising the Speed Limit: U.S. Economic Growth in the Information Age." *Brookings Papers on Economic Activity* 1:125–235.

Jorgenson, Dale, Mun Ho, and Kevin Stiroh. 2003. "Lessons from the U.S. Growth Resurgence." Paper prepared for the First International Conference on the Economic and Social Implications of Information Technology, held at the U.S. Department of Commerce, Washington, D.C., January 27–28, 2003.

Jorgenson, Dale, and Zvi Griliches. 1967. "The Explanation of Productivity Change." *Review of Economic Studies* 34 (July): 249–283.

Jovanovic, Boyan, and Peter L. Rousseau. 2005. "General Purpose Technologies." In *Handbook of Economic Growth*, vol. 1B, ed. P. Aghion and S. N. Durlauf, pp. 1181–1224. Amsterdam: North-Holland. (Earlier version circulated as Working Paper No. 11093, National Bureau of Economic Research, January 2005.)

Kaldor, Nicholas. 1961. "Capital Accumulation and Economic Growth." In *The Theory of Capital*, ed. F. A. Lutz and D. C. Hague. New York: St. Martin's Press.

Katz, Alyssa. 2009. *How Real Estate Came to Own Us*. New York: Bloomsbury.

Kehoe, Timothy J., and Edward Prescott, eds. 2007. *Great Depressions of the Twentieth Century*. Minneapolis: Federal Reserve Bank of Minneapolis.

———. 2008. "Using the General Equilibrium Growth Model to Study Great Depressions." Minneapolis: Federal Reserve Bank of Minneapolis Research Department Staff Report 418 (December).

Kendrick, John W. 1961. *Productivity Trends in the United States*. Princeton: Princeton University Press.

Kendrick, John W., and Elliott S. Grossman. 1980. *Productivity in the United States: Trends and Cycles*. Baltimore: Johns Hopkins University Press.

Keynes, John Maynard. 1973 (1928). "Is There Inflation in the United States?" In *The Collected Writings of John Maynard Keynes*, vol. 13, *The General Theory and After*, part 1, "Preparation," ed. Donald Moggridge, pp. 52–76. London: Macmillan for the Royal Economic Society.

———. 1964 (1936). The *General Theory of Employment, Interest, and Money*. New York: Harcourt Brace.

Khan, Zorina, and Kenneth Sokoloff. 2001. "The Early Development of Intellectual Property Institutions in the United States." *Journal of Economic Perspectives* 15 (Summer): 233–246.

Kindleberger, Charles. 1978. *Manias, Panics, and Crashes: A History of Financial Crises*. New York: Basic Books.

Kleinknecht, Alfred. 1987. *Innovation Patterns in Crisis and Prosperity: Schumpeter's Long Cycle Reconsidered*. New York: St. Martin's Press.

Klenow, Peter, and Andres Rodriquez-Clare. 1997. "Economic Growth: A Review Essay." *Journal of Monetary Economics* 40:597–617.

Krugman, Paul. 2009. "How Did Economists Get It So Wrong?" *New York Times Magazine*, September 6. Available at http://www.nytimes.com/2009/09/06/magazine/06Economic-t.html.

Kuh, Edwin. 1965. "Cyclical and Secular Labor Productivity in United States Manufacturing." *Review of Economics and Statistics* 47 (February): 1–12.

Kuznets, Simon. 1937. *National Income and Capital Formation, 1919–1935: A Preliminary Report.* New York: National Bureau of Economic Research.

———. 1946. *National Product since 1869.* New York: National Bureau of Economic Research.

Lahart, Justin. 2009. "Mr. Rajan Was Unpopular (but Prescient) at Greenspan Party." *Wall Street Journal*, January 2. Available at http://online.wsj.com/article/SB123086154114948151 .html.

Landes, David. 1969. *The Unbound Prometheus: Technological Change and Industrial Development in Western Europe from 1750 to the Present.* Cambridge: Cambridge University Press.

Lebergott, Stanley. 1964. *Manpower in Economic Growth: The American Record since 1800.* New York: McGraw Hill.

Leising, Mathew, and Roger Runnigen. 2008. "Brooksley Born 'Vindicated' as Swap Rules Take Shape." *Bloomberg*, November 13. Available at http://www.bloomberg.com/apps/ news?pid=20601109&sid=aXcq.r6xLf4g&refer=home.

Lipsey, Richard G., and Kenneth Carlaw. 2001. "What Does Total Factor Productivity Measure?" *International Productivity Monitor* (Fall): 23–28.

Lipsey, Richard G., Cliff Bekar, and Kenneth Carlaw. 1998. "What Requires Explanation?" In Helpman, *General Purpose Technologies and Economic Growth*, pp. 15–54.

Lipsey, Richard G., Kenneth Carlaw, and Clifford Bekar. 2005. *Economic Transformations: General Purpose Technologies and Long-Term Economic Growth.* New York: Oxford University Press.

Los Angeles Regional Planning Commission. 1938. "Land Use Survey, County of Los Angeles: A Report on W.P.A. Projects C-2490 and C-5719." Los Angeles: Regional Planning Commission.

Lucas, Robert E., Jr. 1980, 1983. "Methods and Problems in Business Cycle Theory." *Journal of Money, Credit, and Banking* 12 (November 1980): 696–715. In Robert E. Lucas, Jr., *Studies in Business-Cycle Theory.* Cambridge, MA: MIT Press, 1983.

Machlup, Fritz. 1940. *The Stock Market, Credit and Capital Formation.* Trans. Vera C. Smith. New York: Macmillan. (Translation of *Borsenkredit, Industriekredit and Kapitalbildung*, 1931.)

Maddison, Angus. 1982. *Phases of Capitalist Development.* Oxford: Oxford University Press.

Margo, Robert. 1991. "The Microeconomics of Depression Unemployment." *Journal of Economic History* 51 (June): 331–341.

———. 1993. "Employment and Unemployment in the 1930s." *Journal of Economic Perspectives* 7 (Spring): 41–59.

McLean, Bethany. 2009. "Who Really Killed Fannie and Freddie?" *Vanity Fair* (February): 118–147.

McLean, Bethany and Joe Nocera. 2010. *All the Devils Are Here: The Hidden History of the Financial Crisis.* New York: Penguin.

McKinsey Global Institute. 2002. "US Productivity Growth 1995–2000: Understanding the Contribution of Information Technology Relative to Other Factors." Available at http://www.mckinsey.com/mgi/publications/us/index.asp.

Mensch, Gerhard. 1979. *Stalemate in Technology: Innovations Overcome the Depression*. Cambridge, MA: Ballinger.

Michigan State Planning Commission. 1939. *A Study of Subdivision Development in the Detroit Metropolitan Area*. Lansing, MI.

Mills, Geoffrey T., and Hugh Rockoff. 1993. *The Sinews of War: Essays on the Economic History of World War II*. Ames: Iowa State University Press.

Minsky, Hyman. 1964. "Longer Waves in Financial Relations: Financial Factors in the More Severe Depressions." *American Economic Review* 54 (May): 324–335.

——. 1975. *John Maynard Keynes*. New York: Columbia University Press.

——. 1986. *Stabilizing an Unstable Economy*. New Haven: Yale University Press.

Mishkin, Frederick S. 1978. "The Household Balance Sheet and the Great Depression." *Journal of Economic History* 38:918–937.

Mitchell, Broadus. 1947. *Depression Decade: From New Era to New Deal, 1929–1941*. New York: Holt, Rinehart and Winston.

Mokyr, Joel. 2006. Review of Lipsey, Carlaw, and Bekar (2005). Available at http://eh.net/bookreviews.

Morgenstern, Gretchen, and Andrew Martin. 2009. "Citigroup Hires Mr. Inside." *New York Times*, October 11. Available at http://www.nytimes.com/2009/10/11/business/11hohlt.html.

Morgenstern, Gretchen, and Don Van Natta, Jr. 2009. "Even in Crisis, Banks Dig in for Fight against Rules." *New York Times*, June 1. Available at http://www.nytimes.com/2009/06/01/business/01lobby.html.

Mowery, David. 1981. "The Emergence and Growth of Industrial Research in American Manufacturing, 1899–1945." Ph.D. dissertation, Stanford University.

——. 1983. "Industrial Research and Firm Size, Survival, and Growth in American Manufacturing, 1921–1946: An Assessment." *Journal of Economic History* 43 (December): 953–980.

Mowery, David, and Nathan Rosenberg. 1989. *Technology and the Pursuit of Economic Growth*. Cambridge: Cambridge University Press.

——. 2000. "Twentieth Century Technological Change." In Engerman and Gallman, *The Cambridge Economic History of the United States*, vol. 3, pp. 803–926.

Mulligan, Casey B. 2009. "Is Macroeconomics off Track?" *The Economist's Voice*. Available at http://www.bepress.com/ev/vol6/iss10/art6.

Muth, Richard F. 1959. *Cities and Housing: The Spatial Pattern of Urban Residential Land Use*. Chicago: University of Chicago Press.

National Bureau of Economic Research. 2003. "Business Cycle Expansions and Contractions." Http://www.nber.org/cycles/cyclesmain.html.

National Housing Agency. 1945. *Land Assembly for Urban Redevelopment*. Washington, D.C. Government Printing Office.

Nelson, Donald M. 1946. *Arsenal of Democracy: The Story of American War Production*. New York: Harcourt Brace.

New Jersey State Planning Board. 1941. *Premature Land Subdivision a Luxury*. Trenton, NJ.

Nordhaus, William D. 1982. "Economic Policy in the Face of Declining Productivity Growth." *European Economic Review* 18 (May–June): 131–158.

———. 1997. "Traditional Productivity Estimates Are Asleep at the (Technological) Switch." *Economic Journal* 107 (September): 1548–1559.

———. 2002. "Productivity Growth and the New Economy." *Brookings Papers on Economic Activity* 2:211–244.

Ohanian, Lee. 2001. "Why Did Productivity Fall So Much in the Great Depression?" *American Economic Review* 91 (May): 34–38.

———. 2009. "What—or Who—Started the Great Depression?" NBER Working Paper No. 15258.

Okun, Arthur M. 1962. "Potential GNP: Its Measurement and Significance." In American Statistical Association, *Proceedings of the Business and Economic Statistics Section*, 98–104.

Oliner, Steven D., and Daniel E. Sichel. 2000. "The Resurgence of Growth in the Late 1990s: Is Information Technology the Story?" *Journal of Economic Perspectives* 14 (Fall): 3–22.

Olmstead, Alan, and Paul Rhode. 2000. "The Transformation of Northern Agriculture, 1910–1990." In Engerman and Gallman, *The Cambridge Economic History of the United States*, vol. 3, pp. 693–742.

———. 2002. "The Red Queen and the Hard Reds: Productivity Growth in American Wheat, 1800–1940." *Journal of Economic History* 62 (December): 929–966.

Olney, Martha. 1991. *Buy Now Pay Later: Advertising, Credit, and Consumer Durables in the 1920s*. Chapel Hill: University of North Carolina Press.

———. 1999. "Avoiding Default: The Role of Credit in the Consumption Collapse of 1930." *Quarterly Journal of Economics* 114 (February): 319–335.

Owen, Wilfred. 1962. "Transportation and Technology." *American Economic Review* 52 (May): 405–413.

Owens, Richard N., and Charles O. Hardy. 1925. *Interest Rates and Stock Speculation*. New York: Macmillan.

Paxson, Frederic L. 1946. "The Highway Movement, 1916–1935." *American Historical Review* 51 (January): 236–253.

Pensieroso, Luca. 2007. "Real Business Cycle Models of the Great Depression: A Critical Survey." *Journal of Economic Surveys* 21, no. 1:110–142.

Perry, H. W. 1913. "Teams and Motor Trucks Compared." *Scientific American* 108:66.

Philippon, Thomas, and Ariell Reshef. 2009. "Wages and Human Capital in the U.S. Financial Industry: 1909–2006." NBER Working Paper No. 14644 (January).

Posner, Richard. 2009. *A Failure of Capitalism: The Crisis of '08 and the Descent into Depression*. Cambridge, MA: Harvard University Press.

Prescott, Edward. 1986. "Theory ahead of Business Cycle Measurement." *Federal Reserve Bank of Minneapolis Quarterly Review* 10 (Fall): 9–22.

Pulliam, Susan, and Tom McGinty. 2009. "Congress Helped Banks Defang Key Rule." *Wall Street Journal*, June 3. Available at http://online.wsj.com/article/SB124396078596677535.html.

Raff, D. M. G., and M. Trajtenberg. 1997. "Quality-Adjusted Prices for the American Automobile Industry: 1906–1940." In *The Economics of New Goods*, ed. T. Bresnahan and R. J. Gordon. Chicago: University of Chicago Press.

Ratcliff, Richard A. 1949. *Urban Land Economics*. New York: McGraw Hill.

Rebelo, Sergio. 2005. "Real Business Cycle Models: Past, Present, and Future." Working paper.

Reconstruction Finance Corporation. 1946. "Projects Approved by the RFC—Office of Defense Plants as of June 30, 1946." Mimeo, 113 pages.

Reinhart, Carmen, and Kenneth Rogoff. 2009. *This Time Is Different: Eight Centuries of Financial Folly*. Princeton: Princeton University Press.

Reps, John W. 1969. *Town Planning in Frontier America*. Princeton: Princeton University Press.

Rhode, Paul. W. 2002. "Gallman's Annual Output Series for the United States, 1834–1909." NBER Working Paper No. 8860.

Rhode, Paul, and Gianni Toniolo, eds. 2006. *The Global Economy in the 1990s: A Long Run Perspective*. Cambridge: Cambridge University Press.

Rockoff, Hugh M. 1998. "The United States: From Ploughshares to Swords." In *The Economics of World War II*, ed. Mark Harrison, pp. 81–121. Cambridge: Cambridge University Press.

Romer, Christina. 1986. "Spurious Volatility in Historical Unemployment Data." *Journal of Political Economy* 94 (February): 1–37.

———. 1990. "The Great Crash and the Onset of the Great Depression." *Quarterly Journal of Economics* 105 (August): 597–624.

Romer, Paul. 1986. "Increasing Returns and Long Run Growth." *Journal of Political Economy* 94 (October): 1002–1037.

Rosenberg, Nathan. 1998. "Chemical Engineering as a General Purpose Technology." In Helpman, *General Purpose Technologies and Economic Growth*, pp. 167–192.

Rosenberg, Nathan, and Manuel Trajtenberg. 2001. "A General Purpose Technology at Work: The Corliss Steam Engine in the Late 19th Century U.S." NBER Working Paper No. 8485.

Rostow, W. W. 1960. *The Stages of Economic Growth: A Non-Communist Manifesto*. Cambridge: Cambridge University Press.

Rothbard. Murray. 1963. *America's Great Depression*. New York: Van Nostrand.

Rousseau, Peter L. 2006. "GPTs: Then and Now." In Rhode and Toniolo, *The Global Economy in the 1990s*, pp. 118–138.

———. 2008. "General Purpose Technologies." In *The New Palgrave: A Dictionary of Economics*, 2nd ed., ed. S. N. Durlauf and L. Blume. London: Macmillan.

Ruttan, Vernon. 2006. *Is War Necessary for Economic Growth? Military Procurement and Technology Development*. Oxford: Oxford University Press.

Saulnier, Raymond J. 1950. *Urban Mortgage Lending by Life Insurance Companies*. New York: National Bureau of Economic Research.

Schiffman, Daniel A. 2003. "Shattered Rails, Financial Fragility, and Railroad Operations in the Great Depression." *Journal of Economic History* 63 (September): 802–825.

Schmookler, Jacob. 1966. *Invention and Economic Growth*. Cambridge, MA: Harvard University Press.

Schumpeter, Joseph. 1942. *Capitalism, Socialism, and Democracy*. New York: Harper and Row.

Searle, A. D. 1945. "Productivity of Labor and Industry." *Monthly Labor Review* 61 (December): 1132–1147.

Shapiro, Matthew. 1987. "Are Cyclical Fluctuations Due More to Supply Shocks or Demand Shocks?" *American Economic Review* 77 (May): 118–124.

———. 1993. "Cyclical Productivity and the Workweek of Capital." *American Economic Review* 83 (May): 229–233.

Shin, Hyun Song. 2009. "Securitization and Financial Stability." *Economic Journal* 119 (March): 309–332.

Siegan, Bernard H. 1976. *Other People's Property*. Lexington, MA: Lexington Books.

Simpson, Herbert D. 1933. "Real Estate Speculation and the Depression." *American Economic Review* 23 (March): 163–171.

Simpson, Herbert D., and John E. Burton. 1931. *The Valuation of Vacant Land in Suburban Areas*. Chicago: Institute of Economic Research.

Smets, Frank, and Raf Wouters. 2004. "Forecasting with a Bayesian DSGE Model: An Application to the Euro Area." European Central Bank Working Paper No. 389 (September).

Smil, Vaclav. 2001. *Enriching the Earth: Fritz Haber, Carl Bosch, and the Transformation of World Food Production*. Cambridge, MA: MIT Press.

———. 2005. *Creating the Twentieth Century: Technical Innovations of 1867–1914 and Their Lasting Impact*. Oxford: Oxford University Press.

Solow, Robert J. 1957. "Technical Change and the Aggregate Production Function." *Review of Economics and Statistics* 39 (August): 312–320.

Sorkin, Andrew Ross. 2009. *Too Big to Fail*. New York: Viking.

Soulé, George. 1947. *Prosperity Decade: From War to Depression: 1917–1929*. New York: Rinehart and Winston.

Spitz, Peter H. 1988. *Petrochemicals: The Rise of an Industry*. New York: Wiley.

Stover, John F. 1997. *American Railroads*, 2nd ed. Chicago: University of Chicago Press.

Summers, Lawrence H. 1986. "Some Skeptical Observations on Real Business Cycle Theory." *Federal Reserve Bank of Minneapolis Quarterly Review* (Fall).

———. 1998. "Testimony before the Senate Committee on Agriculture, Nutrition, and Forestry on the CFTC Concept Release." July 30. Available at http://www.treas.gov/press/releases/rr2616.htm.

Taylor, John. 2009a. "Monetary Policy and the Recent Extraordinary Measures Taken by the Federal Reserve." Testimony before the Committee on Financial Services, U.S. House of Representatives, February 26. Available at http://www.stanford.edu/~johntayl/House%20FSC%20testimony%20Feb%2026.pdf.

———. 2009b. *Getting off Track: How Government Actions and Interventions Caused, Prolonged, and Worsened the Financial Crisis*. Stanford, CA: Hoover Institution Press.

Temin, Peter. 1976. *Did Monetary Forces Cause the Great Depression?* New York: Norton.

———. 1989. *Lessons from the Great Depression*. Cambridge, MA: MIT Press.

——. 2008. "Real Business Cycle Views of the Great Depression and Recent Events: A Review of Timothy J. Kehoe and Edward C. Prescott's *Great Depressions of the Twentieth Century.*" *Journal of Economic Literature* 46 (September): 669–684.

Temporary National Economic Committee. 1941. *Technology in Our Economy.* U.S. Senate, 76th Congress, 3rd session. Monograph No. 22. Washington, D.C.: Government Printing Office.

Tett, Gillian. 2009. *Fool's Gold: How a Bold Dream of a Small Tribe at J.P. Morgan Was Corrupted by Wall Street Greed and Unleashed a Catastrophe.* New York: Free Press.

Thoma, Grid. 2009. "Striving for a Large Market: Evidence from a General Purpose Technology in Action." *Industrial and Corporate Change* 18:107–138.

Tostlebe, Alvin S. 1957. *Capital in Agriculture: Its Formation and Financing since 1870.* Princeton: Princeton University Press.

Ulmer, Melville J. 1960. *Capital in Transportation, Communication, and Public Utilities: Its Formation and Financing.* Princeton: Princeton University Press.

U.S. Bureau of the Budget. 1946. *The United States at War.* Washington, D.C.: Government Printing Office; reprint edition: New York: Da Capo Press, 1972.

U.S. Bureau of the Census. 1942. *Statistical Abstract of the United States.* Washington, D.C.: Government Printing Office.

——. 1944. *Statistical Abstract of the United States.* Washington, D.C.: Government Printing Office.

——. 1945. *Statistical Abstract of the United States.* Washington, D.C.: Government Printing Office.

——. 1946. *Statistical Abstract of the United States.* Washington, D.C.: Government Printing Office.

——. 1947. *Statistical Abstract of the United States.* Washington, D.C.: Government Printing Office.

——. 1951. *Statistical Abstract of the United States.* Washington, D.C.: Government Printing Office.

——. 1964. *Statistical Abstract of the United States.* Washington, D.C.: Government Printing Office.

——. 1975. *Historical Statistics of the United States: Colonial Times to 1970.* Washington, D.C.: Government Printing Office.

——. 1978. *Statistical Abstract of the United States.* Washington, D.C.: Government Printing Office.

U.S. Council of Economic Advisors. 1951. *Economic Report of the President.* Washington, D.C.: Government Printing Office.

——. 2001. *Economic Report of the President.* Washington, D.C.: Government Printing Office. Available at http://w3.access.gpo.gov/eop/.

——. 2003. *Economic Report of the President.* Washington, D.C.: Government Printing Office. Available at http://w3.access.gpo.gov/eop/.

U.S. Department of Commerce, Bureau of Economic Analysis. 1966. *National Income and Product Accounts of the United States, 1929–1965.* Washington, D.C.: Government Printing Office.

———. 1986. *National Income and Product Accounts of the United States, 1929–1982.* Washington, D.C.: Government Printing Office.

———. 2004. "Gross Domestic Product Originating by Industry: Historic Data." Available at http://www.bea.doc.gov/industry/xls/GDPbyInd_VA_SIC.xls; release date June 17, 2004.

———. 2009. "Gross Domestic Product by Industry Accounts, Value Added by Industry"; release date April 28, 2009.

U.S. Department of Labor, Bureau of Labor Statistics. 1941. "Bulletin No. 699: Changes in Cost of Living in Large Cities in the United States, 1913–41." Washington, D.C.: Government Printing Office.

———. 1946. "Productivity Changes since 1939." *Monthly Labor Review* (December): 893–917.

———. 1997. *Handbook of Methods.* Available at http://stats.bls.gov/opub/hom/homtoc.htm.

———. 2003a. "Capital and Related Measures from the Two Digit Database." Available at www.bls.gov.

———. 2003b. "Industry Productivity Indexes and Values Table." Available at www.bls.gov.

———. 2003c. "Multifactor Productivity Estimates for Wholesale and Retail Trade." Unpublished.

———. 2004. "Multifactor Productivity in U.S. Manufacturing and in 20 Manufacturing Industries, 1949–2001." Dated February 10, 2004. Available at http://www.bls.gov/mfp/ under "Superceded historical SIC measures for manufacturing. . . ." Accessed January 6, 2010.

———. 2008. "Multifactor Productivity and Related KLEMS Measures from the Three Digit Database, 1987–2006, Manufacturing Sector (NAICS 311–339)"; release date May 1, 2008.

———. 2009. "Net Multifactor Productivity and Costs, 1948–2008: SIC 1948–87 Linked to NAICS 1987–2008"; release date May 6, 2009.

U.S. Department of Justice. 1920–1940. *Annual Reports of the Attorney General.* Washington, D.C.: Government Printing Office.

U.S. War Production Board. 1945. *Wartime Production Achievements and the Reconversion Outlook: Report of the Chairman.* October 9, 1945. Washington, D.C.: Government Printing Office.

Vatter, Harold G. 1985. *The U.S. Economy in World War II.* New York: Columbia University Press.

Vernon, J. R. 1994. "World War II Fiscal Policies and the End of the Great Depression." *Journal of Economic History* 54 (December): 850–868.

Von Tunzelmann, George. 1978. *Steam Power and British Industrialization to 1860.* Oxford: Oxford University Press.

Weintraub, David. 1938. "Some Measures of Changing Labor Productivity and Their Uses in Economic Analysis." *Journal of the American Statistical Association* 33 (March): 153–163.

———. 1939. "Effects of Current and Prospective Technological Developments upon Capital Formation." *American Economic Review* 29 (March): 15–32.

Weir, David. 1986. "The Reliability of Historical Macroeconomic Data for Comparing Cyclical Stability." *Journal of Economic History* 46 (June): 353–365.

———. 1992. "A Century of U.S. Unemployment, 1890–1990." *Research in Economic History* 14: 301–346. See also series Ba475, *Historical Statistics of the United States*, vol. 2. Cambridge: Cambridge University Press, 2006.

Weiss, Marc A. 1987. *The Rise of the Community Builders*. New York: Columbia University Press.

White, Eugene N. 2000. "Banking and Finance in the Twentieth Century." In Engerman and Gallman, *The Cambridge Economic History of the United States*, vol. 3, pp. 743–802.

Wigmore, Barry. 2010. "A Comparison of Federal Financial Remediation in the Great Depression and 2008–2009." *Research in Economic History* 27: 255–303.

Williamson, Jeffrey. 1973. "Late Nineteenth-Century American Retardation: A Neoclassical Analysis." *Journal of Economic History* 33 (September): 581–607.

Winston, Gordon. 1974. "The Theory of Capital Utilization and Idleness." *Journal of Economic Literature* 12 (December): 1301–1320.

Woodford, Michael. 2009. "Convergence in Macroeconomics: Elements of the New Synthesis." *American Economic Journal: Macroeconomics* 1 (January): 267–279.

Wright, Gavin. 2000. Review of Helpman (1998). *Journal of Economic Literature* 38 (March): 161–162.

INDEX

Abramovitz, Moses: analysis of nineteenth century, 146–153, 163; analysis of twentieth century, 4, 12, 20–21; dating of productivity slowdown, 116; definition of residual, 13; TFP trend growth rates vary over time, 172; twentieth century differs from nineteenth, 12–13, 146–147, 150; vintage capital adjustment, interwar period, 28–30

Adams, Thomas, 347 n. 33

adversity/hysteresis effect, 15, 150, 297–300, 311

aggregate demand shock: and 1982 recession, 185, 274; defined, 9; during the Depression, 182, 238–241; during World War II, 2, 82–88. *See also* autonomous planned spending; fiscal policy; monetary policy

aggregate supply shock: defined, 10; during the 1920s, 44–46, 70–74; during the 1930s, 3, 36, 40–42, 47–50, 70–78; during World War II, 80–81; oil shocks, 116, 184, 186, 245; posited role as cause of short run fluctuations, 169, 179–187, 189–191. *See also* total factor productivity (TFP); real business cycle theory

agriculture: biological innovation, 212; decline in fertilizer price, 23; during

World War II, 90, 91, 93; share of GDP, 8, 23, 50, 58, 110; TFP growth, nineteenth century, 147, 155, 156, 334 n. 8

aircraft and airframes: B-29, 104; DC-3 (C-47), 23, 41, 104; exports of, 184; fuel requirements during World War II, 113; lead times in building, 174; production during World War II, 22–23, 28, 80–81, 103; productivity growth during Depression, 60, 116; utilization rates affect user cost, 178

airline travel: productivity growth during Depression, 61; radar benefits, 24

airports, 40, 60, 63

Alchian, Armen, 80

Alexopoulos, Michelle, 323 n. 19

Allen, Frederick Lewis, 344 n. 8, n. 13

aluminum: Hall-Herout reduction process, 162; price decline 1890–1913, 162, 164; production during World War II, 22, 24, 28, 65, 93, 204, 328 n.8. *See also* GOPO plant and equipment

Aluminum Corporation of America (Alcoa), 40

American International Group (AIG), 255, 256, 342 n. 27

American Municipal Association, 283